YO-ABH-794

HOME
IMPROVEMENTS &

REFERENCE

DO NOT REMOVE
CARDS FROM POCKET

Not to leave the library

HOME IMPROVEMENTS & PROJECTS INDEX 1990–1993

Highsmith Press Editorial Staff

Highsmith PRESS

Fort Atkinson, Wisconsin

Published by Highsmith Press LLC
W5527 Highway 106
P.O. Box 800
Fort Atkinson, Wisconsin 53538-0800

1-800-558-2110

© Highsmith Press LLC, 1996

Cover art by Frank Neu.

The paper used in this publication meets the minimum requirements of
American National Standard for Information Science —
Permanence of Paper for Printed Library Material.
ANSI/NISO Z39.48-1992.

ISBN 0-917846-30-3

Contents

Introduction   vii

How to Obtain Articles Cited   xi

User's Guide   xiii

Subject Index   1

Title Index   189

Author Index   211

Introduction

This book is intended for anyone who is attracted by the smell of fresh paint or the roar of a table saw! It's designed to provide convenient access to the wealth of information that is available in nine popular magazines on home maintenance and repair, remodeling, craft projects, practical home workshop techniques, selection of tools and materials, and time-saving hints to improve any home and garden. From constructing doll houses and toy trucks, to adding dormers and repairing wobbly chairs, the reader will find articles and illustrations that can save time and money.

While there are numerous books and magazines on home improvements and projects, locating articles on specific projects can be as frustrating as finding an 8/32 nut in the proverbial haystack. Few magazines on these subjects are indexed in the standard reference services found in libraries, and very few indexes provide sufficient entry description to identify the complexity of the project, and whether drawn plans, photographs, illustrations or lists of materials are included.

Home Improvements and Projects Index (*HIPI*) was created to simplify the search for practical solutions to common (and quite a number of uncommon) problems homeowners and craftspersons face in maintaining and improving their homes. It is also intended to provide a rich array of workshop projects of varying complexity for the hobbyist. The 2,900 entries in *HIPI* are arranged alphabetically by subject, and each entry contains the title of the article, author (if cited), a clear and concise description of the article, information on whether plans, illustrations, photographs, lists of materials are included, and a full citation of where the article can be found. Sidebars in each article are described. Separate author and title indexes are also provided to further improve access.

Nine popular home improvements and projects magazines were selected for *HIPI*, based on the quality and diversity of their articles, and on their general availability in U.S. and Canadian libraries as determined by the Union List of serials maintained by the Online Computer Library Center (OCLC). These are: *Better Homes and Garden Wood, Canadian Workshop, Fine Homebuilding, Glass* (*Homeowner's Guide to Glass*), *Home Mechanix* (formerly *Mechanics Illustrated*), *Home Shop Machinist, Practical Homeowner* (formerly *Rodale's Practical*

Homeowner), *Woodwork*, and *Woodworker's Journal*. Another factor in this selection was the availability of the articles as reprints or back issues. Each of publishers of these magazines offered relatively convenient reprint and/or back issue services at reasonable cost. These magazines offered good balance in terms of the type of articles they published, and each offered excellent illustrations, plans, and bills of materials. Articles ranged in complexity from projects for the novice to those suitable for the skilled craftsperson, but each of these magazines used clear language, easy-to follow instructions, and limited their use of technical jargon.

Purely editorial articles and brief notes less than a paragraph in length contained in these publications were not indexed and abstracted in *HIPI*. However, all projects, articles, reports, book and video reviews, computer software evaluations, and other substantive material appearing in these magazines are indexed and annotated in this work.

Selection of appropriate subject headings for *HIPI* was made difficult by the absence of a commonly accepted thesaurus for home improvements and repair, tools, and crafts projects. The most recent editions of the *Library of Congress Subject Headings* and the *Sears List of Subject Headings* offered contradictory advice, and omitted many of the topics that appeared in the selected magazines. Primary reliance was placed on the subject headings contained in *The Complete Illustrated Guide to Everything Sold in Hardware Stores* by Steve R. Ettlinger (New York: Simon & Schuster, 1993), on the basis that these terms and the form of entry would be more familiar to the users. A liberal number of "See" and "See Also" entries were included to further aid the user.

The idea for the initial development of *HIPI* came from Dr. Charles Bunge, Professor, School of Library and Information Studies, University of Wisconsin-Madison. As an authority on library reference materials, past president of the Reference and Adult Services Division of the American Library Association, prolific reference book reviewer, and member of the Highsmith Press Editorial Board, Dr. Bunge observed that there was a paucity of current reference resources on practical subjects such as home improvements, repair, and craft projects. His suggestions led the editors to initiate this project.

Primary credit for the indexing, abstracting, and editorial development of *HIPI* belongs to Helmut Knies, Marcia Lund, and Nancy Wilcox. The editors deeply appreciate their commitment, and the care they took in the development of the manuscript. Valuable technical assistance was obtained from Jim Hinstorff, who provided the answers to various problems experienced in managing the database. The project took over two years, and advice from a wide range of craftspersons was sought to further improve the book. The editors wish to acknowledge their contributions.

Inevitably, the question will arise in a project of this nature as to whether subsequent editions are planned for the future. The editors believe that the subjects and articles indexed and abstracted in this edition, covering the period from 1990-1993, will not become quickly dated. While new home improvement products and tools will emerge, the techniques and craft projects contained in *HIPI* should be of interest and value to craftspersons for many years. As evidence, a great many library collections contain books and other materials on home improvement, repair, and craft projects which were published several decades ago, and they continue to be popular. However, the editors will assess the response to this edition of *HIPI*, and based on feedback we receive from users, consider subsequent editions. Your comments are appreciated, especially suggestions for improvements.

DONALD J. SAGER

How to Obtain Articles Cited in *Home Improvements & Projects Index*

Check at your local library

Check with the library to determine if they subscribe to the journals included in this index and maintain back files. The titles in the *Home Improvements and Projects Index* (*HIPI*) were selected because of their widespread availability in U.S. and Canadian libraries, as well as their quality and balance. If your local library does not have a specific issue, ask a librarian if they have a cooperative agreement with other libraries or a cooperative system pertaining to periodical back issues. Many libraries can obtain specific issues or articles via interlibrary loan.

Contact the magazine publisher

Another alternative is to contact the specific magazine publisher and order the back issue containing the article, or ask them to furnish a photocopy of an individual article. All the publishers of the magazines cited in *HIPI* either offer this service, or have agreements with other agencies to provide back issues or article reprints. The following is the current source and cost at the time of publication.

Better Homes and Gardens Wood
(800/374-4244)

To order individual articles:
Wood Reprint Service
1912 Grand Avenue
Des Moines, IA 50309
U.S.$2/article (Mail orders only)

To order back issues:
Call toll free: 800/572-9350
US $5.95 each
(Major credit cards accepted)

Canadian Workshop
(905/475-8440)

To order individual articles:
Call 905/475-8440
(Ask for Editorial Dept.)

To order back issues:
Call 905/946-0400
Can$4 each
(Major credit cards accepted)

Fine Homebuilding PER
(203/426-8171)   1981-84, 1996 —

To order individual articles:
Call 203/426-8171
(Ask for Customer Service)
US$2.50 each

Fine Homebuilding (cont.)

To order back issues:
Call toll free 800/898-8286
US$5.95 each
(Major credit cards accepted)

Glass (*Homeowner's Guide to Glass*)

(703/442-4890)

Individual articles not available from the publisher.

To order back issues:
Call 703/442-4890 or

Mail to:
National Glass Association
8200 Greensboro Drive
McLean, VA 22102
US$4.95 each
(Major credit cards accepted)

Home Mechanix   PER
(212/779-5000)   1985-1996

Individual articles not available from the publisher.

To order back issues:
Times Mirror Magazines
Attn: Back Issues Dept.
2 Park Avenue
New York, NY 10016
US$4 each
(Mail orders only)

Home Shop Machinist

(616/941-7160)

To order individual articles:
Call toll free (UMI) 800/248-0360

To order back issues:
Call 616/941-7160
US$5.50 each
(Major credit cards accepted)

Practical Homeowner

To order individual articles:
Call toll free: (UMI) at 800/248-0360
US$9.75 each
(Major credit cards accepted)
Individual back issues not available.

Woodwork

(415/382-0583)

Individual articles not available from the publisher.

To order back issues:
Call 415/382-0583 or

Mail to:
Woodwork
42 Digital Drive, Street No. 5
Novato, CA 94949
US$5 each
(Major credit cards accepted)

Woodworker's Journal

(800/765-4119 or 309/682-6626)

To order individual articles:
Call 309/682-6626
(Ask for Editorial Dept.)

To order back issues:
Call toll free 800/634-7720
US$3.95-5.00
(Major credit cards accepted)

All prices and sources are subject to change. Check with the individual publishers if difficulties are experienced in obtaining articles or back issues.

How to Use the *Home Improvements & Projects Index*

All main entries in *HIPI* are arranged in alphabetical order by subject. A liberal number of "See" and "See Also" headings are included as an aid to the user. Articles which are indexed and abstracted in *HIPI* may have several assigned subject headings, and accordingly the article may be cited several times in the book. Multiple articles appearing under the same subject heading are arranged in alphabetical order by title. Following the subject entries section, there are also separate author and title indexes which are in alphabetical order. The initial article (i.e., A, The, etc.) in the title index is ignored in arranging the titles.

Each subject entry has the following elements:

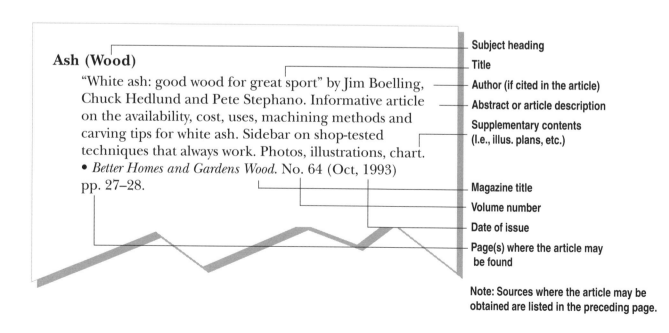

Ash (Wood) — Subject heading

"White ash: good wood for great sport" — Title by Jim Boelling, — Author (if cited in the article) Chuck Hedlund and Pete Stephano. Informative article — Abstract or article description on the availability, cost, uses, machining methods and carving tips for white ash. Sidebar on shop-tested techniques that always work. Photos, illustrations, chart. — Supplementary contents (I.e., illus. plans, etc.)
• *Better Homes and Gardens Wood.* — Magazine title No. 64 — Volume number (Oct, 1993) — Date of issue pp. 27–28. — Page(s) where the article may be found

Note: Sources where the article may be obtained are listed in the preceding page.

Home Improvements & Projects Index

A

Additions

"Adding on to old houses" by Elise Vider. Practical advice for putting on a house addition. Photos. • *Practical Homeowner.* Vol. V, No. 7 (Oct, 1990) pp. 74–78.

"Big Ideas for small spaces" by Howard Katz. Offers ideas for a freestanding addition of 768 sq. ft. Photos, drawings, plans. • *Fine Homebuilding.* No. 75 (July, 1992) pp. 46–49.

"Building from kits" by Bob Wessmiller and Matt Phair. Discusses precut kits and modular rooms for additions to homes. Photos, drawings. • *Home Mechanix.* No. 772 (Feb, 1993) pp. 38–42.

"Growing up in Minnesota" by Steven Jantzen. Presents a cost-cutting method of jacking up a garage roof to build an addition. Photos, drawings. • *Fine Homebuilding.* No. 67 (May, 1991) pp. 64–66.

"Spanning 19 ft." by Christopher F. DeBlois. Brief article discussing what size box beams to span a 19-ft. width of the addition. • *Fine Homebuilding.* No. 76 (Sep, 1992) pp. 16–18.

Additions, Southwest

"A Southwest addition" by Carolyn Robbins Siegel. Offers ideas for a steel and glass addition to an adobe construction. Photos, plans, drawings. Sidebar on using steel-trussed joists. • *Fine Homebuilding.* No. 82 (July, 1993) pp. 64–67.

Additions--Heating of

"Best ways to heat an addition" by Lee Green. Professional advice on heating additions, while keeping excessive heating costs low. Worksheet. • *Home Mechanix.* No. 751 (Dec/Jan, 1990 91) pp. 18–20.

Additions--Natural lighting

"A well-lit addition" by Robert L. Marx. Highlights an addition featuring a glazed cupola and exterior transoms for more light. Photos, diagram. • *Fine Homebuilding.* No. 83 (Sep, 1993) pp. 54–56.

"Sunny additions" by Ann Arnott. Presents three remodeling projects that created more sunlight in the homes. Photos, plans, drawings. • *Home Mechanix.* No. 744 (April, 1990) pp. 38–43.

Additions--Second story

"Make room for Trudy" by Don Price. Construction plans and directions to add an apartment above a garage. Photos, drawings. • *Fine Homebuilding*. No. 69 (Sep, 1991) pp. 62–63.

"Upward mobility" by Roy Barnhart. How to go about adding a second floor onto your home. Photos. • *Practical Homeowner*. Vol. VI, No. 9 (Nov/Dec, 1991) pp. 68–73.

Additions--Stone

"A stone and glass addition" by Christopher Hall. Highlights an addition project using natural fieldstone for a sunporch. Photos, drawing. • *Fine Homebuilding*. No. 77 (Nov, 1992) pp. 74–75.

Adhesives

"Builders' Adhesives" by Ross Herbertson. Provides a guide to job-site bonding. Photos, chart. • *Fine Homebuilding*. No. 65 (March, 1991) pp. 40–45.

"Construction adhesives" by Stephen Smulski. Covers the variety of adhesives used in building projects. Photos. • *Fine Homebuilding*. No. 58 (March, 1990) pp. 72–75.

Adobe Houses

Book Review: *The Earthbuilders' Encyclopedia* by Joseph M. Tibbets. Book review of an encyclopedia providing rammed-earth and adobe terms and a directory of earthbuilders and suppliers. Bosque, NM: Joseph M. Tibbets (PO Box 153) 196 pp. • *Fine Homebuilding*. No. 60 (May, 1990) p. 106.

"Solar adobe" by Benjamin T. Rogers. Construction plans for a greenhouse and solar-heated New Mexico house. Plans, photos. • *Fine Homebuilding*. No. 58 (March, 1990) pp. 80–85.

Air Cleaners

"Electronic air cleaners" by David F. Menicucci. Provides information about furnace-mounted electronic air cleaners.

Photos, drawings, charts. • *Fine Homebuilding*. No. 63 (Nov, 1990) pp. 58–60.

Air Conditioning

Book Review: *Heating, Cooling, Lighting: Design Methods for Architects* by Norbert Lecher. Book review on a valuable guide for designing the heating, cooling, and lighting in homes. New York: John Wiley & Sons, 534 pp. • *Fine Homebuilding*. No. 72 (March, 1992) p. 108.

"Cool improvisation" by Hank Spies. Brief tip explaining a home-made central air-conditioning system. Drawing. • *Home Mechanix*. No. 744 (April, 1990) p. 100.

"Decentralized air conditioning" by Ann Cala. Informative article about a ductless air conditioning system which can cool a room or entire house, yet stays out of sight. Photos, drawings. • *Home Mechanix*. No. 756 (June, 1991) pp. 42–43.

"High-velocity AC systems" by Jay Stein. Offers a brief tip on air-conditioning units with high velocity air flow. • *Fine Homebuilding*. No. 61 (July, 1990) p. 12.

Air-Filtration Cabinets

"Air-filtration cabinet" by Marlen Kemmet and James R. Downing. Building instructions for an air-filtration cabinet that is adjustable and can double as an outfeed table. Photos, diagrams, materials list. • *Better Homes and Gardens Wood*. No. 55 (Oct, 1992) pp. 48–51,74.

Air Hoses

"Air-hose repair" by Jan Lustig. Presents a job-site repair tip for air-hoses on a nail gun or jack hammer. • *Fine Homebuilding*. No. 75 (July, 1992) p. 26.

Air Leaks

Book Review: *Finding and Fixing Hidden Air Leaks: Circular EC 1286* by David Brook. Book review on discovering hidden air leaks in houses. Corvallis, OR: Agricultural Communications, 8 pp. • *Fine*

Homebuilding. No. 65 (March, 1991) p. 108.

Air Quality

"Air-cleaning central" by Henry Spies. Offers information about air-purification systems. • *Home Mechanix.* No. 768 (Sep, 1992) pp. 112–113.

"Air-filtration cabinet" by Marlen Kemmet and James R. Downing. Building instructions for an air-filtration cabinet that is adjustable and can double as an outfeed table. Photos, diagrams, materials list. • *Better Homes and Gardens Wood.* No. 55 (Oct, 1992) pp. 48–51,74.

"Allergy proofing your home" by Gurney Williams. How to improve the air quality in your home and control allergies. • *Practical Homeowner.* Vol. VI, No. 2 (Feb, 1991) pp. 22–24.

"Beating indoor air pollution" by Mike Nuess. Offers a solution for radon in the air in a house. Photos, plans, drawings. • *Fine Homebuilding.* No. 78 (Jan, 1993) pp. 68–71.

"Clean air, healthy air." Presents tips on filtering indoor air to reduce pollution. Photo, drawing. • *Home Mechanix.* No. 749 (Oct, 1990) pp. 16–17.

"Name that fume" by Dave Menicucci. Offers a solution to a problem with fumes in a new house. • *Fine Homebuilding.* No. 78 (Jan, 1993) pp. 16–20.

Air Shafts, Cold

"Gasping for air" by Henry Spies. Addresses a problem with an uninsulated chase, and cold walls and floors next to the chase. • *Home Mechanix.* No. 777 (July/Aug, 1993) pp. 82–84.

Airbrushes

"Airbrush" by Bill Krier and Jim Downing. Provides tips on using an airbrush for painting, applying finishes, and staining. Photos, drawing. • *Better Homes and Gardens Wood.* No. 49 (Jan, 1992) pp. 56–57.

Alarm Systems

"Easily alarmed" by James Lomuscio. A review of new products for home security. Photos. • *Practical Homeowner.* Vol. VI, No. 3 (March, 1991) pp. 38–42.

"You can install a home alarm system" by Bill Phillips. Informative article on installing a home alarm system. Drawing. • *Home Mechanix.* No. 760 (Nov, 1991) pp. 12–15, 97.

Allergies

"Allergy proofing your home" by Gurney Williams. How to improve the air quality in your home and control allergies. • *Practical Homeowner.* Vol. VI, No. 2 (Feb, 1991) pp. 22–24.

See Also Air Quality; Dust Collectors

Alloys, Cerro

"Cerro alloys aid in machining irregular parts" by Ronald E. McBride. This is an examination of the properties of cerro alloys which are composed mainly of bismuth. Photos. • *The Home Shop Machinist.* Vol. 12, No. 6 (Nov/Dec, 1993) pp. 36–38.

Alphabet Blocks (Toy)

"Learning My ABCs" by William Lovett. Describes how to construct a child's wooden bench and alphabet learning toy. Photo. List of materials. Drawn plans. • *Canadian Workshop.* Vol. 15, No. 1 (Oct 1991) pp. 55–56.

Aluminum--History of use

"Aluminum fundamentals, part one" by George Genevro. A history of the use of aluminum as a shop metal. Photos. • *The Home Shop Machinist.* Vol. 12, No. 1 (Jan/Feb, 1993) pp. 26–30.

"Aluminum fundamentals, part two" by George Genevro. See Vol. 12, No. 1 • *The Home Shop Machinist.* Vol. 12, No. 2 (Mar/Apr, 1993) pp. 30–34.

Angels, Wooden

"Christmas angel folk carving" by Rick & Ellen Butz. An outline of the process of carving wooden Christmas ornaments shaped like angels. Photos, drawings, and materials list. • *The Woodworker's Journal.* Vol. 14, No. 6 (Nov/Dec, 1990) pp. 48–51.

Animals (Toy)

"Noah's lovable ark" by Harlequin Crafts and James R. Downing. Plans to make six different kinds of wooden animals and Noah's ark. Photo, diagrams, patterns. • *Better Homes and Gardens Wood.* No. 46 (Oct, 1991) pp. 76–78.

Appliances

"Cutting edge appliances." Product reviews of new ranges, ovens, refrigerators, dishwashers, and washer/dryer combinations. Photos. • *Practical Homeowner.* Vol. VI, No. 7 (Sep, 1991) pp. 38–41.

Appliances, Kitchen

"Features for the '90s" by Sharon Ross. A guide to new kitchen appliances. Photos and drawings. • *Practical Homeowner.* Vol. V, No. 5 (August, 1990) pp. 48–59.

"Liberating the compact kitchen" by Thomas F. Sweeney. A new product guide for space saving appliances. Photos. • *Practical Homeowner.* Vol. VI, No. 7 (Sep, 1991) pp. 49–51.

Appliances, Space Saving

"Space-saving appliances" by Pat McMillan. Presents a look at a group of appliances that fit into small spaces. Photos, plans, chart. • *Home Mechanix.* No. 763 (March, 1992) pp. 66–72.

Aquarium Stands

"An aquarium room divider" by Louise Haberfeld. Provides directions to build an enormous aquarium stand that could also serve as a dividing wall. Photos. • *Fine Homebuilding.* No. 72 (March, 1992) pp. 62–63.

Arbors, Garden

"Made for the shade" by Joseph Truini. Introduces four arbor designs for outdoor plants and vines. Photos, drawings, diagrams. • *Home Mechanix.* No. 763 (March, 1992) pp. 30–36.

"Places in the sun" by Joseph Truini. Highlights construction plans for a shade arbor, rustic deck gazebo, and a patio cover. Photos, diagrams. • *Home Mechanix.* No. 745 (May, 1990) pp. 40–47.

Arbors, Lathe

"Tailstock attachment" by Frank A. McLean. A brief guide to machining arbors as tailstock attachments for lathes. Plans. • *The Home Shop Machinist.* Vol. 12, No. 2 (Mar/Apr, 1993) pp. 36–38.

Arches

"Arch layout" by Spencer Thompson. Presents a handy tip for laying out arches. Drawing. • *Fine Homebuilding.* No. 76 (Sep, 1992) p. 28.

Architects

Book Review: *Fay Jones* by Robert Adams Ivy, Jr. Book review of a compilation of many of Fay Jones' works. Photo. Washington, D.C.: American Institute of Architects Press, 224 pp. • *Fine Homebuilding.* No. 78 (Jan, 1993) p. 110.

"Why homeowners don't hire architects" by Joseph Provey. An analysis of the causes why individual home builders shy away from hiring architects. • *Practical Homeowner.* Vol. VI, No 9 (Nov/Dec, 1991) pp. 40–50.

Architecture

Book Review: *America's Favorite Homes: Mail Order Catalogues as a Guide to Popular Early 20th Century Houses* by Robert Schweitzer and Michael W.R. Davis. Book review on a collection of mail order catalogues and a study of early architectural styles. Detroit, MI: Wayne State University Press, 363 pp. • *Fine Homebuilding.* No. 77 (Nov, 1992) p. 120.

Book Review: *Building Construction Illustrated*, Second Edition by Francis D.K. Ching and Cassandra Adams. Book review on a illustrated manual for residential and light commercial construction. Photo. New York: Van Nostrand Reinhold, 375 pp. • *Fine Homebuilding*. No. 78 (Jan, 1993) p. 110.

Book Review: *Looking Around: A Journey Through Architecture* by Witold Rybczynski. Book review on the design of museums, airports, houses, and other building structures. New York: Viking, 302 pp. • *Fine Homebuilding*. No. 84 (Nov, 1993) p. 124.

Book Review: *Native American Architecture* by Peter Nabokov and Robert Easton. Book review presenting a fascinating account of Native American culture through its architecture. New York: Oxford University Press, 431 pp. • *Fine Homebuilding*. No. 69 (Sep, 1991) p. 110.

Book Review: *Technics and Architecture* by Cecil D. Elliott. Book review highlighting the nontechnical history of building technology. Photo. Cambridge, MA: The MIT Press, 431 pp. • *Fine Homebuilding*. No. 82 (July, 1993) p. 112.

Architecture--Conservation and Restoration *See* Conservation and Restoration

Architecture--Designs and Plans *See* Designs and Plans

Architecture--House Styles

"Homes across America" by Peter Reilly. A description of popular current house styles. Photos and plans. • *Practical Homeowner*. Vol. IV, No. 9 (Jan, 1990) pp. 35–39.

Architecture and the Handicapped

Book Review: *Adaptable Housing: A Technical Manual for Implementing Adaptable Dwelling Unit Specifications*. Book review giving an excellent overview of the history of accessible and adaptable housing.

Rockville, MD: HUD USER, (PO Box 6091) • *Fine Homebuilding*. No. 63 (Nov, 1990) p. 77.

"Building without barriers" by Katie Tamony. A new house design that is wheel chair accessible. Photos and plans. • *Practical Homeowner*. (May/June, 1992) pp. 46–49.

"A house without barriers" by Chuck Williams. Detailed description of a design that offers access for a wheelchair. Photos, plans, drawings. Sidebar on building a cantilevered counter. • *Fine Homebuilding*. No. 76 (Sep, 1992) pp. 54–59.

"Universal kitchens and baths." Provides tips for creating accessibility for handicapped or other special needs. Photos, drawings. • *Home Mechanix*. No. 781 (Dec/Jan, 1993–94) pp. 66 70, 84.

Armoires

"Classic Armoire" by David Riley. Furnishes detailed instructions and plans for a wood armoire. Drawn plans. List of materials. Photos. • *Canadian Workshop*. Vol. 13, No. 5 (Feb 1990) pp. 14–19.

"Tabletop armoire." A step-by-step outline of the procedure for building and finishing a tabletop armoire. Photos, plans and materials list. • *The Woodworker's Journal*. Vol. 14, No. 3 (May/Jun, 1990) pp. 57–60.

Arts and Crafts Houses

"Adapting the craftsman style" by Andre Fontaine. Offers plans for an Arts & Crafts-style home. Photos, plans. • *Fine Homebuilding*. No. 82 (July, 1993) pp. 82–87.

"In the Arts and Crafts tradition" by G. Robert Parker. Offers the design and plans for a combination Maritime vernacular and Arts and Crafts home. Photos, plans. Sidebar on architecture and the Arts and Crafts movement. • *Fine Homebuilding*. No. 73 (Spring, 1992) pp. 51–55.

Asbestos

"Asbestos update" by Hank Spies. Informative article on chrysotile asbestos and how to control it. • *Home Mechanix*. No. 745 (May, 1990) p. 92.

"Clearing the air on home hazards." Updated information on asbestos in houses. • *Home Mechanix*. No. 747 (July/Aug, 1990) p. 12.

"Testing and controlling asbestos" by Stephen Flynn. Learn how to test for asbestos in your house and how to remove it. • *Fine Homebuilding*. No. 70 (Nov, 1991) pp. 18–20.

Ash (Wood)

"White ash: good wood for great sport" by Jim Boelling, Chuck Hedlund and Pete Stephano. Informative article on the availability, cost, uses, machining methods and carving tips for white ash. Sidebar on shop-tested techniques that always work. Photos, illustrations, chart. • *Better Homes and Gardens Wood*. No. 64 (Oct, 1993) pp. 27–28.

Aspen Leaf Houses

"Haertling's aspen leaf house" by Shelley Schlender. Describes the aspen leaf house built with exposed-aggregate walls and a copper roof. Photos, plans. Sidebar on standing for ideals. • *Fine Homebuilding*. No. 58 (March, 1990) pp. 49–53.

Attics

"Adding kneewalls" by Peter H. Guimond. Offers a method of adding kneewalls to an attic. • *Fine Homebuilding*. No. 74 (May, 1992) p. 14.

"Attic art studio" by Kevin Ireton. Offers an inventive plan for dropping the garage ceiling to create a studio or office. Photo, diagrams. • *Fine Homebuilding*. No. 64 (Jan, 1991) pp. 84–87.

"An attic studio apartment" by Robert Malone. Details the results of remodeling an attic. Photos, plans. • *Fine Homebuilding*. No. 60 (May, 1990) pp. 42–45.

"Attic upgrades" by Tom Hanley. An analysis of attic remodeling plans. • *Practical Homeowner*. Vol. V, No. 1 (Feb, 1990) pp. 48–53.

"Energy-efficient attic access" by Jeff Greef. Informative article on installing energy-efficient attic ladders. • *Home Mechanix*. No. 771 (Dec/Jan, 1992–93) pp. 8–9, 80.

"Hot attic" by Henry Spies. Brief tip on how to keep an unfinished attic cool. Drawing. • *Home Mechanix*. No. 755 (May, 1991) pp. 96–97.

"Lights in the attic" by Michael Morris. Detailed plans for adding windows or skylights to bring natural light into attics. Photos, plans. • *Home Mechanix*. No. 751 (Dec/Jan, 1990–91) pp. 32–38.

Audio Systems, Outdoor

"Installing outdoor audio" by Ivan Berger. Brief article on selecting weather resistant speakers for portable or permanent outdoor audio systems. Photos, drawing. • *Home Mechanix*. No. 746 (June, 1990) pp. 30–31, 112.

Awls, Scratch

"Scratch awl" by Jim Boelling. Build your own scratch awl with these instructions. Photo, diagrams, materials list, patterns. • *Better Homes and Gardens Wood*. No. 49 (Jan, 1992) pp. 58–59.

B

Ball Courts

"Home court advantage" by Carolyn Chubet. Advice on using turf or plastic mesh to build backyard courts for badminton, squash, and croquet. Photos. • *Practical Homeowner*. Vol. VI, No. 6 (Jul/Aug, 1991) pp. 68–72.

Band Saw Blades

"Folding bandsaw blades." Instructions and drawing on how to fold band saw blades. Drawing. • *Better Homes and Gardens Wood.* No. 60 (April, 1993) p. 85.

Band Saws

"A band saw slow speed attachment, part one" by Frank A. McLean. A description of the use of Boston change gears to manufacture a slow speed attachment. Photos and plans. • *The Home Shop Machinist.* Vol. 9, No. 2 (Mar/Apr, 1990) pp. 40–45.

"A band saw slow speed attachment, part two" by Frank A. McLean. See Vol. 9, No. 2 • *The Home Shop Machinist.* Vol. 9, No. 3 (May/Jun, 1990) pp. 43–49.

"Band saw transmission" by Richard Torgerson. Plans for using a transmission system to adapt a band saw for metal cutting. Photos and plans. • *The Home Shop Machinist.* Vol. 9, No. 4 (Jul/Aug, 1990) pp. 18–22.

"Bandsaws." Specific guide for choosing a band saw for a particular cutting job. Photos, illustration, chart comparing 26 band saws. • *Better Homes and Gardens Wood.* No. 38 (Oct, 1990) pp. 50–53.

"Bandsaws." Informative article on the specifications of 23 band saws. Photo, chart. • *Better Homes and Gardens Wood.* No. 65 (Nov, 1993) pp. 48–49.

"The great bandsaw roundup" by Bill Krier. Guide to the 12 currently popular models and recommendations. Photos, drawings, chart comparing models. Sidebar on how to make your current band saw work better. • *Better Homes and Gardens Wood.* No. 51 (April, 1992) pp. 66–71.

"Undercover magnet reveals tension on bandsaw blade" by Earl A. Pyle. Handy suggestion for checking on the blade-tension scale without looking inside. Drawing • *Better Homes and Gardens Wood.* No. 60 (April, 1993) p. 12.

"A universal band saw jig" by R. J. DeCristoforo. A concise descriptive article about making jigs and other accessories for band saws. Photos and plans. • *The Woodworker's Journal.* Vol. 16, No. 2 (Mar/Apr, 1992) pp. 30–33.

Bands, Steel

"Steel band hold-ins" by Gothard Knutson. Describes the use of steel bands for ripping wood. Drawing. • *Woodwork.* No. 14 (March/April) p. 6.

Banks, Coin

"Dresser-top coin bank." This beginner's project details the steps in building a small coin bank shaped like a shelf clock. Photo, plans, and materials lists. • *The Woodworker's Journal.* Vol. 15, No. 3 (May/Jun, 1991) pp. 52–53.

Banksia Nut (Wood)

"Turning Australian Wood: The Banksia Nut" by Jeff Parsons. Describes how to use a wood lathe to work with the Australian Banksia nut. Photos. • *Canadian Workshop.* Vol. 13, No. 4 (Jan 1990) pp. 8–9.

Barbecue Fireplaces

"Beyond the basic barbecue" by Pat McMillan. Highlights three designs for outdoor barbecue fireplaces. Photos, drawings. • *Home Mechanix.* No. 757 (July/Aug, 1991) pp. 68–71.

Barkrosing

"Barkrosing" by Larry Johnston. Introduces the carving technique called barkrosing, a Nordic decorative technique for wooden spoons or other objects. Photos. • *Better Homes and Gardens Wood.* No. 61 (June, 1993) pp. 54–55.

Barn Houses

"A big barn at Big River" by John Birchard. Explains how to construct a barn-style house inexpensively and efficiently. Photos, plans. • *Fine Homebuilding.* No. 59 (Spring) pp. 42–47.

Book Review: *The Barn Book: Creative Conversions for Country Living* by Kate Corbett Winder. Book review on converting barns into country-style homes. North Pomfret, VT: Trafalgar Square Publishing, 128 pp. • *Fine Homebuilding.* No. 67 (May, 1991) p. 104.

Barns (Toy)

"Little red tote barn" by Larry Johnston. Directions to construct barn that doubles as a tote carrier for the animals and fence. Photo, drawing, materials list. • *Better Homes and Gardens Wood.* No. 61 (June, 1993) pp. 68–70.

Barns--Remodeling

"Winner's Circle" by Glenn Perrett. Provides information on how the author remodeled an old barn into an efficient stable for horses. List of sources. Photos. • *Canadian Workshop.* Vol. 15, No. 1 (Oct 1991) pp. 66–72.

Barrier-Free Houses

"A house without barriers" by Chuck Williams. Detailed description of a design that offers access for a wheelchair. Photos, plans, drawings. Sidebar on building a cantilevered counter. • *Fine Homebuilding.* No. 76 (Sep, 1992) pp. 54–59.

Barriers, Radiant

"Radiant foil" by Henry Spies. Brief tip on how to install a radiant barrier. Drawing. • *Home Mechanix.* No. 763 (March, 1992) pp. 82–83.

Bars

"Wallace and Hinz" by Deborah Upshaw. Discusses the construction of a typical modular bar. Drawing. Photos. • *Woodwork.* No. 19 (Jan/Feb, 1993) pp. 32–38.

Bars, Knockout

"Knockout Bar" by Jack R. Thompson. A quick tip on making a knockout bar for a lathe. Photo and plans. • *The Home Shop Machinist.* Vol. 12, No. 3 (May/Jun, 1993) p. 37.

Barstools

"Bottoms-up barstools" by Marlen Kemmet and James R. Downing. Explains how to build contemporary-styled barstools featuring mortise-and-tenon joinery. Photos, diagrams, materials list. • *Better Homes and Gardens Wood.* No. 45 (Sep, 1991) pp. 49–53.

Bartering

"Built on barter" by James Lomuscio. An analysis of the growth of bartering organization in recent years. • *Practical Homeowner.* Vol. VI, No. 1 (Jan, 1991) pp. 26–28.

Baseboards

"Baseboard shims" by Ralph W. Brome. Explains how to install baseboards over drywall. Drawing. • *Fine Homebuilding.* No. 62 (Sep, 1990) p. 28.

"Running baseboard efficiently" by Greg Smith. Explains a methodical approach to installing baseboards that is fast and efficient. Photos, drawing. • *Fine Homebuilding.* No. 76 (Sep, 1992) pp. 51–53.

Basements

"After the flood" by Don Best. A troubleshooting guide for leaky basements. Photos. • *Practical Homeowner.* Vol. VI, No. 6 (Jul/Aug, 1991) pp. 76–81.

"Basement condensation" by Henry Spies. Brief tip on how to eliminate condensation on the basement band joist. Drawing. • *Home Mechanix.* No. 753 (March, 1991) p. 80.

"Basement flooding" by Henry Spies. Offers a solution to prevent basement flooding. • *Home Mechanix.* No. 780 (Nov, 1993) pp. 90–91.

"Basement knockout" by Carolyn Chubet. Tips on adding a walkout basement to a house. Photos • *Practical Homeowner.* Vol. VI, No. 5 (May/June, 1991) pp. 50–53.

"Bold, Beautiful Basements" by Rhonda Chant. Reviews the various considerations in renovating a home basement into an attractive living area. Photos. Drawn sample plans. • *Canadian Workshop.* Vol. 13, No. 4 (Jan 1990) pp. 16–20.

"Building a dry basement" by Matt Phair. Offers information on underground drainage products that help keep basements dry. Drawings. • *Home Mechanix.* No. 748 (Sep, 1990) pp. 56–60.

"Digging out the basement" by Hank Spies. Brief tip on building a new retaining wall in a basement. Drawing. • *Home Mechanix.* No. 744 (April, 1990) pp. 101.

"Right from the start" by Don Best. Advice for constructing dry and waterproof basements. Photos and drawings. • *Practical Homeowner.* Vol. VI, No. 5 (May/June, 1991) pp. 64–70.

Basements--Heating

"Cold basement" by Henry Spies. Explains how to increase the temperature of a basement. • *Home Mechanix.* No. 769 (Oct, 1992) p. 80.

Baskets

"Split ash baskets Maine style" by Peter J. Stephano. Offers a fascinating look at the process of making baskets. Photos. • *Better Homes and Gardens Wood.* No. 54 (Sep, 1992) pp. 35–39.

Baskets, Collapsible

"Collapsible basket." How to use a bandsaw to cut a heart-shaped basket out of a single piece of wood. This basket will sag open and collapse flat as needed. Photos, plans, and materials list. • The Woodworker's Journal. Vol. 17, No. 3 (May/Jun, 1993) pp. 33–37.

Bathrooms

"All about steam baths" by Judith Trotsky. Informative article on installing a steam bath in your bathroom. Photos, drawing,

chart. • *Home Mechanix.* No. 752 (Feb, 1991) pp. 78–81.

"Bathroom basics" by Ted Watson. Tips on remodeling bathrooms. Photos. • *Practical Homeowner.* (Nov/Dec, 1992) pp. 46–47.

"Bathroom brushup" by Gene and Katie Hamilton. Lists common bath-surface problems and remedy solutions for cleaning them. Photos. • *Home Mechanix.* No. 769 (Oct, 1992) p. 16.

"Cutting corners to gain bath space" by Pat McMillan. Presents practical designs for bathrooms using corner fixtures. Photos, plans. Sidebar on making room for the bathroom laundry. • *Home Mechanix.* No. 759 (Oct, 1991) pp. 62–69.

"The extra bath" by Roy Barnhart. Space-saving solutions for making a second bath. Photos and plans. • *Practical Homeowner.* Vol. VI, No. 7 (Sep, 1991) pp. 56–62.

"Jewelbox bathroom" by Jeff Morse. Describes a remodeled bathroom tucked in a dormer. Photos, plans, diagrams. • *Fine Homebuilding.* No. 76 (Sep, 1992) pp. 66–69.

"Natural Surroundings." Using natural stone tiles for bath and shower walls. Photos. • *Practical Homeowner.* (Mar/Apr, 1992) pp. 62–65.

"Small bath solutions" by Rich Binsacca. How to get more space out of a small bathroom. Photos and plans. • *Practical Homeowner.* (May/June, 1992) pp. 72–75.

"Universal kitchens and baths." Provides tips for creating accessibility for handicapped or other special needs. Photos, drawings. • *Home Mechanix.* No. 781 (Dec/Jan, 1993–94) pp. 66–70, 84.

Bathrooms--Adding on

"Back-to-back baths" by Pat McMillan. Offers tips on building additional baths and sharing the plumbing lines and electrical wiring. Photos, plans, drawing.

• *Home Mechanix.* No. 760 (Nov, 1991) pp. 63–66.

Bathrooms--Fixtures

"A buyer's guide to faucets, spouts and showerheads" by Pat McMillan. Presents a list of considerations for buying bathroom fixtures. Photos. • *Home Mechanix.* No. 774 (April, 1993) pp. 64–69.

"Small bath solutions" by Pat McMillan. Presents a variety of models and plans for small bathrooms. Photos, drawings, plans. • *Home Mechanix.* No. 765 (May, 1992) pp. 62–67.

"Water-saving showerheads and faucets" by Amy Vickers. In-depth article on the latest models of cost-saving and water-saving showerheads and faucets. Photos, charts. • *Fine Homebuilding.* No. 84 (Nov, 1993) pp. 82–84.

Bathrooms--Natural lighting

"Skylight bath" by Joseph Truini. Offers instructions on adding a skylight to a small bath. Photos. Sidebar on capturing the sun: light-shaft options. • *Home Mechanix.* No. 776 (June, 1993) pp. 56–59.

"Sunbaths" by Ellen Rand. A how-to guide for bringing sunlight into the bathroom. Photos. • *Practical Homeowner.* Vol. V, No. 6 (Sep, 1990) pp. 52–56.

Bathrooms--Safety

"The safety-first bathroom" by Pat McMillan. Presents safety fixtures for bathrooms such as good traction floor coverings and adequate lighting. Photos, diagram. Sidebar—figuring on safety. • *Home Mechanix.* No. 766 (June, 1992) pp. 54–57.

Bathrooms--Storage

"Big improvements for small baths" by Sally Ross. Provides strategies for creating extra storage space in small bathrooms. Photos, plans, drawings, diagrams. • *Home Mechanix.* No. 745 (May, 1990) pp. 36–39.

"Vanity cases" by Pat McMillan. Presents four designs for bathroom storage. Photos, drawings, diagrams. • *Home Mechanix.* No. 774 (April, 1993) pp. 70–73.

Batteries, Rechargeable

"Coming right up." Helpful tips for finding companies that recharge batteries in a short time. Illustration. • *Better Homes and Gardens Wood.* No. 42 (April, 1991) p. 84.

Beam Stairs

"Beam-stair" by Robert Gay. Construction plans to make a beam-stair for making short lifts. Drawing. • *Fine Homebuilding.* No. 70 (Nov, 1991) p. 32.

Beams, Timber

"Glue-laminated timbers" by Stephen Smulski. Offers tips on designing and building with beams. Photos, drawings. Sidebar on sizing up a structural beam. • *Fine Homebuilding.* No. 71 (Jan, 1992) pp. 55–59.

Bedrooms

"Bed alcove" by Tony Simmonds. Offers a plan to convert attic space into a bedroom with a bed that has drawers, bookshelves and a vanity. Photos, drawing. • *Fine Homebuilding.* No. 76 (Sep, 1992) pp. 42–45.

Beds

"A convertible daybed" by Ron Karten. Provides instructions for building a convertible daybed. Drawing. Photos. • *Woodwork.* No. 17 (Sep/Oct, 1992) pp. 36–41.

"Dream keepers" by Matthew Phair. Provides designs and constructions plans for three bed frames with storage. Photos, diagrams. • *Home Mechanix.* No. 780 (Nov, 1993) pp. 60–66.

"Shaker bed" by Marlen Kemmet and James Downing. Describes how to make a queen-sized Shaker-style bed. Photo, drawings, materials list, diagrams. • *Better*

Homes and Gardens Wood. No. 64 (Oct, 1993) pp. 60–65, 78.

"Sleeping beauties" by Matt Phair. Detailed designs and instructions for two bed frames that include built-in storage. Photos, diagrams. • *Home Mechanix.* No. 751 (Dec/Jan, 1990-91) pp. 62–69.

"A use for an odd grease fitting" by Russell H. Smith. Solves the problem of turning a bedpost twice as long as the lathe bed with an old grease fitting. • *Woodwork.* No. 19 (Jan/Feb, 1993) pp. 18–20.

Beds, Baby

"Baby's first bed" by Marlen Kemmet and James R. Downing. Detailed instructions to construct a hardwood crib. Photo, materials list, diagrams. • *Better Homes and Gardens Wood.* No. 59 (Feb, 1993) pp. 34–39.

Beds, Four-Poster

"Provincial four-poster bed." A very detailed article offering plans for the construction of a French Provincial-style, four-poster bed. Photos, plans, and materials list. • *The Woodworker's Journal.* Vol. 4, No. 6 (Nov/Dec, 1990) pp. 41–44.

Belt Clips

"Power-tool belt clip" by Cliff Tillotson. Brief tip on holding a nail gun or a power tool on a tool belt. Drawing. • *Fine Homebuilding.* No. 75 (July, 1992) p. 28.

Belvederes

"The gift of the belvedere." An explanation of a backyard belvedere construction project. Photos. • *Practical Homeowner.* (Mar/Apr, 1992) pp. 82–84.

Benches

"Garden arbor." Tips on how to construct a simple arbor/garden bench. Photo, plans, and materials list. • *The Woodworker's Journal.* Vol. 17, No. 2 (Mar/Apr, 1993) pp. 28–32.

"Gossip bench." This article describes the plans for a one person bench/telephone stand. Photos, plans, and materials list. • *The Woodworker's Journal.* Vol. 17, No. 4 (Jul/Aug, 1993) pp. 36–39.

"Provincial bench." This brief article offers detail for making a small pine bench in the French Provincial style. Photo, plans, and materials list. • *The Woodworker's Journal.* Vol. 15, No. 1 (Jan/Feb, 1991) pp. 52–53.

"Refining rustics" by Joseph Truini and Judith Trotsky. Offers designs and construction plans for a rustic bench and gate made of logs and branches. Photos, diagrams. • *Home Mechanix.* No. 773 (March, 1993) pp. 44–47.

Benches, Children's

"Learning My ABCs" by William Lovett. Describes how to construct a child's wooden bench and alphabet learning toy. Photo. List of materials. Drawn plans. • *Canadian Workshop.* Vol. 15, No. 1 (Oct 1991) pp. 55–56.

"Little folks desk and bench." Clear plans on how to make a child's-size desk and bench. Photos, plans, and materials. • *The Woodworker's Journal.* Vol. 15, No. 6 (Nov/Dec, 1991) pp. 46–47.

Benches, Chopsaw

"Folding chopsaw bench" by Roger Willmann. Brief tip on a design for a folding stand for a power miter box. Drawing. • *Fine Homebuilding.* No. 76 (Sep, 1992) p. 30.

Benches, Colonial

"Colonial bench." This is a simple design for a Colonial-style bench. Photo, plans, and materials list. • *The Woodworker's Journal.* Vol. 15, No. 5 (Sep/Oct, 1991) pp. 40–41.

Benches, Outdoor

"A comfortable outdoor bench" by David Bright. Provides directions to construct a built-in bench for a deck or outdoor porch. Photos, diagram. • *Fine*

Homebuilding. No. 82 (July, 1993) pp. 52–53.

Benches, Potting

"Redwood potting bench." This article describes the steps for making and assembling an outdoor workbench with shelves suitable for gardening. Photos, plans, and materials list. • *The Woodworker's Journal.* Vol. 15, No. 2 (Mar/Apr, 1991) pp. 40–43.

Benches, Santa Fe

"Santa Fe bench." This comprehensive description of the steps in constructing a southwestern-style Santa Fe bench includes a materials list and information on a painted finish. Photos and plans. • *The Woodworker's Journal.* Vol. 14, No. 2 (Mar/Apr, 1990) pp. 32–37.

Benzene

"Is benzene poisoning your home?" by Steve Lyons. An explanation of the uses and dangers of benzene. • *Practical Homeowner.* Vol VI., No. 5 (May/June, 1991) pp. 28-29.

Bevels, Angle

"Angle bevel" by Marlen Kemmet and Jim Boelling. Describes how to make a brass and walnut angle bevel. Photo, diagrams. • *Better Homes and Gardens Wood.* No. 50 (Feb, 1992) pp. 22-24.

Birch (Wood)

"Yellow birch" by Jim Boelling, George Granseth, Else Bigton, and Phil Odden. Provides information on the availability, cost, woodworking uses and carving suggestions. Photos, illustration. • *Better Homes and Gardens Wood.* No. 39 (Dec, 1990) pp. 33-34.

Bird Feeders

"Fine-feathered friend feeder" by Marlen Kemmet. Detailed instructions for a hexagonal shaped feeder measuring 15" in diameter. Diagrams, photo, materials

list. • *Better Homes and Gardens Wood.* No. 36 (Aug, 1990) pp. 76-78.

"Hanging bird feeders." A simple set of instructions for making a hanging bird feeder designed to hold either suet or fruit. Plans. • *The Woodworker's Journal.* Vol. 14, No. 6 (Nov/Dec, 1990) pp. 60-61.

Birdhouses

"Leafy lodging" by David Ashe. Brief instructions to build a tree-shaped birdhouse. Photo, diagrams, pattern. • *Better Homes and Gardens Wood.* No. 59 (Feb, 1993) pp. 68-69.

"Seeds and such snack shop" by Pat Schlarbaum. Instructions to create a bird feeder. Photos, diagrams, materials list. • *Better Homes and Gardens Wood.* No. 63 (Sep, 1993) pp. 46-49.

"Short branch saloon" by James R. Downing. Instructions to build a frontier-style saloon. Photo, diagrams. • *Better Homes and Gardens Wood.* No. 50 (Feb, 1992) pp. 76-77.

"Stars-and-stripes wren house" by Bob and Carolyn Reichert. Brief instructions to build a wren house. Photos, diagrams, pattern. • *Better Homes and Gardens Wood.* No. 42 (April, 1991) pp. 72-73.

"Window-mounted birdhouse." This is an easy-to-make project for a small birdhouse which can be mounted to an window for internal viewing. Photos, plans, and materials list. • *The Woodworker's Journal.* Vol. 15, No. 2 (Mar/ Apr, 1991) pp. 59-61.

Bits, Forstner

"The woodworker's survival guide to buying forstner bits" by Bill Krier. Test results and performance ratings for 18 different forstner bits. Photos, chart. • *Better Homes and Gardens Wood.* No. 41 (Feb, 1991) pp. 72-73, 89.

Bits, Router

"Using router bits in a drill press" by R.J. De Cristoforo. This article describes the advantages of using a drill press to hold router bits instead of a portable router. Photos and drawings. • *The Woodworker's Journal.* Vol. 14, No. 2 (Mar/Apr, 1990) pp. 20-24.

Blocking

"Don't forget the blocks" by Larry Haun. Presents the advantages of blocking a house. Drawings, diagrams. • *Fine Homebuilding.* No. 82 (July, 1993) pp. 48-51.

Blocks, Patio

"Graceful paving" by Jim Rosenau. Practical advice for installing paving blocks for walks and patios without using mortar. Photos. • *Practical Homeowner.* (Jul/Aug, 1992) pp. 84-89.

Blocks (Toy)

"Custom-made building blocks" by Jeff Greef. Provides details on constructing custom-made toy building blocks for children, includes materials list. Photos. • *Woodwork.* No. 18 (Nov/Dec, 1992) pp. 70-74.

"Standing-tall blocks box." Directions to construct wooden blocks tall enough to use as a booster step for toddlers. Photos, materials list, diagram. • *Better Homes and Gardens Wood.* No. 52 (June, 1992) pp. 68-69.

Boards, Cutting

"Culinary Cutting Boards" by Gary Walchuk. Provides instructions on constructing wood cutting boards. Photo. Drawn plans. • *Canadian Workshop.* Vol. 13, No. 4 (Jan 1990) pp. 57 58.

"A cut above the rest" by James R. Downing. Create an attractive, crafted cutting board with this design. Photo, diagrams. • *Better Homes and Gardens Wood.* No. 39 (Dec, 1990) pp. 46 47.

"Sink-top cutting board." This sketch offers a good beginner's project by detailing the steps necessary to make a cutting board. Photo and plans. • *The*

Woodworker's Journal. Vol. 15, No. 2 (Mar/Apr, 1991) pp. 54-55.

Boats

Book Review: *Wooden Boat Building Made Simple* by Kit Bonner. Book review on a guide for building a eight foot wooden pram. Fair Oaks, CA: Author (5129 Ridgegate Way) 46 pp. • *Woodwork.* No. 16 (July/August, 1992) p. 75.

Boats (Model)

"Where realism rides the waves" by Peter J. Stephano. Explains the step-by-step process of creating model boats. Photos. • *Better Homes and Gardens Wood.* No. 64 (Oct, 1993) pp. 29 33.

Bookends

"Bookshelf classics." Offers plans to build bookends in the classical architectural style. Photo, diagram, pattern. • *Better Homes and Gardens Wood.* No. 57 (Dec, 1992) pp. 72-73.

Bookshelves

"Adjustable desktop bookshelf." An easy-to-make project for a single level, portable bookshelf. Photo, plans, and materials list. • *The Woodworker's Journal.* Vol. 17, No. 4 (Jul/Aug, 1993) pp. 52-55.

"Cimarron." This article offers plans for the construction of a full length, southwestern-style open bookcase. Photo, plans, and materials list. • *The Woodworker's Journal.* Vol. 17, No. 1 (Jan/Feb, 1993) pp. 60-63.

"Easy-build bookshelves." Easy-to-follow plans for building open-faced bookshelves. Photos, plans, and materials list. • *The Woodworker's Journal.* Vol. 16, No. 5 (Sep/Oct, 1992) pp. 62-63.

"A home library" by Charles Wardell. Provides an innovative idea for constructing a maple and purpleheart 30 ft. bookcase. Photos, diagrams. • *Fine Homebuilding.* No. 65 (March, 1991) pp. 85-87.

"Shelving showcase" by Marlen Kemmet and Jim Downing. Clear-cut instructions to build a full-length bookcase with fluted face-frame stiles. Photos, diagrams, materials list. • *Better Homes and Gardens Wood.* No. 50 (Feb, 1992) pp. 38-43.

"A study in cherry" by Philip S. Sollman. Explains the process of building a wall unit for books, TV, etc. with cherry. Photos, diagrams. • *Fine Homebuilding.* No. 61 (July, 1990) pp. 72-75.

Borders, Wall

"Border incidents" by Thomas H. Jones. Gives a variety of ideas for decorative wall borders. Photos. • *Home Mechanix.* No. 753 (March, 1991) pp. 44-52.

Boring Machines

"The Butler multiple boring machines" by Harold Mason. A historical look at a revolutionary type of multiple-head boring machine built in 1920. Photos and plans. • *The Home Shop Machinist.* Vol. 12, No. 2 (Mar/Apr, 1993) pp. 14-23.

Bowls

"Lamination sensation" by Larry Johnston. Turn an eye-catching laminated bowl with these directions. Photos, diagrams, materials list. • *Better Homes and Gardens Wood.* No. 60 (April, 1993) pp. 46-49.

Bowls, Ale

"A bird-in-the-hand ale bowl" by Phillip Odden. Carve your own bird-shaped ale bowl. Photos, materials list. • *Better Homes and Gardens Wood.* No. 60 (April, 1993) pp. 50-51, 82.

Bowls, Bricklaid

"Building and turning a bricklaid bowl" by Robert Belke. A description of the method for making a round bowl constructed of wood segments which are assembled and turned on a lathe. Photos, plans, and materials list. • *The Woodworker's Journal.* Vol. 17, No. 6 (Nov/Dec, 1993) pp. 32-35.

Bowls, Potpourri

"Pewter-topped potpourri bowl" by C.I. Gatzke. Brief article on how to turn a potpourri bowl. Photo, pattern, drawing, materials list. • *Better Homes and Gardens Wood.* No. 52 (June, 1992) p. 42.

Bowls, Turned

"From blank bowl to finished bowl" by Bill Krier and Marlen Kemmet. Step-by-step coverage of the process of turning a bowl. Photos, drawings. • *Better Homes and Gardens Wood.* No. 57 (Dec, 1992) pp. 77-80.

Bowls, Wooden

"Faux-turned vessels." An in-depth article detailing the procedure for making round bowls in sections without the use of a lathe. Photos, plans, and drawings. • *The Woodworker's Journal.* Vol. 15, No. 6 (Nov/Dec, 1991) pp. 26-31.

"Faux-turned vessels: 4 patterns." Complete plans for four types of wooden vessels made without using a lathe. Photos and plans. • *The Woodworker's Journal.* Vol. 15, No. 6 (Nov/Dec, 1991) pp. 65-69.

"Turning Australian Wood: The Eucalyptus Slab Bowl" by Jeff Parsons. Provides detailed description of the steps associated with the turning of eucalyptus wood to form a bowl. Photos. • *Canadian Workshop.* Vol. 13, No. 5 (Feb 1990) pp. 8-9.

"Zap! Dry green bowls in minutes" by Peter J. Stephano and Walt Panck. Instructive information on drying green-turned bowls in the microwave, complete with power settings chart. Photos. • *Better Homes and Gardens Wood.* No. 33 (Feb, 1990) pp. 46-49.

Bows

"Making a Northcoast Indian bow" by Jim Tolpin. Describes the process of making a bow and the types of wood that are ideal for the process. Drawing. Photos.

• *Woodwork.* No. 16 (July/August, 1992) pp. 36-42.

Boxes

"The all-wood box" by Marlen Kemmet and Craig Brown. Provides the directions to build a finely crafted wooden box. Photo, diagrams, materials list. • *Better Homes and Gardens Wood.* No. 48 (Dec, 1991) pp. 56-59.

"Audio/video remote rack." A brief tip on making a small wooden tray box for holding remote control units. Photos, plans, and materials list. • *The Woodworker's Journal.* Vol. 16, No. 4 (Jul/Aug, 1992) pp. 44-45.

"Beauty and the box." Learn how to create an attractive box with inlay on the top. Photo, diagrams, materials list. • *Better Homes and Gardens Wood.* No. 61 (June, 1993) pp. 66-67.

"Building boxes" by Roger Holmes. This article describes different techniques for constructing boxes using butt joints, rabbet joints, miters, and dovetail joints. Photo and plans. • *The Woodworker's Journal.* Vol. 17, No. 2 (Mar/Apr, 1993) pp. 13-18.

"Display box." An easy-to-make project for a small display box for miniatures. Photo, plans, and materials list. • *The Woodworker's Journal.* Vol. 17, No. 2 (Mar/Apr, 1993) pp. 51 53.

"Magazine slip cases." An easy-to-make project building box-jointed magazine slip cases. Photo, plans, and materials list. • *The Woodworker's Journal.* Vol. 17, No. 5 (Sep/Oct, 1993) pp. 48-49.

"Museum-quality containers" by Jeffrey Seaton. Directions on how to make a bandsawn box. Drawing. Photos. • *Woodwork.* No. 17 (Sep/Oct, 1992) pp. 30-35.

"Turning small boxes" by Nick Cook. This is a brief description of the process for turning out small round boxes on a lathe.

Photo and drawings. • *The Woodworker's Journal.* Vol. 15, No. 4 (Jul/Aug, 1991) pp. 15-17.

See Also Chests

Boxes, Bread

"Butternut breadbox." How to make a simple breadbox with a sliding tambour door. Photos, plans, and materials list. • The Woodworker's Journal. Vol. 16, No. 3 (May/Jun, 1992) pp. 44 47.

"Wheat-motif bread box" by Jim Boelling. Brief description explaining how to make a breadbox. Photo, materials list, diagrams. • *Better Homes and Gardens Wood.* No. 59 (Feb, 1993) pp. 70-71.

Boxes, Candle

"Colonial candle box." Brief instructions for this pine storage box with a sliding grooved lid. Photos, patterns, diagrams, materials list. • *Better Homes and Gardens Wood.* No. 36 (Aug, 1990) pp. 38-39.

Boxes, Covered

"Heart box." This brief article offers a simple design for a heart-shaped box with a lid. Photos and plans. • *The Woodworker's Journal.* Vol. 16, No. 1 (Jan/Feb, 1992) pp. 59-61.

Boxes, Cutlery

"Well-ordered cutlery case" by Jim Boelling. Directions and assembly for a walnut steak-knife case with a sliding lid. Photo, diagrams, materials list. • *Better Homes and Gardens Wood.* No. 48 (Dec, 1991) pp. 82-83.

Boxes, Jewelry

"Contemporary jewelry box." A brief outline for making a small jewelry box with clean modernistic lines. Photos, plans, and materials list. • *The Woodworker's Journal.* Vol. 17, No. 6 (Nov/Dec, 1993) pp. 53-55.

"Dresser-top delight" by Marlen Kemmet and Jerry Patrasso. Instructions to create a teardrop shaped jewelry box. Photo, diagrams, patterns. • *Better Homes and Gardens Wood.* No. 55 (Oct, 1992) pp. 58-61.

"Heirloom jewelry box." Plans for a small jewelry box with a separate lid. Photos, plans, and materials list. • *The Woodworker's Journal.* Vol. 16, No. 6 (Nov/Dec, 1992) pp. 56-59.

"Jewel of a case" by Marlen Kemmet. Specific directions for a Scandanavian-style jewelry case with sliding trays. Photos, materials list, diagram. • *Better Homes and Gardens Wood.* No. 39 (Dec, 1990) pp. 42-45.

"Jewelry chest." An easy-to-make project for a small jewelry chest with three drawers. Photos, plans, and materials list. • The Woodworker's Journal. Vol. 17, No. 3 (May/Jun, 1993) pp. 42-45.

"Keepsake jewelry box." A simple and easy-to-make design for a small jewelry box. Photos, plans, and materials list. • *The Woodworker's Journal.* Vol. 15, No. 6 (Nov/Dec, 1991) pp. 53-55.

"Koa jewelry chest." A brief analysis of the construction of a small jewelry box made from tropical Koa wood. Plans and materials list. • *The Woodworker's Journal.* Vol. 14, No. 6 (Nov/Dec, 1990) pp. 45-47.

"Octagonal jewelry box." This article presents a design for a small jewelry box with an elaborate wood inlay lid. Photos and plans. • *The Woodworker's Journal.* Vol. 15, No. 2 (Mar/Apr, 1991) pp. 44-47.

Boxes, Miter

"Wooden miter boxes" by Tom Law. Instructions to build a wooden miter box. Photo, diagram. • *Fine Homebuilding.* No. 65 (March, 1991) p. 75.

Boxes, Music

"Masterpiece music box" by C.I. Gatzke. Create a lathe-turned music box with veneer inlays. Photo, diagrams, patterns, materials list. • *Better Homes and Gardens Wood.* No. 53 (Aug, 1992) pp. 69-71.

"Teddy bear music box" by Marlen Kemmet and Richard Gard. Create an adorable music box with walnut base and a teddy bear holding balloons. Photo, diagrams, full-sized patterns. • *Better Homes and Gardens Wood.* No. 48 (Dec, 1991) pp. 66-69.

Boxes, Pine

"A pine box" by Graham Blackburn. Detailed construction instructions on a traditional pine box, complete with materials list. Photo and drawings. • *Woodwork.* No. 18 (Nov/Dec, 1992) pp. 56-60.

Boxes, Recipe

"Four easy-to-make kitchen projects." Four simple designs for kitchen cooling racks, salad tongs, serving boat, and recipe box. Photos, plans, and materials list. • *The Woodworker's Journal.* Vol. 15, No. 5 (Sep/Oct, 1991 pp. 58-66.

Boxes, Shadow

"Country shadow box" by James R. Downing. Brief directions to construct an attractive shadow box to showcase collectibles. Photos, diagram, full-sized patterns. • *Better Homes and Gardens Wood.* No. 40 (Jan, 1991) pp. 68-69, 86.

Boxes, Shaker

"Shaker woodbox." How to build a simple wooden box with attached drawer in the Shaker style. Photos, plans, and materials list. • The Woodworker's Journal. Vol. 14, No. 5 (Sep/Oct, 1990) pp. 42-44.

Boxes, Tissue

"Classy tissue box cover-up" by Larry Johnston. Brief instructions to build a walnut tissue box. Photo, diagrams. • *Better Homes and Gardens Wood.* No. 54 (Sep, 1992) pp. 50-51.

"Tissue box cover." This brief article describes the method of constructing a wooden cover for a tissue box, including parts list. Photo. Plans. • *The Woodworker's*

Journal. Vol. 14, No. 1 (Jan/Feb, 1990) pp. 38-39.

Boxes, Torsion

"Making a torsion box" by Ed Speas. How to build a hollow core wooden structure that is light yet has great strength and stability. Plans. • *The Woodworker's Journal.* Vol. 17, No. 1 (Jan/Feb, 1993) pp. 29-32.

Boxes, Wall

"Pilgrim's-pride wall box." Build a simple colonial wall box for decorative purposes or to hold matches. Full-sized pattern, diagram, photo. • *Better Homes and Gardens Wood.* No. 36 (Aug, 1990) p. 43.

Boxes--Veneering

"Box with marquetry top." This article offers tips on how to use marquetry techniques with wood veneers to create a small box with a contrasting patterned lid. Photo, plans, and drawings. • *The Woodworker's Journal.* Vol. 15, No. 1 (Jan/Feb, 1991) pp. 56-57.

Brackets, Handsaw

"Handsaw bracket" by Sam Yoder. Handy tip to make a handsaw bracket. Drawing. • *Fine Homebuilding.* No. 58 (March, 1990) p. 26.

Brass Inlay

"Brass inlay and brass-covered moulding" by David Loft and Abram Loft. Discusses the methods French craftsmen use in adding brass ornamentation to boxes, mirrors, and other pieces of woodwork. Photos. • *Woodwork.* No. 17 (Sep/Oct, 1992) pp. 42-47.

Brazing

"Brazing band saw blades" by Frank A. McLean. A guide to brazing broken saw blades. Plans. • *The Home Shop Machinist.* Vol. 12, No. 5 (Sep/Oct, 1993) pp. 44-45.

Brick Repointing

"Brick Repointing" by Gary Mayk. Presents the materials, tools, and techniques useful for creating sound brick joints. Photos.

• *Home Mechanix.* No. 773 (March, 1993) pp. 10-13.

Bricklaying

"Matching existing brickwork" by Steven Spratt. Offers instructions on how to match bricks for a remodeling project. Photos. • *Fine Homebuilding.* No. 63 (Nov, 1990) pp. 70-71.

Bricks

"Concrete masonry bricks" by Jacob W. Ribar. Details the value of making homemade bricks for constructing a home. • *Fine Homebuilding.* No. 64 (Jan, 1991) p. 22.

Bridges

"Tassajara makeover" by Gene DeSmidt. Focuses on rebuilding a wooden bridge and an accompanying deck to Tassajara's hot springs. Photos, drawings. • *Fine Homebuilding.* No. 68 (July, 1991) pp. 70-73.

Briefcases

"Hardwood briefcase" by Marlen Kemmet. Provides instructions to build a solid wood briefcase with leather lining. Diagrams, photos, materials list. • *Better Homes and Gardens Wood.* No. 41 (Feb, 1991) pp. 40-46.

Brushes

"Choosing a good brush" by James Barrett. Tips on how to choose a good brush for varnishing. Photo and drawing. • *The Woodworker's Journal.* Vol. 17, No. 2 (Mar/Apr, 1993) pp. 24-27.

"Homemade brush features renewable foam 'bristles'" by Bob Dahlberg. Brief tip on how to make a renewable foam brush. Drawing. • *Better Homes and Gardens Wood.* No. 56 (Nov, 1992) p. 22.

Brushes, Bench

"Bench brushes from old brooms" by Grant Beck. Brief article on how to salvage old brooms to serve as bench brushes.

Drawing. • *Woodwork.* No. 18 (Nov/Dec, 1992) pp. 20-22.

Brushes, Paint

"Perpetual paintbrushes" by Mark White. Handy tips for cleaning paint brushes as you work. • *Fine Homebuilding.* No. 62 (Sep, 1990) p. 30.

Building Codes

Book Review: *The Accessibility Book: Building Code Summary and Products Directory* by Julee Quarve-Peterson. Book review on a handy reference guide to federal accessibility codes. Crystal, MN: Julee Quarve-Peterson (PO Box 28093). • *Fine Homebuilding.* No. 63 (Nov, 1990) p. 106.

Building Materials

"Acrylic-impregnated wood" by Bill Krier. Learn about the process of stabilization, creating hard and solid objects from soft crumbling wood. Photos. • *Better Homes and Gardens Wood.* No. 49 (Jan, 1992) pp. 50-51.

"Air-drying lumber" by Peter J. Stephano. Brief tip on air-drying lumber successfully. Photo, drawings. • *Better Homes and Gardens Wood.* No. 59 (Feb, 1993) pp. 40-41.

"Alternative lumber sources" by Chris Black. Money saving tips on alternative sources for lumber. • *Woodwork.* No. 17 (Sep/Oct, 1992) pp. 54-55.

Book Review: *Construction Materials: Types, Uses and Applications* by Caleb Hornbostel. Book review on a guide to construction materials, the history of the materials, and their physical properties. New York: John Wiley and Sons Inc., 1023 pp. • *Fine Homebuilding.* No. 67 (May, 1991) p. 104.

"Ecoinstruction materials" by Thomas F. Sweeney. Informative article on building materials made from recycled products. Photos. • *Home Mechanix.* No. 765 (May, 1992) pp. 50-54.

"Fabulous fakes" by Megan Connelly. Examines the cost-effectiveness of using alternatives to slate, clay, and natural stone for roofing, patios, and other home projects. Photos, chart. • *Home Mechanix.* No. 748 (Sep, 1990) pp. 34-41.

"Harvesting your own lumber" by Christopher F. DeBlois. Gives information on allowable spans for poplar and air drying vs. kiln-dried lumber. • *Fine Homebuilding.* No. 81 (May, 1993) p. 16.

"Home brews" by Ken Ozimek. Provides homemade nontoxic replacements for woodshop supplies. Illustration. • *Better Homes and Gardens Wood.* No. 44 (August, 1991) p. 68.

"Home-made home" by Henry Spies. Informative article on storing building materials for long periods of time. • *Home Mechanix.* No. 776 (June, 1993) p. 84.

"New again" by Timothy O. Bakke. Brief article on a company that recycles building materials. • *Home Mechanix.* No. 755 (May, 1991) p. 10.

"Preservative-treated wood" by Stephen Smulski. In-depth article on the process and advantages of preserving wood. Photos, charts. • *Fine Homebuilding.* No. 63 (Nov, 1990) pp. 61-65.

"Recycled building blocks" by Timothy O. Bakke. Introduces an energy-efficient and cost effective concrete block with six times the insulating value as a conventional block. Photo. • *Home Mechanix.* No. 760 (Nov, 1991) pp. 26-27.

"Skipping" by Terry Sexton. A primer on the art of skipping, i.e., searching industrial waste skips for recyclable metal. • *The Home Shop Machinist.* Vol. 11, No. 5 (Sep/Oct, 1992) pp. 46 47.

"A two-wheel deal hauls sheet goods." Handy tip to use when trying to move large pieces of stock. Drawing. • *Better Homes and Gardens Wood.* No. 54 (Sep, 1992) p. 17.

"What you really need to know about buying boards." Useful tips for selecting top-quality hardwood boards. Photo. Sidebar on understanding hardwood measures. Sidebar on what you get from a grade. • *Better Homes and Gardens Wood.* No. 51 (April, 1992) pp. 72-73.

"Wood shrinkage" by Henry Spies. Explains the cause of shrinking stock used for cabinets. • *Home Mechanix.* No. 766 (June, 1992) p. 78.

"Wood wins in survey" by Timothy O. Bakke. Brief article on the most preferred material for building. • *Home Mechanix.* No. 753 (March, 1991) p. 9.

See Also by specific name of materials: Wood, Tiles, etc.

Building Materials--Conservation of Resources

Book Review: *g.r.e.b.e.: Guide to Resource-Efficient Building Elements.* Book review on a guide to building products that don't squander resources. Missoula, MT: Center for Resourceful Building Technology, 67 pp. • *Fine Homebuilding.* No. 71 (Jan, 1992) p. 112.

Building Materials--Hazards of

Book Review: *Right-to-Know Pocket Guide for Construction Workers* by Mark Feirer. Book review on a guide to the hazards of commonly used construction materials. Schenectady, NY: Genium Publishing, 78 pp. • *Fine Homebuilding.* No. 62 (Sep, 1990) p. 114.

Buildings — *See* specific parts of building, e.g., Doors, Floors, Windows and specific types of building

Buildings, Underground

Book Review: *An Architect's Sketchbook of Underground Buildings* by Malcolm Wells. Book review on a book filled with 400 hand-drawn sketches of underground buildings. Brewster, MA: Malcolm Wells (673 Satucket Rd.), 200 pp. • *Fine Homebuilding.* No. 65 (March, 1991) pp. 106-108.

Bungalows

"Budget bungalow" by Gerry Copeland. In-depth article on the characteristics and efficiency of a bungalow. Photo, plans, drawings. • *Fine Homebuilding.* No. 59 (Spring, 1990) pp. 52-56.

"A Greene & Greene restoration" by Charles Miller. Presents restoring the Greene's Pratt House. Photos, plans, drawings. Sidebar on the ultimate bungalows. • *Fine Homebuilding.* No. 72 (March, 1992) pp. 36-41.

"Live large, look small" by David Hall. Detailed description of a lakeside house with bungalow features. Photos, plans. • *Fine Homebuilding.* No. 80 (Spring, 1993) pp. 40-45.

Business Card Holders

"Taking care of business" by Marlen Kemmet. Detailed instructions for a business card holder and display stand. Photos, diagrams, material list. • *Better Homes and Gardens Wood.* No. 39 (Dec, 1990) pp. 40-41.

Butternut (Wood)

"Butternut… walnut's kissing cousin" by Jim Boelling and Jim Rose. Informative article covering the cost, availability, uses, machining methods and carving tips. Sidebar on shop-tested techniques. Illustrations, photo, chart. • *Better Homes and Gardens Wood.* No. 55 (Oct, 1992) pp. 23-24.

C

Cabanas

"Coral cabana" by George Brewer. Instructions to build a storm-proof cabana located in the Bahamas. Plans, photos, drawings. • *Fine Homebuilding.* No. 67 (May, 1991) pp. 59-63.

Cabinet Doors

"See-through cabinet doors" by Leon Segal. Increase tool storage area with acrylic doors. • *Woodwork.* No. 15 (May/June, 1992) p. 22.

Cabinet Jacks

"Adjustable cabinet jack" by Robert Francis. Brief instructions to build a hinged cabinet jack for hanging upper cabinets. Drawing. • *Fine Homebuilding.* No. 69 (Sep, 1991) p. 32.

Cabinet Work

Book Review: *52 Weekend Woodworking Projects* by John Nelson. Book review on a projects book filled with a wide range of ideas for beginner to advanced skill levels. New York: Sterling, 160 pp. • *Woodwork.* No. 15 (May/June, 1992) p. 31.

Book Review: *Cabinetry* edited by Robert A. Yoder. Book review on this precise and methodical presentation of 30 cabinetry projects. Emmaus, PA: Rodale, 440 pp. • *Woodwork.* No. 15 (May/June, 1992) p. 28.

Book Review: *Cabinetry Basics* by Sam Allen. Book review introducing the fundamentals of constructing cabinets. New York: Sterling, 128 pp. • *Woodwork.* No. 14 (March/April) p. 19.

"Cutting against the grain" by Larry Haun. Offers methods on successfully cutting materials against the grain. Photos. • *Fine Homebuilding.* No. 76 (Sep, 1992) pp. 63-65.

"Showing off" by Tom Hanley. A presentation of ideas about displaying collections such as shelving and wall units. Photos and drawings. • *Practical Homeowner.* Vol. IV, No. 9 (Jan, 1990) pp. 22-26.

"Thinking like a craftsman" by Roger Holmes. Clear advice and tips on improving woodworking craftsmanship. Drawings. • The Woodworker's Journal. Vol. 16, No. 3 (May/Jun, 1992) pp. 32-35.

Cabinets

"Adaptive behavior" by Matt Phair. Provides information on stock kitchen and bath cabinet that can be adapted to other rooms. Photos, drawings. • *Home Mechanix.* No. 770 (Nov, 1992) pp. 60-63.

"All-star media center" by Marlen Kemmet and Gregory A. Henderson. Construct a beautiful walnut cabinet to hold a T.V., VCR, stereo, tapes, and CDs. Photos, diagrams, materials list. • *Better Homes and Gardens Wood.* No. 46 (Oct, 1991) pp. 50-55.

"Cabinet, cabinet on the wall" by Marlen Kemmet. Detailed instructions for a Shaker-style cherry wall cabinet. Photo, diagrams, materials list. • *Better Homes and Gardens Wood.* No. 41 (Feb, 1991) pp. 74-76.

"Cabinet with punched doors." A design for a side cabinet with punched tin paneled doors. Photos, plans, and materials list. • The Woodworker's Journal. Vol. 14, No. 5 (Sep/Oct, 1990) pp. 45-47.

"Corner for collectibles." A guide to building a corner curio cabinet. Photos and plans. • *Practical Homeowner.* Vol. IV, No. 9 (Jan, 1990) pp. 60-61.

"Cost-effective cabinet makeover" by Jeff Greef. Explains the process of renovating standard face-frame cabinets. Drawing. • *Home Mechanix.* No. 779 (Oct, 1993) pp. 10-13.

"Gun, bookcase, and curio cabinet." A very detailed plan for a large, multi-purpose, floor cabinet. Photos, plans, and materials list. • The Woodworker's Journal. Vol. 15, No. 5 (Sep/Oct, 1991) pp. 48-53.

"How to hang wall cabinets." An analysis of the steps involved in hanging wall cabinets. Drawings. • The Woodworker's Journal. Vol. 14, No. 1 (Jan/Feb, 1990) pp. 17-20.

"Hybrid cabinet construction" by Jim Tolpin. Presents a plan for cabinet construction that combines traditional looks and efficient assembly techniques. Photos, diagrams. Sidebar on glass and lead. • *Fine Homebuilding*. No. 74 (May, 1992) pp. 74-78.

"Pine wall cabinet." This brief article describes the procedure for making a simple wall cabinet with louvered doors. Photos, plans, and materials list. • *The Woodworker's Journal*. Vol. 15, No. 5 (Sep/Oct, 1991) pp. 46-47.

"Shaker-style buffet" by Marlen Kemmet and James R. Downing. Describes the process of constructing a plywood framed in solid cherry buffet cabinet. Photos, diagrams, materials list. • *Better Homes and Gardens Wood*. No. 45 (Sep, 1991) pp. 42-47.

"Universal wall-cabinet system" by James R. Downing, Jim Boelling and Marlen Kemmet. Construct a wall-cabinet system for hand tools, safety equipment, and power-tool accessories with these plans. Photos, diagrams, materials list. Sidebar on how to design customized tool holders. • *Better Homes and Gardens Wood*. No. 54 (Sep, 1992) pp. 74-79.

"Wall cabinet." Plans for using a router to build an Early American-style wall cabinet with doors and drawers. Photos, plans, and materials list. • *The Woodworker's Journal*. Vol. 16, No. 6 (Nov/Dec, 1992) pp. 67-69.

See Also under names of specific types of cabinets, e.g., Kitchen Cabinets, Gun Cabinets, Air-Filtration Cabinets

Cabinets, Spice

"Spiced-up spice cabinet" by Bill Krier. Instructions for an Early-American spice cabinet. Photos, diagrams, pattern. • *Better Homes and Gardens Wood*. No. 42 (April, 1991) pp. 48-51.

Cabins

"Minnesota lake cabin" by Dale Mulfinger and Leffert Tigelaar. Describes the design of a lake cabin with Norwegian themes.

Photos. • *Fine Homebuilding*. No. 80 (Spring, 1993) pp. 59-61.

Calendars, Wall

"Perpetual calendar." An article describing a clever design for a wall-mounted perpetual calender which uses interchangeable wooden blocks. Photos, drawings, plans, and materials list. • *The Woodworker's Journal*. Vol. 14, No. 6 (Nov/Dec, 1990) pp. 57-59.

Candle Holders

"Candle holder" by Michael Mikutowski. This is a brief listing of the steps used in making a five-candle holder. Photo and plans. • *The Woodworker's Journal*. Vol. 14, No. 2, (Mar/Apr, 1990) pp. 46-47.

"Candle holders." A brief tip on making simple candle holders from scrap wood. Photos and plans. • *The Woodworker's Journal*. Vol. 16, No. 4 (Jul/Aug, 1992) p. 39.

Candlestands, Early American

"Early American candlestand." Create a Colonial-style candlestand using an old baluster or turning a pedestal. Diagrams, patterns, photos. • *Better Homes and Gardens Wood*. No. 36 (Aug, 1990) pp. 40-42.

Candlestands, Windsor

"A Windsor candlestand" by Robert J. Treanor. Complete directions on construction of a wood candlestand, including materials list. Photos, drawn plans. • *Woodwork*. No. 18 (Nov/Dec, 1992) pp. 38-43.

Canopies

"Building a shed-roof canopy" by Scott McBride. Instructions to build a canopy for a shed-roof. Drawings. • *Fine Homebuilding*. No. 78 (Jan, 1993) p. 16.

Cape Cod Houses

"Salvaging a small cape" by Rick Moisan. Presents the transformation of a nineteenth-century cape house. Photos, plans, drawings. • *Fine Homebuilding*. No. 78 (Jan, 1993) pp. 56-59.

Carousels, CD

"CD carousel." An easy-to-make project for a tabletop rotating holder for compact discs. Photo, plans, and materials list. • *The Woodworker's Journal*. Vol. 17, No. 1 (Jan/Feb, 1993) pp. 48-50.

Carpentry

Book Review: *Audel Carpenters and Builders Library*, Vols. 1-4 by John E. Ball, edited by John Leeke. Book review covering a handy resource manual for carpenters, joiners, and woodworkers. New York: Macmillan Publishing Co., 269 pp. • *Fine Homebuilding*. No. 76 (Sep, 1992) p. 118.

Book Review: *Carpentry and Construction* by Rex Miller and Glenn E. Baker. Book review on a collection of design and technology techniques for the carpenter. Blue Ridge Summit, PA: TAB Books, 547 pp. • *Fine Homebuilding*. No. 71 (Jan, 1992) p. 112.

Book Review: *Finish Carpentry Basics*. Book review providing the tools and techniques to build, remodel, or repair a home. Photo. Ortho Books, 112 pp. • *Home Mechanix*. No. 766 (June, 1992) p. 16.

Book Review: *Getting a Good Home* by Bob Syvanen. Book review on a guide on checking the quality of workmanship in a home from the perspective of a master carpenter. Old Saybrook, CT: Globe Pequot Press, 112 pp. • *Home Mechanix*. No. 762 (Feb, 1992) p. 25.

Book Review: *Simplified Woodworking I: A Business Guide for Woodworkers* by A. William Benitez. Book review of a guide focusing on the practical side of owning a woodworking business. Austin, TX: Mary Botsford Goens (PO Box 43561) 66 pp. • *Woodwork*. No. 13 (January/February) p. 26.

Book Review: *The Genius of Japanese Carpentry: An Account of a Temple's Construction* by S. Azby Brown. Book review

on temple building, specifically teahouse carpentry and house carpentry. New York: Kodansha International Ltd., 156 pp. • *Fine Homebuilding*. No. 58 (March, 1990) p. 106.

Book Review: *The Technical Carpenter* by Brian Walmsley. Book review on a reference guide to heavy and light construction methods. Scarborough, Ontario: Centennial College Press, 261 pp. • *Fine Homebuilding*. No. 69 (Sep, 1991) p. 108.

"Carpenter's number code" by Jim Chestnut. Brief description of a measurement system for carpentry. • *Fine Homebuilding*. No. 78 (Jan, 1993) pp. 28-30.

"Cutting against the grain" by Larry Haun. Offers methods on cutting materials against the grain successfully. Photos. • *Fine Homebuilding*. No. 76 (Sep, 1992) pp. 63-65.

Carpentry--Tools — *See* Tools; and tools by specific name of tool, e.g., Saws, Clamps

Carpets and Carpeting

"'Greener carpets for better air quality" by Timothy O. Bakke. Brief article on the new classification for carpets that pass the indoor air-quality testing program. Photo. • *Home Mechanix*. No. 770 (Nov, 1992) p. 24.

"How to strip rubber-backed carpet" by Merle Henkenius. Describes the procedure of stripping a rubber-backed carpet. Photos. • *Home Mechanix*. No. 761 (Dec/Jan, 1991-92) pp. 14-15.

"Installing carpet yourself" by Merle Henkenius. Step-by-step instructions to install your own carpeting. Photos. • *Home Mechanix*. No. 761 (Dec/Jan, 1991-92) pp. 12-14.

"Special-effects carpeting" by Judith Trotsky. Presents two creative designs for floor coverings. Photos, drawing, diagrams. • *Home Mechanix.* No. 760 (Nov, 1991) pp. 60-62.

Carriage Stops

"Lathe carriage stop" by Ira J. Neill. A brief description on manufacturing a graduated carriage stop for lathe units. Photos and plans. • *The Home Shop Machinist.* Vol. 10, No. 1 (Jan/Feb, 1991) pp. 36-37.

Carriers

"The Shaker oval carrier" by Jim Downing. Step-by-step directions to create a traditional Shaker carrier. Photos, diagrams. • *Better Homes and Gardens Wood.* No. 40 (Jan, 1991) pp. 54-57.

Carriers, Knitting

"Knitter's companion featuring fine dovetail joinery" by Marlen Kemmet and James R. Downing. Teaches how to construct a walnut and cherry knitting carrier. Photo, diagrams, materials list, drawing. • *Better Homes and Gardens Wood.* No. 51 (April, 1992) pp. 52-53.

Carriers, Protective

"Have nailer, will travel" by William H. Brennen. Brief tip on making a carrying case for a framing nailer. Drawing. • *Fine Homebuilding.* No. 76 (Sep, 1992) p. 28.

Cars

"The great woodie revival" by Peter J. Stephano. Learn how to restore wood-clad cars. Photos, references for woodie sources. • *Better Homes and Gardens Wood.* No. 52 (June, 1992) pp. 64-67.

Cars (Toy)

"Roadster." This brief article outlines an easy-to-make gift project for a child - a roadster. Photos, plans, and materials list. • *The Woodworker's Journal.* Vol. 15, No. 2 (Mar/Apr, 1991) pp. 48-51.

Carts

"Moving sheet goods" by Mark White. Brief tip on building a cart to move heavy sheet goods. Drawing. • *Fine Homebuilding.* No. 83 (Sep, 1993) p. 30.

"Toy airport baggage cart" by Clare Maginley. This is a simple how-to article for making a small child's toy baggage cart and tractor. Photo and plans. • *The Woodworker's Journal.* Vol. 15, No. 3 (May/Jun, 1991) pp. 56-57.

Carts, Outdoor Cooking

"Barbecue work center" by Joseph Truini. Detailed instructions to build a mobile food preparation cart for barbecues, complete with food storage bins, cutting area, and storage for condiments. Photos, diagrams. • *Home Mechanix.* No. 747 (July/Aug, 1990) pp. 70-74.

Carts, Toddler

"Toddler cart." This article provides simple directions for building a four-wheel cart for toddlers and/or toys, including materials list. Photo and plans. • *The Woodworker's Journal.* Vol. 14, No. 2 (Mar/Apr, 1990) pp. 48-49.

Carts, Tool

"Super-simple tool transport." Instructions to build a handy space-saving tool cart for benchtop machines. Diagrams, photos, materials list. • *Better Homes and Gardens Wood.* No. 41 (Feb, 1991) pp. 54-55.

Carts (Toy)

"Tools on wheels" by William Lego, J. Azevedo, Paul Pieper, and Linden Frederick. Provides instructions to make stands with wheels for a miter-saw, radial-arm saw, tool bench, and tool barrow. Photos. • *Fine Homebuilding.* No. 69 (Sep, 1991) pp. 70-75.

Carving — *See* Wood Carving

Cases — *See* Boxes; Carriers; Holders; Storage

Casings

"Making curved casing" by Jonathan F. Shafer. In-depth article on the process of creating curved casing for windows and doors in a Tudor home. Photos, drawings. Sidebar on a reusable jig for curved jambs.

• *Fine Homebuilding.* No. 67 (May, 1991) pp. 82-85.

Cast Iron

"Cast iron repair" by Richard B. Walker. An examination of techniques for repairing cast iron, including brazing, arc welding, and cold welding. Photos and plans. • *The Home Shop Machinist.* Vol. 10, No. 1 (Jan/Feb, 1991) pp. 30-36.

Castings

"Instant access" by James Appleyard. A description of the use of concrete castings to make basement steps. Photos. • *Practical Homeowner.* Vol. IV, No. 9 (Jan, 1990) pp. 62-64.

Casts, Plaster

"Attaching plaster casts" by David Flaharty. Offers a tip on adhesives used for attaching plaster casts to drywall and wood. • *Fine Homebuilding.* No. 60 (May, 1990) p. 16.

Caulking

"Caulking and Sealants" by Bruce Greenlaw. In-depth report on the products available, the tools, and the techniques to apply the sealants or caulking. Photos, drawings, chart. Sidebar on preparation and application tips. • *Fine Homebuilding.* No. 61 (July, 1990) pp. 36-42.

"Smooth caulk joints" by William A. Rolke. Brief tip on a method of caulking a smooth line. • *Fine Homebuilding.* No. 65 (March, 1991) pp. 30-32.

"Substitute caulk gun" by Robert Hausslein. Handy tip for caulking without using a caulking gun. Drawing. • *Fine Homebuilding.* No. 77 (Nov, 1992) p. 30.

Cedar Shakes

"Fire-treating cedar shakes" by Michael M. Westfall. Offers a suggestion on putting fire retardant on cedar shakes. • *Fine Homebuilding.* No. 77 (Nov, 1992) p. 16.

Ceilings

"Building coffered ceilings" by Don Dunkley, Greg Lawrence, and Jay Thomsen. Presents three methods of framing ceilings: single coffer, traditional, and applied coffer. Photos, drawings. • *Fine Homebuilding.* No. 75 (July, 1992) pp. 36-42.

"Ceilings, the last frontier" by Carolyn Chubert. A description of new techniques in ceiling design. Photos. • *Practical Homeowner.* Vol. VI, No. 2 (Feb, 1991) pp. 46-52.

"Cracking up" by Henry Spies. Brief tip on repairing cracks due to truss movement. Drawing. • *Home Mechanix.* No. 781 (Dec/ Jan, 1993-94) p. 87.

"Domes sweet domes" by Michael King. Detailed article on installing a prefabricated dome or building one from scratch. Photos, drawing. • *Home Mechanix.* No. 760 (Nov, 1991) pp. 52-55.

"Framing a cathedral ceiling" by Scott McBride. Brief article on framing a cathedral ceiling. Drawings. • *Fine Homebuilding.* No. 77 (Nov, 1992) pp. 16-20.

"A new skin for a plaster ceiling" by Katie and Gene Hamilton. Step-by-step instructions to repair cracked or sagging plaster. Photos. • *Home Mechanix.* No. 772 (Feb, 1993) pp. 12-13.

"Soaked ceiling" by Henry Spies. Brief suggestion on how to prevent water from entering a house from a second-story deck. Drawing. • *Home Mechanix.* No. 772 (Feb, 1993) p. 80.

"Super ceilings" by Judith Trotsky. Introduces several ways to transform ceilings by adding texture and details. Photos, drawings. • *Home Mechanix.* No. 750 (Nov, 1990) pp. 60-63.

Ceilings, Timbered

"A timbered ceiling" by George Nash. Offers instructions on how to construct a timber-framed ceiling. Photos, diagrams. • *Fine Homebuilding*. No. 65 (March, 1991) pp. 48-51.

Center Finders

"Center finder" by Jim Boelling. Specific directions to build a walnut-and-brass center finder. Photos, diagram. • *Better Homes and Gardens Wood*. No. 40 (Jan, 1991) pp. 60-61, 80.

Chain Saws

"Chainsaws: come out of the woods" by Larry S. Young. Informative article on chain saw safety, maintenance, and techniques. Drawings, photos. • *Fine Homebuilding*. No. 61 (July, 1990) pp. 81-85.

"Using chainsaws on the job site" by Scott McBride. Surveys the cordless chain saws, their capabilities, and maintenance tips. Sidebar on chain saw safety. Sidebar on chain saw maintenance. • *Fine Homebuilding*. No. 78 (Jan, 1993) pp. 38-43.

Chairs

"A better spindle repair" by Asaph Waterman. Describes a method of repairing broken chair spindles. Drawing. • *Woodwork*. No. 19 (Jan/Feb, 1993) p. 20.

"The long and short of it." Offers a solution for wobbly four-legged chairs. Photos. • *Better Homes and Gardens Wood*. No. 53 (Aug, 1992) p. 68.

"Stepstool/chair." How to make a chair that converts into a stepstool. Photos, plans, and materials list. • *The Woodworker's Journal*. Vol. 16, No. 5 (Sep/Oct, 1992) pp. 48-51.

Chairs, Children's

"Child's Windsor." How to make a simple Windsor-style chair for a small child. Photos, plans, and materials list. • *The Woodworker's Journal*. Vol. 16, No. 5 (Sep/Oct, 1992) pp. 40 43.

"Kids' Adirondack Chair & Settee." Plans for a child-sized Adirondack-style garden chair and settee. Photo, plans, and materials list. • *The Woodworker's Journal*. Vol. 17, No. 2 (Mar/Apr, 1993) pp. 58-61.

"Pet-chairs for children" by Jeff Greef. Innovative ideas for creating fun chairs for children, includes a parts list. Drawings. Photos. • *Woodwork*. No. 15 (May/June, 1992) pp. 46-51.

Chairs, Child's Rocking

"Rocking dolphins." An innovative design for a child's rocker shaped like a dolphin. Photos, plans, and materials list. • *The Woodworker's Journal*. Vol. 14, No. 6 (Nov/Dec, 1990) pp. 52-53.

"Smiley the rocking snail" by Marlen Kemmet. Instructions to build a sturdy playroom rocker for a toddler. Photos, diagrams, materials list, patterns. • *Better Homes and Gardens Wood*. No. 61 (June, 1993) pp. 58-61.

Chairs, Dining

"Elegant-oak dining chairs" by Marlen Kemmet. Detailed instructions to build beautiful oak chairs. Photos, diagrams, materials list. • *Better Homes and Gardens Wood*. No. 60 (April, 1993) pp. 72-78.

Chairs, Santa Fe

"Santa Fe chair." This offers a detailed exposition on the steps in cutting, shaping, assembling, and finishing a chair in the Southwestern Santa Fe style. Photos, plans, and materials list. • *The Woodworker's Journal*. Vol. 15, No. 1 (Jan/Feb, 1991) pp. 43-46.

Chairs--Construction of

"An introduction to chairbuilding." A thorough explanation of the steps necessary in the construction of a spindle chair. Photos, plans, and materials list. • *The Woodworker's Journal*. Vol. 16, No. 5 (Sep/Oct, 1992) pp. 16-20.

Chalets, Swiss

"Swiss chalets" by Drew Langsner. Presents an overview of the chalet architectural style and its advantages. Photos, plans. • *Fine Homebuilding.* No. 70 (Nov, 1991) pp. 72-75.

Chapels

"The Sea Ranch Chapel" by Timothy Carpenter. Relates the process of building a wave form sculpture roof for a chapel. Photos, drawings. • *Fine Homebuilding.* No. 64 (Jan, 1991) pp. 50 53.

Chases, Uninsulated

"Gasping for air" by Henry Spies. Addresses a problem with an uninsulated chase, and cold walls and floors next to the chase. • *Home Mechanix.* No. 777 (July/ Aug, 1993) pp. 82-84.

Checkering (Metal)

"Checkering in the mill" by Steve Acker. A description of the process of metal checkering, i.e., incising a non-slip pattern. Photos and plans. • *The Home Shop Machinist.* Vol. 11, No. 5 (Sep/Oct, 1992) pp. 30-32.

Cherry (Wood)

"Black cherry – the poor man's mahogany" by Jim Boelling, Jack Settle, C.L. Gatzke, Rick Beyer and Rick Reeves. Provides information about availability, uses, costs, and carving ideas for black cherry. Photos, illustrations. • *Better Homes and Gardens Wood.* No. 40 (Jan, 1991) pp. 25-26.

Chess Boards

"Chess set." A relatively simple set of plans for making a chess board with a built-in drawer. Photos, plans, and materials list. • *The Woodworker's Journal.* Vol. 16, No. 1 (Jan/Feb, 1992) pp. 48-51.

Chests

"The bachelor chest" by Joseph Olivari. Detailed instructions on building and assembling a chest of drawers. Photos.

Drawings. • *Woodwork.* No. 13 (January/ February) pp. 58-62.

"Cherry lingerie chest." This project offers advice for making a narrow, seven-drawer lingerie chest. Photos, plans, and materials list. • The Woodworker's Journal. Vol. 16, No. 3 (May/Jun, 1992) pp. 36-39.

"Chest/cupboard." Plans for an elaborate, side-by-side, combination chest and cupboard design of cherry wood. Photos, plans, and materials list. • *The Woodworker's Journal.* Vol. 16, No. 4 (Jul/Aug, 1992) pp. 50-55.

"Heirloom blockfront chest." This article outlines an advanced woodworking project for a Wallace Nutting-style four-drawer chest. Photos, plans, and materials list. • *The Woodworker's Journal.* Vol. 17, No. 5 (Sep/Oct, 1993) pp. 36-40.

"Pennsylvania small chest" by Paula Garbarino. How to build a small Colonial-style chest with combination inlays. Photos, plans, and materials list. • *The Woodworker's Journal.* Vol. 15, No. 3 (May-Jun, 1991) pp. 48-51.

"Sample chest." An easy-to-make plan for a three drawer curio chest. Photo, plans, and materials list. • *The Woodworker's Journal.* Vol. 17, No. 2 (Mar/Apr, 1993) pp. 48-50.

"Shaker chest of drawers." A detailed and complex set of plans and instructions for building a Shaker-style chest of drawers. Photos, plans, and materials list. • *The Woodworker's Journal.* Vol. 14, No. 6 (Nov/ Dec, 1990) pp. 65-69.

"Shaker-style tall chest" by Marlen Kemmet and James R. Downing. Construction plans for an elegant and simple Shaker-style chest of drawers. Photos, diagrams, materials list, template. • *Better Homes and Gardens Wood.* No. 55 (Oct, 1992) pp. 36-43.

"Sideboard chest." Complete and detailed instructions for making an Early American-style sideboard. Photos, plans, and materials list. • *The Woodworker's Journal.* Vol. 16, No. 2 (Mar/Apr, 1992) pp. 38-41.

See Also Armoires; Boxes

Chests, Highboy

"Connecticut river valley highboy, parts 1 & 2" by Dennis Preston. This article lays out the steps for making a Colonial-style highboy chest. This project requires advanced woodworking skills. Photos, plans, drawings, and materials list. • *The Woodworker's Journal.* Vol. 15, No. 1 (Jan/Feb, 1991) and No. 2 (Mar/Apr, 1991) pp. 65-71 Part 1 & pp. 44-47 Part 2.

Chests, Tool

"Workbench and portable tool chest" by Dennis Preston. This double article gives details on making a matching workbench and tool chest. Photos, plans, and materials list. • The Woodworker's Journal. Vol. 14, No. 5 (Sep/Oct, 1990) pp. 62-86.

Chests, Toy

"Heirloom toy chest." This is a brief but descriptive article about making a toy chest with a lid and pull-out drawer. Photos, plans, and materials. • *The Woodworker's Journal.* Vol. 15, No. 6 (Nov/Dec, 1991) pp. 60-63.

Chests, Weaver's

"Weaver's chest of drawers." This illustrated article describes how to construct a nineteenth century, Shaker-style chest of drawers, includes parts list. Photo, plans. • *The Woodworker's Journal.* Vol. 14, No. 1 (Jan/Feb, 1990) pp. 34-37.

Children and Carpentry

"Green woodworking with kids" by Roger Holmes. This article offers tips on how to introduce children to woodworking by teaching them to do simple cutting tasks using a shaving horse, a spokeshave, and some green wood. Photos and drawings. • *The Woodworker's Journal.* Vol. 17, No. 1 (Jan/Feb, 1993) pp. 18-23.

Chimney Caps

"Chimney cap" by Henry Spies. Brief instructions on how to repair a cracked brick and mortar cap at the top of a chimney. Drawing. • *Home Mechanix.* No. 776 (June, 1993) pp. 83-84.

Chimney Flues

"Sizing a flue" by Carl Hagstrom. Offers a brief tip on selecting the correct size lining for a flue. • *Fine Homebuilding.* No. 83 (Sep, 1993) pp. 16-18.

Chimneys

"Chimney with a twist" by Carl Hagstrom. Describes a design for a spiral chimney. Photos. Sidebar on chimney codes. • *Fine Homebuilding.* No. 75 (July, 1992) pp. 43-45.

"Hot flashing" by Henry Spies. Helpful tip on preventing leaking with installed flashing. Drawings. • *Home Mechanix.* No. 776 (June, 1993) p. 84.

"Relining a chimney" by Brian Carter. Provides detailed information on a formed-in-place lining system for a chimney. Photos, drawing. Sidebar on burning wood efficiently. • *Fine Homebuilding.* No. 70 (Nov, 1991) pp. 76-79.

Chisels, Bench

"Bench chisels" by Bill Krier and Jim Boelling. Brief article on the basics of chiseling. Illustrations. • *Better Homes and Gardens Wood.* No. 65 (Nov, 1993) pp. 64-65.

Christmas Decorations

"Alpine Santa" by Pam Coffman. Collect small scraps and create a Santa centerpiece for the holidays. Photo, patterns. • *Better Homes and Gardens Wood.* No. 56 (Nov, 1992) pp. 48-49.

"Carve a Santa" by Ron Ransom. Brief instructions and patterns to carve a Santa. Photos, patterns. • *Better Homes and Gardens Wood.* No. 39 (Dec, 1990) p. 78.

"Christmas angel folk carving" by Rick & Ellen Butz. An outline of the process of carving wooden Christmas ornaments shaped like angels. Photos, drawings, and materials list. • *The Woodworker's Journal.* Vol. 14, No. 6 (Nov/Dec, 1990) pp. 48-51.

"Classic shapes for Christmas" by C.L. Gatzke. Instructions to create lightweight bulb-shaped ornaments with a lathe. Photos, drawing, pattern. • *Better Homes and Gardens Wood.* No. 57 (Dec, 1992) pp. 70-71.

"Father Christmas wood carving" by Rick & Ellen Butz. A very complete visual guide for carving a wooden Santa Claus. Photos and drawings. • *The Woodworker's Journal.* Vol. 15, No. 6 (Nov/Dec, 1991) pp. 56-59.

"In-an-instant ornaments" by John Lemieux Rose. Simple designs to scrollsaw a whole set of ornaments. Photos, patterns. • *Better Homes and Gardens Wood.* No. 57 (Dec, 1992) pp. 66 67.

"It's Western Santa" by Larry Johnston and Dave Rushlo. Detailed instructions to carve a cowboy-style Santa. Photos, patterns, materials list. • *Better Homes and Gardens Wood.* No. 48 (Dec, 1991) pp. 76-80.

"Kris Kringle goes cross-country" by Craig Lockwood. Detailed instructions to create a colorful, carved figure. Photo, patterns, materials list. • *Better Homes and Gardens Wood.* No. 57 (Dec, 1992) pp. 38-41.

"Nativity scene." Plans for using a scroll saw to cut out figures for a Nativity scene. Photos, plans, and materials list. • *The Woodworker's Journal.* Vol. 16, No. 6 (Nov/Dec, 1992) pp. 60 63.

"Santa Claus" by Rick and Ellen Butz. A detailed descriptive article on how to carve a wooden Santa Claus figurine. Photos. • *The Woodworker's Journal.* Vol. 17, No. 6 (Nov/Dec, 1993) pp. 38-42.

"Yuletide turnings" by Ron Odegaard. Learn how to turn tree ornaments from leftover scrap wood. Photo, materials list, full-sized templates for four ornaments. • *Better Homes and Gardens Wood.* No. 48 (Dec, 1991) pp. 64-65.

See Also Holiday Decorations

Chucks

"Construct-a-chuck" by Dave Hout. Explains how to construct a homemade chuck. Photos, diagrams. • *Better Homes and Gardens Wood.* No. 43 (June, 1991) pp. 68-69.

"Drill press chuck handles" by Rudy Kouhoupt. This article provides a guide to modifying a drill press chuck with the addition of handles. Photos and plans. • *The Home Shop Machinist.* Vol. 12, No. 2 (Mar/Apr, 1993) pp. 39-41.

"Fitting small drill chucks" by Frank A. McLean. A how-to guide for accurately fitting drill chucks. Photos. • *The Home Shop Machinist.* Vol. 11, No. 1 (Jan/Feb, 1992) pp. 52-55.

"Remounting a four-jaw chuck" by G. Wodham. Advice on increasing the capabilities of a lathe by remounting and increasing the holding capacity of the chuck. Photos and plans. • *The Home Shop Machinist.* Vol. 10, No. 1 (Jan/Feb, 1991) pp. 25-29.

Chucks, Bell

"A bell chuck for your lathe" by Frank A. McLean. A description of the advantages and disadvantages of using a bell chuck as opposed to a usual four-jaw independent chuck. Photos and plans. • *The Home Shop Machinist.* Vol. 11, No. 4 (Jul/Aug, 1992) pp. 54-59.

Chucks, Collet

"Collet chuck turning" by Nick Cook. How to adapt a machinist's collet chuck to hold wood workpieces on a lathe. Photos and plans. • The Woodworker's Journal. Vol. 16, No. 3 (May/Jun, 1992) pp. 26-31.

Chucks, Spigot

"A spigot chuck" by Nick Cook. This offers a simple design for a wooden lathe chuck. Photo and plans. • *The Woodworker's Journal.* Vol. 15, No. 4 (Jul/Aug, 1991) pp. 40-41.

Chutes, Debris

"Spliced debris chute" by Wesley Mulvin and Mary Schendlinger. Brief tip on making a debris chute for a residential renovation project. Drawing. • *Fine Homebuilding.* No. 58 (March, 1990) p. 24.

Circular Saw Blades

"Making the cut" by Joseph Truini. Instructive article discussing how to select the right blade for circular saw projects. Photos. • *Home Mechanix.* No. 752 (Feb, 1991) pp. 64-67.

Circular Saws

"Portable circular saws." Specific guide on 40 different circular saws and their features. Photos, chart comparing various brands, illustrations. • *Better Homes and Gardens Wood.* No. 38 (Oct, 1990) pp. 34-35.

"Portable circular saws." In-depth analysis of 34 portable circular saws. Photo, chart. • *Better Homes and Gardens Wood.* No. 65 (Nov, 1993) pp. 50-51.

"A survey of sidewinders" by Sanford H. Wilk. In-depth evaluation of circular saws. Photos, chart. • *Fine Homebuilding.* No. 63 (Nov, 1990) pp. 72-77.

Clamp Blocks

"An alternative use for swollen biscuits" by Ric Winters. Find old biscuits useful substitutes for clamp blocks. Drawing. • *Woodwork.* No. 15 (May/June, 1992) p. 22.

Clamping

"Basics of clamping, part one" by Edward G. Hoffman. A guide to the basics of clamps as means of locating and holding work pieces. Drawings • *The Home Shop Machinist.* Vol. 10, No. 1 (Jan/Feb, 1991) pp. 59-59.

"Basics of clamping, part two" by Edward G. Hoffman. See Vol. 10, No. 1 • *The Home Shop Machinist.* Vol. 10, No. 2 (Mar/Apr, 1991) pp. 52-53.

"Open the door to convenient clamping" by Lloyd Prailes. Brief tip on clamping small pieces. Drawing. • *Better Homes and Gardens Wood.* No. 62 (Aug, 1993) p. 12.

"Tips for getting the most from your clamps" by Jim Boelling. Handy tips for clamping woodwork properly. • *Better Homes and Gardens Wood.* No. 41 (Feb, 1991) pp. 60-61.

"Wooden clamp corners clamp corner better" by Brian Schaible. Helpful tip on using a wooden clamp for corners. Drawing. • *Better Homes and Gardens Wood.* No. 60 (April, 1993) p. 19.

Clamps

"Alternate clamping devices, part one" by Edward G. Hoffman. A complete description of the different types of clamping devices. Photos and plans. • *The Home Shop Machinist.* Vol. 11, No. 5 (Sep/Aug, 1992) pp. 40-44.

"Alternate clamping devices, part two" by Edward G. Hoffman. See Vol. 11, No. 5 • *The Home Shop Machinist.* Vol. 11, No. 6 (Nov/Dec, 1992) pp. 34-38.

"Anchor-bolt clamps" by Robert J. Dick. Gives a tip on using anchor-bolt clamps for building stairs. Drawing. • *Fine Homebuilding.* No. 74 (May, 1992) p. 24.

"Clamp-fishing" by Brian Carter. Inventive tip for recovering a hammer that has dropped out of reach. Drawing. • *Fine Homebuilding.* No. 67 (May, 1991) p. 28.

"Clamps" by Bill Krier. Pinpoints which clamps are indispensable for the workshop. Photos. • *Better Homes and Gardens Wood.* No. 41 (Feb, 1991) pp. 56-59.

"Clamps on site" by Felix Marti. Informative article describing a variety of clamps and their uses. Photos, drawings. • *Fine Homebuilding.* No. 74 (May, 1992) pp. 70-73.

"Frame-clamping jig" by Gary Walchuk. Describes how to construct a wood frame-clamp jig. Drawn plans. • *Canadian Workshop.* Vol. 13, No. 5 (Feb, 1990) p. 12.

"Handscrew clamps" by Marlen Kemmet. Discover methods on how to construct your own handscrew clamps. Photos, full-sized patterns, diagrams. • *Better Homes and Gardens Wood.* No. 35 (June, 1990) pp. 74-76.

"One-sided clamping with pipe-clamping" by Tara Roopinder. Effective new technique for edge-gluing. Drawing. • *Woodwork.* No. 17 (Sep/Oct, 1992) p. 16.

"Scrapwood eases pressure caused by clamp shortage" by Dan Craney. Instructions to make a clamp out of scrapwood. Drawings. • *Better Homes and Gardens Wood.* No. 51 (April, 1992) p. 20.

"Shopmade handscrews." A clear how-to guide for the manufacture of wooden handscrew clamps. Photos and plans. • *The Woodworker's Journal.* Vol. 16, No. 2 (Mar/Apr, 1992) pp. 54 56.

"Workbench helper." A brief article describing the construction of a floor-standing clamp used for keeping wood boards immobile. Plans and materials list. • *The Woodworker's Journal.* Vol. 14, No. 4 (Jul/Aug, 1990) p. 48.

Clamps, Screw

"Screw clamps" by Edward G. Hoffman. A brief article on the theory and use of screw thread clamps. Drawings. • *The Home Shop Machinist.* Vol. 10, No. 3 (May/Jun, 1991) pp. 56-57.

Clamps, Toggle

"Toggle clamps" by Edward G. Hoffman. This brief article details the uses of toggle clamps. Photos and diagrams. • *The Home Shop Machinist.* Vol. 10, No. 5 (Sep/Oct, 1991) pp. 55-57.

Clamps, Wedge

"Wedge clamps" by Edward G. Hoffman. A brief article on the use of wedge-shaped clamps. Plans. • *The Home Shop Machinist.* Vol. 10, No. 4 (Jul/Aug, 1991) pp. 54-55.

Clamps, Wood

"Clamps." Description of the different types of wood clamps. Drawing. • *The Woodworker's Journal.* Vol. 14, No. 1 (Jan/Feb, 1990 pp. 14-16.

Clamps and Clamping

"Keeping glued panels flat" by Tom E. Moore. Describes the process of using oak or maple bars to clamp boards. Drawing. • *Woodwork.* No. 14 (March/April) p. 12.

Clapboard Siding

"Cutting clapboards" by Loran Smith. Presents a tip on cutting existing clapboard siding. Drawing. • *Fine Homebuilding.* No. 67 (May, 1991) p. 28.

Cleansers, Household

Book Review: *Household Hazards: A Guide to Detoxifying Your Home* by League of Women Voters of Albany County. Book review of a recipes for household cleaners that are non-toxic. League of Women Voters of Albany County, 87 pp. • *Home Mechanix.* No. 762 (Feb, 1992) p. 37.

"Cleanser clean-up" by Lydia Cassidy. Describes several basic cleansers that can be used to resolve a variety of household problems, and provides some safety hints in using a number of commercially available chemicals. • *Canadian Workshop.* Vol. 13, No. 5 (Feb 1990) p. 94.

"Homemade peace of mind." Offers safe substitutes for cleaning products with caustic chemicals. Chart. • *Home Mechanix.* No. 748 (Sep, 1990) p. 22.

Climate Controls

Book Review: *The Quiet Indoor Revolution* by Seichi Konzo and Marylee. Book review on a manual that traces the changes in indoor climate control throughout history. Champaign, IL: Small Homes Council-Building Research Council, 393 pp. • *Fine Homebuilding*. No. 81 (May, 1993) p. 114.

Clockcases

"Pillar & scroll clockcase" by Tom Moore. Detailed instructions to build and assemble a clockcase. Drawings. Photos. • *Woodwork*. No. 13 (January/February) pp. 40-46.

Clocks

"Down-under desk clock" by Larry Johnston. Turn a clock from the seed pod of an Australian tree. Photos, patterns, materials list. • *Better Homes and Gardens Wood*. No. 63 (Sep, 1993) pp. 30-31.

"Echoes of antiquity" by Marlen Kemmet. Provides instructions for a classic columned clock. Photos, diagrams, materials list, patterns. • *Better Homes and Gardens Wood*. No. 59 (Feb, 1993) pp. 30-33.

"Grandchild's clock." This article describes a design for a scaled-down version of a grandfather clock. The resulting Early American-style clock is five feet high. Photo, plans, and materials list. • *The Woodworker's Journal*. Vol. 17, No. 2 (Mar/Apr, 1993) pp. 42-47.

"Man-in-the-moon shelf clock." Whimsical design and directions for a moon-shaped and decorated clock. Photo, drawing, pattern. • *Better Homes and Gardens Wood*. No. 55 (Oct, 1992) pp. 64-65.

"Marbleized masterpiece" by James R. Downing. Create a marble-like modern clock using particleboard. Photos, diagrams, full-sized pattern. • *Better Homes and Gardens Wood*. No. 42 (April, 1991) pp. 74-75.

"Ready-reference calendar/clock." Brief instructions for constructing an attractive oak stand for a digital calendar/clock. Photo, diagram. • *Better Homes and Gardens Wood*. No. 44 (August, 1991) pp. 34-35.

"Seafarer's clock" by James R. Downing. Construct a turned teak timepiece with added maple accents using these plans. Photos, patterns, drawings. • *Better Homes and Gardens Wood*. No. 62 (Aug, 1993) pp. 32-33.

"Tall clock" by Marlen Kemmet and James R. Downing. Create an interpretation of the 'Macintosh clock' with these instructions. Photos, diagrams, materials list. • *Better Homes and Gardens Wood*. No. 63 (Sep, 1993) pp. 32-38.

"Wall clock" by Cary Stage and Marlen Kemmet. Build a wall-mounted pendulum clock with a glass-panel. Photos, diagrams, materials list. • *Better Homes and Gardens Wood*. No. 61 (June, 1993) pp. 39-42.

"Workshop clock" by Jim Boelling. Describes how to construct a handsome clock with a plane ornament. Photo, diagram, pattern. • *Better Homes and Gardens Wood*. No. 54 (Sep, 1992) pp. 80-81.

Clocks, Country

"Country clock." Specific directions to construct a country-style clock with a quartz movement. Photos, drawing. • *Better Homes and Gardens Wood*. No. 36 (Aug, 1990) pp. 44 45.

Clocks, Curio

"Country curio clock." A simple design for a pine wall clock with attached curio shelf. Photos and drawings. • *The Woodworker's Journal*. Vol. 16, No. 3 (May/Jun, 1992) pp. 60-62.

Clocks, Desk

"Desk clock." An easy-to-make project for a desk clock made in a classical style with pillars and a pediment. Photo, plans, and materials list. • *The Woodworker's Journal*. Vol. 17, No. 1 (Jan/Feb, 1993) pp. 51-53.

Clocks, Pendulum

"Free pendulum clock, part four" by Pierre H. Boucheran. See Vol. 10, No. 2

• *The Home Shop Machinist.* Vol. 10, No. 5 (Sep/Oct, 1991) pp. 40-43.

"Free pendulum clock, part one" by Pierce H. Boucheron. Plans for constructing an observatory quality clock based on a free pendulum design. Photos and plans. • *The Home Shop Machinist.* Vol. 10, No. 2 (Mar/Apr, 1991) pp. 20-23.

"Free pendulum clock, part three" by Pierre H. Boucheron. See Vol. 10, No. 2 • *The Home Shop Machinist.* Vol. 10, No. 4 (Jul/Aug, 1991) pp. 40-42.

"Free pendulum clock, part two" by Pierre H. Boucheron. See Vol. 10, No. 2 • *The Home Shop Machinist.* Vol. 10, No. 3 (May/Jun, 1991) pp. 34-37.

Clocks, Shaker

"Shaker tall clock." A very detailed look at the procedure for constructing a floor-standing Shaker clock. Plans and materials list. • *The Woodworker's Journal.* Vol. 14, No. 3 (May/Jun, 1990) pp. 30-35.

Clocks, Shelf

"Eli Terry shelf clock." This detailed article describes the procedure for making a Colonial style, Eli Terry shelf clock. Photos, plans, and materials list. • *The Woodworker's Journal.* Vol. 15, No. 3 (May/Jun, 1991) pp. 40-43.

Clocks, Wall

"Sandblasted wall clock" by James R. Downing. Step-by-step directions for a sandblasted wall clock. Diagrams, photos. • *Better Homes and Gardens Wood.* No. 34 (April, 1990) pp. 40-41.

"Simply stated Shaker wall clock" by Marlen Kemmet and James R. Downing. Offers directions for a cherry Shaker wall clock. Photos, diagrams, materials list, pattern. • *Better Homes and Gardens Wood.* No. 49 (Jan, 1992) pp. 66-70.

"Skeleton wall clock, part one" by W.R. Smith. A complete and in-depth article explaining how to build an all metal, open-sided clock. Photos, plans, and

materials list. • *The Home Shop Machinist.* Vol. 12, No. 6 (Nov/Dec, 1993) pp. 22-28.

Closets

"Closet makeovers" by Pat McMillan. Detailed descriptions to create more space and more efficient use of space in closets. Photos, chart, plans. Sidebar on upgrading a walk-in. Sidebar—open sesame. Sidebar on new closets, old space. • *Home Mechanix.* No. 780 (Nov, 1993) pp. 56-59.

"Secure closet" by Michael Milcahy. Offers advice on building a spacious and security safe closet. • *Fine Homebuilding.* No. 57 (Jan, 1990) pp. 27-28.

"Shelf support" by David Strawderman. Offers a tip on making supports for closet shelves. Drawing. • *Fine Homebuilding.* No. 60 (May, 1990) p. 26.

Clothes Trees

"A clothes tree for youngsters' aquatic playmates." Plans to create a whimsical clothes tree with dolphin-shaped hooks. Photo, pattern, drawing. • *Better Homes and Gardens Wood.* No. 51 (April, 1992) pp. 78-79.

Coatracks

"C-Clamp coatrack" by James R. Downing. Inventive design and instructions to build a coatrack with C-clamps as hooks. Photo, diagrams, pattern. • *Better Homes and Gardens Wood.* No. 55 (Oct, 1992) pp. 62-63.

"Wild-kingdom coatrack" by Marlen Kemmet. Offers three intarsia patterns and instructions to build a coatrack. Photos, patterns. • *Better Homes and Gardens Wood.* No. 63 (Sep, 1993) pp. 54-57.

Coffee Tables

"A coffee table with drawers" by Hugh F. Williamson. Detailed instructions for a coffee table with router-made dovetails. Drawing. Photos. • *Woodwork.* No. 19 (Jan/Feb, 1993) pp. 58-60.

"Early-days sofa table" by Marlen Kemmet. Detailed instructions for this practical, Colonial style table. Diagrams, photos, materials list. • *Better Homes and Gardens Wood*. No. 36 (Aug, 1990) pp. 34-37.

"Fit for a queen cabriole-leg coffee table" by Marlen Kemmet and Jim Boelling. Detailed instructions to build an elegant Queen Anne-style coffee table. Photos, diagrams, materials list, patterns. Sidebar on more Queen Anne designs. • *Better Homes and Gardens Wood*. No. 49 (Jan, 1992) pp. 42-45.

"Santa Fe table." This offers a detailed exposition on the steps in cutting, shaping, assembling, and finishing a small table in the Southwestern Santa Fe style. Photos, plans, and materials list. • *The Woodworker's Journal*. Vol. 15, No. 1 (Jan/Feb, 1991) pp. 47-50.

Cohousing

"Living together." A study of a communal housing development in Washington State. Photos. • *Practical Homeowner*. (Sep/Oct, 1992) pp. 60-65.

Collets

"Adapting the Myford" by R.W. Smith. This article describes the process of using a T-rast to adapt a bench lathe for hand turning. Photos and drawings. • *The Home Shop Machinist*. Vol. 11, No. 3 (May/Jun, 1992) pp. 26-31.

"Rovi expanding mini collets" by Edward G. Hoffman. This is a brief product review for a new type of expanding collet for holding work pieces by their internal diameters. Photo. • *The Home Shop Machinist*. Vol. 9, No. 3 (May/June, 1990) pp. 16-17.

Colonial Architecture

Book Review: *Home Building and Woodworking in Colonial America* by C. Keith Wilbur. Book review on Colonial house-building tools, techniques, and methods. Photo. Saybrook, CT: The Globe Pequot Press, 122 pp. • *Fine Homebuilding*. No. 79 (March, 1993) p. 120.

Colonial Houses

"A Colonial sampler" by Bruce Greenlaw. Details a newly built Colonial house with photos of traditional features. Photos. • *Fine Homebuilding*. No. 63 (Nov, 1990) pp. 45-49.

Columns

"Classical columns outdoors" by Joseph Beals. Brief tip on building classical columns for an outdoor porch. Drawing. • *Fine Homebuilding*. No. 68 (July, 1991) p. 14.

"Making classical columns" by Joseph Beals. Detailed plans on how to construct columns for houses. Photos, drawing. • *Fine Homebuilding*. No. 64 (Jan, 1991) pp. 54-57.

Columns, Lally

"Boxed Lally" by James Whidden. Brief tip on boxing Lally columns. Drawings. • *Fine Homebuilding*. No. 72 (March, 1992) pp. 26-28.

"Lally boxing" by Chet Burgess. Brief tip on an approach to boxing Lally columns. Drawing. • *Fine Homebuilding*. No. 78 (Jan, 1993) p. 30.

Combustion Gases

"Combustion gases: an indoor threat" by Alex Wilson. Detailed information on how to check your home for combustion gases and improve the ventilation in the house. Drawing. • *Home Mechanix*. No. 759 (Oct, 1991) pp. 23-25.

Commercial Construction

Book Review: *Building Construction Illustrated*, Second Edition by Francis D.K. Ching and Cassandra Adams. Book review on an illustrated manual for residential and light commercial construction. Photo. New York: Van Nostrand Reinhold, 375 pp. • *Fine Homebuilding*. No. 78 (Jan, 1993) p. 110.

Communalism

"Living together." A study of a communal housing development in Washington State. Photos. • *Practical Homeowner.* (Sep/Oct, 1992) pp. 60-65.

Compact Disc Holders

"Compact disc holder." This brief article details the method building a rotating base holder for compact discs, includes a materials list. Photo and plans. • *The Woodworker's Journal.* Vol. 14, No. 1 (Jan/Feb, 1990) pp. 44-45.

Compressors

"Tips on keeping your air compressor alive and well." Maintenance tips for air compressors. Illustration. • *Better Homes and Gardens Wood.* No. 34 (April, 1990) pp. 76-78.

Computer-Aided Design (CAD)

"CAD for the small shop" by Edward G. Hoffman. This is a product review of Drafix Windows CAD. • *The Home Shop Machinist.* Vol. 10, No. 1 (Jan/Feb, 1991) p. 12.

"CAD for the small shop" by Edward G. Hoffman. This is review of Drafix Windows CAD program. Drawing. • *The Home Shop Machinist.* Vol. 11, No. 4 (Jul/Aug, 1992); p. 14.

"Removable high performance disks for your computer system" by Edward G. Hoffman. A product review of Bernoulli Disk Drives made by Iomega Corp. • *The Home Shop Machinist.* Vol. 10, No. 2 (Mar/Apr, 1991) pp. 12-13.

"Reviewing CAD systems, part two" by R.W. Friestad. See Vol. 9, No. 6 • *The Home Shop Machinist.* Vol. 10, No. 1 (Jan/Feb, 1991) pp. 53-55.

Computer Applications

"Convert your mill-drill to CNC, part four" by R.W. Friestad. See Vol. 9, No. 2 • *The Home Shop Machinist.* Vol. 9, No. 5 (Sep/Oct, 1990) pp. 46-49.

"Convert your mill-drill to CNC, part one" by R.W. Friestad. An examination of the equipment and electronics changes required before a mill drill can be adapted for computer-controlled operation. Photos and plans. • *The Home Shop Machinist.* Vol. 9, No. 2 (Mar/Apr, 1990) pp. 46-50.

"Convert your mill-drill to CNC, part three" by R. W. Friestad. See Vol. 9, No. 2 • *The Home Shop Machinist.* Vol. 9, No. 4 (Jul/Aug, 1994) pp. 54-55.

"Convert your mill-drill to CNC, part two" by R.W. Friestad. See Vol. 9, No. 2 • *The Home Shop Machinist.* Vol. 9, No. 3 (May/Jun, 1990) pp. 50-56.

Computer Controls

"Build your own CNC controller, part one" by R.W. Friestad. This article gives directions for assembling a 3-axis CNC controller. Plans. • *The Home Shop Machinist.* Vol. 11, No. 5 (Sep/Oct, 1992) pp. 52-55.

"Build your own CNC controller, part three" by R.W. Friestad. See Vol. 11, No. 4 • *The Home Shop Machinist.* Vol. 12, No. 1 (Jan/Feb, 1993) pp. 54-57.

"Build your own CNC controller, part two" by R.W. Friestad. See Vol. 11, No. 5 • *The Home Shop Machinist.* Vol. 11, No. 6 (Nov/Dec, 1992) pp. 51-53.

"Convert a milling machine to CNC control, part five" by R.W. Friestad. See Vol. 10, No. 3 • *The Home Shop Machinist.* Vol. 11, No. 1 (Jan/Feb, 1992) pp. 45-51.

"Convert a milling machine to CNC control, part one" by R.W. Friestad. This is a lengthy series detailing the procedure for adapting a full-sized milling machine to CNC control Plans and photos. • *The Home Shop Machinist.* Vol. 10, No. 3 (May/Jun, 1991) pp. 51-55.

"Convert a milling machine to CNC control, part six" by R.W. Friestad. See

Vol. 10, No. 3 • *The Home Shop Machinist.* Vol. 11, No. 2 (Mar/Apr, 1992) pp. 45-47.

"Convert a milling machine to CNC control, part three" by R.W. Friestad. See Vol. 10, No. 3 • *The Home Shop Machinist.* Vol. 10, No. 5 (Sep/Oct, 1991) pp. 52-55.

"Convert a milling machine to CNC control, part two" by R.W. Friestad. See Vol. 10, No. 3 • *The Home Shop Machinist.* Vol. 10, No. 4 (Jul/Aug, 1991) pp. 44-48.

"Retrofitting Atlas/Craftsman and other lathes to CNC control, part one" by R.W. Friestad. This article offers an in-depth examination of the requirements for retrofitting a lathe for CNC control. Photos and plans. • *The Home Shop Machinist.* Vol. 12, No. 3 (May/Jun, 1993) pp. 48–52.

"Retrofitting Atlas/Craftsmen and other lathes to CNC control, part two" by R.W. Friestad. See Vol. 12, No. 3 • *The Home Shop Machinist.* Vol. 12, No. 5 (Sep/Oct, 1993) pp. 49-53.

Computer Software

Book Review: *Software Directory for Builders: 1992.* Book review listing the categories covered in this valuable directory. Washington, D.C.: Home Builder Press, 88 pp. • *Fine Homebuilding.* No. 75 (July, 1992) p. 110.

Software Review: *AutoSketch 3.0 and AutoSketch for Windows.* Software review on a program that helps produce precise drawings and aids users to visualize details for building homes. Bothell, WA: Autodesk Retail Products. • *Fine Homebuilding.* No. 81 (May, 1993) p. 114.

"Storage by design" by Nancy Cooper. Explains a software resource that helps design storage and cabinet space. Photos. Sample supply list. • *Home Mechanix.* No. 742 (Feb, 1990) pp. 32 37.

Computers

"And now for something completely different" by R.W. Friestad. A brief history of computers and their application to machining through Computer Numerical Control (CNC). • *The Home Shop Machinist.* Vol. 12, No. 2 (Mar/Apr, 1993) pp. 44-47.

"Computers in the shop" by Roland Friestad. An analysis and description of computer programs and applications useful in a machine shop. Photos and plans. • *The Home Shop Machinist.* Vol. 9, No. 1 (Jan/Feb, 1990) pp. 44-51.

Concrete

Book Review: *Concrete Formwork* by Leonard Koel. Book review covering the preparation of building sites, wall forming, and a variety of other projects requiring concrete foundations. Homewood, IL: American Technical Publishers, Inc. 282 pp. • *Fine Homebuilding.* No. 63 (Nov, 1990) p. 106.

Book Review: *The Homeowner's Guide to Building with Concrete, Brick and Stone* by The Portland Cement Association. Book review of a practical, well-written guide on residential masonry. Emmaus, PA: Rodale Press, Inc., 240 pp. • *Fine Homebuilding.* No. 62 (Sep, 1990) p. 112.

"Cleaning concrete" by Jim Barrett. Offers a tip on removing oil spills from concrete without using harsh chemicals. Photos. • *Home Mechanix.* No. 746 (June, 1990) p. 12.

"Crawl-space concrete" by John Campbell. Brief tip on pouring concrete in a small crawl space. • *Fine Homebuilding.* No. 71 (Jan, 1992) pp. 24-26.

"Drying a wet slab" by David Benaroya. Brief tip covering moisture problems on concrete slab flooring. Drawings. • *Fine Homebuilding.* No. 65 (March, 1991) p. 16.

"A lift for sunken concrete" by Matt Phair. Introduces the technique of slabjacking for sunken concrete problems. Photos, drawings. • *Home Mechanix.* No. 756 (June, 1991) p. 13.

"Pouring concrete slabs" by Carl Hagstrom. Provides tips on ordering, placing, screeding, floating, and finishing. Photos. Sidebar on tips for pouring in different kinds of weather. • *Fine Homebuilding.* No. 83 (Sep, 1993) pp. 46-51.

"Standout stakes" by Tony Toccalino. Offers a tip for getting the levels right when pouring concrete for patios, driveways and paths. • *Fine Homebuilding.* No. 82 (July, 1993) pp. 26-28.

Concrete Castings

"Instant access" by James Appleyard. A description of the use of concrete castings to make basement steps. Photos. • *Practical Homeowner.* Vol. IV, No. 9 (Jan, 1990) pp. 62-64.

Concrete Floors

"Coating concrete floors" by Henry Spies. Offers advice on the process of cleaning and then painting a basement floor. • *Home Mechanix.* No. 773 (March, 1993) pp. 83-84.

Concrete Stoops

"Retro-flashing a concrete stoop" by Tim Herrling. Brief tip on how to build a concrete stoop to prevent leaking. Drawing. • *Fine Homebuilding.* No. 57 (Jan, 1990) p. 28.

Concrete Walls

"Designing for tall concrete walls" by William Doran. Offers plans to build on-site panels for tall concrete walls. Photos, diagrams, charts, drawings. Sidebar on calculating concrete pressure. Alternative form ties. • *Fine Homebuilding.* No. 78 (Jan, 1993) pp. 48-53.

"Peeling paint" by Henry Spies. Offers a tip on how to fix peeling paint on concrete walls. • *Home Mechanix.* No. 757 (July/Aug, 1991) p. 81.

"Straightening concrete walls" by Matt Phair. Provides information on how to straighten concrete walls. Drawings.

• *Home Mechanix.* No. 757 (July/Aug, 1991) p. 19.

Condensation

"Condensation on diffusers" by Henry Spies. Offers a way of preventing condensation on ceiling diffusers. • *Home Mechanix.* No. 769 (Oct, 1992) pp. 80-81.

"Hot-surface condensation" by C.K. Wolfert. Offers ideas to solve a condensation problem on the peak of a cathedral ceiling. • *Fine Homebuilding.* No. 63 (Nov, 1990) p. 18.

Conservation and Renovation

Book Review: *A Consumer's Guide to Home Improvement, Renovation & Repair* by Enterprise Foundation. Book review on choosing a cost-effective approach to a home improvement project. Photo. New York: John Wiley & Sons, 270 pp. • *Home Mechanix.* No. 757 (July/Aug, 1991) pp. 18-19.

Book Review: *Repairing Old and Historic Windows.* Book review focusing on renovation and rehabilitation of older buildings. Photo. Washington, D.C.: The Preservation Press, 208 pp. • *Fine Homebuilding.* No. 84 (Nov, 1993) p. 124.

Book Review: *1993 Old-House Journal Catalog.* Book review of the latest Old-House catalog. Gloucester, MA: Dovetale Publishers, 272 pp. • *Fine Homebuilding.* No. 81 (May, 1993) p. 114.

Book Review: *Caring for Your Old House* by Judith L. Kitchen. Book review on a guide for preserving old houses. Washington, D.C.: The Preservation Press, 208 pp. • *Fine Homebuilding.* No. 70 (Nov, 1991) pp. 120-122.

Book Review: *Landmark Yellow Pages: Where to Find All the Names, Addresses, Facts and Figures You Need* by National Trust for Historic Preservation. Book review on a handbook presenting information on preservation and 3,500 contacts serving as a network for preservation. Washington, D.C.: National Trust for Historic

Preservation, 319 pp. • *Fine Homebuilding.* No. 68 (July, 1991) p. 106.

Book Review: *Maintaining Your Old House in Cambridge* by Charles Sullivan, Eileen Woodford and Staff of the Cambridge Historical Commission. Book review on maintaining old houses (pre-1930). Cambridge, MA: Cambridge Historical Commission, 75 pp. • *Fine Homebuilding.* No. 68 (July, 1991) p. 108.

Book Review: *New Life for Old Houses* by George Stephen. Book review of a guide to restoring a house to its original condition. Photo. Washington, DC: Preservation Press, 257 pp. • *Home Mechanix.* No. 754 (April, 1991) p. 17.

Book Review: *Preservation Briefs.* Book review on informative well-written briefs covering a wide range of topics including restoring commercial buildings, old-house restoration. Washington, D.C.: Preservation Assistance Division, National Park Service. • *Fine Homebuilding.* No. 72 (March, 1992) p. 108.

Book Review: *Preserving Porches* by Renee Kahn and Ellen Meagher. Book review on restoring a porch with attention to architectural details and construction methods. Photo. New York: Henry Holt and Co., 148 pp. • *Home Mechanix.* No. 754 (April, 1991) p. 17.

Book Review: *The Complete Home Restoration Manual* by Albert Jackson and David Day. Book review on a manual filled with valuable tips on restoration. Photo. New York: Simon & Schuster, 256 pp. • *Fine Homebuilding.* No. 82 (July, 1993) p. 112.

Book Review: *Traditional Details for Building Restoration, Renovation, and Rehabilitation: From 1932-1951 Editions of Architectural Graphic Standards* edited by John Belle, John Ray Hoke, Jr. and Stephen A. Kliment. Book review on a practical guide to restoration, renovation, and rehabilitation of structures built in the era of 1932-1951. New York: John Wiley and

Sons, Inc., 285 pp. • *Fine Homebuilding.* No. 65 (March, 1991) p. 108.

"Ornamental plaster restoration" by David Flaharty. In-depth article on ornamental plaster restoration. Photos, drawings. • *Fine Homebuilding.* No. 57 (Jan, 1990) pp. 38-42.

"Restoring the east portico of Montgomery Place" by Geoffrey Carter. Explains the devices used to restore the Federal-style mansion, Montgomery Place. Photos, diagrams, drawings. • *Fine Homebuilding.* No. 61 (July, 1990) pp. 67-71.

"Restoring the Jacobs House" by John Eifler. Traces the process of rebuilding the Frank Lloyd Wright house from the outside in. Photos, plans, drawings. • *Fine Homebuilding.* No. 81 (May, 1993) pp. 78-82.

"Row-house renovation" by Robert Van Vranken. Presents open and airy renovation plans for row-houses. Photos. • *Fine Homebuilding.* No. 82 (July, 1993) p. 69.

"Salvaging a small cape" by Rick Moisan. Presents the transformation of a nineteenth-century cape house. Photos, plans, drawings. • *Fine Homebuilding.* No. 78 (Jan, 1993) pp. 56-59.

Consoles

"Get ready...get (T.V.) set...retrofit" by Larry Clayton. Explains how to install a new TV or VCR in an old console. • *Better Homes and Gardens Wood.* No. 50 (Feb, 1992) pp. 82-83.

Construction

Book Review: *Fundamentals of Building Construction: Materials and Methods* (Second Edition) by Edward Allen. Book review with an overview of the construction industry from houses to skyscrapers. Photo. New York: John Wiley & Sons, Inc., 803 pp. • *Fine Homebuilding.* No. 71 (Jan, 1992) p. 112.

Journal Review: *Macintosh Construction Forum: The Journal for Macintosh Users in Construction* by Craig Savage. Journal review of a guide that reviews Macintosh compatible software and Macintosh computers. Sandpoint, ID: Savage Construction Company. • *Fine Homebuilding.* No. 68 (July, 1991) p. 108.

Construction, Panelized

"Fast foundations" by Chuck Silver. A guide to using panelized concrete sections in building a foundation wall. Photos. • *Practical Homeowner.* Vol. VI, No. 7 (Sep, 1991) pp. 90-92.

Construction, Rammed-Earth

"Cooling effects of rammed-earth" by Brian Lockhart. Contrasts the effect of rammed-earth construction versus conventional construction on cooling in the hot season. • *Fine Homebuilding.* No. 63 (Nov, 1990) p. 18.

Containers See Boxes

Contractors

"Before you hire a moonlighter" by James Lomuscio. Advice on hiring a contractor. • *Practical Homeowner.* Vol. V, No. 8 (Nov/ Dec, 1990) pp. 22-23.

Book Review: *Software Directory for Builders: 1992.* Book review listing the categories covered in this valuable directory. Washington, D.C.: Home Builder Press, 88 pp. • *Fine Homebuilding.* No. 75 (July, 1992) p. 110.

"Time and materials contracts" by Charles Smith-Kim. An explanation of the advantages and disadvantages of using time and materials type contracts. • *Practical Homeowner.* (Jul/Aug, 1992) pp. 44-49.

"When not to do it yourself." Advice on how to avoid do-it-yourself pitfalls. Photos. • *Practical Homeowner.* Vol. V, No. 8 (Nov/ Dec, 1990) pp. 62-68.

Contracts, Time and Materials

"Time and materials contracts" by Charles Smith-Kim. An explanation of the advantages and disadvantages of using time and materials type contracts. • *Practical Homeowner.* (Jul/Aug, 1992) pp. 44-49.

Cookie Jar Holders

"Cookie jar holder." Describes an easy-to-make holder for cookie jars, includes materials list. Photo and plans. • *The Woodworker's Journal.* Vol. 14, No. 2 (Mar/ Apr, 1990) pp. 42-43.

Cookie Molds

"Hand-carved cookie molds" by Jim Stevenson. Creative designs and directions for making wooden cookie molds. Photo, diagrams, materials list, full-sized patterns, recipe. • *Better Homes and Gardens Wood.* No. 49 (Jan, 1992) pp. 30-33.

Corrosion

"Metal corrosion" by Ana Diaz. Informative article on corrosion and how to minimize it effects. Photos, chart. • *Fine Homebuilding.* No. 62 (Sep, 1990) pp. 64-67.

Cottages

"A cluster of cottages" by Daniel Milton Hill. Provides details on creating a development of eight cost-efficient houses on an urban lot. Photos, plans. • *Fine Homebuilding.* No. 59 (Spring, 1990) pp. 68-73.

"Cottage in the Cotswolds" by Alasdair G. B. Wallace. Traces the history and changes in a 300-year-old English cottage. Photo, drawings. • *Fine Homebuilding.* No. 60 (May, 1990) pp. 70-73.

Cottonwood (Wood)

"Cottonwood" by Robert McGuffie, Jack Settle, Max Alvarez. Identifies the uses, availability, machining methods, and carving ideas for cottonwood. Photos. • *Better Homes and Gardens Wood.* No. 37 (Sep, 1990) pp. 31-32.

Countertops

"Burned countertop" by Hank Spies. Brief tip on how to repair a burn the size of a quarter on a countertop. Drawing. • *Home Mechanix*. No. 741 (Jan, 1990) p. 84.

"Counter proposals" by Pat McMillan. Offers three space-saving designs for countertops in the kitchen. Photos, diagrams, plans. • *Home Mechanix*. No. 777 (July/Aug, 1993) pp. 60-64.

"Counter punch" by Thomas H. Jones. Specific directions to create countertops with decorative snap-on edging. Photos, drawings. • *Home Mechanix*. No. 748 (Sep, 1990) pp. 62 63.

"Cultured counters" by Joseph Truini. Presents the latest solid-surface materials that can be used for countertops and how to install them. Photos, diagrams. • *Home Mechanix*. No. 754 (April, 1991) pp. 44-48.

"Hardwood edgings for plastic laminate" by Paul Levine. Brief article on how to make hardwood edging for countertops. Photos, drawings. • *Fine Homebuilding*. No. 78 (Jan, 1993) pp. 66-67.

"Making a solid-surface countertop" by Sven Hanson. Presents a countertop made of synthetic materials. Photos, drawings, diagrams. • *Fine Homebuilding*. No. 84 (Nov, 1993) pp. 40-45.

"Making plastic-laminate countertops" by Herrick Kimball. Presents tools and techniques that make working with plastic laminate easier. Photos. • *Fine Homebuilding*. No. 75 (July, 1992) pp. 60-65.

"Wall works" by Sally Ross. Explains how to build wall-mounted counters with drawers for storage. Photos, diagrams, drawing. • *Home Mechanix*. No. 747 (July/Aug, 1990) pp. 46-50.

Countertops, Kitchen

"Choosing kitchen countertops" by Kevin Ireton. In-depth article on the designs and materials available for kitchen countertops. Photos, cost chart. Sidebar on concrete countertops. • *Fine Homebuilding*. No. 77 (Nov, 1992) pp. 40-45.

Cracker-Style Houses

"Cracker house in a hammock" by Robert H. Gore. Offers information on building a cracker style house especially suited for the Florida wetlands. Photos, plans, drawing. • *Fine Homebuilding*. No. 57 (Jan, 1990) pp. 63-67.

Cradles

"A contemporary cradle—designed on the run" by Rod Houston. Demonstrates how to work from a two-dimensional design to full completion. Drawings. Photos. • *Woodwork*. No. 14 (March/April) pp. 48-53.

See Also Beds

Crawl Spaces

"Crawl-space moisture" by Hank Spies. Offers a tip for correcting a moisture problem in a crawl space under a house. Drawing. • *Home Mechanix*. No. 749 (Oct, 1990) p. 93.

"Crawl-space mold" by Henry Spies. Offers advice for controlling mold on floor framing and heating ducts. • *Home Mechanix*. No. 768 (Sep, 1992) p. 113.

"Moisture problems in the crawl space" by David Kaufman. Offers information on how to solve a moisture problem in a crawl space. • *Fine Homebuilding*. No. 64 (Jan, 1991) p. 22.

"Moldy odor" by Henry Spies. Brief tip on reducing the moisture and moldy odor in a crawl space. • *Home Mechanix*. No. 764 (April, 1992) p. 86.

Credenzas

"A credenza with charisma" by Jim Boelling and Marlen Kemmet. Directions to construct a beautiful walnut credenza for displaying collectibles. Photos, diagrams, materials list. • *Better Homes and*

Gardens Wood. No. 60 (April, 1993) pp. 58-64.

See Also Desks

Creosote Odors

"Sealing creosote beams" by Terry Amburgey. Gives advice on a solution for creosote vapors. • *Fine Homebuilding.* No. 62 (Sep, 1990) pp. 18-20.

Cupboards

"Chest/cupboard." Plans for an elaborate, side-by-side, combination chest and cupboard design of cherry wood. Photos, plans, and materials list. • *The Woodworker's Journal.* Vol. 16, No. 4 (Jul/Aug, 1992) pp. 50-55.

"Child's stepped back cupboard." A very comprehensive plan for building a miniature slant-top cupboard sized for a small child. • *The Woodworker's Journal.* Vol. 14, No. 3 (May/Jun, 1990) pp. 51-53.

"Early American corner cupboard." Elaborate plans for a corner cupboard in Early American-style. Photos, plans, and materials list. • *The Woodworker's Journal.* Vol. 17, No. 4 (Jul/Aug, 1993) pp. 31-35.

"Slant-back cupboard." A very detailed plan for constructing a primitive-style, slant-back cupboard. Photos and plans. • *The Woodworker's Journal.* Vol. 14, No. 4 (Jul/Aug, 1990) pp. 32-36.

Cupolas

"Look up!" by Jim Rosenau. A guide to new ideas in cupola design. Photos. • *Practical Homeowner.* (Mar/Apr, 1992) pp. 56-59.

"Topping it off" by Michael Morris. Detailed instructions on how to construct your own cupola. Photos. Sidebar on cupola construction: how to build your own. • *Home Mechanix.* No. 750 (Nov, 1990) pp. 30-33.

Cut-Off Tables

"Band saw cutoff table." A brief article on the uses of a cut-off accessory table to a band saw. Photo, plans, and materials list. • *The Woodworker's Journal.* Vol. 17, No. 4 (Jul/Aug, 1993) pp. 40-41.

Cut-Off Tools

"A saw blade cutoff tool" by Conrad Huard. How to create a lathe cutoff tool using a scrap carbide-tipped saw blades. Photos. • *The Home Shop Machinist.* Vol. 12, No. 1 (Jan/Feb, 1993) p. 31.

Cutting Boards

"Culinary Cutting Boards" by Gary Walchuk. Provides instructions on constructing wood cutting boards. Photo, drawn plans. • *Canadian Workshop.* Vol. 13, No. 4 (Jan 1990) pp. 57 58.

"One whale of a cutting board" by A.J. Hand. Explains how to make a whale-shaped laminated cutting board. Photo, pattern, diagram. • *Better Homes and Gardens Wood.* No. 43 (June, 1991) pp. 72-73.

"One-stop chopping." Instructions to make a cutting board with a slot to hold a knife. Photos, drawings. • *Better Homes and Gardens Wood.* No. 62 (Aug, 1993) pp. 52-53.

D

Dado Cutters

"Dado-cutting tools." Informative article on the specifications of 30 dado-cutting tools. Photo, chart. • *Better Homes and Gardens Wood.* No. 65 (Nov, 1993) pp. 46-47.

"Dado-cutting tools" by Bill Krier. Results of a test of 30 dado blades, blade sets, and router bits. Photos, drawings, chart comparing the tools. Sidebar on how to get the most from dado blades and sets. • *Better Homes and Gardens Wood.* No. 46 (Oct, 1991) pp. 60-65.

"When 3/4 in. isn't 3/4 in." by Arthur A. Corbett. Increase accuracy of dado-cutters with a simple tip. • *Woodwork.* No. 17 (Sep/Oct, 1992) p. 18.

Dado Joints

"Making dadoes" by Roger Holmes. This is an exhaustive study of the use of dado joints in building furniture as an alternative to biscuit joints. Photos and drawings. • *The Woodworker's Journal.* Vol. 15, No. 5 (Sep/Oct, 1991) pp. 21-28.

Daybeds

"A convertible daybed" by Ron Karten. Provides instructions for building a convertible daybed. Drawing. Photos. • *Woodwork.* No. 17 (Sep/Oct, 1992) pp. 36-41.

Decks

"5 easy pieces" by Joseph Truini. Presents five deck designs and construction plans from a modest platform to a multi-level structure. Photos, diagrams. • *Home Mechanix.* No. 777 (July/Aug, 1993) pp. 44-49.

"Another decking persuader" by Phil Cyr. Handy suggestion for aligning deck boards. Drawing. • *Fine Homebuilding.* No. 62 (Sep, 1990) p. 30.

"Clear the deck" by Henry Spies. Brief tip on cleaning mold and mildew from a wood deck. • *Home Mechanix.* No. 773 (March, 1993) pp. 84-85.

"Deck flashing" by Henry Spies. Brief article on installing flashing to protect a deck from decay. Drawing. • *Home Mechanix.* No. 777 (July/Aug, 1993) p. 82.

"Deck-building basics" by Joseph Truini. Specific details and construction techniques for building a deck. Drawings, diagrams. • *Home Mechanix.* No. 747 (July/Aug, 1990) pp. 61-68.

"Deck-cleaning tips" by Joseph Truini. Gives handy tips for cleaning decks. • *Home Mechanix.* No. 777 (July/Aug, 1993) p. 20.

"Decking persuader" by Gregory Tolman. Describes how to lay deck boards with a 1/8" gap. Drawing. • *Fine Homebuilding.* No. 57 (Jan, 1990) p. 26.

"Decks with a difference" by Joseph Truini. Presents six unique deck designs and instructions to build them. Photos, diagrams. • *Home Mechanix.* No. 757 (July/Aug, 1991) pp. 38-47.

"Decks with great details" by Joseph Truini. Offers designs for a treetop, balcony, pool, and hillside deck. Photos, diagrams. • *Home Mechanix.* No. 747 (July/Aug, 1990) pp. 54-60.

"Entry decks" by Elise Vider. How to use decks to customize a house's front yard and entryway. Photos and plans. • *Practical Homeowner.* Vol. V, No. 4 (June, 1990) pp. 56-62.

"Evaluating deck woods" by Scott Grove. Provides information on selecting a stable and long-lasting wood to construct a deck. • *Fine Homebuilding.* No. 61 (July, 1990) pp. 12-14.

"Extend your deck's life" by Roy Barnhart. Practical advice on preserving wooden decks. Photos. • *Practical Homeowner.* Vol. V, No. 5 (August, 1990) pp. 88-89.

"Oasis backyard" by Joseph Truini. Construction plans to build a freestanding deck. Photos, diagrams. • *Home Mechanix.* No. 779 (Oct, 1993) pp. 66-67.

"Places in the sun" by Joseph Truini. Highlights construction plans for a shade arbor, rustic deck gazebo, and a patio cover. Photos, diagrams. • *Home Mechanix.* No. 745 (May, 1990) pp. 40-47.

"A quality deck" by John Baldwin. Instructions to build a deck with built-in benches, recessed lights, and a spacious spa. Photos, diagrams. • *Fine Homebuilding.* No. 69 (Sep, 1991) pp. 46 49.

"The rail thing" by Matt Phair. Provides five designs for railings to add to decks.

Photos, diagrams. • *Home Mechanix.* No. 757 (July/Aug, 1991) pp. 48-57.

"Rejuvenating your deck" by Merle Henkenius. Specific directions for structural reinforcements and refinishing a deck. Drawing, photos. • *Home Mechanix.* No. 777 (July/Aug, 1993) pp. 8-10.

"Shakey, swayey deck" by Jim Thompson. Brief tip on a remedy for a shaky deck. • *Fine Homebuilding.* No. 82 (July, 1993) p. 16.

"Spacing deck boards" by David Bright. Offers a system to space deck boards evenly apart. Drawings. • *Fine Homebuilding.* No. 82 (July, 1993) p. 26.

"Spiked deck joints" by John Trim. Shows how to use aluminum gutter spikes to solve problem joints for decks. Drawing. • *Fine Homebuilding.* No. 75 (July, 1992) p. 26.

"Up on the roof" by Roy Barnhart. Advantages and problems associated with placing a deck on a flat home/garage roof. Photos. • *Practical Homeowner.* Vol. VI, No. 7 (Sep, 1991) pp. 76 82.

"Upper decks" by Matt Phair. Discusses the designs of four second-story decks. Photos, diagrams. • *Home Mechanix.* No. 767 (July/Aug, 1992) pp. 52-57.

"The well-planted deck" by Thomas F. Sweeney. Tips on properly landscaping the area around a new deck. Photos. • *Practical Homeowner.* Vol. VI, No. 8 (Oct, 1991) pp. 36-40.

"Winners" by Timothy O. Bakke. Presents a description of the construction of five prize winning decks. Photos, plans, drawings. • *Home Mechanix.* No. 767 (July/Aug, 1992) pp. 44 50.

"Winners" by Timothy O. Bakke. Highlights the prizewinning designs for decks. Photos, plans, diagrams. • *Home Mechanix.* No. 777 (July/Aug, 1993) pp. 50-53.

"Yardscaping" by Joseph Truini. Provides a glimpse at an example of creating a yardscape complete with a gazebo, sun deck, patio, lattice screens, and tiered planters. Photos, diagrams, drawings. • *Home Mechanix.* No. 775 (May, 1993) pp. 62-69.

Decks, Pool

"Cool pool deck" by Don Vandervort. Detailed instructions to build a multilevel deck especially design for an aboveground pool. Photos, diagrams. • *Home Mechanix.* No. 746 (June, 1990) pp. 48-52, 68.

Decks--Accessories

"All the comforts" by Matt Phair. In-depth look at seven accessories to add to a deck. Photos, drawing. • *Home Mechanix.* No. 777 (July/Aug, 1993) pp. 55-57.

Decks--Hardware and Tools

"Deckware" by Matt Phair. Describes specific tools and hardware designed for decks. Photos, drawings. • *Home Mechanix.* No. 767 (July/Aug, 1992) pp. 58-61.

Decks--Stairs

"Fantail deck stairs" by Jose L. Floresca. Provides instructions to build fantail-shaped deck stairs. Photos, diagram. • *Fine Homebuilding.* No. 83 (Sep, 1993) pp. 74-76.

Decoration and Ornament — *See* Handicraft

Decoys

"Darkhouse decoys" by Peter J. Stephano. In-depth article on Ray Zelinski and his process of creating wooden facsimile fish. Photos. • *Better Homes and Gardens Wood.* No. 60 (April, 1993) pp. 35-39.

"Shoot-over decoys" by Peter J. Stephano. Follow the guidelines of Grayson Chesser, Jr. on making decoys. Photos. Sidebar on more Grayson decoy wisdom. • *Better Homes and Gardens Wood.* No. 55 (Oct, 1992) pp. 28-29.

Design Guidelines

Book Review: *The Architect's Studio Companion: Technical Guidelines for Preliminary Design* by Edward Allen and Joseph Lano. Book review of a guide to technical systems and building codes for architects. New York: John Wiley and Sons, Inc., 468 pp. • *Fine Homebuilding.* No. 57 (Jan, 1990) p. 114.

Designs and Plans

"An A.O.B. House" by Timothy Clark. Presents the plans and design of an energy-efficient home built to an Alternative Owner Builder code. Photos, plans, drawings. • *Fine Homebuilding.* No. 69 (Sep, 1991) pp. 38-43.

"America's most popular house styles." Blueprints for ten of the most popular house plans in the U.S. Plans and drawings. • *Practical Homeowner.* Vol. IV, No. 9 (Jan, 1990) pp. 70-74.

"Annual American Family Home" by Rich Binsacca. A prize-winning design for a single family home. Photos. • *Practical Homeowner.* (Jul/Aug, 1992) pp. 54-65.

"An arc in the woods" by Charles Miller. Offers a unique design for an arc-shaped house in the woods. Photos, plan. • *Fine Homebuilding.* No. 73 (March, 1992) pp. 42-45.

Book and Software Review: *Passive Solar Design Strategies: Guidelines for Home Builders*, and *BuilderGuide Software.* Book and software review on several basic solar designs. Washington, D.C.: Passive Solar Industries Council. • *Fine Homebuilding.* No. 79 (March, 1993) p. 120.

"Built on promises" by Michael Chotiner. Offers the design of a dream home with readers' most-asked-for features. Photos. • *Home Mechanix.* No. 741 (Jan, 1990) pp. 48-57, 85.

"Costly traditions" by Scott Brinckerhoft. A critique of conventional house plans in favor of new uses for rooms. • *Practical Homeowner.* Vol. IV, No. 9 (Jan, 1990) pp. 30-32.

"Designing for a hot climate" by Thomas Leach. Presents a design focusing on the climate control and landscaping. Photos, plans, drawings. Sidebar on building the shadeshelters. • *Fine Homebuilding.* No. 79 (March, 1993) pp. 70-74.

"The Dot houses" by Robert Foulkes. Explains a practical cost-saving design for a cottage house. Photos, plans, drawings. Sidebar on character on a budget. • *Fine Homebuilding.* No. 67 (May, 1991) pp. 34-37.

"Fitting in Seattle" by Richard Beckman. Design and construction plans for an infill lot between two existing homes. Photos, plans. • *Fine Homebuilding.* No. 64 (Jan, 1991) pp. 75-79.

"Home buying in the year 2001" by Joseph Truini. Brief article on the predicted features in homes of the future. Drawing. • *Home Mechanix.* No. 762 (Feb, 1992) p. 34.

"A house in Burnaby" by Fred Thornton Hollingsworth. Offers a design and plan for a building that supports harmonious detailing in cedar, brick and glass. Photos, plans. • *Fine Homebuilding.* No. 66 (Spring, 1991) pp. 40-45.

"A house in Friday Harbor" by Gordon Lagerquist. Describes the design and building of a house with a string of gabled rooms to let in sunlight and a view. Photos, plans. • *Fine Homebuilding.* No. 61 (July, 1990) pp. 50-54.

"A house of light" by Richard M. Beckman. Offers a design with careful window placement to bring in sunlight on a heavily wooded site. Photos, plans. Sidebar on redistributing lateral loads. • *Fine Homebuilding.* No. 81 (May, 1993) pp. 83-87.

"A house on the river" by Steve Taylor. Offers the design of a river house constructed with concrete piers, cantilevered steel and prefab framing. Photos, drawing, plans. Sidebar on a transparent cricket. • *Fine Homebuilding.* No. 73 (Spring, 1992) pp. 71-75.

"The house that healed the land" by Jeff Gold. Offers a design for a home at a site once ravaged by mine shafts and logging. Photos, plans, drawing. Sidebar on carving a creek bed. • *Fine Homebuilding.* No. 80 (Spring, 1993) pp. 62-67.

"In tight" by Denny Abrams. Innovative designs for bringing light and roominess into tight living spaces. Photos. • *Practical Homeowner.* (Nov/Dec, 1992) pp. 30-35.

"Information resources" by Vincent Laurence. Valuable article offering sources for building and design information. • *Fine Homebuilding.* No. 65 (March, 1991) pp. 52-55.

"Inner space." A description of eight modern house plans. • *Practical Homeowner.* Vol. V, No. 1 (Feb, 1990) pp. 74-80.

"Laying out a domed ellipse" by Scott McBride. Presents a plan for building a oval-shaped room with a domed ceiling framed with semicircular arches. Drawing. • *Fine Homebuilding.* No. 71 (Jan, 1992) p. 14.

"More light, more room." Five different plans and blueprints for houses with dormers. • *Practical Homeowner.* Vol. V, No. 3 (April, 1990) pp. 76-80.

"A new 19th-century house" by Aileen L. Barth. Describes the design and construction plans for a reproduction of an 1810 lean-to. Photos, plans. • *Fine Homebuilding.* No. 77 (Nov, 1992) pp. 86-89.

"*Practical Homeowner* builds a house" by Roy Barnhart. This article offers guidance for people planning on designing a home. Photos and plans. • *Practical Homeowner.* Vol. V, No. 8 (Nov/Dec, 1990) pp. 42-50.

"*Practical Homeowner* builds a house, part four" by Roy Barnhart. See Vol. V, No. 6 • *Practical Homeowner.* Vol. VI, No. 4 (April, 1991) pp. 35-50.

"*Practical Homeowner* builds a house, part three" by Roy Barnhart. See Vol. V, No. 6 • *Practical Homeowner.* Vol. VI, No. 3 (March, 1991) pp. 56-59.

"*Practical Homeowner* builds a house, part two" by Roy Barnhart. See Vol. V, No. 8 • *Practical Homeowner.* Vol. VI, No. 1 (Jan, 1991) pp. 36-40.

"Resisting the weather on the Outer Banks" by Frank Harmon. Details the plans and design of a house on the Outer Banks. Photos, diagrams, plans. • *Fine Homebuilding.* No. 59 (Spring, 1990) pp. 78-82.

"Shop at home" by Charles Miller. Highlights a farm-building style home and workspace built with steel. Photos, diagrams, plans. • *Fine Homebuilding.* No. 73 (Spring, 1992) pp. 76-81.

Software Review: *AutoSketch 3.0* and *AutoSketch for Windows.* Software review on a program that helps produce precise drawings and aids users to visualize details for building homes. Bothell, WA: Autodesk Retail Products. • *Fine Homebuilding.* No. 81 (May, 1993) p. 114.

"Storage by design" by Nancy Cooper. Explains a software resource that helps design storage and cabinet space. Photos. Sample supply list. • *Home Mechanix.* No. 742 (Feb, 1990) pp. 32 37.

"Suburban refuge" by Joseph G. Metzler. Details the design of a suburban house constructed to assure comfort and privacy. Photos, plans. • *Fine Homebuilding.* No. 68 (July, 1991) pp. 82 87.

"Unconventional traditions" by Sharon Ross. A study of non-standard house plans including pre-cut log homes and geodesic domes. Photos. • *Practical Homeowner.* Vol. V, No. 7 (Oct, 1990) pp. 34-56.

Designs and Plans--Arts and Crafts Houses

"In the Arts and Crafts tradition" by G. Robert Parker. Offers the design and plans for a combination Maritime vernacular and Arts and Crafts home. Photos, plans. Sidebar on architecture and the Arts and Crafts movement. • *Fine Homebuilding*. No. 73 (Spring, 1992) pp. 51-55.

Designs and Plans--Cracker-Style Houses

"Cracker house in a hammock" by Robert H. Gore. Offers information on building a cracker style house especially suited for the Florida wetlands. Photos, plans, drawing. • *Fine Homebuilding*. No. 57 (Jan, 1990) pp. 63-67.

Designs and Plans--Economy

"Building for unknown clients" by David Carse. Offers designs for a small, cost-conscious spec houses. Photos, plans. • *Fine Homebuilding*. No. 80 (Spring, 1993) pp. 50-53.

Designs and Plans--Energy Efficiency

"When architecture meets energy efficiency" by Marc Rosenbaum. Details an integrated design approach to create an energy efficient house. Photos, plans. • *Fine Homebuilding*. No. 65 (March, 1991) pp. 62-65.

"Wisconsin wizardry" by Kelly Davis. Offers an innovative design creating an energy-efficient house. Photos, drawings, plans. • *Fine Homebuilding*. No. 66 (Spring, 1991) pp. 36-39.

Designs and Plans--Free-Form Buildings

"Rainbow hill" by James T. Hubbell. Describes the plans for a free-form building growing out of the granite. Photos, plans. Sidebar on free-form building. • *Fine Homebuilding*. No. 66 (Spring, 1991) pp. 51-55.

Designs and Plans--Hillside Houses

"Home in the hills" by Cathi and Steven House. Explains the design of a hillside home with an expansive curved deck to appreciate the beautiful scenic view. Photos, plans. • *Fine Homebuilding*. No. 80 (Spring, 1993) pp. 78-81.

Designs and Plans--Kit Homes

"Just add planning" by Michael Morris. Offers tips for the planning stage of building a kit-home. Photos. • *Home Mechanix*. No. 772 (Feb, 1993) pp. 60-61, 67.

Designs and Plans--Small Houses

"Building small" by Charles Wardell. Provides designs and techniques for building houses under 1,500 sq. ft. Photos. Sidebar on the business of building. • *Fine Homebuilding*. No. 74 (May, 1992) pp. 52-56.

Designs and Plans--Solar

"Practical solar design" by Debra G. Rucker. Presents a design of energy efficiency and a traditional look. Photos, plans. Sidebar on determining roof overhangs. • *Fine Homebuilding*. No. 84 (Nov, 1993) pp. 85-89.

"Shop layout" by Olev Edur. The author provides sample workshop floor plans, hints for more efficient work areas, and a template. Drawn plans. • *Canadian Workshop*. Vol. 13, No. 5 (Feb 1990) pp. 31-40.

Designs and Plans--Timber-Frame Houses

"Timber-frame house, shingle-style wrapper" by Lynn Hopkins. Highlights a timber-frame design with porches, dormers and roofs. Photos, plans. • *Fine Homebuilding*. No. 79 (March, 1993) pp. 50-55.

Desk Sets

"Projects with a porpoise" by Marlen Kemmet and Alan Bradstreet. Offers instructions to make a four-piece desk set with a nautical theme. Photos, diagrams. • *Better Homes and Gardens Wood*. No. 64 (Oct, 1993) pp. 39-41.

"Sunset rider deskset." An easy-to-make project for using a scroll saw to fashion a pen and pencil deskset. Photos and plans. • *The Woodworker's Journal.* Vol. 17, No. 5 (Sep/Oct, 1993) pp. 33-35.

"Top-drawer desk set" by Marlen Kemmet. Provides instructions to create beautiful walnut and maple desk accessories. Photos, diagrams, materials list. • *Better Homes and Gardens Wood.* No. 57 (Dec, 1992) pp. 54-59.

Desks

"Oak desk" by Marlen Kemmet. Learn how to construct an oak desk with raised panels. Photos, drawings, materials list. • *Better Homes and Gardens Wood.* No. 62 (Aug, 1993) pp. 42-47.

See Also Credenzas

Desks, Children's

"Little folks desk and bench." Clear plans on how to make a child-size desk and bench. Photos, plans, and materials. • *The Woodworker's Journal.* Vol. 15, No. 6 (Nov/Dec, 1991) pp. 46-47.

Desks, Slant Front

"Slant front desk." This lengthy and thorough article describes all the steps needed to construct a Governor Winthrop-style slant front desk. This project requires advanced cabinetmaking skills. Photos, plans, and materials list. • *The Woodworker's Journal.* Vol. 16, No. 6 (Nov/Dec, 1992) pp. 34-43.

Desks, Wall-Mounted

"Ash wall desk." This piece gives precise guidance for building a wall-mounted desk with doors and a drop-down writing surface. Photos, plans, and materials list. • *The Woodworker's Journal.* Vol. 15, No. 1 (Jan/Feb, 1991) pp. 58-60.

Desks, Writing

"Country pine writing desk." How to guide for making an Early American writing desk. Photos, plans, and materials list.

• *The Woodworker's Journal.* Vol. 15, No. 6 (Nov/Dec, 1991) pp. 40-43.

Die Cutters

"Making threads in wood" by Jim Barrett. A comprehensive description of the use of dies to cut threads in wood. Photos. • *The Woodworker's Journal.* Vol. 16, No. 2 (Mar/Apr, 1992) pp. 25 29.

Dies

"A holder for 13/16" dies, part one" by Rudy Kouhoupt. An explanation of the manufacture of a circular holder for small dies. Photos and plans. • *The Home Shop Machinist.* Vol. 11, No. 1 (Jan/Feb, 1992) pp. 42-44.

"A tapping guide for a unimat" by LeRoy Nessen. A simple procedure for adapting a die holder to fit a Unimat chuck for use as a tapping guide. Plans. • *The Home Shop Machinist.* Vol. 9, No. 4 (Jul/Aug, 1990) p. 27.

Diffusers (Ceiling)

"Condensation on diffusers" by Henry Spies. Offers a way of preventing condensation on ceiling diffusers. • *Home Mechanix.* No. 769 (Oct, 1992) pp. 80-81.

Dining Room Tables

"Cherry dropleaf dining table." A clear, but moderately difficult, set of plans for a large dropleaf table. Photos, plans, and materials list. • *The Woodworker's Journal.* Vol. 16, No. 1 (Jan/Feb, 1992) pp. 44-47.

"Design under glass" by Lars Dalsgaard. Offers directions to build a glass-top dining table with the possibility of changing the underglass inserts. Photos, diagrams, materials list. • *Home Mechanix.* No. 742 (Feb, 1990) pp. 58-61.

"Elegant-oak dining table" by Marlen Kemmet and James R. Downing. Specific plans to construct a sturdy, expandable oak dining table. Photos, diagrams, materials list. • *Better Homes and Gardens Wood.* No. 59 (Feb, 1993) pp. 50-56.

"Harvest table." A very detailed article on the design and construction of an Early American-style dropleaf table. Photos, plans, and materials list. • *The Woodworker's Journal.* Vol. 14. No. 4 (Jul/Aug, 1990) pp. 49-51.

Disabilities — *See* Architecture and the Handicapped

Dishwashers

"More dishwasher disasters" by Steve Brannan. Provides useful solutions to most common types of electrical dishwasher problems. • *Canadian Workshop.* Vol. 13, No. 4 (Jan 1990) p. 10.

Dispensers, Hot-Water

"Staying in hot water" by Merle Henkenius. Describes how to install a hot-water dispenser. Photos, drawing. • *Home Mechanix.* No. 750 (Nov, 1990) pp. 68-70.

Display Cases

"Collector's showcase" by Marlen Kemmet. Construct a showcase for collectible items with these detailed instructions. Diagrams, photos. • *Better Homes and Gardens Wood.* No. 35 (June, 1990) pp. 68-71.

"Pedestal-sized curio showcase" by Marlen Kemmet and James R. Downing. Instructions to build a cherry curio showcase. Photos, diagrams, materials list. • *Better Homes and Gardens Wood.* No. 52 (June, 1992) pp. 47-51.

See Also Cabinets; Boxes

Dollhouses (Toy)

"Classic colonial doll house." A comprehensive and detailed set of plans for building a Colonial-style dollhouse. Photos, plans, and materials list. • *The Woodworker's Journal.* Vol. 15, No. 6 (Nov/Dec, 1991) pp. 48-52.

Domes

Book Review: *Professional Dome Plans*, 2nd edition by Jeffrey O. Hill. Book review on this loose-leaf book covering construction tips for dome builders. Eugene, OR:

Precision Structures, 68 pp. • *Fine Homebuilding.* No. 65 (March, 1991) p. 108.

Door Harps

"Cheery, cherry door harp" by Robert Kiser. Brief description to make a door harp. Photo, diagram. • *Better Homes and Gardens Wood.* No. 41 (Feb, 1991) pp. 66-67.

Doors

"Better backing for doors" by M.F. Marti. Describes a method to create full backing for hinges on doors. Drawing. • *Fine Homebuilding.* No. 70 (Nov, 1991) p. 32.

"Building interior doors" by Joseph Beals. Provides directions to use a shaper to make coped and-sticked frames and raised panels. Photos, drawings. • *Fine Homebuilding.* No. 72 (March, 1992) pp. 50-53.

"Curing unwanted door swings" by Theodore Haendel. Brief tip on how to plumb the hinges to prevent swinging. Drawing. • *Fine Homebuilding.* No. 69 (Sep, 1991) p. 14.

"Doubletakes" by Matthew Phair. Offers tips on purchasing, installing, and finishing double doors. Photos, drawings. Sidebar on problem-solving hinge alternatives. • *Home Mechanix.* No. 778 (Sep, 1993) pp. 124-126, 139.

"An elegant site-built door" by John Birchard. Presents instructions to build interior and exterior doors right on the job site. Photos, drawings. Sidebar on a self-centering router base. • *Fine Homebuilding.* No. 83 (Sep, 1993) pp. 57-61.

"Flush door face lift" by Jim Barrett. Explains a method of upgrading worn interior doors with veneer and decorative moldings. • *Home Mechanix.* No. 750 (Nov, 1990) pp. 18-19.

"A front door and more" by Mark Alvarez. New and classified designs for front doors.

Photos. • *Practical Homeowner*. Vol. VI, No. 4 (April, 1991) pp. 52-60.

"In search of the perfect door" by Timothy O. Bakke. Discusses the advantages of steel and fiberglass doors. Photos. Sidebar on easy door installation system. • *Home Mechanix*. No. 756 (June, 1991) pp. 38-41.

"Installing pre-hung doors" by Armin Rudd. Handy tip for installing the jambs of pre-hung doors. • *Fine Homebuilding*. No. 58 (March, 1990) p. 26.

"Invisible door closer" by Henry Spies. Brief tip on how to prevent doors from swinging shut themselves. Drawing. • *Home Mechanix*. No. 756 (June, 1991) p. 86.

"Ordering and installing prehung doors" by Steve Kearns. Describes the basic carpentry skills needed to install a pre-hung door. Photos, drawing. Sidebar on plumb-bob door hanging. • *Fine Homebuilding*. No. 74 (May, 1992) pp. 62-65.

"Prize doors" by Joseph Truini. Describes a variety of methods of adding a sidelight or transom to a door. Photos, drawings. Sidebar on reframing for a wider door. • *Home Mechanix*. No. 775 (June, 1993) pp. 46-50.

"Refitting a door" by Theodore R. Haendel. Informative tip on refitting old doors. • *Fine Homebuilding*. No. 81 (May, 1993) pp. 26-28.

"Solo level shots" by Lloyd Dorsey. Offers a brief tip on creating an accurate level for installing interior doors. • *Fine Homebuilding*. No. 83 (Sep, 1993) p. 30.

"Stick and cope doorbuilding" by Ernie Conover. This article analyzes the process for using cope and stick cutters to assemble the panel, rail, and stile sections of a panel door. Photos and plans. • *The Woodworker's Journal*. Vol. 16, No. 6 (Nov/Dec, 1992) pp. 20-25.

"Well-rounded door conversions" by Jeff Greef. Presents ideas for transforming a plain door into an elegant arched entryway. Drawings, photos. • *Home Mechanix*. No. 776 (June, 1993) pp. 12-14.

Doors, Fire

"Installing a fire-safe door" by Matt Phair. Detailed directions to install a fire-door. Photos, drawing. • *Home Mechanix*. No. 765 (May, 1992) pp. 24-25.

Doors, French

"For openers" by Ted Jones. Describes how to replace a window with a French door. Photos, drawing. Sidebar on French door interpretations. Sidebar on altering a header. • *Home Mechanix*. No. 750 (Nov, 1990) pp. 55-59.

Doors, Metal-Skinned

"Boring metal-skinned doors" by Robert Countryman. Brief tip on installing locks in metal skinned doors. • *Fine Homebuilding*. No. 83 (Sep, 1993) p. 28.

Doors, Panel

"Making a tombstone frame-and-panel door." A detailed outline of the procedures for constructing a tombstone profile panel section door. Photo and plans. • *The Woodworker's Journal*. Vol. 14, No. 3 (May/Jun, 1990) pp. 22-25.

"Stick and cope doorbuilding" by Ernie Conover. This article analyzes the process for using cope and stick cutters to assemble the panel, rail, and stile sections of a panel door. Photos and plans. • *The Woodworker's Journal*. Vol. 16, No. 6 (Nov/Dec, 1992) pp. 20-25.

Doors, Pocket

"Pocket-door fix" by Bruce G. Koprucki. Brief tip on fixing a pocket door. Drawing. • *Fine Homebuilding*. No. 63 (Nov, 1990) p. 28.

Doors, Screen

"Building wooden screen doors" by Stephen Sewall. Describes the sound joinery and solid materials that create durable and aesthetically beautiful screen doors. Photos, diagrams. • *Fine Homebuilding*. No. 57 (Jan, 1990) pp. 72-75.

"Storm and screen doors" by Judith Trotsky. Describes a variety of designs for storm and screen doors. Photos. Sidebar on the right fit: how to measure a doorway. • *Home Mechanix*. No. 749 (Oct, 1990) pp. 82-88.

Doors, Security

"Doorway defense" by John Warde. Provides instructions on checking doors for the most secure protection. Drawings. • *Home Mechanix*. No. 743 (March, 1990) pp. 20-21, 80.

Doors--Closers

"Installing door closers" by Jim Barrett. Brief instructions on installing a door closer for a home. Photos. • *Home Mechanix*. No. 741 (Jan, 1990) pp. 16-17.

Doors--Decorative Additions

"Pueblo modern" by Craig W. Murray. Presents a method of adding decorative Southwestern motifs to doors using a knife and paintbrush. Photos. • *Fine Homebuilding*. No. 67 (May, 1991) pp. 56-58.

Doors--Patterns

Book Review: *Doormaking Patterns & Ideas* by John Birdhard. Book review of a general guide to designing, building and installing doors. Includes instructions and plans for 47 different types. New York: Sterling Publishing Co. Inc., pp. 192 • *Fine Homebuilding*. No. 68 (July, 1991) p. 106.

Doors--Reinforcers

"Door reinforcers" by Bill Phillips. Informative article on door reinforcers. Photos. • *Home Mechanix*. No. 779 (Oct, 1993) pp. 26-27.

Doorways, Arched

"Create an arch" by Matt Phair. Instructions to create an arched doorway from a typical square doorway. Photos.

• *Home Mechanix*. No. 742 (Feb, 1990) pp. 46-47.

Dormers

"Daring dormers" by James Lomuscio. Creative building applications involving dormer additions. Photos. • *Practical Homeowner*. Vol. VI, No. 5 (May/June, 1991) pp. 54-59.

"Raise the roof" by Mark Alvarez. An innovative technique for using hydraulic jacks to create attic dormers or add an extra story to a building. Photos. • *Practical Homeowner*. Vol. V, No. 3 (April, 1990) pp. 56-59.

"Raising an eyebrow" by James Docker. Offers two methods to frame wave-like dormers. Photos, drawings. • *Fine Homebuilding*. No. 65 (March, 1991) pp. 80-84.

Dormers, Eyebrow

"Steep-slope eyebrow dormers" by David Kane. Brief tip on constructing eyebrow dormers. Drawing. • *Fine Homebuilding*. No. 84 (Nov, 1993) p. 28.

Downspouts

"Dampening drips" by Richard H. Dorn. Offers a solution to noisy dripping raindrops in a downspout. Drawing. • *Fine Homebuilding*. No. 70 (Nov, 1991) pp. 32-34.

Drain Lines

"Thawing frozen drain lines" by Gregory Savas. Presents a method of thawing frozen drain lines. Drawing. • *Fine Homebuilding*. No. 84 (Nov, 1993) p. 30.

Drains

"Appliance drains" by Joseph Fetchko. Presents a method of constructing effective drains under appliances. Drawing. • *Fine Homebuilding*. No. 69 (Sep, 1991) p. 30.

Drawer Boxes

"Single-setup drawer boxes" by Ross Fulmer. Details the process of making drawer boxes. Drawings. • *Fine Homebuilding*. No. 77 (Nov, 1992) p. 30.

Drawers

"Making and installing dovetailed drawers" by Bill Krier and Jim Boelling. In-depth look at making sturdy dovetailed drawers. Photos, diagrams. • *Better Homes and Gardens Wood*. No. 55 (Oct, 1992) pp. 30-35.

"Making drawers." This step-by-step analysis details the process used to construct wooden drawers. Drawings and plans. • *The Woodworker's Journal*. Vol. 14, No. 2 (Mar/Apr, 1990) pp. 16-19.

"Quick drawer fixes" by Jim Barrett. Brief tips on repairing sticking or warped drawers and loose drawer joints. Photos. • *Home Mechanix*. No. 745 (May, 1990) pp. 18-21, 95.

"Wall works" by Sally Ross. Explains how to build wall-mounted counters with drawers for storage. Photos, diagrams, drawing. • *Home Mechanix*. No. 747 (July/Aug, 1990) pp. 46-50.

Dressers — *See* Chests

Drill Bits

"Drill-bit basics" by Joseph Truini. In-depth article on the variety of drill bits available and the functions of these bits. Photos. • *Home Mechanix*. No. 743 (March, 1990) pp. 28-33, 80.

"Drill-bit countersink" by Terence Walker. Brief article on using a drill-bit for attaching plywood countertop substrate to cabinets. Drawings. • *Fine Homebuilding*. No. 78 (Jan, 1993) p. 28.

Drill Bushings

"Drill bushings, part one" by Edward G. Hoffman. This article explains the use of bushings to locate, support, and guide cutting tools. Photos and plans. • *The Home Shop Machinist*. Vol. 12, No. 4 (Jul/Aug, 1993) pp. 54-55.

"Drill bushings, part three" by Edward G. Hoffman. See Vol. 12, No. 4 • *The Home Shop Machinist*. Vol. 12, No. 6 (Nov/Dec, 1993) pp. 54-57.

"Drill bushings, part two" by Edward G. Hoffman. See Vol. 12, No. 4 • *The Home Shop Machinist*. Vol. 12, No. 5 (Sep/Oct, 1993) pp. 54-55.

Drill Guides

"Using a drill guide" by Thomas H. Jones. Offers a tip on increasing the hole-boring accuracy for a portable drill with a drill guide. Photos. • *Home Mechanix*. No. 742 (Feb, 1990) pp. 8-9.

Drill Press Tables

"Drillpress table" by Gary Walchuk. Provides detailed directions on building a wooden drillpress table. Drawn plans. Photos. • *Canadian Workshop*. Vol. 13, No. 4 (Jan 1990) pp. 12 13.

Drill Presses

"Cameron series 164 micro drill press" by John Gascoyne. A product review for a new Cameron micro-sized drill press. • *The Home Shop Machinist*. Vol. 11, No. 4 (Jul/Aug, 1992) pp. 15-17.

"Drill press chuck handles" by Rudy Kouhoupt. This article provides a guide to modifying a drill press chuck with the addition of handles. Photos and plans. • *The Home Shop Machinist*. Vol. 12, No. 2 (Mar/Apr, 1993) pp. 39-41.

"Drill press gets around on an easy-to-build base" by Jeff Masterson. Brief suggestion for moving a drill press. Drawing. • *Better Homes and Gardens Wood*. No. 64 (Oct, 1993) p. 10.

"Drill press quill lock" by Marshall R. Young. A simple left-handed quill lock for use with a drill press. Photos and plans. • *The Home Shop Machinist*. Vol. 11, No. 1 (Jan/Feb, 1992) pp. 40 41.

"Drill press router adapter" by Frank A. McLean. A description of a method to attach a wood router to a drill press for greater spindle control. Photos and plans. • *The Home Shop Machinist*. Vol. 12, No. 3 (May/Jun, 1993) pp. 38-42.

"Drill press vise restraints" by James Berger. A description of two kinds of restraints used to control vise rotation on a drill press—sliding bars and parallel linkage designs. Photos and plans. • *The Home Shop Machinist*. Vol. 11, No. 4 (Jul/Aug, 1992) pp. 45-50.

"Drill presses." Analysis of a drill press and a comparison of 32 different machines. Photo, chart, illustration. • *Better Homes and Gardens Wood*. No. 38 (Oct, 1990) pp. 46-49.

"Drillpress table" by Gary Walchuk. Provides detailed directions on building a wooden drillpress table. Drawn plans. Photos. • *Canadian Workshop*. Vol. 13, No. 4 (Jan 1990) pp. 12 13.

Drilling

"Drilling multiple holes in line" by Bill Wagner. A simple design for a drilling jig. Photos and plans. • *The Home Shop Machinist*. Vol. 10, No. 4 (Jul/Aug, 1991) pp. 18-20.

"Hinge swings into action when holes require spacing" by Ed Abrams. Brief tip on accurately drilling a series of evenly spaced holes. Drawing. • *Better Homes and Gardens Wood*. No. 51 (April, 1992) p. 19.

"Overhead drilling" by Joseph Fetchko. Shows two methods of drilling overhead that reduce damage to arm muscles. Drawing. • *Fine Homebuilding*. No. 67 (May, 1991) p. 26.

Drills

"Cordless drill/drivers." In-depth guide comparing 37 hard-driving drills. Photos, chart, illustration. • *Better Homes and Gardens Wood*. No. 38 (Oct, 1990) pp. 42-45.

"Fitting small drill chucks" by Frank A. McLean. A how-to guide for accurately fitting drill chucks. Photos. • *The Home Shop Machinist*. Vol. 11, No. 1 (Jan/Feb, 1992) pp. 52-55.

"The great electric-drill shoot-out" by Bill Krier. Extensive information about features and specifications of drills. Photos, specification chart. • *Better Homes and Gardens Wood*. No. 36 (Aug, 1990) pp. 66-71.

Drills, Cordless

"Cordless wonders" by Bill Krier. Updated report on battery-operated drills with new innovations. Photos, chart comparing 21 drills. • *Better Homes and Gardens Wood*. No. 42 (April, 1991) pp. 62-67.

Drills, Screw

"Screw drills." Describes the time-saving advantages of screw-hole bits. Photo. • *Better Homes and Gardens Wood*. No. 41 (Feb, 1991) pp. 20-21.

Drills, Twist

"Two new twist drills" by Jim Jedlicka. This is a product review of two new designs for twist drills. Photos. • *The Home Shop Machinist*. Vol. 9, No. 1 (Jan/Feb, 1990) pp. 15-17.

Drills, Variable-Speed

"Survey of $\frac{3}{8}$-in. variable-speed reversible drills" by Herrick Kimball. In-depth evaluation of the latest variable-speed reversible drills. Photos, chart. Sidebar on electrical grounding and shock prevention. • *Fine Homebuilding*. No. 82 (July, 1993) pp. 36-41.

Driveways

"Scenic drives" by Bob Wessmiller. Offers seven paving patterns for driveways. Photos. Sidebar on a drive to build. • *Home Mechanix*. No. 775 (May, 1993) pp. 79-83.

Driveways--Resurfacing

"Asphalt driveway resurfacing" by Matt Phair. Describes the process of chip-seal surface treatments for long-lasting surfaces. Photos, chart. Sidebar about sealers. • *Home Mechanix.* No. 755 (May, 1991) pp. 15-19.

Drop-Leaf Tables

"Shaker drop-leaf table" by Gene Cosloy. This is a brief description of the method of making a drop-leaf side table after a nineteenth-century Shaker pattern. Photo, plans, and materials list. • *The Woodworker's Journal.* Vol. 15, No. 4 (Jul/Aug, 1991) pp. 33-35.

Dryers, Clothes

"Dryer air intake" by Marc Rosenbaum. Offers a tip on finding a vent for the clothes dryer in an energy-efficient house. • *Fine Homebuilding.* No. 81 (May, 1993) pp. 16-18.

Drywall and Drywalling

Book Review: *Drywall: Installation and Applications* by W. Robert Harris. Book review on a the tools and techniques needed in the drywall trade. Photo. Homewood, IL: American Technical Publishers, 168 pp. • *Fine Homebuilding.* No. 70 (Nov, 1991) p. 120.

"Drywall detailing" by Dennis Darrah. Offers instructions on how to add drywall detailing on windows. Photos, drawings. • *Fine Homebuilding.* No. 63 (Nov, 1990) pp. 50-53.

"Drywall edge trimmer" by Brian Bush. Brief tip to remove uniform strips from a sheet of drywall. Drawing. • *Fine Homebuilding.* No. 62 (Sep, 1990) p. 28.

"Installing drywall" by Charles Wardell. Informative tips on keeping sheets flat and eliminating seams when installing drywall. Photos, drawings. Sidebar on cutting holes for outlets, switches and lights. Sidebar on types of drywall. • *Fine Homebuilding.* No. 81 (May, 1993) pp. 38-43.

"A material difference" by Kevin Ireton. Explains the difference between interior and exterior drywall and plywood. • *Fine Homebuilding.* No. 70 (Nov, 1991) p. 14.

"More solo drywall hanging" by Fred Grosser. Brief tip for hanging drywall with cleats. Drawing. • *Fine Homebuilding.* No. 72 (March, 1992) p. 26.

"Pipe-clamp drywall lift" by John D. Leonick. Describes a method of lifting drywall with pipe clamps. Drawing. • *Fine Homebuilding.* No. 74 (May, 1992) p. 26.

"Return backing" by Billy Guild. Offers tips for preparing window openings for drywall. Drawing. • *Fine Homebuilding.* No. 68 (July, 1991) p. 30.

"Solo drywall hanging" by Henry A. Jorgensen. Explains how to hang drywall with the help of three deadmen, cleats and a stepladder. Drawing. • *Fine Homebuilding.* No. 57 (Jan, 1990) p. 26.

"Taping and finishing drywall" by Charles Wardell. Detailed tips for a smooth finish on drywall with minimum sanding. Photos. • *Fine Homebuilding.* No. 82 (July, 1993) pp. 72-77.

"Textured drywall patch" by Kenneth S. Hayes. Brief article on patching a hole in a ceiling and matching the drywall texture. • *Fine Homebuilding.* No. 71 (Jan, 1992) p. 26.

Ducts

"Duct cleaning" by Henry Spies. Describes how a professional duct-cleaning firm cleans ducts. Drawings. • *Home Mechanix.* No. 773 (March, 1993) p. 83.

Dulcimers

"Hammered dulcimer." Complete plans for building a dulcimer using cherry and maple wood. Photos, plans, and materials list. • *The Woodworker's Journal.* Vol. 17, No. 1 (Jan/Feb, 1993) pp. 64-67.

"Mountain dulcimer." This article shows the method of cutting patterns and assembling a dulcimer in a Kentucky mountain pattern. Photos, plans, and materials list. • *The Woodworker's Journal.* Vol. 15, No. 4 (Jul/Aug, 1991) pp. 28-32.

Dump Trucks (Toy)

"Tilt action dump truck." A simple but clever design for a toy dump truck. Photo, plans, and materials list. • *The Woodworker's Journal.* Vol. 15, No. 5 (Sep/Oct, 1991) pp. 54-57.

Dust Collection Hoods

"The dust stops here — portable planer hood" by James R. Downing. Build a simple-to-make hood that attaches to the planer and feeds into a central dust collection system. Photo, diagram, material list. • *Better Homes and Gardens Wood.* No. 43 (June, 1991) pp. 48-49.

Dust Collectors

"Box protects dust collector" by Bob Colpetzer. Instructions to build a drop box to collect large pieces in the dust collection system. Drawing. • *Better Homes and Gardens Wood.* No. 64 (Oct, 1993) p. 16.

"Central dust collection" by Bill Krier and Jim Downing. Presents an affordable and simple central dust collection system. Photos, drawings. • *Better Homes and Gardens Wood.* No. 43 (June, 1991) pp. 40-45.

"Convert pipe couplers into inexpensive blast gates" by David Weissman. Handy tip on creating homemade blast gates for dust-collection systems. Drawing. • *Better Homes and Gardens Wood.* No. 60 (April, 1993) p. 10.

"A down-to-business dust collector" by James R. Downing. Build a dust collector specifically designed for a radial-arm saw blade. Photos, diagrams. • *Better Homes and Gardens Wood.* No. 43 (June, 1991) pp. 46-47.

"Drill-press dust collector" by James R. Downing. Brief tip on making a clamp-down collector. Photo, drawings. • *Better Homes and Gardens Wood.* No. 59 (Feb, 1993) p. 22.

"Dust collectors." Informative article on the specifications of 21 dust collectors. Photo, chart. • *Better Homes and Gardens Wood.* No. 65 (Nov, 1993) pp. 52-53.

"Dust collectors getting the most out of your system" by Grant Beck. Basic guidelines on setting up the most efficient dust collector system. Photos. Drawings. • *Woodwork.* No. 13 (January/February) pp. 55-57.

"Dust collectors: six models for the small shop reviewed" by Grant Beck. Helpful tips on six dust collector models. Photos. Diagram. • *Woodwork.* No. 13 (January/February) pp. 50-54.

"Meet the dust guzzlers" by Bill Krier. In-depth analysis of 11 dust collectors. Photos, chart with comparisons. • *Better Homes and Gardens Wood.* No. 54 (Sep, 1992) pp. 42-47.

"Reducing dust" by Alan Bellamy. Presents a helpful tip on making a dust removal machine from a six inch flexible hose. Drawing. • *Fine Homebuilding.* No. 83 (Sep, 1993) p. 28.

"Scrollsaw picks up dust instead of spreading it" by Donald Diller. Brief tip on collecting dust with a scroll saw. Drawing. • *Better Homes and Gardens Wood.* No. 59 (Feb, 1993) p. 12.

"Sucking up the small stuff" by Rick Stodola. Offers a tip on creating an inexpensive and effective dust collection system. Photo, drawing. • *Fine Homebuilding.* No. 60 (May, 1990) p. 63.

"What's available in low-cost dust collection systems" by Jim Barrett. This review offers a thorough analysis of the type of shop vacs on the market. Photos. • *The Woodworker's Journal.* Vol. 15, No. 3 (May/Jun, 1991) pp. 30-36.

Dust Control

"Dust busting" by James Barrelt. A brief tip on the use of respirators in home workshops. • *Practical Homeowner.* Vol. V, No. 8 (Nov/Dec, 1990) p. 14.

Dust Panels

"Dust panels" by Patrick H. Kelly. Directions on constructing dust panels for woodwork containing drawers. Photo. • *Woodwork.* No. 17 (Sep/Oct, 1992) p. 68.

E

Earth Shelters

"Expressing a site" by Alfredo DeVido. Construction plans to build an energy-efficient earth shelter with materials from the land. Photos, plans, drawing. • *Fine Homebuilding.* No. 71 (Jan, 1992) pp. 36-41.

Earthbuilders--Encyclopedias

Book Review: *The Earthbuilders' Encyclopedia* by Joseph M. Tibbets. Book review of an encyclopedia providing rammed-earth and adobe terms and a directory of earthbuilders and suppliers. Bosque, NM: Joseph M. Tibbets (PO Box 153) 196 pp. • *Fine Homebuilding.* No. 60 (May, 1990) p. 106.

Earthen Houses

"Rammed earth revisited" by Jim Rosenau. An analysis of innovations in building house walls from compacted earth. Photos. • *Practical Homeowner.* (Sep/Oct, 1992) pp. 74-77.

Earthquakes

"Riding out the big one" by Ralph Gareth Gray. Gives an in-depth analysis of the impact of an earthquake on a wood-frame building and how to prevent collapse. Photos, drawings. Sidebar on the load path. • *Fine Homebuilding.* No. 64 (Jan, 1991) pp. 60-65.

Earthships

Book Review: *Earthship, Vol. 1: How to Build Your Own* by Michael Reynolds. Book review that features information on how to build an earthship, a comfortable and energy-efficient home buried in the ground below the frostline. Taos, NM: Solar Survival Press, 229 pp. • *Fine Homebuilding.* No. 69 (Sep, 1991) p. 110.

Eaves

"West coast overhang" by Don Dunkley. Provides information on a framing technique used for soffit-covered eaves. Drawing. • *Fine Homebuilding.* No. 63 (Nov, 1990) p. 69.

Edwardian Houses

"Backyard Edwardian" by Richard Fearn. Explains the process of renovating a Edwardian-era home in Vancouver. Photos, plans, drawings. • *Fine Homebuilding.* No. 59 (Spring, 1990) pp. 48-51.

Electric Discharge Machining (EDM)

"Electric discharge machining" by Hank Meador. A brief discussion of the uses of electric discharge machining (EDM) for precise cutting. Plans and drawings. • *The Home Shop Machinist.* Vol. 10, No. 1 (Jan/Feb, 1991) pp. 41-42.

Electric Generators

Book Review: *More Power to You! A Proven Path to Electric Energy Independence* by H. Skip Thomsen. Book review on a guide that offers step-by-step instructions for building a full-time power system. Manzanita, OR: Oregon Wordworks, 83 pp. • *Fine Homebuilding.* No. 68 (July, 1991) pp. 106-108.

"Off-line electrical systems" by Ezra Auerbach. Provides information on alternative energy sources for remote locations. Photos, drawings, chart. Sidebar on low-tech hydro. • *Fine Homebuilding.* No. 62 (Sep, 1990) pp. 68-71.

Electric Motors

"Junkyard motor junkie" by Ted Myers. A partially tongue-in-cheek article on how to search junkyards for used electric motors. • *The Home Shop Machinist.* Vol. 10, No. 1 (Jan/Feb, 1991) pp. 45-49.

Electric Switches

"Quick switch for receptacles" by Merle Henkenius. Informative article on installing a wall switch with the option of a split receptacle so only one of the outlets is operated by a switch. Photos, drawing. • *Home Mechanix.* No. 751 (Dec/Jan, 1990-91) p. 16.

Electrical Fields

"Electric-radiant slabs and health" by Richard D. Watson. Presents information on whether exposure to weak electrical fields is dangerous to ones health. • *Fine Homebuilding.* No. 82 (July, 1993) p. 20.

Electrical Wiring

"Fish-snake helper" by Larry Wilson. Brief tip on using a fish snake to thread electric wire. Drawing. • *Fine Homebuilding.* No. 63 (Nov, 1990) p. 26.

"Fishtape target" by David Gelderloos. Brief tip on making a target when installing electrical wiring. • *Fine Homebuilding.* No. 77 (Nov, 1992) p. 32.

"Site-built wire spinner" by M. Scott Watkins. Explains how to build a wire spinner in only fifteen minutes. Drawing. • *Fine Homebuilding.* No. 60 (May, 1990) p. 26.

"Wiring three-way switches" by Thomas Johnson. Offers a helpful tip for wiring three-way switches. Drawings. • *Fine Homebuilding.* No. 81 (May, 1993) pp. 48-49.

Elevation Stakes

"Standout stakes" by Tony Toccalino. Offers a tip for getting the levels right when pouring concrete for patios, driveways and paths. • *Fine Homebuilding.* No. 82 (July, 1993) pp. 26-28.

Elm (Wood)

"The mighty elm" by Alasdair Wallace. Describes the different features of working with elm in woodwork projects. Photos. • *Canadian Workshop.* Vol. 13, No. 4 (Jan 1990) pp. 14–15.

End Tables

"Cherry end table." Plans for an end table with a single drawer made of cherry and poplar wood. Photo, plans, and materials list. • *The Woodworker's Journal.* Vol. 17, No. 1 (Jan/Feb, 1993) pp. 41-43.

"Country pine table." This article provides concise instructions for building a small, primitive-style, end table. Photos and plans. • *The Woodworker's Journal.* Vol. 14, No. 6 (Nov/Dec, 1990) pp. 52-64.

"Cutting corners" by Jeff Mathers. Provides detailed instructions on how to build a wooden corner table. Table of materials. Drawn plans. Photo. • *Canadian Workshop.* Vol. 15, No. 1 (Oct 1991) pp. 29-32.

Energy Conservation

"Fifty ways to vitalize your house." A list of 50 products or services that can save energy and improve living. Photos. • *Practical Homeowner.* (Sep/Oct, 1992) pp. 66-73.

"Setback thermostats" by Katie and Gene Hamilton. Detailed instructions on how to save money by setting back the thermostat. (Part one.) Worksheet. • *Home Mechanix.* No. 762 (Feb, 1992) pp. 32-33.

Energy Efficiency

"Beating the heat" by Peter L. Pfeiffer. Highlights a design fit for Texas hot summers. Photos, plans, drawing. • *Fine Homebuilding.* No. 80 (Spring, 1993) pp. 54-58.

Book Review: *1991 Consumer Guide to Home Energy Savings* by Alex Wilson. Book review on a helpful reference guide to energy consumption. American Council for an

Energy-Efficient Economy, 252 pp. • *Fine Homebuilding*. No. 67 (May, 1991) p. 104.

Book Review: *Practical Home Energy Savings* by David Bill and the staff of Rocky Mountain Institute. Book review on low-cost energy-saving tips for homeowners. Snowmass, CO: Rocky Mountain Institute, 48 pp. • *Fine Homebuilding*. No. 76 (Sep, 1992) p. 118.

"Controlling air leakage" by Jim Maloney. Offers suggestions for saving energy in a new construction. Drawings, chart. Sidebar on sealing leaks: what to use. Sidebar on the problem with air leaks. • *Fine Homebuilding*. No. 77 (Nov, 1992) pp. 64-67.

"Cool details" by W. Scott Neely. Building plans for a Texas vernacular home in the tradition of a Texas farmhouse. Photos, plans, diagrams. Sidebar on borrowing designs from the past. • *Fine Homebuilding*. No. 70 (Nov, 1991) pp. 61-65.

"The current cost of energy" by Timothy O. Bakke. Compares the costs of heating with a variety of types of energy. Chart. • *Home Mechanix*. No. 758 (Sep, 1991) p. 19.

"Energy detailing" by Daniel Hill. Analysis of the amount of heat loss in a specific home and solutions to improve the energy efficiency. • *Fine Homebuilding*. No. 65 (March, 1991) p. 18.

"Expert energy inspection" by Matt Phair. Traces the procedure of inspections for energy- and money-wasting air leaks. Photos. • *Home Mechanix*. No. 752 (Feb, 1991) p. 32.

"Guaranteed energy savings" by Timothy O. Bakke. Brief article detailing the Bigelow Homes in which the annual heating bills are guaranteed not to exceed $200. • *Home Mechanix*. No. 760 (Nov, 1991) p. 27.

"Modeling home energy use" by Marc Rosenbaum. Offers strategies to calculate energy loads for houses during the designing stage. Photos, charts, software programs. • *Fine Homebuilding*. No. 71 (Jan, 1992) pp. 46-49.

"Superinsulated in Idaho" by Jonathan Marvel. Describes the plans and the insulation techniques for a home in Idaho. Photos, plans. • *Fine Homebuilding*. No. 66 (Spring, 1991) pp. 64-68.

Energy Efficiency--Lighting

"Compact fluorescent lighting" by Gene and Katie Hamilton. Provides tips on saving energy by using compact fluorescent bulbs. Worksheet. (Part 2) • *Home Mechanix*. No. 763 (March, 1992) pp. 10-11.

Energy Efficiency--Solar

"A photovoltaic test house" by Charles Wardell. This innovative design with solar cells on the roof to generate energy actually sells power back to the power company. Photos. Sidebar on PV past, present and future. Sidebar on making a solar cell. • *Fine Homebuilding*. No. 72 (March, 1992) pp. 70-75.

Energy Efficiency--Windows

"Rooms with a view" by Chris Knowles. Describes how to select and install the most energy efficient windows for the home, as well as window replacement procedures. Photos. • *Canadian Workshop*. Vol. 15, No. 1 (Oct 1991) pp. 42-47.

Energy--Terminology

"Glossary: energy terms" by Glass Magazine Editors. Describes in layperson's language the common terms associated with glass and energy. • *The Homeowner's Guide to Glass*. No. 1 (1989) p. 8.

Engines, Gasoline

"Building the panther pup, part eight" by John Reichart. See Vol. 9, No. 1 • *The Home Shop Machinist*. Vol. 9, No. 3 (May/ Jun, 1990) pp. 31-37.

"Building the panther pup, part nine" by John Reichart. See Vol. 9, No. 1 • *The*

Home Shop Machinist. Vol. 9, No. 4 (Jul/Aug, 1990) pp. 42-47.

"Building the panther pup, part seven" by John Reichert. See Vol. 9, No. 1 • *The Home Shop Machinist.* Vol. 9, No. 2 (Mar/Apr, 1990) pp. 28-32.

"Building the panther pup, part six" by John Reichart. Complete and exhaustive plans for the construction of a four cylinder, four-cycle gasoline engine. Photos and plans. • *The Home Shop Machinist.* Vol. 9, No. 1 (Jan/Feb, 1990) pp. 38-42.

"Gearless hit 'n miss engine, part four" by Philip Duclos. See Vol. 12, No. 3 • *The Home Shop Machinist.* Vol. 12, No. 6 (Nov/Dec, 1993) pp. 29-35.

"Gearless hit 'n miss engine, part one" by Philip Duclos. This article provides comprehensive plans for the construction of a four-cycle, gearless, gasoline engine. Photos, plans, and materials list. • *The Home Shop Machinist.* Vol. 12, No. 3 (May/Jun, 1993) pp. 16-23.

"Gearless hit 'n miss engine, part three" by Philip Duclos. See Vol. 12, No. 3 • *The Home Shop Machinist.* Vol. 12, No. 5 (Sep/Oct, 1993) pp. 18-25.

"Gearless hit 'n miss engine, part two" by Philip Duclos. See Vol. 12, No. 3 • *The Home Shop Machinist.* Vol. 12, No. 4 (Jul/Aug, 1993) pp. 20-29.

"Six-cycle 'oddball' engine, part three" by Phillip Duclos. See Vol. 9, No. 2 • *The Home Shop Machinist.* Vol. 9, No. 5 (Sep/Oct, 1990) pp. 30-37.

"Six-cycle 'oddball' engine, part one" by Phillip Duclos. This article provides detailed instructions on constructing a miniature, six-cycle, air-cooled gas engine with a 3/4" bore. Photos and plans. • *The Home Shop Machinist.* Vol. 9, No. 2 (Mar/Apr, 1990) pp. 20-27.

"Six-cycle 'oddball engine', part three" by Phillip Douglas. See Vol. 9 No. 2 • *The*

Home Shop Machinist. Vol. 9, No. 4 (Jul/Aug, 1990) pp. 36-41.

"Six-cycle 'oddball' engine, part two" by Phillip Duclos. See Vol. 9, No. 2 • *The Home Shop Machinist.* Vol. 9, No. 3 (May/Jun, 1990) pp. 26-30.

"Smallest hit & miss gas engine" by Phillip Duclos. A brief overview of the construction plans for building a miniature gasoline engine with an overall length of four inches. Photos. • *The Home Shop Machinist.* Vol. 9, No. 1 (Jan/Feb, 1990) pp. 34-37.

"Topsy-turvy engine, part five" by Philip Duclos. See Vol. 10, No. 5 • *The Home Shop Machinist.* Vol. 11, No. 3 (May/Jun 1992) pp. 32-36.

"Topsy-turvy engine, part four" by Philip Duclos. See Vol. 10, No. 5 • *The Home Shop Machinist.* Vol. 11, No. 2 (Mar/Apr, 1992) pp. 29-35.

"Topsy-turvy engine, part one" by Philip Duclos. This series provides complete instructions on the building of an inverted, water-cooled, 4-cycle engine. Photos, plans and materials list. • *The Home Shop Machinist.* Vol. 10, No. 5 (Sep/Oct, 1991) pp. 20-27.

"Topsy-turvy engine, part three by Philip Duclos. See Vol. 10, No. 5 • *The Home Shop Machinist.* Vol. 11, No. 1 (Jan/Feb, 1992) pp. 24-28.

Engines, Miniature

"Tiny engines" by Rudy Kouhoupt. A description of two types of miniature engines neither of which is larger than two cubic inches. Photos. • *The Home Shop Machinist.* Vol. 11, No. 6 (Nov/Dec, 1992) pp. 46-49.

Entryways

"Re-entry." Three designs that remodel homes by renovating entryways. Photos. • *Practical Homeowner.* (May/June, 1992) pp. 80-82.

Environmental Hazards

Book Review: *The Complete Book of Home Environment Hazards* by Roberta Altman. Book review on clearly written guide to protect the home from hazards both inside and outside. New York: Facts on File Inc., 290 pp. • *Home Mechanix.* No. 758 (Sep, 1991) p. 23.

Environmental Safety

"An environmental showcase" by Kevin Ireton. Introduces a home built with environmentally safe products from finishes to furnishings. Photos. Sidebar on aquaculture and hydroponics. Sidebar on environmentally responsible building. • *Fine Homebuilding.* No. 73 (Spring, 1992) pp. 66-70.

Epoxies

"Construction epoxies" by Ross Herbertson. In-depth article on what epoxies do, how they work, and how to use them. Photos. Sidebar on syrup, catsup, mayonnaise and peanut butter. • *Fine Homebuilding.* No. 70 (Nov, 1991) pp. 45-49.

"Epoxy: nearly as tough as nails and beautiful, too." Brief article on using epoxy for a finish on wooden bowls. Photos. • *Better Homes and Gardens Wood.* No. 63 (Sep, 1993) pp. 62-63.

"The one glue to have" by Joseph Provey. An explanation of the many uses of epoxy. • *Practical Homeowner.* Vol. VI, No. 1 (Jan, 1991) p. 10.

"Slow-set epoxy." Offers tips on selecting a epoxy that is moisture-proof, weather resistant, and high-strength. Illustration. • *Better Homes and Gardens Wood.* No. 46 (Oct, 1991) p. 71.

Estimates

Book Review: *1991 National Construction Estimator* by Martin D. Kiley and William M. Moselle. Book review on the latest edition of estimates of labor and material costs, including a computer disk with the same information. Carlsbad, CA: Craftsman Book Company, 1990, 573 pp. • *Fine Homebuilding.* No. 67 (May, 1991) p. 104.

Software Review: *Carpenter's Dream* by Dan Heilman. Software review on a materials estimating program. Golden, CO: Workhorses, Inc. • *Fine Homebuilding.* No. 62 (Sep, 1990) p. 112.

Eucalyptus (Wood)

"The eucalyptus affair" by Dennis B. Farrel. Describes how to work with this wood, and its special features. Photos. • *Woodwork.* No. 18 (Nov/Dec, 1992) pp. 61-63.

"Turning Australian wood: The Eucalyptus Slab Bowl" by Jeff Parsons. Provides detailed description of the steps associated with the turning of eucalyptus wood to form a bowl. Photos. • *Canadian Workshop.* Vol. 13, No. 5 (Feb 1990) pp. 8-9.

Exercisers, Aerobic

"Aerobic step." An easy-to-make project for an aerobic exercising step. Photo, plans, and materials list. • *The Woodworker's Journal.* Vol. 17, No. 4 (Jul/Aug, 1993) pp. 48-51.

Exhaust Fans

"Exhaust-fan drip" by Henry Spies. Brief tip on how to prevent dripping from an exhaust fan. Photos. • *Home Mechanix.* No. 760 (Nov, 1991) p. 94.

Extension Cords

"Winding extension cords" by Bob Syvanen. Brief tip offering a method of winding an extension cord. • *Fine Homebuilding.* No. 57 (Jan, 1990) p. 14.

F

Fanlights

Book Review: *Fanlights: A Visual Architectural History* by Alexander Stuart Gray and John Sambrook. Book review highlighting the historical development of fanlights. New York: American Institute of Architects Press, 160 pp. • *Fine Homebuilding*. No. 64 (Jan, 1991) p. 110.

Fans, Ceiling

"Ceiling-fan basics" by Henry Spies. Explains the advantage of using a ceiling fan for heating and cooling. • *Home Mechanix*. No. 766 (June, 1992) p. 78.

Farm Houses

"A contemporary farmhouse" by Charles Miller. Highlights a design featuring complex shapes and unusual materials in a country house in the Sierra Nevada foothills. Photos, plans, drawings. • *Fine Homebuilding*. No. 83 (Sep, 1993) pp. 82-87.

Fasteners

"Knockdown hardware." An exposition of the different types and uses of metal fittings. Photos. Drawings. • *The Woodworker's Journal*. Vol. 14, No. 4 (Jul/Aug, 1990) pp. 25-28.

"Removing reluctant fasteners" by Don Stevenson. Brief tip on removing fasteners from recycled wood. Drawing. • *Fine Homebuilding*. No. 81 (May, 1993) p. 26.

Fasteners, Mechanical

"Mechanical fasteners" by Edward G. Hoffman. An explanation of the types and uses of mechanical fasteners including screws and washers. Photos and plans. • *The Home Shop Machinist*. Vol. 11, No. 2 (Mar/Apr, 1992) pp. 50-52.

"Mechanical fasteners, part two" by Edward G. Hoffman. See Vol. 11, No. 2 • *The Home Shop Machinist*. Vol. 11, No. 3 (May/Jun, 1992) pp. 53-54.

Faucets

"Faucet facelift" by Sally Ross. Presents a step-by-step procedure on changing faucet hardware and replacing it with a new one. Photos. • *Home Mechanix*. No. 746 (June, 1990) pp. 54-59.

Faucets, Outdoor

"Freezeproof outdoor faucets" by Merle Henkenius. Describes how to install freezeproof outdoor faucets. Photos. • *Home Mechanix*. No. 750 (Nov, 1990) p. 16.

Fences

Book Review: *Fences & Retaining Walls* by William McElroy. Book review on a guide to designing and installing fences and retaining walls. Photo. Carlsbad, CA: Craftsman Books, 395 pp. • *Home Mechanix*. No. 757 (July/Aug, 1991) p. 18.

"Custom-made fences for your router-table" by Leon Segal. Diagrams of various fences for a router-table. Diagrams. • *Woodwork*. No. 19 (Jan/Feb, 1993) p. 73.

"Fabulous fences" by Joseph Truini. Describes and offers directions for five attractive fences. Photos, diagrams. • *Home Mechanix*. No. 744 (April, 1990) pp. 46-57.

"Fast fences" by Judith Trotsky. Discusses the variety of ready-to-install unique fences made of wood, aluminum, galvanized steel and PVC plastic. Photos, drawings, diagrams. • *Home Mechanix*. No. 763 (March, 1992) pp. 46-50.

"Fence tips" by Matthew Phair. Describes the procedure of building a picket fence. Photos, drawings. Sidebar on how to cut and assemble a picket fence. • *Home Mechanix*. No. 774 (April, 1993) pp. 74-76.

Fences, Miter

"Miter fence." Plans for building a miter fence and gauge for use with a table saw. Photos, plans, and materials list. • *The Woodworker's Journal*. Vol. 17, No. 6 (Nov/Dec, 1993) pp. 67 69.

Fiberglass

"Fractured fiberglass" by Henry Spies. Addresses a question about what could cause a fiberglass tub to crack. Photo. • *Home Mechanix*. No. 779 (Oct, 1993) pp. 91-92.

Fiddles

"Folk fiddle" by Allene and Harold Westover. This lengthy and detailed article provides instruction in the manner of constructing a fiddle, includes materials list. Photo and plans. • *The Woodworker's Journal*. Vol. 14, No. 2 (Mar/Apr, 1990) pp. 51-57.

File Cleaners

"A handy file cleaner" by Steve Acker. A simple tip for making a file cleaner out of spent cartridge casing. Photo. • *The Home Shop Machinist*. Vol. 12, No. 2 (Mar/Apr, 1993) pp. 42-43.

Files

"Files and how to use them." Advice on the construction and use of hand files. • The Woodworker's Journal. Vol. 14, No. 5 (Sep/Oct, 1990) pp. 16-17.

"A handy file cleaner" by Steve Acker. A simple tip for making a file cleaner out of spent cartridge casing. Photo. • *The Home Shop Machinist*. Vol. 12, No. 2 (Mar/Apr, 1993) pp. 42-43.

"Rasps." A brief overview of the various types and uses of rasp files. • *The Woodworker's Journal*. Vol. 14, No. 4 (Jul/Aug, 1990) pp. 15-17.

Finishes

"5 easy steps to a finish that's glass-smooth" by Bill Krier and James R. Downing. Learn about a polyurethane-finish technique that produces a glass-smooth result. Photos. • *Better Homes and Gardens Wood*. No. 35 (June, 1990) pp. 50-51.

"Decorative painted finishes" by Victor DeMasi. Provides an introduction to glazing, woodgraining, marbleizing and other finish techniques. Photos. Sidebar on marbleizing a mantel. • *Fine Homebuilding*. No. 60 (May, 1990) pp. 78-82.

"Epoxy: nearly as tough as nails and beautiful, too." Brief article on using epoxy for a finish on wooden bowls. Photos. • *Better Homes and Gardens Wood*. No. 63 (Sep, 1993) pp. 62-63.

"Finishing wood problems" by Jim Barrett. An analysis of the types of problems associated with wood finishes especially oiliness and bleeding. • *The Woodworker's Journal*. Vol. 14, No. 6 (Nov/Dec, 1990) pp. 26-30.

"How to choose a finish" by Bob Flexner. Detailed article and chart explaining positive qualities of various finishes. Photos. • *Woodwork*. No. 14 (March/April) pp. 70-75.

"Tabletop finishes" by Jim Barrett. This piece describes and analyses the four types of finishes used for heavy wear surfaces—oil-based, polyurethane, water-based, and epoxy. Source list. • *The Woodworker's Journal*. Vol. 15, No. 2 (Mar/Apr, 1991) pp. 30-33.

Finishes, Clear

"The naturals" by Timothy O. Bakke. Provides information on clear finishes for cedar and redwood siding. Photos, chart. • *Home Mechanix*. No. 773 (March, 1993) pp. 60-62.

Finishes, Country Look

"Country finishes" by Bill Krier, Dick Fitch, Jim Boelling. Clear instructions for creating authentic-looking country finishes. Sidebar on paint: the finish of choice for eighteenth century Americans. Photos. • *Better Homes and Gardens Wood*. No. 36 (Aug, 1990) pp. 46 50.

Finishes, Deck

"High performance finishes" by Timothy O. Bakke. In-depth evaluation of new-formula deck protectors. Photo, chart.

Sidebar on cleaning your deck. • *Home Mechanix*. No. 757 (July/Aug, 1991) pp. 60-63, 84.

Finishes, Faux

"Faux antique crackled finish." This article describes the process of using wood finish to create the appearance of age and distress. Photos. • *The Woodworker's Journal*. Vol. 17, No. 5 (Sep/Oct, 1993) pp. 25-26.

"Painted stone finishes" by Bill Krier. Step-by-step directions to paint particleboard so it appears to be granite or marble. Photos. • *Better Homes and Gardens Wood*. No. 42 (April, 1991) pp. 76-78.

Finishes, Fir

"Finishes for fir floors" by Don Bollinger. Offers information on selecting a finish for a fir floor. • *Fine Homebuilding*. No. 65 (March, 1991) pp. 16-18.

Finishes, Floor

"Performance testing of floor finishes" by Michael W. Purser. Presents a floor finisher's approach to testing finishes and discusses his results. Photos. Sidebar on VOC compliance. Sidebar on coping with abrasion. • *Fine Homebuilding*. No. 67 (May, 1991) pp. 52-55.

Finishes, Gel

"Working with gel stains" by Jim Barrett. This analysis outlines the pro's and con's of using a gelled wood stain product. Photos. • *The Woodworker's Journal*. Vol. 15, No. 4 (Jul/Aug, 1991) pp. 53-57.

Finishes, Maple

"Finishes for maple" by Jim Barrett. An analysis of the different types of finishes that work well on maple, including mineral oil, nut oils, gel stains, and dyes. Photos. • *The Woodworker's Journal*. Vol. 16, No. 4 (Jul/Aug, 1992) pp. 22-25.

Finishes, Oak

"Three easy finishes for oak." A brief but thorough description of the properties of three different types of finishes used on oak furniture—natural, antique, and faux pickled. • *The Woodworker's Journal*. Vol. 15, No. 1 (Jan/Feb, 1991) pp. 20-22.

Finishes, Outdoor

"Finishing outdoor projects" by Jim Barrett. This article details the variety of protective finishes available for use with outdoor wood projects. • *The Woodworker's Journal*. Vol. 14, No. 2 (Mar/Apr, 1990) pp. 25-29.

Finishes, Water-Based

"Water-based finishes" by Jim Barrett. An analysis of the types and uses of water-based finishes. • The Woodworker's Journal. Vol. 14, No. 5 (Sep/Oct, 1990) pp. 24-26.

"The wave of the future water-based finishes" by Bill Krier, Wade Sundeen, Jim Downing, and Jim Boelling. In-depth report on how water-based finishes work. Photos. Sidebars on covering a large surface and points to keep in mind when spraying. • *Better Homes and Gardens Wood*. No. 42 (April, 1991) pp. 42-47.

Finishes, Wood

"Tips for mess-free finishing" by Jim Barrett. This brief article provides helpful suggestions for improving wood finishing techniques. Photos and drawings. • *The Woodworker's Journal*. Vol. 15, No. 3 (May/Jun, 1991) pp. 21-23.

Finishes--Nontoxic

"Food-safe finishes." Informative article on nontoxic finishes for salad bowls and other food containers. Illustration. • *Better Homes and Gardens Wood*. No. 64 (Oct, 1993) p. 74.

Finishes--Removal of

"Finish removers" by Bill Krier. Informative article describing the effectiveness of 59 finish removers. Photos, chart on the six types of finish removers, comparison chart. • *Better Homes and*

Gardens Wood. No. 53 (Aug, 1992) pp. 54-59.

Finishes--Safety Risks

"Safety: workshop finishes pose risk" by Jim Barrett. An analysis of the dangers associated with wood finishes and the proper methods for their use. • *The Woodworker's Journal.* Vol. 14, No. 4 (Jul/Aug, 1990) pp. 18-21.

Fireplace Dampers

"Retrofit damper" by Henry Spies. Explains the type of damper to install in a masonry fireplace. Drawing. • *Home Mechanix.* No. 767 (July/Aug, 1992) p. 82.

Fireplace Inglenooks

"Baronial inglenook" by Scott Wynn. Presents a remodeled inglenook with laminated mahogany arches and detailed carvings. Photos, diagrams, drawings. Sidebar on pilasters and fretwork. • *Fine Homebuilding.* No. 69 (Sep, 1991) pp. 82-87.

Fireplaces

"Add-on fireplace" by Henry Spies. Brief instructions on adding a prefab, zero-clearance fireplace to a brick house. Drawings. • *Home Mechanix.* No. 751 (Dec/Jan, 1990-91) p. 80.

"Beyond the basic barbecue" by Pat McMillan. Highlights three designs for outdoor barbecue fireplaces. Photos, drawings. • *Home Mechanix.* No. 757 (July/Aug, 1991) pp. 68-71.

"Fireplace and chimney codes" by John Lloyd. Presents a fireplace that meets the code and keeps the fire in the right spot. Photos, diagrams. • *Fine Homebuilding.* No. 69 (Sep, 1991) pp. 76-78.

"Fireplace facelift" by Joseph Truini. Describes the process of renovating an old fireplace with a new mantle, marble hearth and woodstove insert. Photos, diagram, drawings. Sidebar on taking critical dimensions. • *Home Mechanix.* No. 768 (Sep, 1992) pp. 48-52.

"Fireplace facing" by Henry Spies. Brief tip on how to install birch boards correctly to reface a fireplace. Drawing. • *Home Mechanix.* No. 754 (April, 1991) p. 92.

"Fireplace odor" by Henry Spies. Brief article addressing the problem of smoke odors lingering for weeks after using the fireplace. • *Home Mechanix.* No. 752 (Feb, 1991) p. 82.

"Floor framing for fireplaces" by Scott McBride. Offers instructions on building two fireplaces with two flues in one chimney. Drawing. • *Fine Homebuilding.* No. 82 (July, 1993) pp. 16-20.

"Hearth and mantel masterpiece" by John Decker. Offer directions to build and install a hearth and mantel. Photos, diagram. • *Home Mechanix.* No. 750 (Nov, 1990) pp. 37-40.

"Hearths of stone" by Matt Phair. Presents four masonry fireplace designs and instructions for building them. Photo, drawings. • *Home Mechanix.* No. 768 (Sep, 1992) pp. 55-59.

"Spreading on the charm" by Jane Cornell. Introduces new stucco-like materials for fireplace surrounds. Photos, diagram. • *Home Mechanix.* No. 760 (Nov, 1991) pp. 56-59.

Fireproofing

"Fire-treating cedar shakes" by Michael M. Westfall. Offers a suggestion on putting fire retardant on cedar shakes. • *Fine Homebuilding.* No. 77 (Nov, 1992) p. 16.

Fittings

"Knockdown hardware." An exposition of the different types and uses of metal fittings. Photos. Drawings. • *The Woodworker's Journal.* Vol. 14, No. 4 (Jul/Aug, 1990) pp. 25-28.

Fixtures

"Basics of locating, part five" by Edward G. Hoffman. See Vol. 9, No. 2 • *The Home Shop Machinist.* Vol. 9, No. 3 (May/Jun, 1990) pp. 57-59.

"Basics of locating, part four" by Edward G. Hoffman. An explanation of the use of jigs and fixtures to properly load and locate parts. Plans. • *The Home Shop Machinist.* Vol. 9, No. 2 (Mar/Apr, 1990) pp. 52-53.

"Jigs and fixtures, part three" by Edward Hoffman. An analysis of the importance of using proper jigs and fixtures to accurately locate and hold work. Plans. • *The Home Shop Machinist.* Vol. 9, No. 1 (Jan/Feb, 1990) pp. 54-55.

"Tool bodies, part one" by Edward G. Hoffman. A descriptive look at the types and manufactures of jigs and fixtures. Drawings. • *The Home Shop Machinist.* Vol. 12, No. 2 (Mar/Apr, 1993) pp. 48-49.

"Tool bodies, part two" by Edward G. Hoffman. See Vol. 12, No. 2 • *The Home Shop Machinist.* Vol. 12, No. 3 (May/Jun, 1993) pp. 46-47.

Flame Cutters

"Flame cutter" by Thomas Verity. Complete sketches and description for constructing a flame cutter for cutting steel parts. Photos and plans. • *The Home Shop Machinist.* Vol. 9, No. 5 (Sep/Oct, 1990) pp. 50-54.

Flashing

"Flashing a wall" by Stephen D. Dahlin. Offers a tip on flashing a wall on an enclosed porch. Drawings. • *Fine Homebuilding.* No. 58 (March, 1990) p. 14.

"Hot flashing" by Henry Spies. Helpful tip on preventing leaking with installed flashing. Drawings. • *Home Mechanix.* No. 776 (June, 1993) p. 84.

Flasks, Perfume

"Jewel of a vial" by Deborah Doyle. Create an elegant looking perfume flask with these instructions. Photos, drawings. • *Better Homes and Gardens Wood.* No. 61 (June, 1993) pp. 28-29.

Floodlights

"The ABCs of PIR sensors" by Roger Dooley. Explains the features of passive-infrared sensors for indoor and outdoor lighting systems. Drawing. • *Home Mechanix.* No. 745 (May, 1990) pp. 24-27.

Floor Plans — *See* Designs and Plans

Floor Vent Covers

"A wood floor-vent cover" by David Donnelly. Describes how to quickly construct a simple wooden floor cover. Photos. • *Woodwork.* No. 18 (Nov/Dec, 1992) pp. 54-55.

Floors

"Cold-floor cure" by Henry Spies. Brief tip on keeping a floor above a crawl space warmer. Drawings. • *Home Mechanix.* No. 771 (Dec/Jan, 1992-93) p. 81.

"Create your own custom floor" by Mary Golden. New trends in vinyl floor design. Photos and plans. • *Practical Homeowner.* Vol. VI, No. 2 (Feb, 1991) pp. 60-65.

"Dampening a bouncy floor" by William A. Burdick. Offers a tip for a bouncy floor problem. • *Fine Homebuilding.* No. 73 (Spring, 1992) p. 14.

"Decorative floor inlays" by Don Bollinger. Gives tips on selecting decorative materials and how to install the inlay. Photos. • *Fine Homebuilding.* No. 63 (Nov, 1990) pp. 78-80.

"Upgrade a floor" by Michael Chotiner. Presents a method of upgrading floors with prefinished wood flooring. Photos, drawings. • *Home Mechanix.* No. 742 (Feb, 1990) pp. 38-40, 89.

Floors, Hardwood

"3 fast floors" by Pat McMillan. Highlights three hardwood flooring systems and how to install them. Photos, drawings. Sidebar on how to make a slip-notch. • *Home Mechanix.* No. 777 (July/Aug, 1993) pp. 66-69.

"Wood over slab" by Henry Spies. Offers a tip on installing wood flooring over a concrete slab. • *Home Mechanix.* No. 755 (May, 1991) p. 96.

Floors, Radiant Heat

"Electric radiant floors" by Bruce C. Kaercher, Jr. Presents the advantages of radiant heat floors. Photos, cost comparison chart. Sidebar on the advantages of radiant heat. • *Fine Homebuilding.* No. 75 (July, 1992) pp. 68-72.

Floors, Stone

"Installing a hammer-cut stone floor" by Paul Holloway. Shows how to produce a quartzite floor using hammers and chisels. Photos, drawings. • *Fine Homebuilding.* No. 68 (July, 1991) pp. 47-49.

Floors, Terrazzo

"Floor guard" by Matt Jackson. Brief tip on protecting a terrazzo floor during remodeling. Drawing. • *Fine Homebuilding.* No. 64 (Jan, 1991) p. 30.

Floors, Vinyl

"Floor fashions" by Mary Golden. New ideas for vinyl floor patterns. Photos. • *Practical Homeowner.* Vol. V, No. 3 (April, 1990) pp. 30-32.

"Repairs for sheet-vinyl flooring" by Michael Morris. Brief article on making a patch for vinyl flooring that has been scratched or marred. Photos. • *Home Mechanix.* No. 749 (Oct, 1990) p. 36.

"Resilient flooring" by Olivia Bell Buehl. In-depth description of the advantages of vinyl flooring. Photos. Sidebar on asbestos alert. Sidebar on vintage linoleum. • *Home Mechanix.* No. 770 (Nov, 1992) pp. 64-67.

"Vinyl's revived" by Mary Golden. A look at new trends in vinyl flooring. Photos. • *Practical Homeowner.* Vol. VI, No. 2 (Feb, 1991) pp. 54-58.

"Waxy buildup" by Henry Spies. Brief tip on removing a waxy finish from a vinyl floor. • *Home Mechanix.* No. 765 (May, 1992) pp. 80-81.

Floors--Noise Control

"Noisy floor" by Henry Spies. Presents a way to stiffen trusses and reduce noise from squeaking floors. • *Home Mechanix.* No. 761 (Dec/Jan, 1991-92) p. 73.

"Squeaking parquet floors" by Henry Spies. Offers several methods to stop squeaking in a wood-parquet floor. • *Home Mechanix.* No. 751 (Dec/Jan, 1990-91) p. 81.

Floors--Painting

"Fantasy floors" by Sherry Spear. Describes the process of painting and varnishing floors to create a faux granite or marble appearance. Photos, drawings. • *Home Mechanix.* No. 762 (Feb, 1992) pp. 58-62, 78.

Floors--Patching

"Patching a hardwood strip floor" by Ted Garner. Brief instruction on how to make a convincing patch in a hardwood strip floor. Drawing. • *Fine Homebuilding.* No. 64 (Jan, 1991) pp. 30-32.

Floors--Remodeling

"This old floor" by Joseph Truini. Brief article on remodeling old floors safely. • *Home Mechanix.* No. 773 (March, 1993) p. 22.

Flues

"Strap-clamp for flues" by David Strawderman. Offers a helpful tip for assembling and disassembling interlocking metal flue sections. Drawing. • *Fine Homebuilding.* No. 74 (May, 1992) pp. 24-26.

Fluorescent Bulbs

"Fluorescent fixes" by Hank Spies. Offers a solution for fluorescent fixtures that fail to light on days when the weather is damp. Drawing. • *Home Mechanix.* No. 748 (Sep, 1990) p. 89.

Footpaths

"Private paths" by Joseph Truini. Presents seven paving projects for a lawn or garden. Photos, drawings. Sidebar on cutting stone and brick. • *Home Mechanix*. No. 763 (March, 1992) pp. 38-41.

Foundations

Book Review: *Builder's Foundation Handbook* by John Carmody, Jeffrey Christian, and Kenneth Labs. Review of book on the three most common foundation systems. Springfield, VA: National Technical Information Service, 112 pp. • *Fine Homebuilding*. No. 74 (May, 1992) p. 98.

"Deep foundations" by Alvin M. Sacks. Presents a method of building on soft ground using driven piles and grade beams. Photos, drawings. Sidebar on brickbats and freefalls. • *Fine Homebuilding*. No. 69 (Sep, 1991) pp. 58-61.

"Fast foundations" by Chuck Silver. A guide to using panelized concrete sections in building a foundation wall. Photos. • *Practical Homeowner*. Vol. VI, No. 7 (Sep, 1991) pp. 90-92.

"Foundation drain" by Hank Spies. Brief tip on building a foundation with adequate drainage to prevent rotting. Drawing. • *Home Mechanix*. No. 741 (Jan, 1990) p. 84.

"Foundation forms that insulate" by Mark Feirer. Informative article on insulating panels that double as formwork. Photos, drawing. Sidebar on XEPS and your health. • *Fine Homebuilding*. No. 76 (Sep, 1992) pp. 36-41.

"Foundation jacking" by John Gaynor. New techniques for jacking up foundation walls. Photos and drawings. • *Practical Homeowner*. Vol. V, No. 4 (June, 1990) p. 24.

"Foundation materials" by Henry Spies. Discusses the benefits of using poured concrete or concrete blocks for foundations. Drawing. • *Home Mechanix*. No. 775 (May, 1993) pp. 98-99.

"Foundation-wall reinforcement" by Donald L. Anderson. Brief tip on restoring a wall without dismantling it. Drawing. • *Fine Homebuilding*. No. 61 (July, 1990) p. 24.

"Framing a crawl-space foundation" by Larry Haun. Provides tips on setting sills, posts, and girders. Photos, drawings, chart. • *Fine Homebuilding*. No. 77 (Nov, 1992) pp. 80-85.

"Permanent wood foundations" by Bill Eich. Details the steps to build a permanent wood foundation. Photos, drawings. • *Fine Homebuilding*. No. 68 (July, 1991) pp. 62-66.

"Shoring settled foundations" by Matt Phair. Highlights a new anchoring system to stop settling and correct problems related to settling. Drawings. • *Home Mechanix*. No. 757 (July/Aug, 1991) pp. 17-19.

"A slab-on-grade foundation for cold climates" by George Nash. Describes the advantages of the slab-on-grade foundation. Photos, drawing. • *Fine Homebuilding*. No. 60 (May, 1990) pp. 52-55.

"Stabilizing a cracked slab" by Alvin Sacks. Offers information on how to repair a cracked slab foundation and cracked bathroom tiles. • *Fine Homebuilding*. No. 68 (July, 1991) pp. 14-16.

"Waterproofing a stone foundation" by Stephen Kennedy. Brief instructions on sealing a stone foundation to stop water seepage. Drawing. • *Fine Homebuilding*. No. 69 (Sep, 1991) pp. 14 16.

Foundations, Deck

"Deck foundations that last" by Scott Schuttner. Highlights a deck foundation design with footings and piers to match the load and bearing capacity of the soil. Photos, drawings. Sidebar on calculating the footings and concrete for a sample deck. • *Fine Homebuilding*. No. 79 (March, 1993) pp. 64-69.

Foundations, Wood

"The right foundation" by Merle Henkinius. A study of the advantages of using permanent wood foundations (PWF) over concrete. Photos. • *Practical Homeowner*. Vol. V, No. 4 (June, 1990) pp. 75-77.

Foundations--Insulating

"Cutting costs of cold floors" by Hank Spies. Provides a tip for insulating a concrete garage foundation. Drawing. • *Home Mechanix*. No. 742 (Feb, 1990) p. 70.

Foundations--Repairs

"Battling a bulge in a foundation wall" by Dick Kreh. Explains a solution to a crack in a foundation wall. Drawing. • *Fine Homebuilding*. No. 81 (May, 1993) p. 16.

Frame Clamps

"Frame-clamping jig" by Gary Walchuk. Describes how to construct a wood frame-clamp jig. Drawn plans. • *Canadian Workshop*. Vol. 13, No. 5 (Feb 1990) p. 12.

Frames, Picture

"Four easy picture frames." This article gives step-by-step illustrations of how to make the following types of frames: rustic, built-up, burnt veneered, and cove & bead. Photos and plans. • *The Woodworker's Journal*. Vol. 15, No. 4 (Jul/Aug, 1991) pp. 36-39.

"Framing with purpleheart" by Dennis Darrah. Describes a framing structure built with the dense tropical hardwood, purpleheart. Photos, drawings. • *Fine Homebuilding*. No. 57 (Jan, 1990) pp. 68-70.

"Hearts-and-hares picture frame" by Harlequin Crafts. Explains how to cut hearts and rabbits in a picture frame with a stand. Photo, diagrams, full-sized

pattern. • *Better Homes and Gardens Wood*. No. 45 (Sep, 1991) pp. 80-81.

"High-flying photo frame." Brief article on creating a dove-patterned scrollsawed frame. Photo, drawings, diagram. • *Better Homes and Gardens Wood*. No. 52 (June, 1992) pp. 70-71.

"Low-tech picture frames" by Roger Holmes. This in-depth article focuses on the tools needed to construct simple wood frames. Photos and plans. • *The Woodworker's Journal*. Vol. 15, No. 4 (Jul/Aug, 1991) pp. 18-23.

"Olympian display." Match the frame of a favorite picture with this temple-shaped frame. Photo, diagrams. • *Better Homes and Gardens Wood*. No. 61 (June, 1993) pp. 64-65.

"A picture-book project" by David Ashe. Instructions to make a photo frame resembling a leather-bound book. Photo, diagrams, materials list. • *Better Homes and Gardens Wood*. No. 59 (Feb, 1993) pp. 66-67.

"Quick clamping jig makes fuss-free frame corners" by Joe B. Godfrey. Brief tip on assembling a frame with a C-clamp. Drawing. • *Better Homes and Gardens Wood*. No. 53 (Aug, 1992) p. 22.

Frames, Rectangular

"Breaking the rules" by Dick Dorn. Reverse the direction of the router travel in order to avoid splintering and tearout. Drawing. • *Woodwork*. No. 19 (Jan/Feb, 1993) pp. 24.

Frames, Window

"Shop-built window frames" by Joseph Beals III. Describes how to build your own window frames with simple joinery. Photos, drawings. • *Fine Homebuilding*. No. 84 (Nov, 1993) pp. 76 79.

Framing

"Economical framing" by E. Lee Fisher. Describes a cost-effective method of framing. Photos, charts, drawings. • *Fine*

Homebuilding. No. 84 (Nov, 1993) pp. 46-49.

"Room to mingle" by Michael Corlis. Offers accents to a living space such as laminated post and-beam walls, custom roof trusses, and headerless clerestories. Photos, diagrams, plans. • *Fine Homebuilding.* No. 75 (July, 1992) pp. 80-85.

Framing (Houses)

"Basic frame work" by Dean Johnson. A brief tip on the steps to take in framing a house. Photos and drawings. • *Practical Homeowner.* Vol. IV, No. 9 (Jan, 1990) pp. 16-18.

"Livable sculpture" by Ashley Smith. Describes hybrid framing techniques for California floodplains. Photos, drawing, plans. • *Fine Homebuilding.* No. 57 (Jan, 1990) pp. 52-57.

"Skin-tight homes." A guide to the options in timber-framed homes. Photos. • *Practical Homeowner.* Vol. V, No. 2 (Mar, 1990) pp. 60-68.

Framing (Roofs)

Book Review: *Roof Framing* by Marshall Gross. Book review offering solid instruction on roof framing. Carlsbad, CA: Craftsman Book Company, 475 pp. • *Fine Homebuilding.* No. 60 (May, 1990) p. 106.

"Falling eaves" by Scott McBride. Describes five methods of framing a difficult roof. Photos, diagrams. • *Fine Homebuilding.* No. 74 (May, 1992) pp. 82-85.

"Simplified valley framing" by Larry Haun. Provides instructions for constructing a blind valley roof. Photos, drawings. • *Fine Homebuilding.* No. 79 (March, 1993) pp. 58-61.

"Valley framing for unequally pitched roofs" by George Nash. Describes a method of framing unequally pitched roofs without using extensive mathematical calculations. Drawings.

Sidebar on making cheek cuts. • *Fine Homebuilding.* No. 68 (July, 1991) pp. 74-78.

Freezers

"The deep freeze" by Steve Brannan. Provides basic solutions to more common home freezer problems. • *Canadian Workshop.* Vol. 13, No. 5 (Feb 1990) p. 10.

French Doors

"French-door retrofit" by David Strawderman. Follows the procedure of opening a wall to create a French door. Photos, drawings. • *Fine Homebuilding.* No. 68 (July, 1991) pp. 42-46.

Fumes

"Name that fume" by Dave Menicucci. Offers a solution to a problem with fumes in a new house. • *Fine Homebuilding.* No. 78 (Jan, 1993) pp. 16-20.

Furniture

"All-star media center" by Marlen Kemmet and Gregory A. Henderson. Construct a beautiful walnut cabinet to hold a T.V., VCR, stereo, tapes, and CDs. Photos, diagrams, materials list. • *Better Homes and Gardens Wood.* No. 46 (Oct, 1991) pp. 50-55.

Book Review: *Creative Designs in Furniture.* Book review on a color picture book featuring 125 furnituremakers. Madison, WI: Kraus Sikes Inc., 160 pp. • *Woodwork.* No. 17 (Sep/Oct, 1992) p. 26.

"Cabriole legs" by Bill Krier and Jim Boelling. Clear, well-written article tracing the steps to fashion a cabriole leg. Photos, diagrams, patterns. • *Better Homes and Gardens Wood.* No. 49 (Jan, 1992) pp. 36-41.

"Casual classics —mahogany outdoor furniture that will last and last" by Marlen Kemmet. Detailed instructions to build solid, mahogany outdoor furniture, specifically chairs in this issue. Photos, diagrams. • *Better Homes and Gardens Wood.* No. 42 (April, 1991) pp. 56-61.

"Shaker-style buffet" by Marlen Kemmet and James R. Downing. Describes the process of constructing a plywood framed in solid cherry buffet cabinet. Photos, diagrams, materials list. • *Better Homes and Gardens Wood.* No. 45 (Sep, 1991) pp. 42-47.

"Southwest tables" by James R. Downing and Marlen Kemmet. Directions to build a sofa, end, and coffee table in a Southwest design. Photo, diagrams, materials list, patterns. • *Better Homes and Gardens Wood.* No. 44 (August, 1991) pp. 36-41.

"Tehal Virk's wonderful willow works" by Peter J. Stephano. Follow Tehal Virk's description of creating furniture with willow sticks. Photos. • *Better Homes and Gardens Wood.* No. 61 (June, 1993) pp. 23-27.

"Warm up to Southwest." Some of the decorative designs from Santa Fe and Taos that are influencing the furniture market. Photos. • *Better Homes and Gardens Wood.* No. 37 (Sep, 1990) pp. 40-41.

"A William and Mary sideboard?" by Steven M. Lash. Presents an intriguing account of building a seventeenth-century William and Mary sideboard without having a model to reproduce. Drawings. Photos. Dimension specifications. • *Woodwork.* No. 14 (March/April) pp. 42-47.

See Also specific types of furniture, e.g., Chairs, Cabinets

Furniture, Bedroom

"Class room" by Joseph Truini. Detailed instructions to build furniture that has the flexibility to expand in size as the child grows and needs larger pieces. Photos, diagrams, drawings. Sidebar on platform paneling. • *Home Mechanix.* No. 746 (June, 1990) pp. 32-41.

Furniture, Children's

"Child's stepped back cupboard." A very comprehensive plan for building a miniature slant-top cupboard sized for a small child. • *The Woodworker's Journal.* Vol. 14, No. 3 (May/Jun, 1990) pp. 51-53.

"Kids' Adirondack chair & settee." Plans for a child-sized Adirondack-style garden chair and settee. Photo, plans, and materials list. • *The Woodworker's Journal.* Vol. 17, No. 2 (Mar/Apr, 1993) pp. 58-61.

"Kids' modular furniture set." A brief description for building a modular chair and table for little children. Photos, plans, and materials list. • *The Woodworker's Journal.* Vol. 17, No. 6 (Nov/Dec, 1993) pp. 70-72.

"Little folks desk and bench." Clear plans on how to make a child's size desk and bench. Photos, plans, and materials. • *The Woodworker's Journal.* Vol. 15, No. 6 (Nov/Dec, 1991) pp. 46-47.

Furniture, Outdoor

"English garden set." Description of the steps in constructing an English-style garden table, garden chair, and planter box. • *The Woodworker's Journal.* Vol. 14, No. 3 (May/Jun, 1990) pp. 36-45.

"Fun-in-the-sun furniture" by James R. Downing and Marlen Kemmet. Instructions to build a handsome table and chair for your deck. Photos, diagrams, materials list. Sidebar on how to build a table to match the chair. • *Better Homes and Gardens Wood.* No. 61 (June, 1993) pp. 48-53.

"Lawn glider." How to build a large, double-sided lawn glider. Plans, photos, and materials list. • *The Woodworker's Journal.* Vol. 16, No. 4 (Jul/Aug, 1992) pp. 30-35.

Furniture, Rustic

Book Review: *Making Rustic Furniture* by Daniel Mack. Book review on building rustic furniture. Asheville, NC: Altamont Press, 160 pp. • *Woodwork.* No. 17 (Sep/Oct, 1992) p. 29.

Furniture--Compartments in

"Secret compartments" by Tim Faner. A description of how to install secret compartments inside of clocks, desks, cabinets, and stools. Photos and plans. • *The Woodworker's Journal.* Vol. 15, No. 5 (Sep/Oct, 1991) pp. 29-34.

Furniture--Refinishing

Video Review: *Refinishing Furniture* with Bob Flexner by Bob Flexner. Video review on a guide to stripping, surface preparation, bleaching, staining, finishing, and sealing. Photo. Newton, CT: Taunton. • *Home Mechanix.* No. 751 (Dec/Jan, 1990-91) p. 17.

Furniture--Repairing

Video Review: *Repairing Furniture* with Bob Flexner by Bob Flexner. Videotape review focusing on assembly and disassembly, glue choice, clamping jigs and joint repair. Photo. Newton, CT: Taunton Press. • *Home Mechanix.* No. 751 (Dec/Jan, 1990-91) p. 17.

Furniture--Storage

"Fun furniture" by Matt Phair. Introduces a set of storage modules for a child's room that can double as imaginative play props. Photos, drawing. • *Home Mechanix.* No. 746 (June, 1990) pp. 60-61.

Futons

"The fabulous futon." Clear and direct plans for making a convertible couch/bed-type futon. Photos, plans, and materials list. • *The Woodworker's Journal.* Vol. 16, No. 6 (Nov/Dec, 1992) pp. 44-46.

G

Gages, Centering

"A new centering gage" by Frank A. McLean. A brief article on constructing a brass centering gage. Plans. • *The Home*

Shop Machinist. Vol. 10, No. 2 (Mar/Apr, 1991) pp. 50-51.

Games

"Home court advantage" by Carolyn Chubet. Advice on using turf or plastic mesh to build backyard courts for badminton, squash, and croquet. Photos. • *Practical Homeowner.* Vol. VI, No. 6 (Jul/Aug, 1991) pp. 68-72.

"What a Racket!" by Phil Barley. Provides information on how to build a wooden racketeer game. Materials list. Photo. • *Canadian Workshop.* Vol. 15, No. 1 (Oct 1991) pp. 50-52.

See Also Toys

Garage Doors

"Framing for garage doors" by Steve Riley. Offers a guide to framing a garage door accurately and with structural integrity. Photos, drawings. Sidebar on framing with steel. • *Fine Homebuilding.* No. 74 (May, 1992) pp. 57-59.

"Garage-door update" by Bob Wessmiller. Introduces new vinyl and steel garage doors providing easy installation and less maintenance. Photos, drawings. Sidebar on easy door installation. • *Home Mechanix.* No. 755 (May, 1991) pp. 83-85.

Garages

"Adding a garage" by Samuel Greer and Gerald Kaye. Professional advice on adding a garage through a contractor, a prefab-garage builder, or building it yourself. Photos. • *Home Mechanix.* No. 743 (March, 1990) pp. 24-27.

"Converting a garage into living space" by Neil Hartzler. Presents the process of converting a garage into a library with a bay window. Photos, drawing, diagrams, plans. • *Fine Homebuilding.* No. 77 (Nov, 1992) pp. 76-79.

"Cutting costs of cold floors" by Hank Spies. Provides a tip for insulating a garage concrete foundation. Drawing. • *Home Mechanix.* No. 742 (Feb, 1990) p. 70.

"Garage conversions" by James Lomuscio. Ideas on converting your garage into a habitable room. Photos. • *Practical Homeowner.* Vol. VI, No. 9 (Nov/Dec, 1991) pp. 60-67.

"Keeping burglars out of the garage" by Vivian Valbuena. Detailed descriptions of ways to secure a garage from break-ins. Drawings. • *Home Mechanix.* No. 766 (June, 1992) pp. 17-19.

"Warm garage" by Hank Spies. Brief explanation of the possible causes of a warm garage. • *Home Mechanix.* No. 750 (Nov, 1990) p. 95.

Garden Ornaments and Furniture

"Casual classics—a distinctive and durable mahogany table" by Marlen Kemmet. Detailed instructions to build a 48" sturdy mahogany table for a deck or backyard. Photos, diagrams, materials list. • *Better Homes and Gardens Wood.* No. 43 (June, 1991) pp. 64-67.

"Casual classics —mahogany outdoor furniture that will last and last" by Marlen Kemmet. Detailed instructions to build solid, mahogany outdoor furniture, specifically chairs in this issue. Photos, diagrams. • *Better Homes and Gardens Wood.* No. 42 (April, 1991) pp. 56-61.

"English garden set." Description of the steps in constructing an English-style garden table, garden chair, and planter box. • *The Woodworker's Journal.* Vol. 14, No. 3 (May/Jun, 1990) pp. 36-45.

"Finishing outdoor projects" by Jim Barrett. This article details the variety of protective finishes available for use with outdoor wood projects. • *The Woodworker's Journal.* Vol. 14, No. 2 (Mar/Apr, 1990) pp. 25-29.

"Garden arbor." Tips on how to construct a simple arbor/garden bench. Photo, plans, and material list. • *The Woodworker's Journal.* Vol. 17, No. 2 (Mar/Apr, 1993) pp. 28-32.

"Home court advantage" by Carolyn Chubet. Advice on using turf or plastic mesh to build backyard courts for badminton, squash, and croquet. Photos. • *Practical Homeowner.* Vol. VI, No. 6 (Jul/Aug, 1991) pp. 68-72.

"Lawn glider." How to build a large, double-sided lawn glider. Plans, photos, and materials list. • *The Woodworker's Journal.* Vol. 16, No. 4 (Jul/Aug, 1992) pp. 30-35.

"Made for the shade" by Joseph Truini. Introduces four arbor designs for outdoor plants and vines. Photos, drawings, diagrams. • *Home Mechanix.* No. 763 (March, 1992) pp. 30-36.

"Refining rustics" by Joseph Truini and Judith Trotsky. Offers designs and construction plans for a rustic bench and gate made of logs and branches. Photos, diagrams. • *Home Mechanix.* No. 773 (March, 1993) pp. 44-47.

"Return of the trellis" by Jonathan Fast. New ideas in designing and building garden trellises. Photos. • *Practical Homeowner.* Vol. V, No. 5 (August, 1990) pp. 74-78.

"Tassajara makeover" by Gene DeSmidt. Focuses on rebuilding a wood bridge and an accompanying deck at Tassajara's hot springs. Photos, drawings. • *Fine Homebuilding.* No. 68 (July, 1991) pp. 70-73.

"Yardscaping" by Joseph Truini. Provides a glimpse at an example of creating a yardscape complete with a gazebo, sun deck, patio, lattice screens, and tiered planters. Photos, diagrams, drawings. • *Home Mechanix.* No. 775 (May, 1993) pp. 62-69.

Garden Tools

"The no waste yard" by Michael Ferrara. A description of all the tools and equipment needed to effectively recycle yard waste. Photos and plans. • *Practical Homeowner.* Vol. VI, No. 3 (March, 1991) pp. 66-81.

Gardening

"A front yard of food, flowers, and friends" by Susan Bryan. A plan for converting a front lawn into a garden. Photos.
• *Practical Homeowner.* (Jul/Aug, 1992) pp. 66-71.

"In praise of the well-raised bed" by Channing Dawson. An explanation of intensive gardening using raised beds. Photos. • *Practical Homeowner.* (Mar/Apr, 1992) pp. 77-79.

Gas — *See* Radon

Gas Logs

"Gas-log retrofit" by Hank Spies. Brief suggestion on trying to install a gas log in an air-tight fireplace insert. • *Home Mechanix.* No. 750 (Nov, 1990) p. 95.

Gauges

"A finely crafted cutting gauge" by Edwin P. Sheriff. Step-by-step instructions on making a gauge including a list of suppliers. Photos. • *Woodwork.* No. 16 (July/August, 1992) pp. 43-45.

"Set your fence accurately with this shop-made gauge" by Edward Rinaldo. Brief tip on making a jig to rip accurately on a table saw. Drawing. • *Better Homes and Gardens Wood.* No. 63 (Sep, 1993) p. 17.

Gauges, Giant-Contour

"Giant-contour gauge" by Dan Tishman and Andy Williamson. Provides instructions on gauging levels of a rocky ledge when pouring concrete. Drawing. • *Fine Homebuilding.* No. 65 (March, 1991) p. 32.

Gauges, Miter

"The accu-miter" by Dennis Preston. A brief tip on the uses of the accu-miter gauge. • *The Woodworker's Journal.* Vol. 15, No. 6 (Nov/Dec, 1991) p. 18.

"Brassy solution for a sloppy miter gauge" by Mel Morabito. Brief tip to improve the accuracy of a miter gauge. Drawing.

• *Better Homes and Gardens Wood.* No. 62 (Aug, 1993) p. 14.

Gazebos

"Innovative outbuildings" by Rick Mastelli. Four designs for gazebos, greenhouses, and potting sheds. Photos. • *Practical Homeowner.* Vol. V, No. 3 (April, 1990) pp. 50-54.

"Places in the sun" by Joseph Truini. Highlights construction plans for a shade arbor, rustic deck gazebo, and a patio cover. Photos, diagrams. • *Home Mechanix.* No. 745 (May, 1990) pp. 40-47.

"Pondside gazebo" by Alan Guazzoni. Describes construction plans to build a gazebo on wet, unstable soil. Photos, drawings. • *Fine Homebuilding.* No. 75 (July, 1992) pp. 57-59.

"Summer rooms" by Norman Kolpas. Ideas for building open porches, gazebos, and trellises. Photos. • *Practical Homeowner.* (Jul/Aug, 1992) pp. 78-83.

"Yardscaping" by Joseph Truini. Provides a glimpse at an example of creating a yardscape complete with a gazebo, sun deck, patio, lattice screens, and tiered planters. Photos, diagrams, drawings.
• *Home Mechanix.* No. 775 (May, 1993) pp. 62-69.

Generators

"Backup power" by Ezra Auerbach. Explains the kinds of backup power to use when storms shut down electricity. • *Fine Homebuilding.* No. 74 (May, 1992) p. 16.

Girders

"Rectifying a rotted girder" by George Nash. Brief article suggesting a solution for a rotting girder. • *Fine Homebuilding.* No. 79 (March, 1993) pp. 22-24.

Glass

"Glass additions" by Fran Rensbarger. Explains how architects integrate various glass products into homes to add variety to the design and solve problems. Photos.

• *The Homeowner's Guide to Glass.* No. 1 (1989) pp. 34-39.

"The house that glass built…" by Debra Levy. An overview of the types of residential glass products. Photos. • *The Homeowner's Guide to Glass.* No. 1 (1989) pp. 14-21.

"Reflections" by Joyce Grimley. Answers to frequently asked questions on using glass in homes. Photo. • *The Homeowner's Guide to Glass.* No. 1 (1989) pp. 6-7.

Glass Blocks

"Block party" by Matt Phair. Presents four innovations to help install glass blocks. Photos, drawings. • *Home Mechanix.* No. 770 (Nov, 1992) pp. 52-58.

Glass, Leaded

"Leaded glass-the easy way" by Matt Phair. Presents a method of creating a leaded glass with ordinary windows. Photos. • *Home Mechanix.* No. 758 (Sep, 1991) p. 20.

"Leaded-glass panels" by Bill Krier and Jim Downing. Directions to make leaded panels with clear, stained, or beveled glass. Photos, drawings, materials list. • *Better Homes and Gardens Wood.* No. 61 (June, 1993) pp. 32-38.

Glazing

"Decorative painted finishes" by Victor DeMasi. Provides an introduction to glazing, woodgraining, marbleizing and other finish techniques. Photos. Sidebar on marbleizing a mantel. • *Fine Homebuilding.* No. 60 (May, 1990) pp. 78-82.

Gliders

"Lawn glider." How to build a large, double-sided lawn glider. Plans, photos, and materials list. • *The Woodworker's Journal.* Vol. 16, No. 4 (Jul/Aug, 1992) pp. 30-35.

Glue Guns

"Hot-melt glue guns" by August Capotosto. Surveys a variety of glue guns. Photos. • *Home Mechanix.* No. 744 (April, 1990) p. 14.

Glues

"Gluing oily woods." A description of the proper techniques for gluing woods that have a high oil content. Photo and drawings. • *The Woodworker's Journal.* Vol. 14, No. 3 (May/June, 1990) pp. 18-20.

Gluing

"Hot-melt gluing hard-to-clamp pieces" by Manuel Avalos. Helpful tips for gluing joining arms to chair-backs, legs to aprons and other projects. Drawing. • *Woodwork.* No. 13 (January/February) p. 20.

Graders (Toy)

"Rugged road grader" by Marlen Kemmet and James R. Downing. Detailed instructions to construct an ideal toy for the sandbox or home. Photos, diagrams, full-sized pattern, materials list. • *Better Homes and Gardens Wood.* No. 45 (Sep, 1991) pp. 62-65.

Greenhouses

"Innovative outbuildings" by Rick Mastelli. Four designs for gazebos, greenhouses, and potting sheds. Photos. • *Practical Homeowner.* Vol. V, No. 3 (April, 1990) pp. 50-54.

"Solar adobe" by Benjamin T. Rogers. Construction plans for a greenhouse and solar-heated New Mexico house. Plans, photos. • *Fine Homebuilding.* No. 58 (March, 1990) pp. 80-85.

Grinders

"A tool post grinder" by Frank A. McLean. A simple design for attaching a grinder to a lathe. Photos and plans. • *The Home Shop Machinist.* Vol. 10, No. 3 (May/Jun, 1991) pp. 44-47.

Grinding Rests

"A grinding rest for precise tools, part one" by Rudy Kouhoupt. How to build a customized grinding rest for precision work. Photos. • *The Home Shop Machinist.* Vol. 9, No. 3 (May/Jun, 1990) pp. 40-42.

"A grinding rest for precise tools, part two" by Rudy Kouhoupt. See Vol. 9, No. 3 • *The Home Shop Machinist.* Vol. 9, No. 4 (Jul/Aug, 1990) pp. 48-49.

Grinding, Surface

"Surface grinding on the drill press" by Ray E. Starnes. A brief tip on adapting a drill press for grinding applications. Photo. • *The Home Shop Machinist.* Vol. 9, No. 2 (Mar/Apr, 1990) p. 54.

Groundwater

"Groundwater heating and cooling" by Steven J. Strong. Explains the advantages and disadvantages of using groundwater for heating or cooling. • *Fine Homebuilding.* No. 69 (Sep, 1991) p. 18.

Guides, Ruler

"Rule guide for easier layout" by Edward G. Hoffman. A brief tip for making a scribing guide for a steel ruler. • *The Home Shop Machinist.* Vol. 10, No. 4 (Jul/Aug, 1991) pp. 39.

Gumball Machine

"Gumball machine." A simple, yet clever, design for a small wooden gumball machine with clear plexiglass sides. Photo, plans, and materials list. • *The Woodworker's Journal.* Vol. 15, No. 4 (Jul/Aug, 1991) pp. 50-52.

Gun Cabinets

"A high-caliber gun cabinet" by Marlen Kemmet. Detailed instructions and assembly directions for a handsome wall-hung gun cabinet. Photos, materials list, diagrams and sandblast pattern. • *Better Homes and Gardens Wood.* No. 40 (Jan, 1991) pp. 44-51.

Gussets

"Gusset blocks" by Ron Milner. Brief tip on using gusset blocks for building a rafter on a cottage. Drawing. • *Fine Homebuilding.* No. 82 (July, 1993) p. 28.

Gutters

"Goodbye to gutters" by Henry Spies. Presents an alternative to cleaning clogged gutters every week. Drawing. • *Home Mechanix.* No. 758 (Sep, 1991) p. 81.

"Replacing an inlaid gutter" by Rob Paral. Explains the process of making and installing a lead-coated copper drainage system. Photos, diagrams. Sidebar on selecting lead-coated copper. • *Fine Homebuilding.* No. 61 (July, 1990) pp. 46-49.

"Replacing rain gutters" by Les Williams. Offers a professional's advice on installing aluminum and galvanized steel gutters. Photos, drawings. Sidebar on soldering galvanized sheet-metal. • *Fine Homebuilding.* No. 67 (May, 1991) pp. 38-43.

"Rethinking the cornice return" by Scott McBride. Offers recent developments in constructing effective gutters. Photos, drawings. • *Fine Homebuilding.* No. 77 (Nov, 1992) pp. 46-49.

H

Hall Trees

"Hall tree" by W. Curtis Johnson. Detailed instructions for building an elegant hall tree. Drawings. Photos. • *Woodwork.* No. 16 (July/August, 1992) pp. 70-74.

Hammers

"Getting a handle on hammers" by Larry Haun. Brief tips on buying and maintaining a hammer. • *Fine Homebuilding.* No. 84 (Nov, 1993) p. 30.

Handicap Access — *See* Architecture and the Handicapped

Handicraft

Book Review: *Art for Everyday: The New Craft Movement* by Patricia Conway. Book review on a craft book containing photos of projects of glass, furniture, tile or metal work. Clarkson Potter Publishers, 264 pp. • *Fine Homebuilding.* No. 65 (March, 1991) p. 108.

"Cheery, cherry door harp" by Robert Kiser. Brief description to make a door harp. Photo, diagram. • *Better Homes and Gardens Wood.* No. 41 (Feb, 1991) pp. 66-67.

"Decorator duck" by Howard and Mariann Eggleston. Brief directions to make a duck-shaped desk statue. Photo, pattern. • *Better Homes and Gardens Wood.* No. 63 (Sep, 1993) pp. 66-67.

"Exhibit under glass" by James R. Downing. Directions to create an attractive wooden-inlay base to display collectibles or flowers. Diagrams, photos. • *Better Homes and Gardens Wood.* No. 42 (April, 1991) pp. 68-69.

"Fanciful flowers from found wood" by Don Hart. How to turn found wood into attractive flowers. Photo, diagram. • *Better Homes and Gardens Wood.* No. 41 (Feb, 1991) p. 61.

"Graceful goose." Directions to construct a goose-shaped country-style napkin holder. Photo, full-sized pattern. • *Better Homes and Gardens Wood.* No. 41 (Feb, 1991) pp. 66-67.

"Inside-out twists" by Robert L. Calvert. Create inventive gift items and ornaments with unusual shapes of wood. Photos. • *Woodwork.* No. 15 (May/June, 1992) pp. 74-76.

"Petal-powered wall hanging" by Jeff and Leonila Girdler. Complete instructions and full-sized pattern offered for a hummingbird and flower wall hanging.

Photos, grid pattern, drawings. • *Better Homes and Gardens Wood.* No. 34 (April, 1990) pp. 58-59.

"Reincarnating hockey sticks" by Denis Roy. Describes various handicraft projects that could be constructed from used hockey sticks. Photos. Drawn plans. • *Canadian Workshop.* Vol. 13, No. 4 (Jan, 1990) pp. 28-31.

"Ride the wind" by Larry Raiche. Instructions to build an air balloon wall hanging. Photo, drawing, full-sized pattern. • *Better Homes and Gardens Wood.* No. 41 (Feb, 1991) pp. 64-65.

"Save a whale." Brief article on making a wooden whale with pine, fir, or cedar. Photo, pattern, drawing. • *Better Homes and Gardens Wood.* No. 50 (Feb, 1992) pp. 80-81.

"Thanks for the memories" by Sherry Connors. Brief description of an attractive wall hanging for old toys. Photo, full-sized pattern, drawing. • *Better Homes and Gardens Wood.* No. 45 (Sep, 1991) pp. 78-79.

"Toucan-on-a-branch." How to use a scroll saw to cut a tropical bird design. Photos, plans, and materials list. • *The Woodworker's Journal.* Vol. 16, No. 1 (Jan/Feb, 1992) pp. 66-69.

"Wildfowl fridge magnets" by Judy Gale Roberts. Creative bird designs and instructions to scrollsaw refrigerator magnets. Photos. • *Better Homes and Gardens Wood.* No. 60 (April, 1993) pp. 68-69.

See Also Holiday Decorations; and specific types of project materials, e.g., Wood Carving.

Handles

"Hands-on handles" by Rus Hurt. Create your own custom-built handles with these instructions. Photo, diagram, materials list. • *Better Homes and Gardens Wood.* No. 56 (Nov, 1992) p. 88.

Handles, Bag

"Plastic grocery bag handles." How to construct a pair of wooden hand grips for holding onto plastic shopping bags. Photos and plans. • *The Woodworker's Journal.* Vol. 16, No. 5 (Sep/Oct, 1992) pp. 52-53.

Handles, Knife

"Sharp steak knives" by Walt Easley. Cut your own teak handles for steak knives with these instructions. Photo, diagram. • *Better Homes and Gardens Wood.* No. 48 (Dec, 1991) pp. 70 71.

Handrails

"Reducing springback" by Klaus Matthies. Handy tip to keep a laminated curved handrail from losing its shape. Drawing. • *Fine Homebuilding.* No. 62 (Sep, 1990) p. 30.

Handsaws

"Using a handsaw" by Tom Law. Explains the effectiveness and safety of a handsaw for certain projects. Photos. • *Fine Homebuilding.* No. 78 (Jan, 1993) pp. 60-61.

Hangers, Joist

"Installing joist hangers" by Fred Misner, Todd Sauls, Fred Mocking, Steve Chassereau, and Chris Cartwright. Provides several methods of installing joist hangers. Drawing. • *Fine Homebuilding.* No. 75 (July, 1992) p. 14.

Hardware

"Homemade hardware" by Chip Rosenblum. Instructions to make homemade hinges and other types of hardware. Photos. • *Fine Homebuilding.* No. 63 (Nov, 1990) pp. 66-68.

"Knockdown hardware." An exposition of the different types and uses of metal fittings. Photos. Drawings. • *The Woodworker's Journal.* Vol. 14, No. 4 (Jul/ Aug, 1990) pp. 25-28.

Hardware, Wooden

"For projects that hinge upon their good looks: wooden hardware" by Bill Krier and Jim Boelling. Describes how to build and install a wooden hinge, lid support, and handles. Photos, diagrams. • *Better Homes and Gardens Wood.* No. 48 (Dec, 1991) pp. 50-55.

Harps

"Aeolian harp." A brief description for building a rectangular, wooden, wind harp also known as an Aeolian harp. Photos, plans, and materials list. • *The Woodworker's Journal.* Vol. 16, No. 4 (Jul/Aug, 1992) pp. 36-38.

Hazardous Materials Disposal

"Getting rid of CFCs" by Timothy O. Bakke. Update on the elimination of using CFCs in insulation and refrigerators. • *Home Mechanix.* No. 756 (June, 1991) pp. 18-19, 46.

"Hazardous waste disposal hotlines" by Timothy O. Bakke. Phone numbers and state agencies to contact for disposing of hazardous wastes in all U.S. states. Chart. • *Home Mechanix.* No. 753 (March, 1991) p. 9.

Health Hazards

Book Review: *The Complete Book of Home Environment Hazards* by Roberta Altman. Book review on clearly written guide to protect the home from hazards both inside and out. New York: Facts on File Inc., 290 pp. • *Home Mechanix.* No. 758 (Sep, 1991) p. 23.

"Safety: Workshop finishes pose risk" by Jim Barrett. An analysis of the dangers associated with wood finishes and the proper methods for their use. • *The Woodworker's Journal.* Vol. 14, No. 4 (Jul/ Aug, 1990) pp. 18-21.

"Worrisome little additions" by Lisa Iannuci. An analysis of some of the health hazards involved in remodeling, especially for pregnant women. • *Practical*

Homeowner. Vol. V, No. 4 (June, 1990) pp. 16-18.

Heat Conservation

"Rooms with a view" by Chris Knowles. Describes how to select and install the most energy efficient windows for the home, as well as window replacement procedures. Photos. • *Canadian Workshop.* Vol. 15, No. 1 (Oct 1991) pp. 42-47.

Heat Ducts

"Heat-seeking ducts" by Henry Spies. Offers instructions on how to make a heat duct system more effective so rooms furthest from the furnace receive enough heat. • *Home Mechanix.* No. 781 (Dec/Jan, 1993-94) pp. 87-88.

Heat Pumps

"Efficient heat pumps" by Timothy O. Bakke. Describes the heat pumps that use a refrigerant instead of water to make them more efficient. Photo. • *Home Mechanix.* No. 777 (July/Aug, 1993) pp. 17-18.

Heat Treating

"Heat treating basics" by Steve Acker. A basic introduction to the processes of hardening steel through heat treating. Diagrams. • *The Home Shop Machinist.* Vol. 10, No. 5 (Sep/Oct, 1991) pp. 28-31.

Heating and Ventilation

"Best ways to heat an addition" by Lee Green. Professional advice on heating additions, while keeping excessive heating costs low. Worksheet. • *Home Mechanix.* No. 751 (Dec/Jan, 1990 91) pp. 18-20.

Book Review: *Heating, Cooling, Lighting: Design Methods for Architects* by Norbert Lecher. Book review on a valuable guide for designing the heating, cooling, and lighting in homes. New York: John Wiley & Sons, Inc., 534 pp. • *Fine Homebuilding.* No. 72 (March, 1992) p. 108.

Book Review: *The Quiet Indoor Revolution* by Seichi Konzo and Marylee. Book review on a manual that traces the changes in indoor climate control throughout history. Champaign, IL: Small Homes Council-Building Research Council, 393 pp. • *Fine Homebuilding.* No. 81 (May, 1993) p. 114.

"The breathable home" by Lydia Cassidy. Describes factors that should be considered in improving home ventilation, including vents, fans, and insulation. Drawings. • *Canadian Workshop.* Vol. 13, No. 4 (Jan 1990) pp. 38-43.

"Building a tiled masonry heater" by Vladimir Popovac. Fashioned after the Finnish masonry heater, this design offers an energy-efficient clean-burning fireplace. Photos, drawing. Sidebar on masonry-heater emissions and the EPA. • *Fine Homebuilding.* No. 71 (Jan, 1992) pp. 50 54.

"Create zones for your hot-water heating system" by Gene and Katie Hamilton. Informative article on installing electrically operated zone valves to control a hot-water heating system. Drawings, photos. • *Home Mechanix.* No. 768 (Sep, 1992) pp. 16-18.

"Efficiency zones for heating and cooling" by Timothy O. Bakke. Informative article on zoned heating and cooling systems so temperatures in different rooms can have separate thermostats. Photo, drawing. • *Home Mechanix.* No. 754 (April, 1991) pp. 18-19.

"Heat for less" by Don Best. Tips and new product ideas for home heating. Photos. • *Practical Homeowner.* Vol. VI, No. 7 (Sep, 1991) pp. 66-72.

"Hot tips on home heating systems" by Anne Cala. Evaluates forced-air, gas, oil, and hydronic furnaces as well as, gas boilers. Illustrations. Sidebar on new standards for home heaters. • *Home Mechanix.* No. 751 (Dec/Jan, 1990-91) pp. 40-47.

"Hydronic coils for forced-air heating" by Denny Adelman. Provides information on the installation of forced-air heating. • *Fine Homebuilding*. No. 74 (May, 1992) pp. 14-16.

"Small house, big heater" by Albie Barden. Detailed article on a multipurpose masonry heater. Photos, plans, drawings. • *Fine Homebuilding*. No. 76 (Sep, 1992) pp. 76-79.

"Warming trends" by Michael Morris. Offers three alternative home heating systems. Photos, drawings. • *Home Mechanix*. No. 751 (Dec/Jan, 1990-91) pp. 48-51, 86.

"Weatherization" by Joseph Truini. Helpful tips on improving the heating efficiency of a home. • *Home Mechanix*. No. 764 (April, 1992) pp. 20-21.

Heating, Radiant-Floor

"Heat at your feet" by Alan Saunders. Discusses the advantage of radiant-floor heating and how to install it. Drawing. • *Home Mechanix*. No. 780 (Nov, 1993) pp. 68-72.

Herbicides

"Winning the weed war." A basic guide to the use of herbicides. Photos. • *Practical Homeowner*. Vol. V, No. 5 (August, 1990) pp. 30-33.

Hickory (Wood)

"Hickory: tougher than nails, and versatile, too" by Walt Hudson and Tommy Glades. Informative article covering the cost, availability, uses, machining and carving methods. Illustration, chart. Sidebar on shop-tested techniques. • *Better Homes and Gardens Wood*. No. 51 (April, 1992) pp. 33-34.

Highchairs

"Happy-days highchair" by Marlen Kemmet and Bruce Pierce. In-depth description on how to construct a sturdy and safe hardwood highchair. Photos, diagrams, materials list. • *Better Homes and Gardens Wood*. No. 51 (April, 1992) pp. 56-63.

Hinges, Wood

"An easy to make wood hinge." These are brief and easy-to-follow instructions for the manufacture of wooden hinges for boxes or decorative purposes. Drawings and plans. • *The Woodworker's Journal*. Vol. 15, No. 2 (Mar/Apr, 1991) pp. 38-39.

Historic Buildings

Book Review: *Caring for Your Old House* by Judith L. Kitchen. Book review on a guide for preserving old houses. Washington, D.C.: The Preservation Press, 208 pp. • *Fine Homebuilding*. No. 70 (Nov, 1991) pp. 120-122.

Book Review: *Landmark Yellow Pages: Where to Find All the Names, Addresses, Facts and Figures You Need* by National Trust for Historic Preservation. Book review on a handbook presenting information on preservation and 3,500 contacts serving as a network for preservation. Washington, D.C.: National Trust for Historic Preservation, 319 pp. • *Fine Homebuilding*. No. 68 (July, 1991) p. 106.

Holders

"Forstner bit holders" by Jim Boelling. Brief tip on making forstner bit holders for a drill press cabinet. Photo, diagrams, materials list. • *Better Homes and Gardens Wood*. No. 54 (Sep, 1992) p. 32.

Holders, Bandsaw Blade

"Bandsaw blade holder" by Chuck Hedlund. Brief directions to make a band saw blade holder. Photo, diagram. • *Better Homes and Gardens Wood*. No. 60 (April, 1993) p. 84.

Holiday Decorations

"Holiday horn of plenty" by Charles Sommers and Ellen Herrington. Create your own carved intarsia based on a Thanksgiving theme. Photo, pattern. • *Better Homes and Gardens Wood*. No. 56 (Nov, 1992) pp. 40-41.

"Nativity scene." Plans for using a scroll saw to cut out figures for a Nativity scene.

Photos, plans, and materials list. • *The Woodworker's Journal.* Vol. 16, No. 6 (Nov/Dec, 1992) pp. 60 63.

"Santa Claus" by Rick and Ellen Butz. A detailed descriptive article on how to carve a wooden Santa Claus figurine. Photos. • *The Woodworker's Journal.* Vol. 17, No. 6 (Nov/Dec, 1993) pp. 38-42.

"Tabletop Tom" by George Hans. Two-step process to create a Thanksgiving centerpiece. Photo, pattern. • *Better Homes and Gardens Wood.* No. 56 (Nov, 1992) pp. 42-43.

Home Inspections

"Effective do-it-yourself home inspection" by Timothy O. Bakke. In-depth article presenting the procedures of a home inspection. Checklist. • *Home Mechanix.* No. 764 (April, 1992) pp. 22 25.

"How home inspectors can help" by John Heyn. Professional advice on the benefits of home inspections and how they are conducted. • *Home Mechanix.* No. 745 (May, 1990) pp. 8-13.

Home Ownership

"The big money game of home ownership" by Guney Williams. The ins and outs of buying and financing your own home. • *Practical Homeowner.* Vol. VI, No. 1 (Jan, 1991) pp. 32-34.

Honing

"To hone or not to hone" by Jeff Parsons. Discusses how to properly sharpen lathe tools. Photos. • *Canadian Workshop.* Vol. 15, No. 1 (Oct 1991) p. 9.

Hooks

"Adjustable bench hook" by Anthony P. Matlosz. Basic instructions on how to construct a bench hook. Drawing. • *Woodwork.* No. 15 (May/June, 1992) p. 20.

"Siding hooks" by Roy Rider. Brief tip on angle-iron hooks used for putting up

siding. Drawing. • *Fine Homebuilding.* No. 78 (Jan, 1993) p. 30.

Horse Barns

"Winner's circle" by Glenn Perrett. Provides information on how the author remodeled an old barn into an efficient stable for horses. List of sources. Photos. • *Canadian Workshop.* Vol. 15, No. 1 (Oct 1991) pp. 66-72.

Horses, Rocking

"A stylized rocking horse" by W. Curtis Johnson. Detailed construction plans of a stylized sturdy rocking horse for children. Drawing. Photos. • *Woodwork.* No. 19 (Jan/Feb, 1993) pp. 39-41.

Hoses

"New life for old hose" by Scott N. Ayres. Brief article on recycling old hoses to repair new ones. Drawing. • *Fine Homebuilding.* No. 76 (Sep, 1992) p. 30.

Hot Tubs

"An energy-efficient hot tub" by Ron Miller. Details the on-site construction of a concrete, tile and foam hot tub. Diagram, photo. • *Fine Homebuilding.* No. 69 (Sep, 1991) pp. 64-65.

"Taking the plunge" by Dean Johnson. Practical advice for installing an outdoor spa or hot tub. Photos and drawings. • *Practical Homeowner.* Vol. V, No. 4 (June, 1990) pp. 14-15.

Hourglasses

"Hourglass." This article briefly outlines how to make a spindle frame for an hourglass. Photo and drawing. • *The Woodworker's Journal.* Vol. 14, No. 2 (Mar/Apr, 1990) pp. 44-45.

House Construction

"An Acadian cottage" by Leslie Barry Davidson. Construction plans and development of an Acadian-style home. Photos, plans, drawings. Sidebar about building on clay. Sidebar on the Acadian style. • *Fine Homebuilding*. No. 73 (Spring, 1992) pp. 36-41.

Book and Video Review: *R-2000: The Better-Built House*. Book and video review on a set of twenty 15-minute videos, a trainer's guide, and a learner's guide all focusing on constructing R-2000 homes. Arlington, MA: Cutter Information Corp. • *Fine Homebuilding*. No. 61 (July, 1990) p. 106.

Book Review: *Basic Home Building*. Book review on this basic guide to building or remodeling a home. Photo. Ortho Books, 352 pp. • *Home Mechanix*. No. 766 (June, 1992) p. 16.

Book Review: *Building Construction Illustrated*, Second Edition by Francis D.K. Ching and Cassandra Adams. Book review on an illustrated manual for residential and light commercial construction. Photo. New York: Van Nostrand Reinhold, 375 pp. • *Fine Homebuilding*. No. 78 (Jan, 1993) p. 110.

Book Review: *Fundamentals of Building Construction: Materials and Methods* (Second Edition) by Edward Allen. Book review with an overview of the construction industry from houses to skyscrapers. Photo. New York: John Wiley & Sons, Inc., 803 pp. • *Fine Homebuilding*. No. 71 (Jan, 1992) p. 112.

Book Review: *Shelter* by Lloyd Kahn. Book review on this updated book focusing on the art and spirit of housebuilding. Bolinas, CA: Shelter Publications, pp. 176 • *Fine Homebuilding*. No. 62 (Sep, 1990) p. 114.

"Building a pole house" by John Terrell. Introduces an approach to building a weekend retreat with 20 ft. poles. Photos, drawing. • *Fine Homebuilding*. No. 83 (Sep, 1993) pp. 77-79.

"Building for unknown clients" by David Carse. Offers designs for a small, cost-conscious spec houses. Photos, plans. • *Fine Homebuilding*. No. 80 (Spring, 1993) pp. 50-53.

"Elegance on a shoestring" by John Brooks. Tells how Brooks built a four-bedroom home with state-of-the-art framing and bold detailing for $38 per sq. ft. Photos, plans, drawings. Sidebar on production soffit framing. • *Fine Homebuilding*. No. 73 (Spring, 1992) pp. 56-59.

"Escape from Manhattan" by Jeffrey Dale Bianco. Describes techniques for building a retreat home with a gabled roof and circular porch. Photos, drawings, plans. • *Fine Homebuilding*. No. 66 (Spring, 1991) pp. 78-81.

"The lookout house" by John S. MacDonald. Details the construction of a house on a rocky ledge of an island in Maine. Photo, plans. Sidebar on fastening piers to rock. • *Fine Homebuilding*. No. 74 (May, 1992) pp. 66-69.

"Manhattan comes to Sun Valley" by Steve Kearns and Stephen Riley. Details the construction of a Manhattan style house in Sun Valley, Idaho. Photos, drawings. • *Fine Homebuilding*. No. 62 (Sep, 1990) pp. 58-61.

"Panelized frame, customized finish" by Richard Irland. Describes the process of building a home with a prefab insulated wall system. Photos, plans. • *Fine Homebuilding*. No. 62 (Sep, 1990) pp. 72-77.

"Rainbow hill" by James T. Hubbell. Describes the plans for a free-form building growing out of granite. Photos, plans. Sidebar on free-form building. • *Fine Homebuilding*. No. 66 (Spring, 1991) pp. 51-55.

"Rammed earth revisited" by Jim Rosenau. An analysis of innovations in building house walls from compacted earth. Photos. • *Practical Homeowner*. (Sep/Oct, 1992) pp. 74-77.

"Salvaged in Ohio" by Clyde R. Kennedy. Details the process of building a house almost exclusively from salvaged materials.

Photos, plans. • *Fine Homebuilding*. No. 66 (Spring, 1991) pp. 74-77.

"A small house on a rocky hillside" by Kathleen Kenny. Presents construction plans for a house built on a canyon ledge. Photos, drawings, plans. • *Fine Homebuilding*. No. 82 (July, 1993) pp. 78-81.

"A small house to serve a richer life" by Ted Trinkaus. Follows the construction of a small house with a translucent roof and a movable wall to expand the floor plan. Photos, plans. • *Fine Homebuilding*. No. 65 (March, 1991) pp. 36-39.

See Also Architecture and Designs and Plans

House Plans — *See* Designs and Plans

House Plants

"Healthier house plants" by Jeff Ball. Advice on the ways to grow healthier house plants. Photos. • *Practical Homeowner*. Vol. VI, No. 1 (Jan, 1991) pp. 18-22.

Houses

"The American home" by Michael Morris. Showcases builders' show house as a model for future homes. Photos, plans. • *Home Mechanix*. No. 773 (March, 1993) pp. 66-73.

Book Review: *America's Favorite Homes: Mail Order Catalogues as a Guide to Popular Early 20th Century Houses* by Robert Schweitzer and Michael W.R. Davis. Book review on a collection of mail order catalogues and a study of early architectural styles. Detroit, MI: Wayne State University Press, 363 pp. • *Fine Homebuilding*. No. 77 (Nov, 1992) p. 120.

Book Review: *Getting a Good Home* by Bob Syvanen. Book review of a guide on checking the quality of workmanship in a home from the perspective of a master carpenter. Old Saybrook, CT: Globe Pequot Press, 112 pp. • *Home Mechanix*. No. 762 (Feb, 1992) p. 25.

Book Review: *The Natural House Book: Creating a Healthy, Harmonious, and Ecologically Sound Home Environment* by David Pearson. Book review on a ecologically sound houses. New York: Simon and Schuster Inc., 287 pp. • *Fine Homebuilding*. No. 61 (July, 1990) p. 106.

"Courtyard connections" by Murray Silverstein. Describes the layout of a house and a guest cottage linked with outdoor rooms. Photos, drawings, plans. Sidebar on finding a builder. • *Fine Homebuilding*. No. 80 (Spring, 1993) pp. 82-87.

"Designing for a hot climate" by Thomas Leach. Presents a design focusing on climate control and landscaping. Photos, plans, drawings. Sidebar on building shadeshelters. • *Fine Homebuilding*. No. 79 (March, 1993) pp. 70-74.

"House on the river" by Steve Taylor. Offers the design of a river house constructed with concrete piers, cantilevered steel and prefab framing. Photos, drawing, plans. Sidebar on a transparent cricket. • *Fine Homebuilding*. No. 73 (Spring, 1992) pp. 71-75.

"Live large, look small" by David Hall. Detailed description of a lakeside house with bungalow features. Photos, plans. • *Fine Homebuilding*. No. 80 (Spring, 1993) pp. 40-45.

"A modest house in Bucks County" by Jeremiah Eck. Detailed description of country house built in the tradition of the Old Congress-style houses. Photos, plans. Sidebar on interior and exterior millwork. • *Fine Homebuilding*. No. 59 (Spring, 1990) pp. 36-41.

"A new 19th-century house" by Aileen L. Barth. Describes the design and construction plans for a reproduction of an 1810 lean-to. Photos, plans. • *Fine Homebuilding*. No. 77 (Nov, 1992) pp. 86-89.

"Resisting the weather on the Outer Banks" by Frank Harmon. Details the plans and design of a house on the Outer Banks. Photos, diagrams, plans. • *Fine Homebuilding.* No. 59 (Spring, 1990) pp. 78-82.

"Sam Maloof's House" by Charles Miller. Offers a tour through Sam Maloof's house highlighting inventive uses of wood for furniture, the exterior, and doors. Photos, drawings. Sidebar on an American woodworker. • *Fine Homebuilding.* No. 68 (July, 1991) pp. 36-41.

"Suburban refuge" by Joseph G. Metzler. Details the design of a suburban house constructed to assure comfort and privacy. Photos, plans. • *Fine Homebuilding.* No. 68 (July, 1991) pp. 82 87.

See Also Architecture; Specific styles of houses, e.g., Arts and Crafts Houses, Colonial Houses

Houses, Acadian

"An Acadian cottage" by Leslie Barry Davidson. Construction plans and development of an Acadian-style home. Photos, plans, drawings. Sidebar about building on clay. Sidebar on the Acadian style. • *Fine Homebuilding.* No. 73 (Spring, 1992) pp. 36-41.

Houses, Bay

"The buzzards bay house" by Peter Adrian Thomas. Describes an architect's design for a Cape Cod location. Photos, plans. Sidebar on the eyebrow dormer. • *Fine Homebuilding.* No. 59 (Spring, 1990) pp. 62-67.

Houses, Beach

"Camino con corazon" by Steve Badanes. Details the process of building a butterfly-roof, Baja beach house. Photos, plans. • *Fine Homebuilding.* No. 63 (Nov, 1990) pp. 36-41.

Houses, Cantilevered

"Cantilevered hillside house" by Eliot Goldstein. Highlights a house of cantilevers. Photos, plans, drawings. • *Fine*

Homebuilding. No. 79 (March, 1993) pp. 80-84.

Houses, Country

"Louisiana country house" by Errol Barron. Offers a plan for an attractive country house with a traditional facade and an environmentally conscious design. Photos, plans. • *Fine Homebuilding.* No. 59 (Spring, 1990) pp. 57-61.

Houses, Desert

"Desert house" by Les Wallach. Gives the design and construction plans for a desert house with a very large roof span and an enclosed bridge. Photos, plans, drawings. • *Fine Homebuilding.* No. 66 (Spring, 1991) pp. 82-87.

Houses, Hawaiian Ohana

"Hawaiian ohana house" by Sue Ellen White-Hansen. Describes flexible plans for housing on an island with a limited amount of buildable land. Photos, drawing. Sidebar on the furo. • *Fine Homebuilding.* No. 61 (July, 1990) pp. 58-61.

Houses, Hillside

"Simplicity with style" by Duo Dickinson. Practical design on a realistic budget for a hillside house. Photos, plans, drawing. • *Fine Homebuilding.* No. 66 (Spring, 1991) pp. 69-73.

Houses, Modular

"Builders' blocks" by Mark Alvarez. An article describing the latest advances in modular home construction. Photos. • *Practical Homeowner.* Vol. V, No. 5 (August, 1990) pp. 62-69.

Houses, Panelized

"Building by numbers" by Craig Canine. A guide to wood-frame panelized housing. Photos. • *Practical Homeowner.* Vol. IV, No. 9 (Jan, 1990) pp. 48-53.

Houses, Post-and-Beam

"Post-and-beam houses" by Joseph Truini. Shows examples of post-and-beam houses

from five kit manufacturers. Photos.
• *Home Mechanix*. No. 772 (Feb, 1993) pp. 44-47.

Houses, Prefab

"Panelized frame, customized finish" by Richard Irland. Describes the process of building a home with a prefab insulated wall system. Photos, plans. • *Fine Homebuilding*. No. 62 (Sep, 1990) pp. 72-77.

Houses, Split Level

"Living on different levels." Three different house plans featuring split level homes. • *Practical Homeowner*. Vol. V, No. 6 (Sep, 1990) pp. 70-74.

Houses, Tower

"High living in a small space" by Harry J. Wirth. Imitating Indian shelters, this design introduces new storage and cooling techniques. Photos, plans, drawings. • *Fine Homebuilding*. No. 80 (Spring, 1993) pp. 68-71.

Houses, Usonian

"Adapting Usonian" by J. Stewart Roberts. Gives plans and instructions for a blend of Frank Lloyd Wright's ideas with today's construction techniques. Photos, plans. • *Fine Homebuilding*. No. 66 (Spring, 1991) pp. 56-59.

"Beneath green gable roofs" by John Eifler. Highlights a Usonian-type design with waferboard siding and barn-style shingles. Photos, plans. • *Fine Homebuilding*. No. 80 (Spring, 1993) pp. 46-49.

Houses, Vernacular

"A small, Maine house" by Ted Marks. Follows the process of selecting a site and building a house in the style of Maine houses. Photos, plans, drawing. • *Fine Homebuilding*. No. 73 (Spring) pp. 46-50.

Houses--Acoustics

"Quiet please" by Russell DuPree. Offers strategies for toning down sound

transmission in wood-framed floors and ceilings. Drawings, charts. • *Fine Homebuilding*. No. 58 (March, 1990) pp. 54-57.

Houses--Air Quality

Book Review: *Residential Indoor Air Quality & Energy* by Peter DuPont and John Morrill. Book review of a handbook covering research on health, air quality, and energy-efficient housing. Berkeley, CA: American Council for an Energy-Efficient Economy, 267 pp. • *Fine Homebuilding*. No. 75 (July, 1992) p. 110.

See Also Air Quality; Heating and Ventilation; Dust Collectors

Houses--Barrier Free Environments

Book Review: *Adaptable Housing: A Technical Manual for Implementing Adaptable Dwelling Unit Specifications*. Book review giving an excellent overview of the history of accessible and adaptable housing. Rockville, MD: HUD USER, (PO Box 6091) • *Fine Homebuilding*. No. 63 (Nov, 1990) p. 77.

Houses--Conservation and Restoration *See* Conservation and Restoration

Houses--Dating

"Dating vintage houses" by Dan Marvin and Karey Solomon. Provides methods of uncovering the age of a house. Drawings, photos. Sidebar on one home's story. • *Home Mechanix*. No. 757 (July/Aug, 1991) pp. 72-77.

Houses--Energy Efficiency — *See* Energy Efficiency

Houses--Framing

"Framing a second-story addition" by Alexander Brennen. Describes the process of framing a quartet of gables linked by California-style valleys. Photos, drawings, plans. • *Fine Homebuilding*. No. 58 (March, 1990) pp. 76-77.

Houses--Maintenance and Repair — *See* **Maintenance and Repair**

Houses--Modern Features

"Home buying in the year 2001" by Joseph Truini. Brief article on some of the features in homes of the future are expected to include. Drawing. • *Home Mechanix.* No. 762 (Feb, 1992) p. 34.

Houses--Remodeling — *See* **Remodeling**

Houses--Solar

Book and Software Review: *Passive Solar Design Strategies: Guidelines for Home Builders*, and *BuilderGuide Software*. Book and software review on several basic solar designs. Washington, D.C.: Passive Solar Industries Council. • *Fine Homebuilding.* No. 79 (March, 1993) p. 120.

Humidity Control

"Basement rust" by Michael M. Ambrosino. A guide to inhibiting rust formation in basement workshops. • *The Home Shop Machinist.* Vol. 11, No. 6 (Nov/Dec, 1992) pp. 40-41.

Hurricanes

"Hurricane warnings" by Charles Miller. Informative article on the wreckage of Hurricane Andrew and why some houses survived. Photos, drawings. Sidebar on emergency power. • *Fine Homebuilding.* No. 78 (Jan, 1993) pp. 82-87.

Hutches

"Pine hutch." A very detailed and advanced design for an Early American-style pine hutch. Photos, plans, and materials list. • *The Woodworker's Journal.* Vol. 16, No. 5 (Sep/Oct, 1992) pp. 34-39.

See Also Cabinets

I

Ice Dams

"Framing a cold roof" by Steve Kearns. Instructions on how to build a cold roof, one that prevents ice damming and roof leaks. Photos, drawings. • *Fine Homebuilding.* No. 63 (Nov, 1990) pp. 42-44.

"Ice-dam defense" by Henry Spies. Explains how ice dams form in roof eaves and how to prevent them. Drawing. • *Home Mechanix.* No. 769 (Oct, 1992) p. 78.

"Ice-damming myths" by Gene Leger. Offers a solution to an ice-damming problem. • *Fine Homebuilding.* No. 71 (Jan, 1992) p. 14.

Iceboxes

"Old-time icebox" by Gary Graziani. A thorough description of the steps in building an exact replica of an old-fashioned home icebox. • *The Woodworker's Journal.* Vol. 17, No. 6 (Nov/Dec, 1993) pp. 43-47.

Indexes

"An indexing device" by Ed Dubosky. A thorough examination of the uses of an indexing device for holding small parts while machining. Photos and plans. • *The Home Shop Machinist.* Vol. 9, No. 5 (Sep/Oct, 1990) pp. 20-25.

Indexing Tables

"A simple indexing rotary table" by Michael F. Hoff, Jr. The manufacture and application of a precise indexing device for machine shop work. Photos. • *The Home Shop Machinist.* Vol. 11, No. 1 (Jan/Feb, 1992) pp. 32-37.

Injuries

"Working without pain" by Daniel Wing. Examines injuries that occur over many years incorrect posture or holding tools improperly. Photos, drawings. • *Fine Homebuilding.* No. 64 (Jan, 1991) pp. 66-69.

Inlays

"Two traditional inlay techniques" by Paula Garbarino. Provides a brief but complete description of both the banding and the line methods of producing inlay. Photos and plans. • *The Woodworker's Journal.* Vol. 15, No. 3 (May/Jun, 1991) pp. 17-20.

Inlays, Mother-of-Pearl

"Inlaying mother-of-pearl." An exhaustive description of the methods of putting mother-of pearl inlay in decorative woodwork. Drawings • *The Woodworker's Journal.* Vol. 14, No. 6 (Nov/Dec, 1990) pp. 35-38.

Insecticides

"Medicine kit for the yard" by Jeff Ball. Recommendations for the application of various insecticides. • *Practical Homeowner.* Vol. VI, No. 5 (May/June, 1991) pp. 24-26.

Insects

Book Review: *The Termite Report: A Guide for Homeowners & Homebuyers on Structural Pest Control* by Donald V. Pearman. Book review on a comprehensive guide to repair pest related structural problems. Pearman Publishing, 139 pp. • *Home Mechanix.* No. 764 (April, 1992) p. 29.

"Bug busters" by Gurney Williams. How to use high temperatures to kill termites. Photos. • *Practical Homeowner.* Vol. VI, No. 5 (May/June, 1991) pp. 82-88.

"Long horn beetles" by Phil Pellitteri. Helpful advice on how to prevent beetles from causing structural damage to wood. • *Fine Homebuilding.* No. 58 (March, 1990) p. 18.

"Termite Termination." Brief tips on warning signs of termite damage and how to prevent infestation. Chart. • *Home Mechanix.* No. 744 (April, 1990) p. 16.

"Wood-infesting insects" by Phil Pellitteri. In-depth article on controlling termites, carpenter ants, and powderpost beetles. Photos, drawings. • *Fine Homebuilding.* No. 60 (May, 1990) pp. 64-69.

Inserts, Threaded

"Threaded inserts go straight with simple installation jig" by Paul R. Cook. Brief tip on driving threaded inserts on a workpiece too big for a drill press. Drawing. • *Better Homes and Gardens Wood.* No. 59 (Feb, 1992) p. 12.

Insulating

"Re-siding with wood" by Hank Spies. Brief tip on re-siding and insulating a two-story house. • *Home Mechanix.* No. 744 (April, 1990) pp. 100-101.

"After-the-fact insulation" by Thomas F. Sweeney. Practices and pitfalls of adding blown-in insulation to an older home. Photos. • *Practical Homeowner.* Vol. VI, No. 8 (Oct, 1991) pp. 14 18.

Insulation

"Alphabet soup: what are those R's, U's and low-E's?" by Jim Crisci. Offers a summary description of the acronyms and abbreviations used in insulation. • *The Homeowner's Guide to Glass.* No. 1 (1989) pp. 10-11.

"Blown-in wall insulation" by Hank Spies. Addresses a question on whether it is possible to add blown-in insulation to exterior walls that are insulated with batts to R-13. • *Home Mechanix.* No. 748 (Sep, 1990) pp. 90-91.

"Building with pumice-crete" by Vishu Magee. Offers instructions to make pumice-crete, an insulating concrete. Photos, drawing. • *Fine Homebuilding.* No. 77 (Nov, 1992) pp. 55-57.

"Cutting costs of cold floors" by Hank Spies. Provides a tip for insulating a garage concrete foundation. Drawing. • *Home Mechanix.* No. 742 (Feb, 1990) p. 70.

"Energy barriers" by Mark Alvarez. An explanation of the different types of insulation products. Drawing. • *Practical Homeowner.* Vol. VI, No. 1 (Jan, 1991) pp. 42-50.

"Insul-vines" by Henry Spies. Brief tip on the value of growing vines as insulation. Drawing. • *Home Mechanix.* No. 778 (Sep, 1993) p. 128.

"Insulating a tight spot" by John Ross. Offers a suggestion on insulating a small area. Drawing. • *Fine Homebuilding.* No. 79 (March, 1993) p. 20.

"Insulating beneath a slab" by William A. Randall. Brief tip on whether it is necessary to insulate floor slabs. • *Fine Homebuilding.* No. 81 (May, 1993) p. 18.

"Insulating with recycled glass" by Timothy O. Bakke. Presents a kind of insulation created from recycled glass. Photo. • *Home Mechanix.* No. 777 (July/Aug, 1993) p. 17.

"Insulation upgrades" by John Ingersoll. Provides professional advice on upgrading a home's insulation. Photos, chart. • *Home Mechanix.* No. 748 (Sep, 1990) pp. 10-15.

"Itch-free insulation" by Jane A. Havsy. Introduces a new fiberglass insulation that is encased in a pink polyethylene wrapping to minimize fly-away glass fibers. Photo. • *Home Mechanix.* No. 779 (Oct, 1993) pp. 30-31.

"Timberframe sound insulation" by Russell Dupree. Detailed instructions to construct a floating floor to reduce sound between floors in a timberframe house. Drawings. • *Fine Homebuilding.* No. 62 (Sep, 1990) p. 18.

"Wrapping up your house." Brief article on the R-value or the expression of resistance to heat flow for home insulation according to the climate in the area. Chart. • *Home Mechanix.* No. 743 (March, 1990) p. 16.

Insulation (Windows)

"Rooms with a view" by Chris Knowles. Describes how to select and install the most energy efficient windows for the home, as well as window replacement procedures. Photos. • *Canadian Workshop.* Vol. 15, No. 1 (Oct 1991) pp. 42-47.

Insulation, Fiberglass

"Insulation declaration" by Joseph Truini. Brief article on safety tips for installing fiberglass insulation. • *Home Mechanix.* No. 764 (April, 1992) p. 14.

Intarsia

"Carved intarsia" by Peter J. Stephano. Informative article about Ellen Harrington and her development of carved intarsia. Photos. • *Better Homes and Gardens Wood.* No. 56 (Nov, 1992) pp. 37-39.

"Intarsia project-American eagle" by Robert Hlavacek. An explanation of the intarsia process of cutting and fitting together pieces of wood in a puzzle fashion to make an eagle. Photos, plans, and materials list. • *The Woodworker's Journal.* Vol. 17, No. 5 (Sep/Oct, 1993) pp. 27 32.

"Intarsia: The Judy Gale Roberts way" by Judy Gale Roberts. Step-by-step instructions and two specially designed patterns available for an intarsia project. Photos, diagrams, full-sized pattern. • *Better Homes and Gardens Wood.* No. 44 (August, 1991) pp. 28-33.

"The knothole gang." Directions for a beginners intarsia project involving a large knothole and jigsaw cut pieces which form a scene with two raccoons. Photos and drawings. • The Woodworker's Journal. Vol. 16, No. 3 (May/Jun, 1992) pp. 54-57.

Intercoms

"Speak easy" by Matt Phair. Presents a variety of models of intercoms to install in a home. Photos, diagram. • *Home Mechanix.* No. 741 (Jan, 1990) pp. 74-77.

Interior Design

"Finishing with the best." A guide to finishing various home elements including floors, cabinets, painting, and stripping. • *Practical Homeowner.* Vol. V, No. 7 (Oct, 1990) pp. 58-70.

"Making space" by Carolyn Chubert. Practical schemes for gaining space by rearranging furnishings. Photos and plans. • *Practical Homeowner.* Vol. V, No. 1 (Feb, 1990) pp. 42-47.

"Remodeling with paint" by Gary Mayk. Offers remodeling designs for exteriors using paint. Photos, drawings, chart. • *Home Mechanix.* No. 764 (April, 1992) pp. 48-52.

"Sam Maloof's house" by Charles Miller. Offers a tour through Sam Maloof's house highlighting the inventive use of wood for furniture, the exterior, and doors. Photos, drawings. Sidebar on an American woodworker. • *Fine Homebuilding.* No. 68 (July, 1991) pp. 36-41.

Interior Design--Color Schemes

"Fear of color" by Jim Rosenau. Advice on choosing the right color scheme for your house exterior. Photos • *Practical Homeowner.* (May/June, 1992) pp. 51-55.

Ironing Boards

"Wall-hung ironing board." Complete instructions on how to make an ironing board which folds up into a wall mounted compartment. Includes materials list. Plans. • *The Woodworker's Journal.* Vol. 14, No. 1 (Jan/Feb, 1990) pp. 50-52.

Ironwork

"Architectural ironwork" by Tom Joyce. Informative article on the many uses for ironwork in homes and the process of making the ironwork. Photos. Sidebar on mortise and tenon. Sidebar on the language of ironwork. • *Fine Homebuilding.* No. 75 (July, 1992) pp. 75-79.

"Cast iron repair" by Richard B. Walker. An examination of techniques for repairing cast iron, including brazing, arc welding, and cold welding. Photos and plans. • *The Home Shop Machinist.* Vol. 10, No. 1 (Jan/Feb, 1991) pp. 30-36.

J

Jambs, Door

"Replacing a door jamb" by Chris Dahle. Presents a method of repairing a door jamb when only one jamb leg is damaged. Drawings. • *Fine Homebuilding.* No. 75 (July, 1992) p. 28.

Jambs, Extension

"Scribing extension jambs" by Steve Becker. Brief tip on fitting extension jambs to irregular walls. Drawing. • *Fine Homebuilding.* No. 58 (March, 1990) p. 26.

Jewelry

"Autumn delight" by Marie Fredrickson. Brief tip on making a wooden necklace. Photo. • *Better Homes and Gardens Wood.* No. 37 (Sep, 1990) p. 76.

"Belt buckle and bolo set." A description of the technique for making belt buckles and bolo tie clasps with inlaid eagle and skull designs. Photos, plans, and materials list. • *The Woodworker's Journal.* Vol. 16, No. 4 (Jul/Aug, 1992) pp. 46-49.

"Bring on the bracelets" by Ab Odnokon. Brief description of using a lathe to make wooden bracelets. Diagram, photos. • *Better Homes and Gardens Wood.* No. 33 (Feb, 1990) p. 71.

"Carve a colorful feather pin" by Larry Johnston and Harold Rosauer. Instructions to carve and paint a feather pin. Photos, patterns. • *Better Homes and Gardens Wood.* No. 55 (Oct, 1992) pp. 44-47.

"Resplendent pendant" by Jim Boelling. Explains how to make a maple pendant case for a timepiece. Photo, drawings.

• *Better Homes and Gardens Wood.* No. 44 (August, 1991) pp. 66-67.

Jewelry Boxes — *See* Boxes, Jewelry

Jig Saw Tables

"Right height for a router/jigsaw table" by C. E. Rannefeld. With plywood brackets and clamps a router/jigsaw table can match the height of the work bench. Drawing. • *Woodwork.* No. 17 (Sep/Oct, 1992) p. 12.

Jig Sawing

"Jig and templates duplicate irregular shapes" by Mike Jagielo. Brief tip on cutting irregular shapes with a jig and templates. Drawing. • *Better Homes and Gardens Wood.* No. 39 (Dec, 1990) p. 20.

Jig Saws

"Jigsaws." Helpful information on the specifications of 31 jigsaws. Photo, chart. • *Better Homes and Gardens Wood.* No. 65 (Nov, 1993) pp. 54-55.

Jigs

"Basics of locating, part five" by Edward G. Hoffman. See Vol. 9, No. 2 • *The Home Shop Machinist.* Vol. 9, No. 3 (May/Jun, 1990) pp. 57-59.

"Basics of locating, part four" by Edward G. Hoffman. An explanation of the use of jigs and fixtures to properly load and locate parts. Plans. • *The Home Shop Machinist.* Vol. 9, No. 2 (Mar/Apr, 1990) pp. 52-53.

"Jigs and fixtures, part three" by Edward Hoffman. An analysis of the importance of using proper jigs and fixtures to accurately locate and hold work. Plans. • *The Home Shop Machinist.* Vol. 9, No. 1 (Jan/Feb, 1990) pp. 54-55.

"Tool bodies, part one" by Edward G. Hoffman. A descriptive look at the types and manufactures of jigs and fixtures. Drawings. • *The Home Shop Machinist.* Vol. 12, No. 2 (Mar/Apr, 1993) pp. 48-49.

"Tool bodies, part two" by Edward G. Hoffman. See Vol. 12, No. 2 • *The Home Shop Machinist.* Vol. 12, No. 3 (May/Jun, 1993) pp. 46-47.

"Box joint jig." This article describes the process for building a jig to hold parts for cutting box joints. Photos, plans, and materials list. • *The Woodworker's Journal.* Vol. 17, No. 5 (Sep/Oct, 1993) pp. 44-47.

"Door jig" by Steve Prince. Instructions to build a jig to use when making interior doors. Drawing. • *Fine Homebuilding.* No. 65 (March, 1991) p. 32.

"Essential jigs for the table saw" by R.J. DeCristoforo. This article provides a run-down on various types of jig accessories for table saws including. pushsticks, hold-downs, extensions, etc. • *The Woodworker's Journal.* Vol. 15, No. 5 (Sep/Oct, 1991) pp. 35-39.

"An exact finger-joint jig" by Arthur W. Keely. Describes a method to make an exact jig. Drawing. • *Woodwork.* No. 15 (May/June, 1992) p. 18.

"Frame-clamping jig" by Gary Walchuk. Describes how to construct a wood frame clamp jig. Drawn plans. • *Canadian Workshop.* Vol. 13, No. 5 (Feb 1990) p. 12.

"High and mighty tablesaw jig" by Marlen Kemmet and James R. Downing. Instructions to construct a plywood jig. Photos, diagrams, materials list. • *Better Homes and Gardens Wood.* No. 62 (Aug, 1993) pp. 34-35.

"Incra jig pro" by Dennis Preston. A brief product tip on the uses of an Incra jig linear positioning device. • *The Woodworker's Journal*. Vol. 17, No. 4 (Jul/Aug, 1993) pp. 10-11.

"Jigs and fixtures, part three" by Edward Hoffman. An analysis of the importance of using proper jigs and fixtures to accurately locate and hold work. Plans. • *The Home Shop Machinist.* Vol. 9, No. 1 (Jan/Feb, 1990) pp. 54-55.

"Mitered-moulding jig" by Tom E. Moore. Explains construction of a jig to pare and fit any mitered moulding on cabinet doors. Drawing. • *Woodwork*. No. 14 (March/April) p. 10.

"Multipurpose doorpull jig" by Mark Hallock. Brief suggestion for a jig to locate the screw holes for cabinet pulls. Drawing. • *Fine Homebuilding*. No. 71 (Jan, 1992) p. 26.

"Picture-hanging jig eliminates guesswork." Brief tip on constructing a jig to make picture hanging easier and more accurate. Drawing. • *Better Homes and Gardens Wood*. No. 39 (Dec, 1990) p. 23.

"Pipe-cutting jig" by V.A. Maletic. Brief tip on making a jig for cutting a pipe. Drawing. • *Fine Homebuilding*. No. 63 (Nov, 1990) p. 26.

"The safe and simple thin-strip ripper" by Loyal Downing. Useful tip for ripping thin strips between the tablesaw blade and fence with a jig. Photos, drawings, diagrams. • *Better Homes and Gardens Wood*. No. 45 (Sep, 1991) pp. 58-59.

m-shingle jig" by John Kraft. Brief tip on making shim shingles from scraps of wood. Drawing. • *Fine Homebuilding*. No. 58 (March, 1990) p. 26.

"Tablesaws tenoning jig" by Dana Martin Batory. Assembly instructions for a jig including a cutting list. Drawings. Photos. • *Woodwork*. No. 16 (July/August, 1992) pp. 59-61.

"Tool bodies, part one" by Edward G. Hoffman. A descriptive look at the types and manufactures of jigs and fixtures. Drawings. • *The Home Shop Machinist*. Vol. 12, No. 2 (Mar/Apr, 1993) pp. 48-49.

"Tool bodies, part two" by Edward G. Hoffman. See Vol. 12, No. 2 • *The Home Shop Machinist*. Vol. 12, No. 3 (May/Jun, 1993) pp. 46-47.

"Turning jig for better bottoms" by Marlen Kemmet, Lanny Lyell and John Lea.

Describes a method to turn bottoms of plates expertly. Photo, diagrams. • *Better Homes and Gardens Wood*. No. 45 (Sep, 1991) p. 84.

"Universal table saw jig." How to make a tabletop jig for cutting miters. Photos, plans, and materials list. • *The Woodworker's Journal*. Vol. 16, No. 5 (Sep/Oct, 1992) pp. 44-47.

Jigs, Band Saw

"A universal band saw jig" by R. J. DeCristoforo. A concise descriptive article about making jigs and other accessories for band saws. Photos and plans. • *The Woodworker's Journal*. Vol. 16, No. 2 (Mar/Apr, 1992) pp. 30-33.

Jigs, Dovetail

"Six dovetail jigs." A tool review of six different jigs that act like routers in cutting dovetail joints. Photos. • The Woodworker's Journal. Vol. 14, No. 5 (Sep/Oct, 1990) pp. 32-37.

"Tilting-table dovetail jig" by Marlen Kemmet and James R. Downing. Directions to build a tilting-table to use while cutting dovetails. Photo, diagrams, drawings, materials list. • *Better Homes and Gardens Wood*. No. 51 (April, 1992) pp. 49-51.

Jigs, Doweling

"Doweling jigs" by Jim Barrett. A product description of various types of commercial jigs used to drill dowel holes. Photos. • The Woodworker's Journal. Vol. 17, No. 3 (May/Jun, 1993) pp. 21-27.

Jigs, Tenon

"Tenon jig." A thorough article providing details on the construction of a tenon jig for use with a table saw. Photo, plans, and materials list. • *The Woodworker's Journal*. Vol. 17, No. 2 (Mar/Apr, 1993) pp. 36-41.

Joiners, Biscuit

"The biscuit joiner" by Jim Barrett. This is a comprehensive assessment of the various models of biscuit joiner power tools. Photos and plans. • *The Woodworker's Journal*. Vol. 15, No. 6 (Nov/Dec, 1991) pp. 70-76.

"Buying a biscuit joiner" by Bill Krier. In-depth report on the basic components of a biscuit joiner and tips on the latest models. Photos, drawings, chart with comparisons. • *Better Homes and Gardens Wood*. No. 57 (Dec, 1992) pp. 42-47.

Joinery

Book Review: *Purpose-made joinery*. 2nd edition by E.V. Foad. Book review on a guide for apprentice cabinetmakers or architectural woodworkers. Fresno, CA: Linden Publishing Co. Inc., 317 pp. • *Fine Homebuilding*. No. 69 (Sep, 1991) pp. 108-110.

"Mortise-and-tenon joinery" by Bill Krier and Jim Boelling. Presents a method of cutting a four shouldered tenon and mating mortise without a fancy jig. Photos, drawings. • *Better Homes and Gardens Wood*. No. 48 (Dec, 1991) pp. 38-41.

"Splayed joinery" by Graham Blackburn. Detailed instructions for measuring and constructing joints with splayed sides. Diagrams. • *Woodwork*. No. 17 (Sep/Oct, 1992) pp. 56-61.

Joinery, Biscuit

"Biscuit joinery basics" by Bill Krier. Highlight how to make seven basic joints with a biscuit joiner. Photo, drawings. Sidebar on biscuit joinery with a router. • *Better Homes and Gardens Wood*. No. 57 (Dec, 1992) pp. 48-53.

Joinery, End-Grain

"Here's a plug for end-grain joinery" by Tom E. Moore. Explains how to drive screws into the end of the board to create a strong joint. Drawing. • *Better Homes and Gardens Wood*. No. 60 (April, 1993) p. 21.

Joinery, Plate

"Plate joinery on the job site" by Kevin Ireton. Offers basic instructions for plate joinery. Photos, diagrams. • *Fine Homebuilding*. No. 70 (Nov, 1991) pp. 50-53.

Joining

"Joining tops to tables and case pieces" by Roger Holmes. This articles describes the practices for joining wood tops to furniture using screws, buttons, or slide fasteners. Photos and drawings. • *The Woodworker's Journal*. Vol. 16, No. 4 (Jul/Aug, 1992) pp. 26-29.

Jointer Tables

"Dial 0 to align jointer tables" by John Platania. Brief tip on how to adjust the infeed table accurately. Drawing. • *Better Homes and Gardens Wood*. No. 60 (April, 1993) p. 14.

Jointers

"Jointers." Basic guide for selecting a jointer. Photos, illustrations, chart comparing sixteen machines. • *Better Homes and Gardens Wood*. No. 38 (Oct, 1990) pp. 66-69.

Joints

Book Review: *Joinery Basics* by Sam Allen. Review of the latest in the Basics Book Series featuring clear and descriptive information for beginning woodworkers. New York: Sterling, 128 pp. • *Woodwork*. No. 19 (Jan/Feb, 1993) p. 31.

"Router tenoning jig" by John K. Schilaty. Learn a fast and accurate way to cut tenons. Drawings. Photos. • *Woodwork*. No. 16 (July/August, 1992) pp. 56-58.

Joints, Box

"Box joint jig." This article describes the process for building a jig to hold parts for cutting box joints. Photos, plans, and materials list. • *The Woodworker's Journal*. Vol. 17, No. 5 (Sep/Oct, 1993) pp. 44-47.

"Box joints on the radial-arm saw." by C. E. Rannefeld. Brief tip on how to use radial saws to cut joints. Drawing. • *Woodwork*. No. 18 (Nov/Dec, 1992) pp. 16-18.

Joints, Dovetail

"Compound angle dovetails." A description of the method of cutting angled dovetail joints using a table saw. Drawings. • The Woodworker's Journal. Vol. 14, No. 5 (Sep/Oct, 1990) pp. 20-23.

"Hand-cut dovetails." This article offers a complete analysis of the methods, layouts, and cutting steps required for making dovetail joints. Drawings. • *The Woodworker's Journal.* Vol. 15, No. 1 (Jan/Feb, 1991) pp. 26-30.

Joints, Edge-Lap

"Edge-lap joints." Provides basic instruction on how to make edge-lap joints. Photos. • *Home Mechanix.* No. 749 (Oct, 1990) pp. 22-25.

Joints, Half-Lap

"Making half-lap joints" by Thomas H. Jones and August Capotosto. Instructive article on making half-lap joints. Photos. • *Home Mechanix.* No. 747 (July/Aug, 1990) p. 24.

Joints, Mortise and Tenon

"Boring square holes" by Roger Holmes. This article provides information on using a drill press to cut mortise-and-tenon joints. Photos and plans. • *The Woodworker's Journal.* Vol. 15, No. 3 (May/Jun, 1991) pp. 24-29.

"Shop built mortise/tenoning table" by R.J. DeCristoforo. An analysis of how to build a jig to transform a portable router into a tool for making mortise/tenon joints. Photos, plans, and materials list. • *The Woodworker's Journal.* Vol. 15, No. 5 (Sep/Oct, 1991) pp. 42-45.

Joints, Scarf

"Clamping scarf joints" by James A. Berg. Brief article on securing scarf joints. Drawing. • *Fine Homebuilding.* No. 76 (Sep, 1992) p. 28.

Joints, Slip

"Making the slip joint." A description of the method of cutting a simple slip joint, also called an open mortise and tenon joint. Drawings. • The Woodworker's Journal. Vol. 14, No. 5 (Sep/Oct, 1990) pp. 28-31.

Joints, Through-Dovetail

"Bandsawed: through-dovetail joints" by Bill Krier and Jim Downing. Detailed description of how to cut a through-dovetail joint with a jig. Photos, drawings. • *Better Homes and Gardens Wood.* No. 51 (April, 1992) pp. 44-48.

Joists

"Beefing up old joists" by Richard E. Reed. Brief tip on strengthening old joists. Drawing. • *Fine Homebuilding.* No. 62 (Sep, 1990) p. 28.

"On beefing up joists" by Daniel Brown. Provides suggestions on beefing up joists set between ripped plywood. Drawing. • *Fine Homebuilding.* No. 68 (July, 1991) p. 16.

"Strengthening old joists" by David Wallace. Handy tip for beefing up old joists. Drawing. • *Fine Homebuilding.* No. 64 (Jan, 1991) p. 30.

Joists, Ceiling

"Ceiling joists for a hip roof" by Larry Haun. Offers three problem-solving framing techniques for making ceiling joists for a hip roof. Photos. • *Fine Homebuilding.* No. 69 (Sep, 1991) pp. 44 45.

Jones, Fay

Book Review: *Fay Jones* by Robert Adams Ivy, Jr. Book review of a compilation of many of Fay Jones' works. Photo. Washington, D.C.: American Institute of Architects Press, 224 pp. • *Fine Homebuilding.* No. 78 (Jan, 1993) p. 110.

K

Kachina Dolls

"Carve Shalako" by Bobbie K. Thurman. Learn how to carve a Southwest Native American symbol called a kachina doll. Photo, pattern. • *Better Homes and Gardens Wood.* No. 53 (Aug, 1992) p. 53.

Kalimba

"Kalimba." A description of the process for building a Kalimba - an African thumb piano. Photos and materials list. • *The Woodworker's Journal.* Vol. 16, No. 2 (Mar/Apr, 1992) pp. 48 49.

Key Chains

"Letter perfect key chains." Scrollsaw a letter key chain as a gift or for yourself with these tips. Photo, drawing, illustration. • *Better Homes and Gardens Wood.* No. 46 (Oct, 1991) p. 79.

Keys, Fixture

"Fixture keys" by Edward G. Hoffman. An examination of the use of machined keys as aids in properly locating work pieces. Drawings. • *The Home Shop Machinist.* Vol. 11, No. 4 (Jul/Aug, 1992) pp. 58-59.

Kitchen Cabinets

"Beyond the box" by Sharon Ross. Innovative options for creating more cabinet space. Photos. • *Practical Homeowner.* Vol. VI, No. 3 (March, 1991) pp. 46-49.

"Cabinet shopper's survival guide" by Lisa Harbatkin. A list of do's and don'ts of buying kitchen cabinets. • *Practical Homeowner.* Vol. V, No. 6 (Sep, 1990) pp. 60-63.

"Cold cabinets" by Henry Spies. Offers a solution to cold kitchen cabinets during the winter. Drawing. • *Home Mechanix.* No. 774 (April, 1993) p. 95.

"Installing kitchen cabinets" by Matt Phair. Offers do-it-yourself directions to construct kitchen cabinets. Drawings, diagrams. • *Home Mechanix.* No. 743 (March, 1990) pp. 52-55, 81,87.

"Jazz-up your kitchen" by Jerry Walker. Provides advice on replacing wood kitchen cabinets. Photos. • *Canadian Workshop.* Vol. 13, No. 4 (Jan 1990) pp. 32-37.

"Kitchen cabinetry" by Judith Trotsky. Presents two creative designs that help solve layout problems. Photos, plans, diagrams. • *Home Mechanix.* No. 749 (Oct, 1990) pp. 42-47.

"Kitchen cupboard facelift" by Coralie Adams. Furnishes those considering replacement of their kitchen cabinets with insight into the work involved with the projects, and other helpful hints. List of materials. Photos. • *Canadian Workshop.* Vol. 13, No. 5 (Feb 1990) pp. 23-29.

"Manufactured kitchen cabinets" by Kevin Ireton. Covers a wide range of choices for kitchen cabinets. Photos, diagrams. Sidebar on certified cabinets. • *Fine Homebuilding.* No. 65 (March, 1991) pp. 69-74.

"Refacing kitchen cabinets" by Rex Alexander and Herrick Kimball. Offers tips on giving kitchen cabinets a face-lift. Photos. Sidebar on another option: pressure-sensitive veneer. • *Fine Homebuilding.* No. 81 (May, 1993) pp. 72-77.

"Stock options" by Don Vandervort. A guide to picking kitchen cabinets. Photos and plans. • *Practical Homeowner.* (May/June, 1992) pp. 66-71.

Kitchen Islands

"Fantasy islands" by Joseph Truini. Demonstrates how to build a custom kitchen island using stock cabinets. Photos, diagrams. Sidebar on design guide to kitchen islands. • *Home Mechanix.* No. 759 (Oct, 1991) pp. 52-56.

"Hideaway island" by Matthew Phair. Offers a design and directions to build a kitchen island that can be stored as a hideaway when not in use. Photos, diagrams. • *Home Mechanix.* No. 779 (Oct, 1993) pp. 54-57.

"Your own special island" by Ted Jones. Provides information on creating a design for a kitchen island. Photo, drawings. Sidebar on how to design and build an island with a cooking cove. • *Home Mechanix.* No. 772 (Feb, 1993) pp. 62-67.

Kitchen Projects

"Four easy-to-make kitchen projects." Four simple designs for kitchen cooling racks, salad tongs, serving boat, and recipe box. Photos, plans, and materials list. • *The Woodworker's Journal.* Vol. 15, No. 5 (Sep/Oct, 1991 pp. 58-66.

"Noodle cutter" by Russ Hurt. Describes how to turn a noodle cutter on a lathe. Photo, diagram, pattern, recipe for noodles. • *Better Homes and Gardens Wood.* No. 46 (Oct, 1991) pp. 72-73, 88.

Kitchen Utensils

"Wooden kitchen utensils" by Diane Beetler. Instructions for carving kitchen utensils. Drawing. Photos. • *Woodwork.* No. 15 (May/June, 1992) pp. 56-58.

Kitchens

"31 new rules for kitchen design" by Pat McMillan. Detailed article on the latest planning tips for designing kitchens. Photos, plans. • *Home Mechanix.* No. 769 (Oct, 1992) pp. 38-46.

Book Review: *The Smart Kitchen: How to Design a Comfortable, Safe, Energy-Efficient, and Environment-Friendly Workspace* by David Goldbeck. Book review of a work on designing kitchens. New York: Kodansha International Ltd., 156 pp. • *Fine Homebuilding.* No. 58 (March, 1990) p. 106.

"Building a butternut kitchen" by Rex Alexander. Describes the directions to build a kitchen with hand-planed hardwoods. Photos, diagrams. Sidebar on

a simple tenoning jig. Sidebar on solid wood and humidity. • *Fine Homebuilding.* No. 69 (Sep, 1991) pp. 50-54.

"A cantilevered kitchen addition" by Robert Gleason. Describes adding a 4-ft. by 30-ft. addition to the back of a two-story gambrel-roof house. Photos, drawings. • *Fine Homebuilding.* No. 70 (Nov, 1991) pp. 82-85.

"Character at cost" by Charlie Posoneil. A colorful and inexpensive kitchen remodeling project. Photos. • *Practical Homeowner.* (March/April, 1992) pp. 60-61.

"Design at a discount" by Pat McMillan. Discusses ways to get a design for a kitchen at lower rates. Photos, plans. Sidebar on tips for getting design help. • *Home Mechanix.* No. 759 (Oct, 1991) pp. 44-50.

"Eco-kitchen" by Timothy O. Bakke. Offers an example of an environmentally friendly remodeled kitchen. Photos, plans. Sidebar on the ultimate recycler. • *Home Mechanix.* No. 765 (May, 1992) pp. 56-60.

"The heart of the house" by Bill Mastin. Details the process of merging a kitchen and breakfast room. Photos, plans, diagrams. • *Fine Homebuilding.* No. 63 (Nov, 1990) pp. 54-57.

"Kitchen basics" by Stephan Keach. How to design functional kitchens in tight spaces. Photos. • *Practical Homeowner.* (Nov/Dec, 1992) pp. 42-45.

"Kitchen planning made perfect" by Elaine Petrowski. Offers professional layout strategies for an efficient kitchen work space. Plans, drawings. • *Home Mechanix.* No. 743 (March, 1990) pp. 34-37, 81.

"Kitchens that work" by Ann Arnott. Remodeling solutions for problems in kitchens. Photos, plans. • *Home Mechanix.* No. 743 (March, 1990) pp. 38-45.

"Liberating the compact kitchen" by Thomas F. Sweeney. A new product guide

for space saving appliances. Photos.
• *Practical Homeowner.* Vol. VI, No. 7 (Sep, 1991) pp. 49-51.

"More than a kitchen" by Pat McMillan. Offers design ideas to create a multi-function kitchen center. Photos, plans. • *Home Mechanix.* No. 762 (Feb, 1992) pp. 64-67.

"New kitchen for an old house" by Philip S. Sollman. Presents a remodeling idea for an old house adding a kitchen with cherry cabinets. Photos, drawing. • *Fine Homebuilding.* No. 71 (Jan, 1992) pp. 42-45.

"Open country" by Charlie Posoneil. Remodeling a 1940s kitchen to achieve a sense of openness. Photos. • *Practical Homeowner.* (Jul/Aug, 1992) pp. 73-75.

"Quieter kitchens" by Pat McMillan. Describes how to add noise-absorbing acoustical materials to kitchen walls, ceilings, and floors as well as other methods to reduce noise. Photos, drawings. Sidebar on how to build a sound-rated door. • *Home Mechanix.* No. 770 (Nov, 1992) pp. 68-74.

"Site-built kitchen" by Tony Simmonds. Describes how to construct base cabinets and drawers for a site-built kitchen. Photos, diagrams, drawings. • *Fine Homebuilding.* No. 79 (March, 1993) pp. 76-79.

"Space-smart kitchens" by Michael Hartnett. Presents three kitchen storage designs. Photos, diagrams. • *Home Mechanix.* No. 780 (Nov, 1993) pp. 50-54.

"Three smart money kitchens" by Charlie Posoneil. A description of three do-it-yourself kitchen projects. Photos and plans. • *Practical Homeowner.* (May/June, 1992) pp. 56-65.

"Universal kitchens and baths." Provides tips for creating accessibility for handicapped or other special needs. Photos, drawings. • *Home Mechanix.* No. 781 (Dec/Jan, 1993-94) pp. 66 70, 84.

"Unusual kitchens" by Pat McMillan. Explains ways to cut costs of building custom cabinets when remodeling a kitchen. Photos, diagrams, plans. Sidebar on perfecting the pediments and playing the angles. Sidebar on creating a chase. • *Home Mechanix.* No. 752 (Feb, 1991) pp. 48-54.

Kitchens, Outdoor

"Cookout kitchens" by Matthew Phair. Detailed designs for three outdoor cooking centers. Photos, diagrams. Sidebar on barbecue tune-up. • *Home Mechanix.* No. 776 (June, 1993) pp. 62-65.

"Kitchen in the garden" by Joseph R. Provey. Complete instructions for building an outdoor kitchen in a small pavilion. Photos and plans. • *Practical Homeowner.* Vol. V, No. 3 (April, 1990) pp. 46-48.

Kitchens--Lighting

"The light touch for kitchens" by Pat McMillan. Presents two designs to bring a balance of natural and artificial light into a kitchen. Photos, plans. Sidebar on energy conservation tips. Sidebar on lighting tips. • *Home Mechanix.* No. 754 (April, 1991) pp. 36-42.

Kneewalls

"Adding kneewalls" by Peter H. Guimond. Offers a method of adding kneewalls to an attic. • *Fine Homebuilding.* No. 74 (May, 1992) p. 14.

Knives, Jointer

"How to install jointer knives" by Bill Krier. Brief tip on installing jointer knives. Drawings. • *Better Homes and Gardens Wood.* No. 52 (June, 1992) pp. 56-57.

Knots

"Cargo knots" by Glenn Bowan. Brief article on knots used to tie down truck loads. Drawing. • *Fine Homebuilding.* No. 78 (Jan, 1993) p. 28.

Knurling

"Knurls and knurling" by Eric Carver. An explanation of the technique of impressing a design onto a cylinder of metal—known as knurling. Photos and plans. • *The Home Shop Machinist.* Vol. 11, No. 2 (Mar/Apr, 1992) pp. 38-41.

L

Lacquers

"Lacquer that's music to your ears." Identifies some of the characteristics of fine-quality, durable lacquers. Photos. • *Better Homes and Gardens Wood.* No. 41 (Feb, 1991) pp. 52-53.

"Water-based lacquers: the safe finish that goes on fast." Informative suggestions on using water-based lacquers including a buying guide. • *Better Homes and Gardens Wood.* No. 34 (April, 1990) pp. 42-43.

Ladder Baskets

"Basket case" by Paul Penfield. Handy tip to make a basket to attach to the top of a ladder, avoiding trips up and down. Drawing. • *Fine Homebuilding.* No. 61 (July, 1990) p. 26.

Ladders

"Energy-efficient attic access" by Jeff Greef. Informative article on installing energy-efficient attic ladders. • *Home Mechanix.* No. 771 (Dec/Jan, 1992-93) pp. 8-9, 80.

"Ladders" by Bruce Greenlaw. In-depth article on how to select ladders and how to use them. Photos. Sidebar on safety resources. • *Fine Homebuilding.* No. 84 (Nov, 1993) pp. 50-55.

Laminates, Plastic

"Repairing plastic laminate" by Thomas H. Jones. Explains how to repair edges or cosmetic damage on plastic laminate.

Drawings, photos. • *Home Mechanix.* No. 744 (April, 1990) pp. 18-21.

Laminating

"Laminating structural timbers" by Stephen Smulski. Offers information on laminating boards together to make posts and beams. • *Fine Homebuilding.* No. 64 (Jan, 1991) p. 20.

Lamps

"Spotlight your work with a reading lamp" by Roger Jewell. Brief tip on mounting a lamp to work areas. Drawing. • *Better Homes and Gardens Wood.* No. 56 (Nov, 1992) p. 20.

Lamps, Hurricane

"Lathe-turned hurricane lamp." A simple design for a classic Christmas gift. Photo and plans. • *The Woodworker's Journal.* Vol. 15, No. 6 (Nov/Dec, 1991) pp. 44-45.

Lamps, Oil

"Decorator oil lamps" by Warren Vienneau. Instructions to turn two tulip-shaped oil lamps. Photos, patterns, drawings. • *Better Homes and Gardens Wood.* No. 51 (April, 1992) pp. 64 65.

Lamps, Table

"Affordable elegance" by Marlen Kemmet and Tim Connors. Describes the process of making a quality table lamp for under $50. Photo, diagrams, materials list. • *Better Homes and Gardens Wood.* No. 56 (Nov, 1992) pp. 58-59.

"Colonial-style ratchet table lamp." Clear instructions and a simple design for an adjustable height table lamp. Photos, plans, and materials list. • *The Woodworker's Journal.* Vol. 16, No. 2 (Mar/Apr, 1992) pp. 34-37.

"Table lamp." A brief tip on how to make a columnar table lamp using a lathe and router. Photo, plans, and materials list. • *The Woodworker's Journal.* Vol. 17, No. 2 (Mar/Apr, 1993) pp. 33-35.

Landscaping

"Build a garden pond" by Jim Barrett. Offers instructions to build a garden pond in your own backyard. Photos, drawing. Sidebar on concrete coverup. • *Home Mechanix.* No. 747 (July/Aug, 1990) pp. 42-44.

"Designing for a hot climate" by Thomas Leach. Presents a design focusing on the climate control and landscaping. Photos, plans, drawings. Sidebar on building the shadeshelters. • *Fine Homebuilding.* No. 79 (March, 1993) pp. 70-74.

"A front yard of food, flowers, and friends" by Susan Bryan. A plan for converting a front lawn into a garden. Photos. • *Practical Homeowner.* (Jul/Aug, 1992) pp. 66-71.

"Laid-back landscape" by Larry Carlsen. Inexpensive landscaping ideas. Photos. • *Practical Homeowner.* Vol. VI, No. 6 (Jul/Aug, 1991) p. 54.

"Low-water landscapes" by Jeff Boll. How to choose the right plants for low moisture environments. Photos and plans. • *Practical Homeowner.* Vol. V, No. 4 (June, 1990) pp. 26-28.

"Protecting your trees" by Linda P. Williams. A guide to protecting trees during construction periods. Photos. • *Practical Homeowner.* Vol. IV, No. 9 (Jan, 1990) pp. 58-59.

"Reclaiming your front yard" by Thomas Sweeney. Three innovative front yard landscaping plans. Photos and plans. • *Practical Homeowner.* Vol. VI, No. 6 (Jul/Aug, 1991) pp. 48-53.

"Smart technologies for the outdoors" by Jeff Ball. Practical landscaping ideas for a small yard. Drawing. • *Practical Homeowner.* Vol. V, No. 1 (Feb, 1990) pp. 32-35.

"The well-planted deck" by Thomas F. Sweeney. Tips on properly landscaping the area around a new deck. Photos. • *Practical Homeowner.* Vol. VI, No. 8 (Oct, 1991) pp. 36-40.

"Yardscaping" by Joseph Truini. Provides a glimpse at an example of creating a yardscape complete with a gazebo, sun deck, patio, lattice screens, and tiered planters. Photos, diagrams, drawings. • *Home Mechanix.* No. 775 (May, 1993) pp. 62-69.

See Also Lawn Care; Yards

Lanterns

"Wall lantern" by Marlen Kemmet and James R. Downing. Instructions to build an outdoor lantern with stained glass, a decorative grill, and a large overhanging roof. Photo, diagrams, materials list. • *Better Homes and Gardens Wood.* No. 62 (Aug, 1993) pp. 69-73.

Lasers

"The lure of the laser" by Peter J. Stephano. Describes costs and features of a laser machine and introduces the uses for a laser in woodworking. Photos. Sidebar on lasers and hot light. • *Better Homes and Gardens Wood.* No. 37 (Sep, 1990) pp. 74-75.

Lateral Supports

"Lateral support for wood beams" by Christopher DeBlois. Provides rules on lateral support for wood beams. Chart. • *Fine Homebuilding.* No. 70 (Nov, 1991) p. 14.

Lathe Dogs

"Making a catch plate" by Rudy Kouhoupt. A description of the use of a protective catch plate in conjunction with a lathe dog. Photos and plans. • *The Home Shop Machinist.* Vol. 11, No. 4 (Jul/Aug, 1992) pp. 51-54.

"Two useful lathe dogs" by Rudy Kouhoupt. This brief article describes the use of devices called lathe dogs to drive a work piece between the centers of a lathe in order to machine it. Photos. • *The Home Shop Machinist.* Vol. 10, No. 5 (Sep/Oct, 1991) pp. 48-51.

"An unusual lathe dog" by Frank A. McLean. A how-to article for making a lathe dog. Plans. • *The Home Shop Machinist.* Vol. 11, No. 3 (May/Jun, 1992) pp. 50-52.

Lathe Drives

"An improved lathe drive" by G. Wadham. How to improve lathe operations by modifying pulleys and drive shafts. Photos. • *The Home Shop Machinist.* Vol. 11, No. 5 (Sep/Oct, 1992) pp. 24-29.

Lathe Rests

"A useful follower rest." Instructions for building a follower rest for a lathe. Photo, plans and materials list. • *The Home Shop Machinist.* Vol. 10, No. 2 (Mar/Apr, 1991) pp. 28-29.

Lathe Tables

"A lathe table" by Rudy Kouhoupt. A simple set of instructions for making a rectangular work table for a lathe. Photos and plans. • *The Home Shop Machinist.* Vol. 12, No. 3 (May/Jun, 1993) pp. 43-45.

Lathe Tools--Sharpening

"To hone or not to hone" by Jeff Parsons. Discusses how to properly sharpen lathe tools. Photos. • *Canadian Workshop.* Vol. 15, No. 1 (Oct 1991) p. 9.

Lathes

"Benchtop lathes" by Jim Barrett. This is a new product review of six different models of benchtop lathe. Photos. • *The Woodworker's Journal.* Vol. 17, No. 5 (Sep/Oct, 1993) pp. 55 60.

"Combination tools-plus" by Olev Edur. Evaluates the various features of the Shopsmith Power Station. Photos. • *Canadian Workshop.* Vol. 13, No. 4 (Jan 1990) pp. 25-27.

"Enco 12X26" geared head engine lathe" by Clifton Lawson. This article offers a thorough review of the features of an Enco lathe. Photos. • *The Home Shop Machinist.* Vol. 12, No. 6 (Nov/Dec, 1993) pp. 44-49.

"The grizzly 8X18" lathe" by Glenn M. Schultz. A product guide to a Grizzly Imports 8X18" lathe. Photos. • *The Home Shop Machinist.* Vol. 12, No. 1 (Jan/Feb, 1993) pp. 39-43.

"A larger steady rest" by Glenn Wilson. A description of the steps required to construct a sheet metal rest for use with a lathe. Photos. • *The Home Shop Machinist.* Vol. 9, No. 1 (Jan/Feb, 1990) pp. 24-28.

"Lathes." Analysis of the basic components of a lathe. Photos, illustration, chart comparing 29 varieties. • *Better Homes and Gardens Wood.* No. 38 (Oct, 1990) pp. 70-73.

"Low cost lathes" by Bill Krier. In-depth analysis of ten lathes priced under $600. Photos, chart. • *Better Homes and Gardens Wood.* No. 64 (Oct, 1993) pp. 42-47.

"Poshing up a Taiwanese lathe" by Walt Warren and Guy Lautard. This article offers advice on how to upgrade the components of a Taiwanese-built lathe. Photos. • *The Home Shop Machinist.* Vol. 10, No. 3 (May/Jun, 1991) pp. 23-27.

"A spigot chuck" by Nick Cook. This offers a simple design for a wooden lathe chuck. Photo and plans. • *The Woodworker's Journal.* Vol. 15, No. 4 (Jul/Aug, 1991) pp. 40-41.

Video Review: *Fun at the Lathe* by John I. Timby. Video review on how to use the lathe for wood projects. Deming, NM: Author (PO Box 1904) 2hrs. • *Woodwork.* No. 18 (Nov/Dec, 1992) p. 31.

Lathes, Jeweler's

"Topics in micromachining" by Ted Roubal. This article offers a product explanation of the uses of a jeweler's lathe. Photos. • *The Home Shop Machinist.* Vol. 9, No. 3 (May/Jun, 1990) pp. 20-23.

Lathework

"Adapting the myford" by R.W. Smith. This article describes the process of using a T-rast to adapt a bench lathe for hand turning. Photos and drawings. • *The Home Shop Machinist*. Vol. 11, No. 3 (May/Jun, 1992) pp. 26-31.

"A bell chuck for your lathe" by Frank A. McLean. A description of the advantages and disadvantages of using a bell chuck as opposed to a usual four-jaw independent chuck. Photos and plans. • *The Home Shop Machinist*. Vol. 11, No. 4 (Jul/Aug, 1992) pp. 54-59.

"Building and turning a bricklaid bowl" by Robert Belke. A description of the method for making a round bowl constructed of wood segments which are assembled and turned on a lathe. Photos, plans, and materials list. • *The Woodworker's Journal*. Vol. 17, No. 6 (Nov/Dec, 1993) pp. 32-35.

"Checking lathe alignment" by Rudy Kouhoupt. A guide to the steps necessary for insuring that a lathe's headstock and tailstock are aligned. Photos and plans. • *The Home Shop Machinist*. Vol. 11, No. 5 (Sep/Oct, 1992) pp. 48-51.

"Collet chuck turning" by Nick Cook. How to adapt a machinist's collet chuck to hold wood workpieces on a lathe. Photos and plans. • The Woodworker's Journal. Vol. 16, No. 3 (May/Jun, 1992) pp. 26-31.

"Dutch turning." A descriptive article of how to achieve the appearance of lathework by using power drills and saws. Photos, plans, and drawings. • *The Woodworker's Journal*. Vol. 16, No. 1 (Jan/Feb, 1992) pp. 17-22.

"Faux-turned vessels." An in-depth article detailing the procedure for making round bowls in sections without the use of a lathe. Photos, plans, and drawings. • *The Woodworker's Journal*. Vol. 15, No. 6 (Nov/Dec, 1991) pp. 26-31.

"A fixture plate for a lathe or mill" by Ray E. Starnes. Brief tips on constructing a fixture plate. Photos. • *The Home Shop Machinist*. Vol. 10, No. 2 (Mar/Apr, 1991) pp. 30-31.

"From blank bowl to finished bowl" by Bill Krier and Marlen Kemmet. Step-by-step coverage of the process of turning a bowl. Photos, drawings. • *Better Homes and Gardens Wood*. No. 57 (Dec, 1992) pp. 77-80.

"An improved lathe drive" by G. Wadham. How to improve lathe operations by modifying pulleys and drive shafts. Photos. • *The Home Shop Machinist*. Vol. 11, No. 5 (Sep/Oct, 1992) pp. 24-29.

"Knockout bar" by Jack R. Thompson. A quick tip on making a knockout bar for a lathe. Photo and plans. • *The Home Shop Machinist*. Vol. 12, No. 3 (May/Jun, 1993) p. 37.

"Lathe carriage stop" by Ira J. Neill. A brief description on manufacturing a graduated carriage stop for lathe units. Photos and plans. • *The Home Shop Machinist*. Vol. 10, No. 1 (Jan/Feb, 1991) pp. 36-37.

"Lathe operations on a vertical mill" by Stephan Thomas. An examination of the uses of a vertical spindle type milling machine for lathe operations. Photos. • *The Home Shop Machinist*. Vol. 9, No. 1 (Jan/Feb, 1990) pp. 29-33.

"Lathe operations on a vertical mill" by Stephan Thomas. See Vol. 9, No. 1 • *The Home Shop Machinist*. Vol. 9, No. 2 (Mar/Apr, 1990) pp. 33-37.

"A lathe table" by Rudy Kouhoupt. A simple set of instructions for making a rectangular work table for a lathe. Photos and plans. • *The Home Shop Machinist*. Vol. 12, No. 3 (May/Jun, 1993) pp. 43-45.

"Making a catch plate" by Rudy Kouhoupt. A description of the use of a protective catch plate in conjunction with a lathe dog. Photos and plans. • *The Home Shop Machinist*. Vol. 11, No. 4 (Jul/Aug, 1992) pp. 51-54.

"Making a cutoff toolholder, part one" by Rudy Kouhoupt. A how-to guide for making a holder for a lathe cut-off tool. Photos and plans. • *The Home Shop Machinist.* Vol. 12, No. 4 (Jul/Aug, 1993) pp. 49-51.

"Milling on the lathe" by Frank A. McLean. A description of how to set milling attachments on a standard lathe. Photos. • *The Home Shop Machinist.* Vol. 9, No. 4 (Jul/Aug, 1990) pp. 51-53.

"Pewter-topped potpourri bowl" by C.I. Gatzke. Brief article on how to turn a potpourri bowl. Photo, pattern, drawing, materials list. • *Better Homes and Gardens Wood.* No. 52 (June, 1992) p. 42.

"A quick-change tool post system, part one" by Richard Torgerson. This descriptive article looks at the different types of quick-change tool post systems available. Photos. • *The Home Shop Machinist.* Vol. 12, No. 4 (Jul/Aug, 1993) pp. 36-42.

"A quick-change tool post system, part three" by Richard Torgerson. See Vol. 12, No. 4 • *The Home Shop Machinist.* Vol. 12, No. 6 (Nov/Dec, 1993) pp. 39-43.

"A quick-change tool post system, part two" by Richard Torgerson. See Vol. 12, No. 4 • *The Home Shop Machinist.* Vol. 12, No. 5 (Sep/Oct, 1993) pp. 39-43.

"Radius turning attachment, part one" by Glenn L. Wilson. The article describes the uses of a radius attachment for turning spherical objects. Photos and plans. • *The Home Shop Machinist.* Vol. 11, No. 4 (Jul/Aug, 1992) pp. 20-26.

"Radius turning attachment, part two" by Glenn L. Wilson. See Vol. 11, No. 4 • *The Home Shop Machinist.* Vol. 11, No. 5 (Sep/Oct, 1992) pp. 18-23.

"Remounting a four-jaw chuck" by G. Wodham. Advice on increasing the capabilities of a lathe by remounting and increasing the holding capacity of the chuck. Photos and plans. • *The Home Shop*

Machinist. Vol. 10, No. 1 (Jan/Feb, 1991) pp. 25-29.

"Starting turning, part five" by Audrey Mason. See Vol. 11, No. 2 • *The Home Shop Machinist.* Vol. 12, No. 5 (Sep/Oct, 1993) pp. 30-38.

"Starting turning, part four" by Audrey Mason. See Vol. 11, No. 2 • *The Home Shop Machinist.* Vol. 11, No. 6 (Nov/Dec, 1992) pp. 24-33.

"Starting turning, part one" by Audrey Mason. An introduction into the use of the lathe. Photos and plans. • *The Home Shop Machinist.* Vol. 11, No. 2 (Mar/Apr, 1992) pp. 20-28.

"Starting turning, part three" by Audrey Mason. See Vol. 11, No. 2 • *The Home Shop Machinist.* Vol. 11, No. 4 (Jul/Aug, 1992) pp. 27-33.

"Starting turning, part two" by Audrey Mason. See Vol. 11, No. 2 • *The Home Shop Machinist.* Vol. 11, No. 3 (May/Jun, 1992) pp. 19-25.

"Tailstock attachment" by Frank A. McLean. A brief guide to machining arbors as tailstock attachments for lathes. Plans. • *The Home Shop Machinist.* Vol. 12, No. 2 (Mar/Apr, 1993) pp. 36-38.

"Tailstock attachments for the lathe, part one" by Frank A. McLean. A guide to the manufacture of a variety of tailstock arbors and die holders. Photos and plans. • *The Home Shop Machinist.* Vol. 12, No. 1 (Jan/Feb, 1993) pp. 46-48.

"Thread cutting on the lathe" by Rudy Kouhoupt. An explanation of how to use a lathe to cut threads. Photos and plans. • *The Home Shop Machinist.* Vol. 12, No. 1 (Jan/Feb, 1993) pp. 18 25.

"A thread tooling system and wiggler for the lathe" by D.E. Johnson. A thorough guide to the author's system for cutting threads on a lathe. Photo, plans, and materials list. • *The Home Shop Machinist.* Vol. 11, No. 6 (Nov/Dec, 1992) pp. 18-23.

"Turning a morse taper, part three" by Rudy Kouhoupt. See Vol. 10, No. 6 • *The Home Shop Machinist*. Vol. 11, No. 2 (Mar/Apr, 1992) pp. 42-44.

"Turning Australian wood: The Eucalyptus Slab Bowl" by Jeff Parsons. Provides detailed description of the steps associated with the turning of eucalyptus wood to form a bowl. Photos. • *Canadian Workshop*. Vol. 13, No. 5 (Feb 1990) pp. 8-9.

"Two useful lathe dogs" by Rudy Kouhoupt. This brief article describes the use of devices called lathe dogs to drive a work piece between the centers of a lathe in order to machine it. Photos. • *The Home Shop Machinist*. Vol. 10, No. 5 (Sep/Oct, 1991) pp. 48-51.

"An unusual lathe dog" by Frank A. McLean. A how-to article for making a lathe dog. Plans. • *The Home Shop Machinist*. Vol. 11, No. 3 (May/Jun, 1992) pp. 50-52.

"A use for an odd grease fitting" by Russell H. Smith. Solves the problem of turning a bedpost twice as long as the lathe bed with an old grease fitting. • *Woodwork*. No. 19 (Jan/Feb, 1993) pp. 18-20.

"A useful follower rest" Instructions for building a follower rest for a lathe. Photo, plans and materials list. • *The Home Shop Machinist*. Vol. 10, No. 2 (Mar/Apr, 1991) pp. 28-29.

"Using a cutoff tool" by Rudy Kouhoupt. A guide to the proper use of a lathe cut-off tool. Photos and plans. • *The Home Shop Machinist*. Vol. 12, No. 5 (Sep/Oct, 1993) pp. 46-48.

"Vacuum turning" by Nick Cook. A detailed examination of the use of vacuum systems to hold an object on a lathe without using fasteners. Photos and plans. • *The Woodworker's Journal*. Vol. 16, No. 5 (Sep/Oct, 1992) pp. 24-32.

Laundry Rooms

"Relocating the laundry" by Elaine Martin Petrowski. Presents three designs for upstairs laundry rooms. Photos, diagrams. Sidebar on design tips for efficiency and safety. • *Home Mechanix*. No. 758 (Sep, 1991) pp. 59-62.

Lawn and Garden Equipment

"Your next yard tool" by Ken Boness. A guide to everything about brushcutters. Photos. • *Practical Homeowner*. Vol. V, No. 1 (Feb, 1990) pp. 64-72.

"The no waste yard" by Michael Ferrara. A description of all the tools and equipment needed to effectively recycle yard waste. Photos and plans. • *Practical Homeowner*. Vol. VI, No. 3 (March, 1991) pp. 66-81.

"Yard power" by Mike Ferara. A descriptive article about all the newest in lawn and garden power tools. Photos. • *Practical Homeowner*. Vol. V, No. 2 (Mar, 1990) pp. 44-58.

Lawn Care

"Lawn care safety" by John Harrington. A basic guide to the use of lawn chemicals. • *Practical Homeowner*. Vol. V, No. 5 (August, 1990) pp. 14-19.

"Renovate your lawn" by Jeff Ball. An explanation of the seven steps in overseeding a lawn. Drawings. • *Practical Homeowner*. Vol. V, No. 6 (Sep, 1990) pp. 28-30.

"Waste not" by Jeff Ball. Description of how to build a home compost bin. Drawings. • *Practical Homeowner*. Vol. V, No. 8 (Nov/Dec, 1990) pp. 24-26.

"Winning the weed war." A basic guide to the use of herbicides. Photos. • *Practical Homeowner*. Vol. V, No. 5 (August, 1990) pp. 30-33.

Lead Dust

"Deadly lead dust" by Timothy O. Bakke. Updated report on the health risks of lead dust in homes. • *Home Mechanix.* No. 759 (Oct, 1991) pp. 25,39.

Leaks

"Double joist cause leak" by Will Rainey. Handy tip to prevent leakage on a deck. Drawing. • *Fine Homebuilding.* No. 61 (July, 1990) p. 26.

"Sherlock ohms" by Jim Albertson. Brief suggestion for finding a leak electrically. • *Fine Homebuilding.* No. 76 (Sep, 1992) p. 30.

Leaks, Sub-Surface Piping

"Slab leak" by Henry Spies. Brief tip on how to locate leaks in sub-surface piping. • *Home Mechanix.* No. 757 (July/Aug, 1991) p. 81.

Legs, Cabriole

"Making a cabriole leg" Provides complete specifications and outline for making a furniture leg in the animal shaped, or cabriole, style.   Plans and drawings. • *The Woodworker's Journal.* Vol. 15, No. 1 (Jan/ Feb, 1991) pp. 23-25.

Letter Boxes

"Cherry letterbox" by Rick and Ellen Butz. A description of a cherry wood letterbox with a carved relief of a mountain scene on the front panel. Photos, plans, and materials list. • *The Woodworker's Journal.* Vol. 17, No. 4 (Jul/Aug, 1993) pp. 56-60.

"Superstamp letter holder." Scrollsaw an enlarged postage stamp to hold letters. Photos, pattern. • *Better Homes and Gardens Wood.* No. 62 (Aug, 1993) pp. 56-57.

See Also Boxes

Letter Holders

"Special delivery: letter/napkin holder" by Keith Raivo Designs. Provides construction plans for a walnut and oak letter/napkin holder. Photo, diagram, drawing, materials list. • *Better Homes and Gardens Wood.* No. 45 (Sep, 1991) pp. 76-77.

Letter Openers

"Fun-to-fashion letter openers" by Deborah Doyle. Directions and full-sized patterns to make letter openers. Photo, patterns. • *Better Homes and Gardens Wood.* No. 54 (Sep, 1992) pp. 52-53.

Lettering, Ornamental

"Ornamental lettering" by Mark Van Stone. Brief instructions for painting lettering on interior walls. Photo. • *Fine Homebuilding.* No. 72 (March, 1992) pp. 48-49.

Levelers

"Lag-bolt cabinet leveler" by Don Jensen. Describes an inexpensive way to level a cabinet without using a shim. Drawing. • *Fine Homebuilding.* No. 81 (May, 1993) p. 26.

Leveling

"How to level glued-up stock." Brief, helpful tip on leveling glue-ups without removing much material. Drawings • *Better Homes and Gardens Wood.* No. 59 (Feb, 1993) pp. 57-.

Levels

"Spirit levels" by Dan Rockhill. In-depth article on how to select a level and maintain it. Photos. Sidebar on glass vials. Sidebar on specialty levels. • *Fine Homebuilding.* No. 58 (March, 1990) pp. 42-45.

"Tuning an adjustable level" by Jim Tolpin. Brief tip on checking a level to make sure it is adjusted properly. Drawings. • *Fine Homebuilding.* No. 81 (May, 1993) p. 28.

Lichens

"Roof lichens" by Henry Spies. Brief tip on removing lichens from an asphalt-shingle roof. • *Home Mechanix.* No. 754 (April, 1991) p. 92.

Lifts

"Beam-stair" by Robert Gay. Construction plans to make a beam-stair for making short lifts. Drawing. • *Fine Homebuilding.* No. 70 (Nov, 1991) p. 32.

"A water counterbalance" by Max Wolf. Describes a water lift useful for up to 1,000 lbs. of stock. Drawing. • *Fine Homebuilding.* No. 62 (Sep, 1990) p. 30.

Light Bulbs

"The right light" by Michael Cala. Offers information on how to select the right bulb for economy and effect. Photos, charts. Sidebar on how to calculate savings. • *Home Mechanix.* No. 741 (Jan, 1990) pp. 78-82.

Light Switches

"Light switch glitches" by Merle Henkenius. Presents five most common trouble spots with light switches. Photos, drawing. • *Home Mechanix.* No. 742 (Feb, 1990) pp. 14-16.

Light Wells

"Making curved crown" by Scott McBride. Describes a method of making a curved crown on a circular recessed light well. Drawings. • *Fine Homebuilding.* No. 67 (May, 1991) p. 12.

Lighting

"Accent on lighting" by Lydia Cassidy. Discusses factors which should be considered in planning home lighting, and describes the different types of lighting that can be used. Photos. • *Canadian Workshop.* Vol. 13, No. 5 (Feb 1990) pp. 54-68.

Book Review: *Heating, Cooling, Lighting: Design Methods for Architects* by Norbert Lecher. Book review on a valuable guide for designing the heating, cooling, and lighting in homes. New York: John Wiley & Sons, Inc., 534 pp. • *Fine Homebuilding.* No. 72 (March, 1992) p. 108.

"Points of light" by Edward Effron. Using low-voltage spot lights to add emphasis to a home. Photos and drawings. • *Practical*

Homeowner. Vol. VI, No. 8 (Oct, 1991) pp. 46-53.

Lighting, Fluorescent

"The newest wave in compact fluorescent lighting" by Alex Wilson. Discusses the latest energy-efficient compact fluorescents. Photos, drawing. • *Home Mechanix.* No. 765 (May, 1992) pp. 30-32.

Lighting, Solar-Powered

"Daylight savings" by Steve Lowe. A new product guide to different types of solar-powered lighting fixtures. Photos. • *Practical Homeowner.* Vol. V, No. 4 (June, 1990) pp. 36-38.

Lighting, Track

"Off the beaten track" by Edward Effron. New ideas for using track lighting. Photos and plans. • *Practical Homeowner.* Vol. VI, No. 3 (March, 1991) pp. 30-32.

Lightning Rods

"Lightning protection for your home" by Merle Henkenius. Brief article on how to install a lightning rod and an arrester system to prevent damage to a home. Photos, drawing. • *Home Mechanix.* No. 753 (March, 1991) p. 16.

Lights

"Work light" by Steve Harman. Brief article on making a work light that takes a 300- to 500- watt quartz halogen lamp. Drawing. • *Fine Homebuilding.* No. 60 (May, 1990) p. 26.

Lintels

"Site-casting concrete lintels" by Joe Fetchko. Presents the advantages of site-casting concrete lintels. Photos. • *Fine Homebuilding.* No. 74 (May, 1992) pp. 50–51.

Locks

"Higher-security, lower-cost locks" by Bill Phillips. Discusses the latest high-security locks available. Photo, drawing. • *Home Mechanix.* No. 775 (May, 1993) pp. 38–39.

"Picking a good lock" by Bill Phillips. Informative article on how locks work and the features that make them strong. Photos, drawing. • *Home Mechanix.* No. 753 (March, 1991) pp. 10–12.

Locks, Magnetic

"Magnetic locks are hard to beat" by Bill Phillips. Provides information on electromagnetic locks that are available for residential use. Photos, diagram. • *Home Mechanix.* No. 755 (May, 1991) pp. 20–23.

Locks, Quill

"Drill press quill lock" by Marshall R. Young. A simple left-handed quill lock for use with a drill press. Photos and plans. • *The Home Shop Machinist.* Vol. 11, No. 1 (Jan/Feb, 1992) pp. 40–41.

Locks, Spindle

"A spindle lock for your mill/drill" by Bill Lowery. How to fabricate and install a spindle lock on a mill/drill. Photos and plans. • *The Home Shop Machinist.* Vol. 12, No. 2 (Mar/Apr, 1993) pp. 28–29.

Locksets

"Boring metal-skinned doors" by Robert Countryman. Brief tip on installing locks in metal skinned doors. • *Fine Homebuilding.* No. 83 (Sep, 1993) p. 28.

"Installing locksets" by Gary M. Katz. Describes how to install locksets with jigs and routers. Drawings, photos. Sidebar on making router templates. • *Fine Homebuilding.* No. 79 (March, 1993) pp. 40–45.

"Installing mortise locksets" by Gary M. Katz. Provides detailed instructions for installing mortise locksets. Photos, drawings. • *Fine Homebuilding.* No. 81 (May, 1993) pp. 60–63.

Log Houses

"Log houses" by Joseph Truini. Offers design ideas and tips for constructing log homes. Photos, drawings, diagrams. • *Home Mechanix.* No. 772 (Feb, 1993) pp. 48–55.

"Out of the woods" by Joseph Truini. Informative article on construction kits for log cabins. Photos, plans, drawing. • *Home Mechanix.* No. 768 (Sep, 1992) pp. 68–72.

Lumber

"Buying wood" by Roger Holmes. This article offers advice on how to make knowledgeable purchases of wood stock. • *The Woodworker's Journal.* Vol. 17, No. 4 (Jul/Aug, 1993) pp. 17–21.

M

Machine Shops

"Setting up shop" by Rudy Kouhoupt. Practical suggestions for starting a home machine shop. • *The Home Shop Machinist.* Vol. 11, No. 3 (May/Jun, 1992) pp. 47-49.

Machines, Multipurpose

"Shopsmith vs. Total Shop" by Bill Krier. Informative guide comparing the two top-selling multipurpose machines. Photos, chart. • *Better Homes and Gardens Wood.* No. 35 (June, 1990) pp. 35-39.

Machines, Woodworking

"The jack-shaft speed-reducer" by Jacob Schulzinger. Describes the solution for powering old machines at slow speeds. Drawing. Photos. • *Woodwork.* No. 14 (March/April) pp. 39-41.

Machining

"Cerro alloys aid in machining irregular parts" by Ronald E. McBride. This is an examination of the properties of cerro alloys which are composed mainly of bismuth. Photos. • *The Home Shop Machinist.* Vol. 12, No. 6 (Nov/Dec, 1993) pp. 36-38.

Machining Tables

"The rotary, dual cross-slide drill press and milling machine table, part one" by John Gascoyne. This in-depth article describes the types and features of rotary, dual cross-slide machining tables. Photos and drawings. • *The Home Shop Machinist.* Vol. 10, No. 2 (Mar/Apr, 1991) pp. 40-44.

"The rotary, dual cross-slide drill press and milling machine table, part two" by John Gascoyne. See Vol. 10, No. 2 • *The Home Shop Machinist.* Vol. 10, No. 3 (May/Jun, 1991) pp. 38-43.

"The rotary, dual cross-slide drill press and milling machine table" by John Gascoyne. See Vol. 10, No. 2 • *The Home Shop Machinist.* Vol. 10, No. 4 (Jul/Aug, 1991) pp. 36-38.

Magnets

"Wildfowl fridge magnets" by Judy Gale Roberts. Creative bird designs and instructions to scroll saw refrigerator magnets. Photos. • *Better Homes and Gardens Wood.* No. 60 (April, 1993) pp. 68-69.

Mahogany (Wood)

"Casual classics—a distinctive and durable mahogany table" by Marlen Kemmet. Detailed instructions to build a 48" sturdy mahogany table for a deck or backyard. Photos, diagrams, materials list. • *Better Homes and Gardens Wood.* No. 43 (June, 1991) pp. 64-67.

"Honduras mahogany" by Jim Boelling, Jim Downing, Robert St. Pierre, Jim Rose and Gary Zeff. Identifies the availability, cost, uses, plus machining, carving, and turning methods for mahogany. Photos, illustration. • *Better Homes and Gardens Wood.* No. 42 (April, 1991) pp. 31-32.

Maintenance and Repair

Book Review: *A Consumer's Guide to Home Improvement, Renovation & Repair* by Enterprise Foundation. Book review on choosing a cost-effective approach to a home improvement project. Photo. New York: John Wiley & Sons, 270 pp. • *Home Mechanix.* No. 757 (July/Aug, 1991) pp. 18-19.

Book Review: *Complete Do-It-Yourself Manual.* Book review on this comprehensive guide to home improvement. Photo. Pleasantville, NY: Reader's Digest, 538 pp. • *Home Mechanix.* No. 760 (Nov, 1991) p. 21.

Book Review: *Finish Carpentry Basics.* Book review providing the tools and techniques to build, remodel, or repair a home. Photo. Ortho Books, 112 pp. • *Home Mechanix.* No. 766 (June, 1992) p. 16.

Book Review: *Quick Fix Home Repair Handbook* by Gene and Katie Hamilton. Book review of a homeowner's manual for home repairs. Photo. New York: Harper & Row, 167 pp. • *Home Mechanix.* No. 752 (Feb, 1991) p. 33.

Book Review: *The Termite Report: A Guide for Homeowners & Homebuyers on Structural Pest Control* by Donald V. Pearman. Book review on a comprehensive guide to repair pest related structural problems. Pearman Publishing, 139 pp. • *Home Mechanix.* No. 764 (April, 1992) p. 29.

Book Review: *The Walls Around Us* by David Owen. Book review on an owner's manual for houses, especially paint, lumber, and electricity. New York: Vintage Books, 308 pp. • *Fine Homebuilding.* No. 83 (Sep, 1993) p. 120.

"Cleaning concrete" by Jim Barrett. Offers a tip on removing oil spills from concrete without using harsh chemicals. Photos. • *Home Mechanix.* No. 746 (June, 1990) p. 12.

"Cracking up" by Henry Spies. Brief tip on repair cracks due to truss movement. Drawing. • *Home Mechanix.* No. 781 (Dec/Jan, 1993-94) p. 87.

"Curing the chronic crack" by Walter Jowers. How to use fiberglass mesh tape to fix wall cracks. Photos. • *Practical Homeowner.* Vol. V, No. 3 (April, 1990) pp. 42-43.

"Detailing for wood shrinkage" by Stephen Smulski. Provides valuable information about avoiding nail pops, cracked drywall and sloping floors. Photos, drawings, diagrams. Sidebar on how moisture content changes with humidity levels. • *Fine Homebuilding.* No. 81 (May, 1993) pp. 54-59.

"Don't let upkeep get you down." Brief tip on planning maintenance costs for your household. Chart. • *Home Mechanix.* No. 742 (Feb, 1990) p. 10.

"Hurricane warnings" by Charles Miller. Informative article on the wreckage of Hurricane Andrew and why some houses survived. Photos, drawings. Sidebar on emergency power. • *Fine Homebuilding.* No. 78 (Jan, 1993) pp. 82-87.

"A lift for sunken concrete" by Matt Phair. Introduces the technique of slabjacking for sunken concrete problems. Photos, drawings. • *Home Mechanix.* No. 756 (June, 1991) p. 13.

"Metal corrosion" by Ana Diaz. Informative article on corrosion and how to minimize it effects. Photos, chart. • *Fine Homebuilding.* No. 62 (Sep, 1990) pp. 64-67.

"Pitched-roof sag" by Henry Spies. Brief tip on repairing a sagging garage roof. Drawings. • *Home Mechanix.* No. 762 (Feb, 1992) p. 74.

"Power washing a house" by Jim Barrett. Describes equipment and procedures for cleaning the exterior of a home. Photos. • *Home Mechanix.* No. 746 (June, 1990) p. 10.

"Riding out the big one" by Ralph Gareth Gray. Gives an in-depth analysis of the impact of an earthquake on a wood-frame building and how to prevent collapse. Photos, drawings. Sidebar on the load path. • *Fine Homebuilding.* No. 64 (Jan, 1991) pp. 60-65.

"Roof lichens" by Henry Spies. Brief tip on removing lichens from an asphalt-shingle roof. • *Home Mechanix.* No. 754 (April, 1991) p. 92.

"Soaked ceiling" by Henry Spies. Brief suggestion on how to prevent water from entering a house from a second-story deck. Drawing. • *Home Mechanix.* No. 772 (Feb, 1993) p. 80.

"Standing up to salt water" by Scott King. Solves a problem with salt water eating away at the paint and hardware on a home built on an island. • *Fine Homebuilding.* No. 68 (July, 1991) p. 16.

"Taking a load off" by W. Whitie Gray. Offers three basic shoring techniques for making structural repairs. Photos, drawings. • *Fine Homebuilding.* No. 69 (Sep, 1991) pp. 67-69.

"Termite termination." Brief tips on warning signs of termite damage and how to prevent infestation. Chart. • *Home Mechanix.* No. 744 (April, 1990) p. 16.

"Unique home services" by Linda Williams. A description of unusual home repair services. Photos. • *Practical Homeowner.* Vol. V, No. 5 (August, 1990) pp. 36-40.

"Wood-destroying fungi" by Terry Amburgey. Informative article on the fungi that can destroy wood and hints on how to prevent destruction. Photos. • *Fine Homebuilding.* No. 72 (March, 1992) pp. 64-66.

See Also specific tasks

Maintenance and Repair--Scheduling

"Hearing yourself keeps extended projects on track" by Dan Wilks. Brief tip on keeping track of your place in the process of extended projects with long interruptions. Drawing. • *Better Homes and Gardens Wood.* No. 57 (Dec, 1992) p. 23.

Mallets

"The friendly persuader: a turned mallet for your shop" by Haroldo Martins. Provides directions and a full-sized pattern for turning a handy mallet. Photo, patterns. • *Better Homes and Gardens Wood.* No. 46 (Oct, 1991) pp. 6-7.

Mantels, Fireplace

"Mantels in minutes" by Joseph Truini. Offers step-by-step mantel installation with kit-built mantels. Photos. • *Home Mechanix.* No. 750 (Nov, 1990) pp. 42-44.

Maple (Wood)

"Sugar maple" by Jim Boelling, Paul McClure, Don Wipperman, Phil Odden, Rick Reeves. Learn essential details about the workability, cost, durability and other features useful for carving, turning, or building with sugar maple. • *Better Homes and Gardens Wood.* No. 36 (Aug, 1990) pp. 31-32.

Marble

"Boneyard marble" by Jay Latta. Useful tips for adding cast-off marble tiles to a bathroom or sunspace. Photos, drawings. • *Fine Homebuilding.* No. 69 (Sep, 1991) pp. 55-57.

Marble Drops (Toy)

"Marble drop" by Don Koppin. Describes how to construct a simple wooden marble drop toy for a child. Photo. List of materials. Drawn plans. • *Canadian Workshop.* Vol. 13, No. 5 (Feb 1990) pp. 49-52.

Marbleizing

"Decorative painted finishes" by Victor DeMasi. Provides an introduction to glazing, woodgraining, marbleizing and other finish techniques. Photos. Sidebar on marbleizing a mantel. • *Fine Homebuilding.* No. 60 (May, 1990) pp. 78-82.

Marquetry

"Box with marquetry top." This article offers tips on how to usc marquetry techniques with wood veneers to create a small box with a contrasting patterned lid. Photo, plans, and drawings. • *The Woodworker's Journal.* Vol. 15, No. 1 (Jan/Feb, 1991) pp. 56-57.

"The Major's marquetry" by Peter J. Stephano. Craftsman Dave Peck describes how to decorate surfaces with designs or pictures made from thin veneers. Photos, drawing. • *Better Homes and Gardens Wood.* No. 52 (June, 1992) pp. 27-31.

"Marquetry: the direct method" by Nicholas Mariana. Directions for the direct method of producing marquetry-type wooden pictures. Drawings. • *The Woodworker's Journal.* Vol. 14, No. 1 (Jan/Feb, 1990) pp. 21-24.

Masks

Book Review: *Carving Totem Poles and Masks* by Alan and Gill Bridgewater. Book review on the techniques of carving projects like totem poles and masks. New York: Sterling, 191 pp. • *Woodwork.* No. 16 (July/August, 1992) pp. 26-29.

Masonry

Book Review: *Masonry: How to Care for Old and Historic Brick and Stone* by Mark London. Book review on a complete guide to the use of brick and stone for building houses. Washington, DC: Preservation Press, 208 pp. • *Home Mechanix.* No. 756 (June, 1991) p. 14.

Book Review: *The Homeowner's Guide to Building with Concrete, Brick and Stone* by The Portland Cement Association. Book review of a practical, well-written guide on residential masonry. Emmaus, PA: Rodale Press, Inc., 240 pp. • *Fine Homebuilding.* No. 62 (Sep, 1990) p. 112.

"Make it masonry" by Bob Wessmiller and Matthew Phair. Introduces five new finishing systems for home exteriors. Photos. • *Home Mechanix.* No. 774 (April, 1993) pp. 51-54.

Materials Estimating

Software Review: *Carpenter's Dream* by Dan Heilman. Software review on a material estimating program. Golden, CO:

Workhorses, Inc. • *Fine Homebuilding*. No. 62 (Sep, 1990) p. 112.

Measuring Systems

"Carpenter's number code" by Jim Chestnut. Brief description of a measurement system for carpentry. • *Fine Homebuilding*. No. 78 (Jan, 1993) pp. 28-30.

Measuring Tools

"Ultrasonic measuring tools" by Karl Riedel. Explains the features of ultrasonic measuring tools. Photos, chart. • *Fine Homebuilding*. No. 78 (Jan, 1993) pp. 54–55.

Mechanical Devices

Book Review: *Making Mechanical Marvels in Wood* by Raymond Levy. Book review on constructing wooden mechanical devices, such as a stationary steam engine. New York: Author (387 Park Avenue South) 200 pp. • *Woodwork*. No. 14 (March/April) pp. 20-22.

Mediterranean-Style Houses

"Airtight in Massachusetts" by Paul Fisette. Describes the construction of an energy-efficient Mediterranean-style house. Photos, drawings. • *Fine Homebuilding*. No. 63 (Nov, 1990) pp. 81-85.

Mercury

"Mercury banned" by James Lomuscio. An examination of the use of mercury in house paints. • *Practical Homeowner*. Vol. V, No. 7 (Oct, 1990) pp. 24-25.

Mesquite (Wood)

"Turning mesquite" by Billy S. Cook. Describes the process of turning mesquite into bowls. Photos. • *Woodwork*. No. 17 (Sep/Oct, 1992) pp. 48-53.

Message Boards

"Kitchen message center." An easy-to-make project for a wall-mounted message board. Photos, plans, and materials list. • *The Woodworker's Journal*. Vol. 17, No. 1 (Jan/Feb, 1993 pp. 54-57.

Metals

"Skipping" by Terry Sexton. A primer on the art of skipping, i.e., searching industrial waste skips for recyclable metal. • *The Home Shop Machinist*. Vol. 11, No. 5 (Sep/Oct, 1992) pp. 46 47.

Micromachining

"A grinding rest for precise tools, part one" by Rudy Kouhoupt. How to build a customized grinding rest for precision work. Photos. • *The Home Shop Machinist*. Vol. 9, No. 3 (May/Jun, 1990) pp. 40-42.

"A grinding rest for precise tools, part two" by Rudy Kouhoupt. See Vol. 9, No. 3 • *The Home Shop Machinist*. Vol. 9, No. 4 (Jul/Aug, 1990) pp. 48-49.

"A holder for 13/16" dies, part one" by Rudy Kouhoupt. An explanation of the manufacture of a circular holder for small dies. Photos and plans. • *The Home Shop Machinist*. Vol. 11, No. 1 (Jan/Feb, 1992) pp. 42-44.

"Topics in micromachining" by Ted Roubal. This article offers a product explanation of the uses of a jeweler's lathe. Photos. • *The Home Shop Machinist*. Vol. 9, No. 3 (May/Jun, 1990) pp. 20-23.

"Topics in micromachining, part two" by Ted Roubal. An explanation of the uses of a pivot polisher. Photos and plans. • *The Home Shop Machinist*. Vol. 9, No. 4 (Jul/Aug, 1990) pp. 23-26.

"Topics in micromachining, part three" by Ted Roubal. See Vol. 9, No. 3 • *The Home Shop Machinist*. Vol. 9, No. 5 (Sep/Oct, 1990) pp. 38-41.

Mill Drills

"Convert your mill-drill to CNC, part four by R.W. Friestad. See Vol. 9, No. 2 • *The Home Shop Machinist*. Vol. 9, No. 5 (Sep/Oct, 1990) pp. 46-49.

"Convert your mill-drill to CNC, part one" by R.W. Friestad. An examination of the equipment and electronics changes required before a mill-drill can be adapted for computer-controlled operation.

Photos and plans. • *The Home Shop Machinist.* Vol. 9, No. 2 (Mar/Apr, 1990) pp. 46-50.

"Convert your mill-drill to CNC, part three" by R. W. Friestad. See Vol. 9, No. 2 • *The Home Shop Machinist.* Vol. 9, No. 4 (Jul/Aug, 1994) pp. 54-55.

"Convert your mill-drill to CNC, part two" by R.W. Friestad. See Vol. 9, No. 2 • *The Home Shop Machinist.* Vol. 9, No. 3 (May/Jun, 1990) pp. 50-56.

"A spindle lock for your mill/drill" by Bill Lowery. How to fabricate and install a spindle lock on a mill/drill. Photos and plans. • *The Home Shop Machinist.* Vol. 12, No. 2 (Mar/Apr, 1993) pp. 28-29.

Milling Machine Stands

"A mill-drill stand" by Gerald Mulholland. A brief tip on building a machine stand from scrap iron. Photos. • *The Home Shop Machinist.* Vol. 9, No. 2 (Mar/Apr, 1990) p. 51.

Milling Machines

"Ball turning in the mill" by Norman H. Bennett. A description of how to use a milling machine to turn a spheroid. Photos and diagrams. • *The Home Shop Machinist.* Vol. 11, No. 3 (May/Jun, 1992) pp. 44-46.

"Cutting vee notches" by John A. Cooper. A brief tip on how to cut vee notches with an end mill. • *The Home Shop Machinist.* Vol. 12, No. 4 (Jul/Aug, 1993) p. 48.

"A homemade bench mill" by James S. McNight. This brief article describes a homemade bench milling machine. • *The Home Shop Machinist.* Vol. 10, No. 4 (Jul/Aug, 1991) pp. 42-43.

"Lathe operations on a vertical mill" by Stephan Thomas. An examination of the uses of a vertical spindle-type milling machine for lathe operations. Photos. • *The Home Shop Machinist.* Vol. 9, No. 1 (Jan/Feb, 1990) pp. 29-33.

"Lathe operations on a vertical mill" by Stephan Thomas. See Vol. 9, No. 1 • *The Home Shop Machinist.* Vol. 9, No. 2 (Mar/Apr, 1990) pp. 33-37.

"A milling machine conversion" by Larry Shull. This article describes the process of converting a horizontal milling machine for vertical work. Photos and plans. • *The Home Shop Machinist.* Vol. 12, No. 2 (Mar/Apr, 1993) pp. 24-27.

"Rounding the ends" by Frank A McLean. Tips on using a pivot handle to make milling operations quicker. Photos and plans. • *The Home Shop Machinist.* Vol. 12, No. 4 (Jul/Aug, 1993) pp. 52-53.

"Thoughts on selecting vertical mills, part one" by Thomas F. Howard. An introduction to the variables involved in purchasing a vertical milling machine. • *The Home Shop Machinist.* Vol. 12, No. 4 (Jul/Aug, 1993) pp. 30-33.

"Thoughts on selecting vertical mills, part two" by Thomas F. Howard. See Vol. 12, No. 4 • *The Home Shop Machinist.* Vol. 12, No. 5 (Sep/Oct, 1993) pp. 26-29.

"Two useful milling accessories" by Rudy Kouhoupt. This article offers designs for two accessories for milling machines–an end mill holder and an auxiliary milling table. Photos and plans. • *The Home Shop Machinist.* Vol. 10, No. 3 (May/Jun, 1991) pp. 48-50.

"X and Y stops for the mill" by Rudy Kouhoupt. A guide to the use of metal stops on a milling machine table. Photos. • *The Home Shop Machinist.* Vol. 12, No. 1 (Jan/Feb, 1993) pp. 49-51.

Milling Techniques

"Milling on the lathe" by Frank A. McLean. A description of how to set milling attachments on a standard lathe. Photos. • *The Home Shop Machinist.* Vol. 9, No. 4 (Jul/Aug, 1990) pp. 51-53.

Mills, End

"Sharpen your end mills, part one" by Rudy Kouhoupt. A brief description of the technique for sharpening an end mill tool. Photos and plans. • *The Home Shop*

Machinist. Vol. 9, No. 5 (Sep/Oct, 1990) pp. 42-45.

Mills, Multi-Cutter

"Building a multi cutter face mill, part one" by Rudy Kouhoupt. This article offers detailed information on constructing and using a four-cutter face mill for use on a Sherline vertical mill. Photos and drawings. • *The Home Shop Machinist.* Vol. 10, No. 1 (Jan/Feb, 1991) pp. 50-52.

Mills, Vertical

"Elevating a vertical mill" by Rudy Kouhoupt. An explanation of a technique to fit an elevator block onto a milling machine table. Photos and drawings. • *The Home Shop Machinist.* Vol. 10, No. 2 (Mar/Apr, 1991) pp. 54-59.

Millwork

"A fixture plate for a lathe or mill" by Ray E. Starnes. Brief tips on constructing a fixture plate. Photos. • *The Home Shop Machinist.* Vol. 10, No. 2 (Mar/Apr, 1991) pp. 30-31.

"High-style low-maintenance millwork" by Matt Phair. Highlights the latest materials available to recreate traditional moldings. Photos, drawing. • *Home Mechanix.* No. 755 (May, 1991) pp. 44-47.

"Turning short tapers on a mill" by Stephen Thomas. This article describes a method of turning short tapers on a mill/drill or other vertical spindle machine. Photos. • *The Home Shop Machinist.* Vol. 11, No. 1 (Jan/Feb, 1992) pp. 18-23.

Mirrors

"Charming Cheval mirror" by Marlen Kemmet and James R. Downing. Describes how to build a beautiful stand-up mirror. Photo, diagrams, materials list. • *Better Homes and Gardens Wood.* No. 49 (Jan, 1992) pp. 52-55.

"Country pine mirror and shelf." A brief article describing the process of constructing a primitive pine mirror. Photos, plans, and materials list. • *The*

Woodworker's Journal. Vol. 16, No. 1 (Jan/Feb, 1992) pp. 41-43.

"Ladies' cosmetic mirror" by Don Bailey. Describes how to make a durable cosmetic mirror. Photos, diagrams, full-sized pattern. • *Better Homes and Gardens Wood.* No. 43 (June, 1991) pp. 76-77.

"Remodel with mirrors" by James Lomuscio. Advice on using large wall mirrors in remodeling plans. Photos. • *Practical Homeowner.* Vol. VI, No. 8 (Oct, 1991) pp. 58-63.

Mirrors, Early American

"Early American mirror." This is a brief outline on building an Early American-style mirror with dovetailed joints, includes materials list. Photo and plans. • *The Woodworker's Journal.* Vol. 14, No. 2 (Mar/Apr, 1990) pp. 38-39.

Mirrors, Hand

"Walnut hand mirror." A description of the steps needed to carve and shape a small, walnut, hand mirror and add mother-of-pearl inlay. Photos and drawings. • *The Woodworker's Journal.* Vol. 14, No. 6 (Nov/Dec, 1990) pp. 54-56.

Mirrors, Mortised

"Mortise and tenon mirror." Details the procedures involved in building a mirror frame with mortise and tenon joints, includes parts list. Plans. • *The Woodworker's Journal.* Vol. 14, No. 1 (Jan/Feb, 1990) pp. 31-33.

Mirrors, Sunburst

"Sunburst mirrors." A brief look at the method of making a wall mirror with a sunburst-style crest. Photo and plans. • *The Woodworker's Journal.* Vol. 14, No. 4 (Jul/Aug, 1990) pp. 29-31.

Mirrors, Vanity

"Pine vanity." This descriptive article outlines the procedure for making a dresser-top vanity with drawers. Photo, plans, and materials list. • *The Woodworker's*

Journal. Vol. 15, No. 2 (Mar/Apr, 1991) pp. 56-58.

Mirrors, Windowpaned

"Windowpaned mirrors." A project for cutting and assembling trim and molding to give a French-window-like appearance to an ordinary wall mirror. Photos, plans, and materials list. • *The Woodworker's Journal.* Vol. 17, No. 6 (Nov/Dec, 1993) pp. 64-66.

Mirrors--Hanging of

"Hanging frameless mirrors" by Jim Barrett. Detailed instructions on installing frameless mirrors. Drawing. • *Home Mechanix.* No. 748 (Sep, 1990) pp. 18-19.

Miters

"Getting an angle on compound miters" by David DeCristoforo. Evaluates portable saws that can make complex cuts. Photos, chart. • *Fine Homebuilding.* No. 57 (Jan, 1990) pp. 58-62.

Mitersaw Cabinets

"Custom mitersaw cabinet" by Marlen Kemmet and James R. Downing. Explains how to build a mitersaw cabinet complete with a stand and roll-out bin for chips and cut-offs. Photos, diagrams, materials list. • *Better Homes and Gardens Wood.* No. 50 (Feb, 1992) pp. 56-61.

Mitersaws

"Mitersaws." Detailed analysis of the features of 26 mitersaws. Photo, chart. • *Better Homes and Gardens Wood.* No. 65 (Nov, 1993) pp. 56-57.

Mitersaws, Power

"Power mitersaws" by Bill Krier. Analysis of the value of power mitersaws and a comparison of the different brands. Chart with comparisons, photos, drawings. Sidebar on why we have a power mitersaw in the wood shop. • *Better Homes and Gardens Wood.* No. 50 (Feb, 1992) pp. 48-53.

Mobiles

"Feathered friends mobile." An easy-to-make project for using a scroll saw to cut out bird designs for a mobile. Photo and plan. • *The Woodworker's Journal.* Vol. 17, No. 1 (Jan/Feb, 1991) pp. 58-59.

"High flying balloon mobile" by Marlen Kemmet. Explains how to turn laminated wood to create checkered-pattern hot air balloons. Photos, diagrams, full-sized template. • *Better Homes and Gardens Wood.* No. 43 (June, 1991) pp. 50-52.

Models

"Where realism rides the waves" by Peter J. Stephano. Explains the step-by-step process of creating model boats. Photos. • *Better Homes and Gardens Wood.* No. 64 (Oct, 1993) pp. 29 33.

Moisture Control

Book Review: *Moisture Control for Homes: A Primer for Designers and Builders* by J.D. Ned Nisson. Book review on a collection of articles focusing on moisture control. Arlington, MA: Cutter Information Corp., 54 pp. • *Fine Homebuilding.* No. 70 (Nov, 1991) p. 122.

Book Review: *Moisture Control Handbook: New, Lowrise, Residential Construction* by Joseph Lstiburek and John Carmody. Book review providing information on moisture causing problems and strategies to prevent them. Springfield, VA: National Technical Information Service, 248 pp. • *Fine Homebuilding.* No. 74 (May, 1992) p. 98.

Moisture Problems

"Basement condensation" by Henry Spies. Brief tip on how to eliminate condensation on the basement band joist. Drawing. • *Home Mechanix.* No. 753 (March, 1991) p. 80.

"Clear the deck" by Henry Spies. Brief tip on cleaning mold and mildew from a wood deck. • *Home Mechanix.* No. 773 (March, 1993) pp. 84-85.

"Condensation on diffusers" by Henry Spies. Offers a way of preventing condensation on ceiling diffusers. • *Home Mechanix.* No. 769 (Oct, 1992) pp. 80-81.

"Controlling spa-room moisture" by M. Scott Watkins. Presents information on moisture control for a spa room in a humid climate. • *Fine Homebuilding.* No. 79 (March, 1993) p. 24.

"Crawl-space moisture" by Hank Spies. Offers a tip for correcting a moisture problem in a crawl-space under a house. Drawing. • *Home Mechanix.* No. 749 (Oct, 1990) p. 93.

"Crawl-space moisture" by Henry Spies. Explains the reason for moisture problems inside a house situated above an uninsulated crawl space. • *Home Mechanix.* No. 771 (Dec/Jan, 1992-93) p. 81.

"Crawl-space mold" by Henry Spies. Offers advice for controlling mold on floor framing and heating ducts. • *Home Mechanix.* No. 768 (Sep, 1992) p. 113.

"Damp masonry" by Stephen Kennedy. Offers a tip for solving a problem with moisture on the interior of a chimney. • *Fine Homebuilding.* No. 76 (Sep, 1992) pp. 18-20.

"Detecting moisture problems" by Jim Barrett. Introduces equipment that detects water moisture in homes. Photos, drawing. • *Home Mechanix.* No. 748 (Sep, 1990) pp. 17-18.

"Drying a wet slab" by David Benaroya. Brief tip covering moisture problems on concrete slab flooring. Drawings. • *Fine Homebuilding.* No. 65 (March, 1991) p. 16.

"Moisture problems in the crawl space" by David Kaufman. Offers information on how to solve a moisture problem in a crawl space. • *Fine Homebuilding.* No. 64 (Jan, 1991) p. 22.

"Moldy odor" by Henry Spies. Brief tip on reducing the moisture and moldy odor in a crawl space. • *Home Mechanix.* No. 764 (April, 1992) p. 86.

"Mysterious moisture" by Henry Spies. Offers suggestions on discovering the cause of moisture in a basement. Drawing. • *Home Mechanix.* No. 761 (Dec/Jan, 1991-92) p. 72.

"Soaked ceiling" by Henry Spies. Brief suggestion on how to prevent water from entering a house from a second-story deck. Drawing. • *Home Mechanix.* No. 772 (Feb, 1993) p. 80.

"Waterproofing woes" by Henry Spies. Brief tip on how to prevent water seepage on concrete walls. Drawing. • *Home Mechanix.* No. 757 (July/Aug, 1991) p. 80.

Molding Machines

"Plastic injection molding machine, part one" by Rodney S. Hanson. Complete and thorough layout of the steps for building a small plastic injection molding machine. Photos and plans. • *The Home Shop Machinist.* Vol. 10, No. 3 (May/Jun, 1991) pp. 16-22.

"Plastic injection molding machine, part three" by Rodney W. Hanson. See Vol. 10, No. 3 • *The Home Shop Machinist.* Vol. 10, No. 5 (Sep/Oct, 1991) pp. 44-47.

"Plastic injection molding machine, part two" by Rodney Hanson. See Vol. 10, No. 3 • *The Home Shop Machinist.* Vol. 10, No. 4 (Jul/Aug, 1991) pp. 32-35.

Moldings

"Add the crowning touch to your projects large-scale moldings" by Bill Krier, Jim Boelling and Jim Downing. Detailed instructions for constructing large-scale moldings. Photos, diagrams, guide for cutting coves. Sidebar on six quick steps to a bullnose. • *Better Homes and Gardens Wood.* No. 40 (Jan, 1991) pp. 38-43.

Book Review: *Walls & Moldings: How to Care for Old and Historic Wood and Plaster* by Natalie Shivers. Book review on fixing up plaster walls, moldings, and other areas in old homes. Washington, D.C.: The Preservation Press, 198 pp. • *Fine Homebuilding.* No. 77 (Nov, 1992) pp. 120-122.

"Cutting crown molding" by Stephen Nuding. Offers a method of calculating miter and bevel angles for any crown and for any angle. Photos, drawings. Sidebar on coping with big crown. • *Fine Homebuilding.* No. 68 (July, 1991) pp. 79-81.

"Estimating and buying molding" by Craig Savage. Informative article on the quantity, quality, and cost of molding. Photos, chart on wood suitable for trim. • *Fine Homebuilding.* No. 57 (Jan, 1990) pp. 48-51.

"Hardwood edgings for plastic laminate" by Paul Levine. Brief article on how to make hardwood edging for countertops. Photos, drawings. • *Fine Homebuilding.* No. 78 (Jan, 1993) pp. 66-67.

"How to clamp tricky mitered moldings." Introduces a method clamping a difficult mitered joint. Drawings. • *Better Homes and Gardens Wood.* No. 61 (June, 1993) p. 47.

"Making curved crown molding" by John La Torre, Jr. Describes two approaches to making curved trim. Photos. • *Fine Homebuilding.* No. 74 (May, 1992) pp. 79-81.

"Mitered-moulding jig" by Tom E. Moore. Explains construction of a jig to pare and fit any mitered moulding on cabinet doors. Drawing. • *Woodwork.* No. 14 (March/April) p. 10.

"Mitering curved moldings" by Scott McBride. Detailed instructions on how to cut miter joints for an arch-shaped piece surrounding windows. • *Fine Homebuilding.* No. 63 (Nov, 1990) pp. 16-18.

"Replicating moldings" by Gene and Katie Hamilton. Describes the process of reproducing vintage moldings with a router or a combination plane. Photos, drawings. • *Home Mechanix.* No. 766 (June, 1992) pp. 14-16.

Moldings, Crown

"Crowning touches" by Thomas H. Jones. Presents professional advice and techniques for installing crown moldings. Photos. • *Home Mechanix.* No. 751 (Dec/Jan, 1990-91) pp. 52-57.

"Installing two-piece crown" by Dale F. Mosher. Presents a method for running wide, paint grade crown moldings. Photos. • *Fine Homebuilding.* No. 71 (Jan, 1992) pp. 85-87.

"Window dressing" by John Decker. Step-by-step instructions to make custom moldings for windows. Photos, diagrams, drawings. • *Home Mechanix.* No. 753 (March, 1991) pp. 40-43.

Molds, Pattern

"Shaping on a table saw" by R. J. DeCristoforo. A description of how to adapt a table saw using molding-head knives to shape pattern molds. Photos and drawings. • *The Woodworker's Journal.* Vol. 15, No. 4 (Jul/Aug, 1991) pp. 24-27.

Mortises

"Chiseling hinge mortises" by Daniel E. Hill. Offers a tip for small jobs dealing with mortises. Drawing. • *Fine Homebuilding.* No. 78 (Jan, 1993) p. 28.

Mortising Machines

"Boring square holes" by Roger Holmes. This article provides information on using a drill press to cut mortise-and-tenon joints. Photos and plans. • *The Woodworker's Journal.* Vol. 15, No. 3 (May/Jun, 1991) pp. 24-29.

Motor Mounts

"A homemade electric motor mount" by Ralph T. Walker. A description of how to adapt a used appliance motor for machine shop use. Photos. • *The Home Shop Machinist.* Vol. 11, No. 3 (May/Jun, 1992) pp. 42-43.

Motors, Electric

"Amps versus horsepower" by Jim Barrett. This article explains the differences between amperage and horsepower as it affects the operation of electric motors.

• *The Woodworker's Journal.* Vol. 16, No. 5 (Sep/Oct, 1992) p. 22.

"An inexpensive power feed" by Melvin L. Kalb. A description of the application of a small electric motor to control a lathe feed table. Photos. • *The Home Shop Machinist.* Vol. 11, No. 2 (Mar/Apr, 1992) pp. 52-54.

"Troubleshooting electric motors" by Jim Barrett. A brief article that looks at the problems to which electric motors are susceptible. Photos and drawings. • *The Woodworker's Journal.* Vol. 17, No. 2 (Mar/Apr, 1993) pp. 19-23.

Mounting Strips

"Mounting strips for walls" by John Roccanova. Brief instruction on a mounting system that makes hanging posters, artwork, and other wall pieces easier. Drawing. • *Fine Homebuilding.* No. 65 (March, 1991) p. 32.

Music Boxes

"Mr. Music box." Highlights a woodworker who designed wooden music boxes and presents instructions on how to make them. Sidebar on the process of making the boxes. Photos, diagrams, materials list. • *Better Homes and Gardens Wood.* No. 43 (June, 1991) pp. 31-35.

Music Stands

"Oak music stand." This brief article offers a simple plan for making an oak music stand. Photo, plans, and materials list. • *The Woodworker's Journal.* Vol. 15, No. 3 (May/Jun, 1991) pp. 54-55.

Musical Instruments

"Aeolian harp." A brief description for building a rectangular, wooden, wind harp also known as an Aeolian harp. Photos, plans, and materials list. • *The Woodworker's Journal.* Vol. 16, No. 4 (Jul/Aug, 1992) pp. 36-38.

"The bowed psaltery" by Marlen Kemmet. Learn how to construct and play a Renaissance instrument. Diagrams, photos, materials list. • *Better Homes and Gardens Wood.* No. 34 (April, 1990) pp. 68-73.

"Hammered dulcimer." Complete plans for building a dulcimer using cherry and maple wood. Photos, plans, and materials list. • *The Woodworker's Journal.* Vol. 17, No. 1 (Jan/Feb, 1993) pp. 64-67.

"Kalimba." A description of the process for building a Kalimba - an African thumb piano. Photos and materials list. • *The Woodworker's Journal.* Vol. 16, No. 2 (Mar/Apr, 1992) pp. 48 49.

"Mountain dulcimer." This article shows the method of cutting patterns and assembling a dulcimer in a Kentucky mountain pattern. Photos, plans, and materials list. • *The Woodworker's Journal.* Vol. 15, No. 4 (Jul/Aug, 1991) pp. 28-32.

N

Nail Stains

"Nail stains" by Henry Spies. Brief tip on removing nail stains from cedar siding. • *Home Mechanix.* No. 769 (Oct, 1992) pp. 78-79.

Nailer, Framing

"Have nailer, will travel" by William H. Brennen. Brief tip on making a carrying case for a framing nailer. Drawing. • *Fine Homebuilding.* No. 76 (Sep, 1992) p. 28.

Nails

"Nail pickup" by Raja Abusharr. Handy tip for collecting nails and screws. Drawing. • *Fine Homebuilding.* No. 77 (Nov, 1992) p. 32.

"Patience and recycling" by Brad R. Johnson. Brief tip on removing nails from pressure-treated lumber. • *Fine Homebuilding.* No. 71 (Jan, 1992) p. 24.

Napkin Holders

"Band-sawn napkin holder." This brief article describes how to make a wooden napkin holder. Photo and plans. • *The Woodworker's Journal.* Vol. 14, No. 1 (Jan/Feb, 1990) pp. 40-41.

"Graceful goose." Directions to construct a goose-shaped country-style napkin holder. Photo, full-sized pattern. • *Better Homes and Gardens Wood.* No. 41 (Feb, 1991) pp. 66-67.

"Napkin holder" by Gunther Keil. A brief tip on an easy-to-make design for a napkin holder. Photo and plans. • *The Woodworker's Journal.* Vol. 15, No. 4 (Jul/Aug, 1991) pp. 42-43.

"Pussycat napkin holder." An easy-to-make project for a cat-shaped napkin holder. Photo and materials list. • *The Woodworker's Journal.* Vol. 17, No. 4 (Jul/Aug, 1993) pp. 46-47.

"Special delivery: letter/napkin holder" by Keith Raivo Designs. Provides construction plans for a walnut and oak letter/napkin holder. Photo, diagram, drawing, materials list. • *Better Homes and Gardens Wood.* No. 45 (Sep, 1991) pp. 76-77.

Napkin Rings

"Four novel napkin rings." Design and directions for four sets of napkin rings including full sized patterns. Photos, patterns. • *Better Homes and Gardens Wood.* No. 43 (June, 1991) pp. 12-13.

Needlework Organizers

"Needleworks" by Don Boufford. Describes how to construct a wooden sewing/needlework organizer. Table of materials. Drawn plans. Photo. • *Canadian Workshop.* Vol. 15, No. 1 (Oct 1991) pp. 34-39.

Noise Problems

"Damping duct noise" by Hank Spies. Brief tip on fixing a noisy heat duct. Drawing. • *Home Mechanix.* No. 750 (Nov, 1990) p. 95.

"Nixing noises" by Hank Spies. Offers a solution to reduce noise for a bedroom

situated above a garage. Drawings. • *Home Mechanix.* No. 748 (Sep, 1990) p. 91.

"Noise in the shop" by Jim Barrett. An analysis of the dangers associated with noise levels and tips on how to reduce wood shop machine noise. Drawings. • *The Woodworker's Journal.* Vol. 15, No. 6 (Nov/Dec, 1991) pp. 21-25.

"Sound solutions" by Bob Wessmiller. Informative article on remodeling ideas to control noise around the house. Drawings. Sidebar on Do you live near an airport? • *Home Mechanix.* No. 758 (Sep, 1991) pp. 64-71.

Noodle Cutter

"Noodle cutter" by Russ Hurt. Describes how to turn a noodle cutter on a lathe. Photo, diagram, pattern, recipe for noodles. • *Better Homes and Gardens Wood.* No. 46 (Oct, 1991) pp. 72-73, 88.

Notches, V-Shaped

"Cutting vee notches" by John A. Cooper. A brief tip on how to cut vee notches with an end mill. • *The Home Shop Machinist.* Vol. 12, No. 4 (Jul/Aug, 1993) p. 48.

Nutcrackers

"Nutcrackers suite as can be" by Peter J. Stephano. Describes the process of creating miniature nutcrackers. Photos. Sidebar on how nutcrackers weren't always made to crack nuts. • *Better Homes and Gardens Wood.* No. 65 (Nov, 1993) pp. 27-29.

Nuts

"Small t-slot nuts" by John Williams. A brief examination of the uses for t-slot nuts. • *The Home Shop Machinist.* Vol. 9, No. 1 (Jan/Feb, 1990) pp. 59-61.

Oak (Wood)

"Northern red oak" by Jim Boelling and Don Wipperman, Ron Mackey and Cleat Christiansen. Uses, cost, availability, and carving guide for using northern red oak. Chart, diagram. • *Better Homes and Gardens Wood*. No. 34 (April, 1990) pp. 27-28.

"White oak: The weatherproof stock of Old Iron sides, barrels, and mission furniture" by Jim Boelling and Don Wipperman. Informative article on the availability, cost, uses, machining methods and carving suggestions. Illustrations, photos, chart. • *Better Homes and Gardens Wood*. No. 60 (April, 1993) pp. 33-34.

Odors

"Fireplace odor" by Henry Spies. Brief article addressing the problem of smoke odors lingering for weeks after using the fireplace. • *Home Mechanix*. No. 752 (Feb, 1991) p. 82.

"Foiling oil odor" by Hank Spies. Presents a solution to oil fumes in a upper level bedroom. Drawing. • *Home Mechanix*. No. 749 (Oct, 1990) p. 92.

"Moldy odor" by Henry Spies. Brief tip on reducing the moisture and moldy odor in a crawl space. • *Home Mechanix*. No. 764 (April, 1992) p. 86.

"Moldy odor" by Henry Spies. Brief tip on reducing the moisture and moldy odor in a crawl space. • *Home Mechanix*. No. 764 (April, 1992) p. 86.

"Name that fume" by Dave Menicucci. Offers a solution to a problem with fumes in a new house. • *Fine Homebuilding*. No. 78 (Jan, 1993) pp. 16-20.

"Plumbing odors" by Peter Hemp. Brief explanation on the possible causes of a plumbing odor. • *Fine Homebuilding*. No. 62 (Sep, 1990) p. 18.

"Sealing creosote beams" by Terry Amburgey. Gives advice on a solution for creosote vapors. • *Fine Homebuilding*. No. 62 (Sep, 1990) pp. 18-20.

Offices, Home

"Attic art studio" by Kevin Ireton. Offers an inventive plan for dropping the garage ceiling to create a studio or office. Photo, diagrams. • *Fine Homebuilding*. No. 64 (Jan, 1991) pp. 84-87.

Book Review: *The Home Office Book: How to Set Up and Use an Efficient Personal Workspace in the Computer Age* by Mark Alvarez. Book review on a guide to designing and choosing equipment of a workspace. Woodbury, CT: Goodwood Press, 304 pp. • *Fine Homebuilding*. No. 65 (March, 1991) p. 108.

"Creative home offices" by Ted Jones and Pat McMillan. Detailed descriptions and plans for three home offices. Photos, diagrams. • *Home Mechanix*. No. 753 (March, 1991) pp. 34-39.

"Office assembly" by Joseph Truini. Provides a tip on creating a home office with ready-to assemble furniture. Photos. • *Home Mechanix*. No. 741 (Jan, 1990) pp. 42-44.

"Strike three against home offices?" by Mark E. Battersby. An analysis of recent IRS changes affecting home machine shops. • *The Home Shop Machinist*. Vol. 12, No. 4 (Jul/Aug, 1993) pp. 34-35.

"Working spaces" by Ann Arnott. Presents six home-office designs and plans. Photos, plans. • *Home Mechanix*. No. 741 (Jan, 1990) pp. 36-42.

Ohmmeters

"Low range ohmmeters" by Theodore J. Myers. Plans for building a simple pocket ohmmeter that can read at a single ohm level. Photos. • *The Home Shop Machinist*. Vol. 10, No. 2 (Mar/Apr, 1991) pp. 24-27.

Oil Fumes

"Foiling oil odor" by Hank Spies. Presents a solution to oil fumes in a upper level

bedroom. Drawing. • *Home Mechanix.*
No. 749 (Oct, 1990) p. 92.

Old Congress-Style Houses

"A modest house in Bucks County" by
Jeremiah Eck. Detailed description of
country house built in the tradition of the
Old Congress-style houses. Photos, plans.
Sidebar on interior and exterior millwork.
• *Fine Homebuilding.* No. 59 (Spring, 1990)
pp. 36-41.

Organizers

"Basket case" by Paul Penfield. Handy tip
to make a basket to attach to the top of a
ladder to save trips up and down. Drawing.
• *Fine Homebuilding.* No. 61 (July, 1990)
p. 26.

"Handy hardware hauler" by Philip
Belanger. Offers instructions to make a
hardware carrier from recyclable
materials. Photo, diagram. • *Better Homes
and Gardens Wood.* No. 61 (June, 1993)
p. 16.

"Plastic light grid shines for screwdriver
storage" by Harvey Charbonneau. Brief tip
on how to organizer screwdrivers, awls,
and other tools. Drawing. • *Better Homes
and Gardens Wood.* No. 65 (Nov, 1993)
p. 12.

"Power-cord straps" by John Schmidt. Brief
tip on how to make a strap to keep
extension cords coiled neatly. Drawing.
• *Fine Homebuilding.* No. 82 (July, 1993)
p. 28.

"Sanding-supply organizer" by Marlen
Kemmet and James R. Downing. Offers six
easy-to-build projects to organize sanding
supplies. Photos, diagrams, patterns,
materials list. • *Better Homes and Gardens
Wood.* No. 56 (Nov, 1992) pp. 80-84.

"Scrollsaw-blade organizer" by John M.
Turok. Brief instructions to build an
organizer for scrollsaw blades. Photo,
diagram. • *Better Homes and Gardens Wood.*
No. 56 (Nov, 1992) p. 90.

Ornaments — *See* Holiday Decorations; Handicraft

Ovens and Stoves

"Masonry bake ovens" by Albie Barden.
Specific instructions for building a small
brick oven in a basement. • *Fine
Homebuilding.* No. 64 (Jan, 1991) pp. 20-
22.

"New-wave cooking" by Elaine Martin
Petrowski. In-depth report on the latest
technology in ranges and ovens. Photos,
drawings. Sidebar on the new technology
how it works. Sidebar on self-cleaning
ovens. • *Home Mechanix.* No. 754 (April,
1991) pp. 56-60, 92.

P

Paint

"Fear of color" by Jim Rosenau. Advice on
choosing the right color scheme for your
house exterior. Photos • *Practical
Homeowner.* (May/June, 1992) pp. 51-55.

"The fine print" by Walt Gozdan. An
analysis of how price affects the quality of
house paints. • *Practical Homeowner.* Vol. V,
No. 3 (April, 1990) pp. 64-65.

"Mercury banned" by James Lomuscio. An
examination of the use of mercury in
house paints. • *Practical Homeowner.* Vol. V,
No. 7 (Oct, 1990) pp. 24-25.

"Peeling paint" by Henry Spies. Offers a
tip on how to fix peeling paint on
concrete walls. • *Home Mechanix.* No. 757
(July/Aug, 1991) p. 81.

"Problem-solving paints and coatings" by
Gene and Katie Hamilton. Brief article
presenting a table of paints that can be
used in problem areas, such as slippery
surfaces or stopping moisture. Chart.
• *Home Mechanix.* No. 763 (March, 1992)
p. 22.

"Strokes of genius" by Carolyn Chubet.
New ideas in artistic interior paint
schemes. • *Practical Homeowner.* Vol. VI,
No. 2 (Feb, 1991) pp. 40-45.

"Understanding color" by Jill Pilaroscia. In-depth information on selecting a specific color for exterior painting. Photos, chart. Sidebar on the color wheel. Sidebar on applying color schemes. • *Fine Homebuilding.* No. 74 (May, 1992) pp. 40-45.

Paint, Low-Pollution

"Low-pollution paints" by Timothy O. Bakke. Discusses the latest paints with no volatile organic compounds. Chart. • *Home Mechanix.* No. 773 (March, 1993) pp. 64-65.

Paint Pads

"Perfect-edge painting pads." Presents the advantages of using painting pads. Photos. • *Home Mechanix.* No. 749 (Oct, 1990) pp. 26-29.

Paint, Spray

"Enamel spray paint." Provides data on the performance of eighteen different kinds of spray paint. Photos, chart showing comparison. • *Better Homes and Gardens Wood.* No. 40 (Jan, 1991) pp. 58-59.

Paint Sprayers

"Power painting" by Robert Walker and Matt Phair. Informative article on airless sprayers. Photos, drawings. • *Home Mechanix.* No. 748 (Sep, 1990) pp. 51-55.

"Wagner finecoat sprayer" by Dennis Preston. A product review of a high volume, low pressure paint sprayer. • *The Woodworker's Journal.* Vol. 16, No. 5 (Sep/Oct, 1992) p. 21.

Paint Strainer

"Paint strainer" by Bob Simpson. Brief tip on how to make paint strainers. Drawing. • *Fine Homebuilding.* No. 63 (Nov, 1990) p. 28.

Paint Strippers

"Finish removers" by Bill Krier. Informative article describing the effectiveness of 59 finish removers. Photos, chart on the six types of finish removers, comparison chart. • *Better Homes and Gardens Wood.* No. 53 (Aug, 1992) pp. 54-59.

"The new safe strippers" by Jim Barrett. This article tests the qualities of five leading brands of chemical paint strippers. Photos. • *The Woodworker's Journal.* Vol. 15, No. 5 (Sep/Oct, 1991) pp. 67-69.

"Removing exterior paint" by Stephen Mead. Offers tips on removing exterior paint with chemical treatments. Photos. Sidebar on the hazards of lead paint. • *Fine Homebuilding.* No. 84 (Nov, 1993) pp. 72-75.

"Sawdust stripping" by Clyde R. Kennedy. Brief suggestion on using sawdust to strip paint off picture frames, fancy baseboards, trim and carved furniture. • *Fine Homebuilding.* No. 69 (Sep, 1991) pp. 30-32.

Painting

Book Review: *Painter's Handbook* by William McElroy. Book review covering technical advice on painting. Carlsbad, CA: Craftsman Books, 318 pp. • *Home Mechanix.* No. 755 (May, 1991) p. 19.

"Finishing with the best." A guide to finishing various home elements including floors, cabinets, painting, and stripping. • *Practical Homeowner.* Vol. V, No. 7 (Oct, 1990) pp. 58-70.

"Garage door painting" by Henry Spies. Brief article on painting a wood-framed garage door. Drawing. • *Home Mechanix.* No. 756 (June, 1991) p. 86.

"House-painting myth buster" by Matt Phair. Detailed chart with important facts setting the record straight about painting. Chart. • *Home Mechanix.* No. 756 (June, 1991) p. 15.

"Masking before painting" by Don Vandervort. Helpful article on using masking tape to protect surfaces from paint. Photos. • *Home Mechanix.* No. 743 (March, 1990) pp. 14-15.

"Painting exteriors" by Robert Dufort. Informative article on the process of painting exteriors. Photos. • *Fine Homebuilding*. No. 62 (Sep, 1990) pp. 36-41.

"Painting paneling" by Henry Spies. Describes the procedure of painting paneling. Drawing. • *Home Mechanix*. No. 765 (May, 1992) p. 80.

"Painting stone" by Stephen M. Kennedy. Provides ideas for those interested in painting stone. • *Fine Homebuilding*. No. 62 (Sep, 1990) pp. 20-22.

"Painting trim like a pro" by Don Vandervort and Joseph Truini. Detailed instructions on painting trim. Photos, drawings. • *Home Mechanix*. No. 745 (May, 1990) pp. 22-23.

"Painting, without the pain" by Larry Johnston. Handy tips on painting with acrylics from a carver's perspective. Photos. • *Better Homes and Gardens Wood*. No. 59 (Feb, 1993) pp. 48-49.

"Perpetual paintbrushes" by Mark White. Handy tips for cleaning paintbrushes as you work. • *Fine Homebuilding*. No. 62 (Sep, 1990) p. 30.

"Remodeling with paint" by Gary Mayk. Offers remodeling designs for exteriors using paint. Photos, drawings, chart. • *Home Mechanix*. No. 764 (April, 1992) pp. 48-52.

"Rolling interior latex wall paint" by Byron Papa. Offers tips from a professional painter's perspective on applying latex wall paint. Photos. • *Fine Homebuilding*. No. 67 (May, 1991) pp. 67-71.

"Wiping paint brushes" by Michael R. Hogan. Provides a quick tip for wiping a paint brush without using the rim on a paint can. Drawing. • *Fine Homebuilding*. No. 82 (July, 1993) p. 26.

Paneling

"Custom paneling" by Jane Cornell. Describes three approaches to custom paneling using different types of materials.

Photos, diagrams. • *Home Mechanix*. No. 779 (Oct, 1993) pp. 68-71.

"Recipe for raised-panel walls" by Rich Ziegner. Brief tip on making ornate oak paneling for walls. Drawing. • *Fine Homebuilding*. No. 82 (July, 1993) pp. 14-16.

Panels

"Composition panels" by Charles Wardell. Comprehensive article on the major composition panels and what they can do. Photos. Sidebar on reinventing the tree. Sidebar on particleboard and formaldehyde. • *Fine Homebuilding*. No. 67 (May, 1991) pp. 77-81.

"Foam-core panels" by Steve Andrews. In-depth article on the foam-core products available, installation methods, and the controversies about them. Photos, drawings. Sidebar on installation options. • *Fine Homebuilding*. No. 62 (Sep, 1990) pp. 52-57.

"The frame and the panel" by Roger Holmes. A very detailed article on the process for making panel sections and frames. • *The Woodworker's Journal*. Vol. 15, No. 6 (Nov/Dec, 1991) pp. 32-39.

"High-styled raised panels and frames" by Bill Krier. In-depth article covering techniques to make raised panels and frames. Photos, diagrams. • *Better Homes and Gardens Wood*. No. 62 (Aug, 1993) pp. 36-41.

"Make raised panels with your tablesaw." Brief instruction tips on how to make raised panels with a table saw. Illustrations, diagrams. • *Better Homes and Gardens Wood*. No. 36 (Aug, 1990) pp. 72-73.

Panels, Cabinet

"How to create made-to-match cabinet panels." Brief tip on how to make cabinet panels that have matching cathedral or "V" patterns. Illustrations. • *Better Homes and Gardens Wood*. No. 45 (Sep, 1991) p. 48.

Panels, Leaded-Glass

"Leaded-glass panels" by Bill Krier and Jim Downing. Directions to make leaded panels with clear, stained, or beveled glass. Photos, drawings, materials list. • *Better Homes and Gardens Wood.* No. 61 (June, 1993) pp. 32-38.

Pantries

"Pantry plus" by Joseph Truini. Offers instructions for a pantry toolbox and provides creative ideas for maximizing small space storage. Photos, diagrams. • *Home Mechanix.* No. 743 (March, 1990) pp. 46-48, 61.

Patios

"Brick-mosaic patios" by Scott Ernst. Offers instructions and tips on creating patterns and pictures with dry-laid brick for a patio. Photos, diagrams. • *Fine Homebuilding.* No. 64 (Jan, 1991) pp. 80-83.

"Prize patios" by Joseph Truini. Focuses on three designs for outdoor patios. Photos, plans, drawings. • *Home Mechanix.* No. 755 (May, 1991) pp. 35-43.

See Also Decks

Paving

"Graceful paving" by Jim Rosenau. Practical advice for installing paving blocks for walks and patios without using mortar. Photos. • *Practical Homeowner.* (Jul/Aug, 1992) pp. 84-89.

Pegboards

"Pegboard & mallet" by Alasdair Wallace. Furnishes detailed plans and instructions for building a wood child's toy pegboard and mallet. Photo, drawn plans. • *Canadian Workshop.* Vol. 13, No. 4 (Jan 1990) pp. 54-55.

Pen Barrels

"The write stuff." Provides directions to make pen barrels using a drill press or a lathe. Photos, diagrams. • *Better Homes and Gardens Wood.* No. 44 (August, 1991) pp. 60-61.

Pendants

"Resplendent pendant" by Jim Boelling. Explains how to make a maple pendant case for a timepiece. Photo, drawings. • *Better Homes and Gardens Wood.* No. 44 (August, 1991) pp. 66-67.

Periscopes

"Sneak-a-peek periscope" by Marlen Kemmet and James R. Downing. Detailed instructions to make your own periscope. Photos, diagrams, materials list. • *Better Homes and Gardens Wood.* No. 57 (Dec, 1992) pp. 68-69.

Pest Control

Book Review: *Common-Sense Pest Control* by William Olkowski, Sheila Daar and Helga Olkowski. Book review on how to eliminate pests with non-toxic methods. Taunton Press, 736 pp. • *Home Mechanix.* No. 758 (Sep, 1991) p. 23.

"Critter proof your home" by Joseph Crane. Tips on ridding homes of unwelcome visitors. • *Practical Homeowner.* Vol. VI, No. 4 (April, 1991) pp. 62-68.

See Also Insects; Insecticides

Phase Convertors

"A simple phase convertor" by Steve Acker. A primer on the principles of phase conversion as well as a guide to building one. Photos and plans. • *The Home Shop Machinist.* Vol. 10, No. 1 (Jan/Feb, 1991) pp. 34-40.

Physical Disabilities — *See* Architecture and the Handicapped

Picnic Tables

"Picnic table." Instructions for building the classic picnic table. Photos, plans, and materials list. • *The Woodworker's Journal.* Vol. 16, No. 3 (May/Jun, 1992) pp. 40-43.

Picture Hanging

"Picture-hanging jig eliminates guesswork." Brief tip on constructing a jig to make picture hanging easier and more accurate. Drawing. • *Better Homes and Gardens Wood.* No. 39 (Dec, 1990) p. 23.

Pie Safes

"Country pie safe." Instructions for building a classic pie safe with pierced tin door panels. Photos, plans, and materials list. • *The Woodworker's Journal.* Vol. 17. No. 3 (May/Jun, 1993) pp. 28-32.

Piers

"Waterproofing brick piers" by Matthew Scolforo. Brief explanation on how to waterproof brick piers. • *Fine Homebuilding.* No. 82 (July, 1993) p. 20.

Pillartools

"Building the universal pillartool" by Harold Mason. This exhaustive article features complete plans and parts list for the construction of a versatile pillartool. Photos. • *The Home Shop Machinist.* Vol. 10, No. 1 (Jan/Feb, 1991) pp. 16-24.

"Building the universal pillartool, part five" by Harold Mason. See Vol. 10, No. 1 • *The Home Shop Machinist.* Vol. 10, No. 5 (Sep/Oct, 1991) pp. 32-39.

"Building the universal pillartool, part four" by Harold Mason. See Vol. 10, No. 1 • *The Home Shop Machinist.* Vol. 10, No. 4 (Jul/Aug, 1991) pp. 21-27.

"Building the universal pillartool, part three" by Harold Mason. See Vol. 10, No. 1 • *The Home Shop Machinist.* Vol. 10, No. 3 (May/Jun, 1991) pp. 28-33.

"Building the universal pillartool, part two" by Harold Mason. See Vol. 10, No. 1 • *The Home Shop Machinist.* Vol. 10, No. 2 (Mar/Apr, 1991) pp. 32-37.

Pincushions

"Turn scraps into pincushions" by S. Gary Roberts. Brief tip on using blocks of scrap wood to create pincushions. Photos, patterns. • *Better Homes and Gardens Wood.* No. 52 (June, 1992) p. 74.

Pine (Wood)

"Eastern white pine" by Jim Boelling, Tom Becraft, and Harley Refsal. Informative article covering the cost, availability, uses, machining methods, and carving tips. Photo, chart, illustrations. Sidebar on shop-tested techniques. • *Better Homes and Gardens Wood.* No. 53 (Aug, 1992) pp. 35-36.

Pipe Clamps

"Keeping pipe-clamps upright" by Tara Roopinder. Handy and inexpensive directions on how to make pipe-clamp holders. Drawing. • *Woodwork.* No. 17 (Sep/Oct, 1992) p. 18.

Pipes

"No-freeze piping" by Henry Spies. Brief instructions on how to keep bathroom pipes from freezing when remodeling. Drawing. • *Home Mechanix.* No. 773 (March, 1993) p. 85.

"Noisy pipes" by Peter Hemp. Brief tip on replacing ABS plastic drainage pipes due to noise above the dining room. • *Fine Homebuilding.* No. 79 (March, 1993) p. 20.

"Underground piping tips" by Jay Stein. Offer information about pipe installation. • *Fine Homebuilding.* No. 65 (March, 1991) p. 18.

Pivots

"Rounding the ends" by Frank A McLean. Tips on using a pivot handle to make milling operations quicker. Photos and plans. • *The Home Shop Machinist.* Vol. 12, No. 4 (Jul/Aug, 1993) pp. 52-53.

Pizza Paddles

"No-problem pizza paddle." Provides instructions to create pizza paddle. Photo, drawings, pattern. • *Better Homes and Gardens Wood.* No. 51 (April, 1992) pp. 76-77.

Planers

"Planers/molders" by Bill Krier. Examines some of the combination planer/molders and their accessories. Photos, drawings, chart with comparisons of the models. Sidebar on some nifty accessories. • *Better Homes and Gardens Wood.* No. 62 (Aug, 1993) pp. 62-68.

"Thickness planers." In-depth analysis of the components of a planer. Photos, illustration, chart comparing 29 different planers. • *Better Homes and Gardens Wood.* No. 38 (Oct, 1990) pp. 54-57.

"Thickness planers under $500" by Bill Krier. Informative guide on the task of thickness planers and a comparison of models under $500. Photos, chart. • *Better Homes and Gardens Wood.* No. 34 (April, 1990) pp. 64-67.

"Wagner safe-t-planer" by Dennis Preston. A product review for a Wagner wood planer. Photo. • *The Woodworker's Journal.* Vol. 17, No. 5 (Sep/Oct, 1993) p. 14.

Planers and Planing

"Struttin' your stuff for smoother planing." Brief tip on providing support under an extension table when working with long stock. Drawing. • *Better Homes and Gardens Wood.* No. 41 (Feb, 1991) p. 14.

Planers, Portable

"A talented new trio of... portable planers" by Bill Krier. Handy article for tool buyers interested in the capacities of portable planers. Photos, chart with comparisons. • *Better Homes and Gardens Wood.* No. 51 (April, 1992) pp. 54-55.

Planes

Book Review: *Patented Traditional & Metallic Planes in America, Volume II* by Roger K. Smith. Book review on an examination of woodworking planes. Athol, MA: Author (PO Box 177) 400 pp. • *Woodwork.* No. 18 (Nov/Dec, 1992) p. 28.

"Hand planes for trim carpentry" by Scott Wynn. Explains how to tune and adjust hand planes for smooth trimming. Photos, drawings. Sidebar on making a miter-shooting board. Sidebar on sharpening plane blades. • *Fine Homebuilding.* No. 76 (Sep, 1992) pp. 80-85.

"The making of a Japanese-style plane" by Scott Wynn. Provides information on the design of a versatile plane. Drawings. • *Woodwork.* No. 15 (May/June, 1992) pp. 38-45.

Planes (Toy)

"Sea skipper" by David Lanford. Brief article on building an easy-to-assemble floatplane. Photo, drawing, patterns. • *Better Homes and Gardens Wood.* No. 46 (Oct, 1991) pp. 58-59.

Plant Hangers

"Plant hanger from paradise" by Bill Zaun. Brief article on how to make a colorful scrollsawed plant hanger. Photo, pattern, drawing. • *Better Homes and Gardens Wood.* No. 63 (Sep, 1993) pp. 64-65.

Plant Stands

"Plant stand." This very brief illustrated article defines the steps in making an Early American plant stand. Photo and plans. • *The Woodworker's Journal.* Vol. 14, No. 2 (Mar/Apr, 1990) pp. 58-59.

"Stickley-style plant stand" by Marlen Kemmet. Plans to construct a stylish, sturdy oak plant stand. Photos, diagrams, materials list. • *Better Homes and Gardens Wood.* No. 48 (Dec, 1991) pp. 42-45.

Planters

"Bloom boxes" by Matt Phair. Provides directions to build a window box planter with sturdy brackets. Photos, diagrams. • *Home Mechanix.* No. 756 (June, 1991) pp. 58-60.

"Deck railing planters." How to build rectangular planter pots for installation on a porch deck railing. Photos, plans, and materials list. • *The Woodworker's Journal.* Vol. 16, No. 2 (Mar/Apr, 1992) pp. 44-47.

Plaques

"Cozy fireplace plaque" by Roy King and Scott Kochendorfer. Scrollsaw a 3-D fireplace setting plaque with these instructions. Photos, pattern. • *Better Homes and Gardens Wood.* No. 59 (Feb, 1993) pp. 28-29.

"Duck under glass" by Jamie Downing. Provides detailed instructions and a pattern for an extraordinary plaque. Photos, diagrams, pattern. • *Better Homes and Gardens Wood.* No. 43 (June, 1991) pp. 57-59.

"Nature's goodness wall plaque" by Larry Johnston and Jim Barnett. Provides instructions to carve and finish a kitchen or dining room plaque. Photos, materials list. • *Better Homes and Gardens Wood.* No. 44 (August, 1991) pp. 48-51.

"Old-world windmill" by Roy King and Scott Kochendorfer. Patterns and instructive guide to scrollsaw a windmill scene. Photo, patterns. • *Better Homes and Gardens Wood.* No. 55 (Oct, 1992) pp. 66-67.

"V.I.P. door plaque" by Perry McFarlin. Designs and patterns to create your own door plaque. Photo, patterns. • *Better Homes and Gardens Wood.* No. 60 (April, 1993) pp. 70-71.

Plaster

"Drywall booster shot" by David O. Hasek. Offers a tip on repairing a hole in a veneer-plaster wall. • *Fine Homebuilding.* No. 79 (March, 1993) pp. 30-32.

"Faster plaster" by Timothy O. Bakke. Presents a skim-coat system that can be applied in less time than conventional plaster or drywall, yet provides a high-quality finish. Photos. Sidebar on pro tips for a smooth finish. • *Home Mechanix.* No. 752 (Feb, 1991) pp. 68-71, 86.

"Ornamental plaster restoration" by David Flaharty. In-depth article on ornamental plaster restoration. Photos, drawings. • *Fine Homebuilding.* No. 57 (Jan, 1990) pp. 38-42.

"Plaster problems" by Hank Spies. Brief tip on stripping paint, treating the plaster, and repainting. • *Home Mechanix.* No. 743 (March, 1990) p. 78.

Plastering

Book Review: *Plastering Skills* by F. Van Den Branden and Thomas L. Hartsell. Book review on a complete guide to plastering skills. Homewood, IL: American Technical Publishers, 543 pp. • *Fine Homebuilding.* No. 77 (Nov, 1992) p. 120.

"Gluing plaster" by Mark Shilling. Provides a tip on gluing plaster when restoring an old house. • *Fine Homebuilding.* No. 77 (Nov, 1992) p. 30.

"A new skin for a plaster ceiling" by Katie and Gene Hamilton. Step-by-step instructions to repair cracked or sagging plaster. Photos. • *Home Mechanix.* No. 772 (Feb, 1993) pp. 12-13.

"Scribe-fit plaster patch" by Mark Benzel. Offers a scribing method to make an accurate patch for plaster. Drawing. • *Fine Homebuilding.* No. 68 (July, 1991) p. 28.

Plastics

"Recycled plastics find new homes" by Bob Wessmiller. Informative article on the latest uses for recycled plastic bottles. Photos. • *Home Mechanix.* No. 756 (June, 1991) p. 16.

"Repairing plastic laminate" by Thomas H. Jones. Explains how to repair edges or cosmetic damage on plastic laminate. Drawings, photos. • *Home Mechanix.* No. 744 (April, 1990) pp. 18-21.

Plate Racks

"Prize-winning plate rack" by Timothy Burke. Directions to build a decorative red oak corner plate holder. Photo, drawings, pattern. • *Better Homes and Gardens Wood.* No. 51 (April, 1992) pp. 74-75.

Plates, Fixture

"A fixture plate for a lathe or mill" by Ray E. Starnes. Brief tips on constructing a fixture plate. Photos. • *The Home Shop*

Machinist. Vol. 10, No. 2 (Mar/Apr, 1991) pp. 30-31.

Plates, Pivot

"Pivot plates on carpet" by Glenn J. Goldey. Offers an alternative to a wood block under a pivot bifold-door pivot foot. Drawing. • *Fine Homebuilding.* No. 70 (Nov, 1991) p. 34.

Plates, Wooden

"Plate-turning stock." Offers suggestions on the type of stock suitable for turning wooden plates. Illustration. • *Better Homes and Gardens Wood.* No. 45 (Sep, 1991) p. 88.

"A short course in flat-out fun: plate turning 101" by Hopkins Associates. Teaches how to turn a wooden plate with a special turning jig. Photo, drawings. • *Better Homes and Gardens Wood.* No. 45 (Sep, 1991) pp. 82-83.

Play Structures

"Child's play" by Joseph Truini. Offers construction plans to build a sky-high playhouse and a fun train as backyard play structures. Photos, diagrams. Sidebar on pressure-treated precautions. • *Home Mechanix.* No. 756 (June, 1991) pp. 47-54.

Playhouses

"Building a Gothic playhouse" by Stephen Elkins. Provides directions to construct a Gothic style playhouse. Photos, drawings. Sidebar on carpenter gothic. • *Fine Homebuilding.* No. 61 (July, 1990) pp. 43-45.

"Kid's castle" by Carolyn Chubet. How to build a plywood playhouse. Photos and plans • *Practical Homeowner.* Vol. VI, No. 6 (Jul/Aug, 1991) pp. 74-75.

"The playful playhouse" by Ted Jones. Provides design ideas for constructing playhouses. Photos. • *Home Mechanix.* No. 767 (July/Aug, 1992) pp. 72-75.

Playrooms

"Designing with kids" by Linda P. Williams. Ideas on how to work together with children to design appropriate playrooms. • *Practical Homeowner.* Vol. VI,. No. 9 (Nov/Dec, 1991) pp. 52-59.

Plugs

"Screw plugs" by Bill Krier and Jim Downing. Brief tip on making wooden plugs to match the color and grain of the wood surrounding it. Drawings. • *Better Homes and Gardens Wood.* No. 63 (Sep, 1993) p. 39.

"Trench plugs" by Glen Carlson. Brief tip on how to seal open gaps near trenches or embankments. Drawing. • *Fine Homebuilding.* No. 63 (Nov, 1990) p. 26.

Plumbing

Book Review: *Home Plumbing Projects and Repairs.* Book review of a step-by-step manual for repairing plumbing systems. Photo. 128 pp. • *Home Mechanix.* No. 752 (Feb, 1991) p. 33.

Book Review: *The Homeowner's Guide to Plumbing* by Merle Henkenius. Book review on a handy guide to plumbing emergencies and problems from the perspective of a licensed master plumber. Popular Science/Meredith Press, 307 pp. • *Home Mechanix.* No. 756 (June, 1991) pp. 13-14.

"Hot water quicker" by Peter Hemp. Brief article on solving the problem of getting hot water to a second-floor bathroom quicker. • *Fine Homebuilding.* No. 72 (March, 1992) p. 14.

"Plumbing odors" by Peter Hemp. Brief explanation on the possible causes of a plumbing odor. • *Fine Homebuilding.* No. 62 (Sep, 1990) p. 18.

"Plumbing secrets" by Merle Henkenius. Offers eighteen tips and techniques for plumbing repair projects. Photos. • *Home Mechanix.* No. 753 (March, 1991) pp. 60-63.

"Plumbing with flexible pipe" by Rex Cauldwell. Introduces the features of polybutylene pipe and how to install it. Photos. Sidebar on types of fittings. Sidebar on crimping: the key to leak free installations. • *Fine Homebuilding.* No. 78 (Jan, 1993) pp. 74-78.

Plumbing Fixtures

"Plumbing fixtures get the lead out." Brief article on the alternative plumbing fixtures available to prevent lead poisoning. Photo. • *Home Mechanix.* No. 767 (July/Aug, 1992) p. 14.

Plywood

"10 winning ways to work with plywood" by Bill Krier, Jim Boelling and Jim Downing. Ten helpful guidelines for cutting, making dadoes, and getting the edge on plywood. Photos, diagrams, materials list. • *Better Homes and Gardens Wood.* No. 46 (Oct, 1991) pp. 46-49.

"Curled plywood roof" by Henry Spies. Explains why plywood sheathing curls. • *Home Mechanix.* No. 761 (Dec/Jan, 1991-92) p. 72.

"The lowdown on Asian plywood" by David Elbert. Identifies the woodworking uses and methods of sawing Asian plywood. Photos. Sidebar on sawing. • *Better Homes and Gardens Wood.* No. 37 (Sep, 1990) pp. 68-69.

"Plywood siding" by Henry Spies. Brief tip on how to prevent cracking in plywood siding. • *Home Mechanix.* No. 777 (July/Aug, 1993) pp. 84-85.

Poles, Wood

"Poles for building" by Warren Johnson. Explains the advantages of using wooden poles to build roof beams. Photos. • *Fine Homebuilding.* No. 64 (Jan, 1991) pp. 58-59.

Polishers

"Topics in micromachining" by Ted Roubat. An explanation of the uses of a pivot polisher. Photos and plans. • *The*

Home Shop Machinist. Vol. 9, No. 4 (Jul/Aug, 1990) pp. 23-26.

Polishing, French

"Sal Marino's friction-film finish for turned objects." Offers tips on French polishing. Photos. • *Better Homes and Gardens Wood.* No. 59 (Feb, 1993) pp. 58-59.

Ponds, Garden

"Build a garden pond" by Jim Barrett. Offers instructions to build a garden pond in your own backyard. Photos, drawing. Sidebar on concrete cover-up. • *Home Mechanix.* No. 747 (July/Aug, 1990) pp. 42-44.

Pools

"Just add water" by Don Vandervort. Informative article on installing an aboveground pool. Photos. • *Home Mechanix.* No. 746 (June, 1990) pp. 42-47.

"Pools that do more" by Roy Barnhart. Innovative ideas in pool design. Photos. • *Practical Homeowner.* Vol. VI, No. 6 (Jul/Aug, 1991) pp. 56-57.

Porcelain Fixtures

"Renewing porcelain fixtures" by Merle Henkenius. Describes how to refinish old porcelain fixtures. Photos. • *Home Mechanix.* No. 774 (April, 1993) pp. 26-28.

Porch Swings

"Porch/yard swing." How to build a swing set with an A-frame suspension. Photos, plans, and materials list. • *The Woodworker's Journal.* Vol. 17, No. 3 (May/Jun, 1993) pp. 49-53.

Porches

"Bringing up the rear." New ideas for porch construction. Photos. • *Practical Homeowner.* (Nov/Dec, 1992) pp. 48-51.

"Fixing footings and piers" by Henry Spies. Presents directions to build footings and piers for a small porch. Photos. • *Home Mechanix.* No. 754 (April, 1991) p. 17.

"Frugal four-square fixup" by Linda Mason Hunter. Describes the procedure of adding a porch to a four-square house. Photos. Sidebar on square architecture. • *Fine Homebuilding.* No. 71 (Jan, 1992) pp. 60-63.

"Porch reconstruction" by Gene and Katie Hamilton. Offers tips on correcting the structural details when reconstructing a porch. Photos. • *Home Mechanix.* No. 754 (April, 1991) p. 16.

"Porches that won't rot" by Kevin M. Mahoney. Construction tips for porches to prevent rotting. Photos, drawings. • *Fine Homebuilding.* No. 81 (May, 1993) pp. 44-47.

"Renovating old porches" by George Nash. Provides solutions to common problems when renovating old porches. Drawings. • *Fine Homebuilding.* No. 75 (July, 1992) pp. 73-74.

"A screened-porch addition" by Jerry Germer. Offers instructions to add a screened porch to a home with simple detailing and inexpensive materials. Photos, drawings. • *Fine Homebuilding.* No. 72 (March, 1992) pp. 81-83.

"A stone and glass addition" by Christopher Hall. Highlights an addition project using natural fieldstone for a sun porch. Photos, drawing. • *Fine Homebuilding.* No. 77 (Nov, 1992) pp. 74-75.

"Summer rooms" by Norman Kolpas. Ideas for building open porches, gazebos, and trellises. Photos. • *Practical Homeowner.* (Jul/Aug, 1992) pp. 78-83.

Porches--Conservation and Restoration

Book Review: *Preserving Porches* by Renee Kahn and Ellen Meagher. Book review on restoring a porch with attention to architectural details and construction methods. Photo. New York: Henry Holt and Co., 148 pp. • *Home Mechanix.* No. 754 (April, 1991) p. 17.

Post Pulling

"Improved post puller" by Thomas Ricci. Offers an effective method of post extraction. Drawing. • *Fine Homebuilding.* No. 79 (March, 1993) p. 30.

"More post pulling" by Eric Roth. Brief variation on a method of post extraction. Drawing. • *Fine Homebuilding.* No. 81 (May, 1993) p. 28.

Post-and-Beam Houses

"Post-and-beam houses" by Joseph Truini. Shows examples of post-and-beam houses from five kit manufacturers. Photos. • *Home Mechanix.* No. 772 (Feb, 1993) pp. 44-47.

Posts, Newel

"Building an exterior newel post" by Peter Carlson. Offers instructions to build newel posts for a Victorian style house or other styles. Photos, drawing. • *Fine Homebuilding.* No. 84 (Nov, 1993) pp. 60-63.

Posts, Timber-Frame

"Supporting timber-frame posts" by Robert L. Brungraber. Brief tip on calculating the compression capabilities of a concrete block wall to which the timber-frame posts are mounted. • *Fine Homebuilding.* No. 83 (Sep, 1993) p. 18.

Pots

"Weed pots" by Marlen Kemmet. Step-by-step turning method for weed pots. Photos, diagrams, drawings. Sidebar on proportions for weed pots. • *Better Homes and Gardens Wood.* No. 37 (Sep, 1990) pp. 64-67.

Potting Sheds

"Innovative outbuildings" by Rick Mastelli. Four designs for gazebos, greenhouses, and potting sheds. Photos. • *Practical Homeowner.* Vol. V, No. 3 (April, 1990) pp. 50-54.

Power Tools

"Mechanical advantages" by Roy Barnhart. An explanation of the uses of various home shop power tools. • *Practical Homeowner.* Vol. V, No. 8 (Nov/Dec, 1990) pp. 52-60.

"The shaper" by R. J. DeCristoforo. This lengthy article describes the various woodworking uses for a power shaper. Photos and drawings. • *The Woodworker's Journal.* Vol. 14, No. 6 (Nov/Dec, 1990) pp. 20-24.

Power Tools, Cordless

"The cordless tool revolution" by Jim Barrett. A review of new products and standards in cordless drills and other power tools. Photos. • *The Woodworker's Journal.* Vol. 16, No. 4 (Jul/Aug, 1992) pp. 15-21.

Power Tools--Repair of

Book Review: *Troubleshooting and Repairing Power Tools* by Homer L. Davidson. Book review covering this in-depth guide to repairing power tools. Tab Books, 243 pp. • *Home Mechanix.* No. 760 (Nov, 1991) p. 21.

Prams

Book Review: *Wooden Boat Building Made Simple* by Kit Bonner. Book review on a guide for building a eight-foot wooden pram. Fair Oaks, CA: Author (5129 Ridgegate Way) 46 pp. • *Woodwork.* No. 16 (July/August, 1992) p. 75.

Preservation

"Decay resistance of exterior wood" by Stephen Smulski. Offers information on which woods resist decaying the most. Table. • *Fine Homebuilding.* No. 69 (Sep, 1991) p. 16.

"Post treatment" by Henry Spies. Brief suggestion for treating lumber with chemicals rather than pressure. • *Home Mechanix.* No. 755 (May, 1991) p. 97.

Preservation — *See* Conservation and Restoration

Presses, Hydraulic

"Building a hydraulic press twice, part one" by Steve Acker. A detailed examination of the manufacture of a hydraulic press using a six-ton bottle jack. Photos and plans. • *The Home Shop Machinist.* Vol. 12, No. 3 (May/Jun, 1993) pp. 31-35.

"Building a hydraulic press twice, part two" by Steve Acker. See Vol. 12, No. 3 • *The Home Shop Machinist.* Vol. 12, No. 4 (Jul/Aug, 1993) pp. 43-47.

Protractors, Vernier

"A vernier protractor" by Guy Lautard. A product review for a newly designed protractor with a vernier scale. Photos. • *The Home Shop Machinist.* Vol. 11, No. 5 (Sep/Oct, 1992) p. 12.

Psaltery

"The bowed psaltery" by Marlen Kemmet. Learn how to construct and play a Renaissance instrument. Diagrams, photos, materials list. • *Better Homes and Gardens Wood.* No. 34 (April, 1990) pp. 68-73.

Punch Works

"Cabinet with punched doors." A design for a side cabinet with punched tin paneled doors. Photos, plans, and materials list. • *The Woodworker's Journal.* Vol. 14, No. 5 (Sep/Oct, 1990) pp. 45-47.

Punches

"Making pin punches" by Steve Acker. A description of the process of making a punch from a discarded Allen wrench. Photos. • *The Home Shop Machinist.* Vol. 12, No. 1 (Jan/Feb, 1993) pp. 32-37.

Pushsticks, Jointer

"Jointer pushstick" by James R. Downing. Brief instructions to make a jointer pushstick. Photo, diagram. • *Better Homes and Gardens Wood.* No. 62 (Aug, 1993) p. 22.

Putty

"Workable window putty" by Daniel Wing. Handy tips from an expert on making putty of one consistency. • *Fine Homebuilding.* No. 60 (May, 1990) pp. 26-28.

Puzzles, Jigsaw

"Steve Malavolta's playable artwork" by Steve Malavolta. Describes how to design, construct, and finish wood jigsaw puzzles. Photos, drawings. • *Woodwork.* No. 18 (Nov/Dec, 1992) pp. 32-37.

Puzzles (Toy)

"King of the caterpillars." Instructions to cut a king-size caterpillar puzzle ideal for toddlers. Photo, pattern. • *Better Homes and Gardens Wood.* No. 53 (Aug, 1992) pp. 72-73.

"The lighter side of woodworking" by Graham Blackburn. Ideas for woodworking techniques when building toys, puzzles, games, and other whimsical projects. Drawings. Photos. • *Woodwork.* No. 16 (July/August, 1992) pp. 50-53.

"Scrollsawn bunny rabbit puzzle." An easy-to-make project for a scroll saw. Photo. • *The Woodworker's Journal.* Vol. 17, No. 5 (Sep/Oct, 1993) p. 41.

Q

Queen Anne Coffee Tables

"Fit for a queen cabriole-leg coffee table" by Marlen Kemmet and Jim Boelling. Detailed instructions to build an elegant Queen Anne-style coffee table. Photos, diagrams, materials list, patterns. Sidebar on more Queen Anne designs. • *Better Homes and Gardens Wood.* No. 49 (Jan, 1992) pp. 42-45.

Queen Anne Furniture

Book Review: *Queen Anne Furniture* by Norman Vandal. Book review on the history, design, and construction of Queen Anne furniture. Newtown, CT: Taunton Press, 247 pp. • *Better Homes and Gardens Wood.* No. 49 (Jan, 1992) p. 75.

Quilt Hangers

"Country quilt hanger" by James R. Downing. Instructions and assembly for a walnut on-wall hanger. Photo, diagrams. • *Better Homes and Gardens Wood.* No. 49 (Jan, 1992) pp. 60-61.

"Tumbling block quilt hanging" by Marlen Kemmet. Instructions to make a tumbling block patterned quilt wall hanging. Photo, patterns, drawing. • *Better Homes and Gardens Wood.* No. 65 (Nov, 1993) pp. 68-70.

Quilt Stands

"Country-colors quilt stand" by David Ashe. Brief article on constructing a quilt stand designed to hold one or more quilts. Photo, diagrams, pattern. • *Better Homes and Gardens Wood.* No. 52 (June, 1992) pp. 72-73.

R

Racketeer

"What a racket!" by Phil Barley. Provides information on how to build a wood racketeer game. Materials list. Photo. • *Canadian Workshop.* Vol. 15, No. 1 (Oct 1991) pp. 50-52.

Racks

"Audio/video remote rack." A brief tip on making a small wooden tray box for holding remote control units. Photos, plans, and materials list. • *The Woodworker's Journal.* Vol. 16, No. 4 (Jul/Aug, 1992) pp. 44-45.

"A clothes tree for youngsters' aquatic playmates." Plans to create a whimsical clothes tree with dolphin-shaped hooks. Photo, pattern, drawing. • *Better Homes and*

Gardens Wood. No. 51 (April, 1992) pp. 78-79.

"Hall tree" by W. Curtis Johnson. Detailed instructions for building an elegant hall tree. Drawings. Photos. • *Woodwork.* No. 16 (July/August, 1992) pp. 70-74.

"Space-saving clamp rack" by Loyal Downing. Brief description of how to make a wall mounted clamp rack. Drawing. • *Better Homes and Gardens Wood.* No. 64 (Oct, 1993) p. 25.

"The three rack-a-tiers" by James R. Downing. Simple directions to construct a rack for cassettes, videos, and CDs. Diagrams, photos. • *Better Homes and Gardens Wood.* No. 39 (Dec, 1990) pp. 54-55.

See Also Storage–Tools

Racks, Chisel

"Safe-and-sound customized chisel rack" by Richard Baker. Explains how to make a free standing or wall-mounted chisel rack. Photo, diagram. • *Better Homes and Gardens Wood.* No. 55 (Oct, 1992) p. 76.

Racks, Clamp

"Clamp rack." This is a brief note on how to assemble a clamp rack for a workbench. Plans. • *The Woodworker's Journal.* Vol. 15, No. 1 (Jan/Feb, 1991) p. 51.

Racks, Dish

"Oak dish rack." An easy-to-build design for a wall-mounted plate rack. Plans and materials list. • *The Woodworker's Journal.* Vol. 14, No. 4 (Jul/Aug, 1990) pp. 52-53.

Racks, Drying

"Drying rack." An easy-to-make project for a fold-up drying rack for the kitchen or bathroom. Photos, plans, and materials list. • *The Woodworker's Journal.* Vol. 17, No. 2 (Mar/Apr, 1993) pp. 54-57.

Racks, Fishing Equipment

"Fishing rod rack." A description of all the steps necessary to construct a wall rack for holding fishing rods and tackle. Photos,

plans, and materials list. • *The Woodworker's Journal.* Vol. 16, No. 2 (Mar/Apr, 1992) pp. 50-53.

Racks, Lumber

"On-site lumber rack" by M. Felix Marti. Directions on building a sturdy lumber rack to store wood on-site. Drawing. • *Fine Homebuilding.* No. 67 (May, 1991) p. 26.

Racks, Plate

"Prizewinning plate rack" by Timothy Burke. Directions to build a decorative red oak corner plate holder. Photo, drawings, pattern. • *Better Homes and Gardens Wood.* No. 51 (April, 1992) pp. 74-75.

Racks, Saw

"Saw stay straight, sharp in hanging rack" by E.Q. Smith. Brief tip on how to organize saws with a wall-mounted rack. Drawings. • *Better Homes and Gardens Wood.* No. 57 (Dec, 1992) p. 18.

"Simple saw rack" by Merwin Snyder. Organize the saws in your woodshop by building a saw rack. Photos, diagrams. • *Better Homes and Gardens Wood.* No. 48 (Dec, 1991) p. 14.

Racks, Spoon

"A stirring display" by David Ashe. Instructions for a display rack for teaspoons or demitasse spoons. Photo, pattern, drawings, materials list. • *Better Homes and Gardens Wood.* No. 63 (Sep, 1993) pp. 68-69.

Racks, Wrench

"Ready wrench rack." Brief article on how to build a wrench rack that holds up to 16 wrenches. Photo, diagram. • *Better Homes and Gardens Wood.* No. 51 (April, 1992) p. 12.

Radial Arm Saws

Book Review: *Radial Arm Saw Basics* by Roger W. Cliffe. Book review on the basics of using a radial arm saw. New York, New York: Sterling, 128 pp. • *Woodwork.* No. 14 (March/April) p. 19.

"Radial-arm saws." Detailed analysis of the radial arm saw and its components. Photos, comparison chart, illustration. • *Better Homes and Gardens Wood.* No. 38 (Oct, 1990) pp. 34-37.

Radial Arm Saw Stands

"Radial-arm saw stand" by Karl Juul. Brief tip on how to make a sturdy radial-arm saw stand. Drawing. • *Fine Homebuilding.* No. 58 (March, 1990) p. 24.

Radon

"Beating indoor air pollution" by Mike Nuess. Offers a solution for radon in the air in a house. Photos, plans, drawings. • *Fine Homebuilding.* No. 78 (Jan, 1993) pp. 68-71.

Book Review: *Make Your House Radon Free* by Carl and Barbara Giles. Book review on this handbook covering the effects of radon and how to test for it in your home. Photo. Tab Books, 134 pp. • *Home Mechanix.* No. 755 (May, 1991) p. 10.

Book Review: *Practical Radon Control for Homes* by Terry Brennan and Susan Galbraith. Book review on a technical treatment of radon control. Cutter Information Corp. • *Home Mechanix.* No. 755 (May, 1991) p. 10.

"Our readers and radon" by Timothy O. Bakke. Updated report on radon analysis in homes throughout the United States. Chart. • *Home Mechanix.* No. 760 (Nov, 1991) pp. 24-26.

"Radon alert" by Joseph Truini. Brief article on the hazards of radon and information on a do it-yourself radon kit. • *Home Mechanix.* No. 763 (March, 1992) p. 14.

"Radon mitigation in existing homes" by Christopher Meehan. Informative article on dangerous radon levels and making a choice on mitigating or not. Photos, drawing. Sidebar on finding a radon contractor. Sidebar on testing for radon. • *Fine Homebuilding.* No. 67 (May, 1991) pp. 47-51.

"Rating your radon risk" by William M. Turner. In-depth article on the risk of radon in a home. Chart. • *Home Mechanix.* No. 752 (Feb, 1991) pp. 8-9, 91.

"Retrofit radon reduction" by Hank Spies. Brief tip on cleaning radon out of a basement. • *Home Mechanix.* No. 748 (Sep, 1990) p. 90.

"State-by-state radon update" by Timothy O. Bakke. Informative article on the effects of radon and steps for radon reduction. Drawing. • *Home Mechanix.* No. 753 (March, 1991) pp. 8-9.

Railings

"The rail thing" by Matt Phair. Provides five designs for railings to add to decks. Photos, diagrams. • *Home Mechanix.* No. 757 (July/Aug, 1991) pp. 48-57.

"Railing against the elements" by Scott McBride. Describes how to build long-lasting exterior railings. Photos, drawings. • *Fine Homebuilding.* No. 70 (Nov, 1991) pp. 68-71.

"Replace a stair railing" by Michael Morris. Offers information about prefabricated stairway railing kits. Photos, drawings. • *Home Mechanix.* No. 742 (Feb, 1990) pp. 42-45.

Rain Forests

"Tropical woods under fire." A critique of the controversy surrounding the continued use of wood from tropical forests for making furniture. • *The Woodworker's Journal.* Vol. 14, No. 3 (May/Jun, 1990) pp. 26-29.

Ranch Houses

"Transforming a suburban ranch" by Jack Wilbern. Traces the transformation of a 1950 ranch house using `cheap-chic' ideas. Photos, plans. • *Fine Homebuilding.* No. 80 (Spring, 1993) pp. 72-77.

Rasps

"Rasps." A brief overview of the various types and uses of rasp files. • *The*

Woodworker's Journal. Vol. 14, No. 4 (Jul/Aug, 1990) pp. 15-17.

Re-Siding

"Re-siding with wood" by Hank Spies. Brief tip on re-siding and insulating a two-story house. • *Home Mechanix.* No. 744 (April, 1990) pp. 100-101.

Reamers

"Making tap and reamer handles" by Rudy Kouhoupt. Plans for construction of handles for taps and reamers. Photos. • *The Home Shop Machinist.* Vol. 10, No. 4 (Jul/Aug, 1991) pp. 49-53.

Recycled Materials

"Skipping" by Terry Sexton. A primer on the art of skipping, i.e., searching industrial waste skips for recyclable metal. • *The Home Shop Machinist.* Vol. 11, No. 5 (Sep/Oct, 1992) pp. 46-47.

Redwood (Wood)

"Redwood: The forest's elder statesman" by Peter Malokoff, Robert Crevelon and Jack Schultz. Provides information on the availability, cost, woodworking uses, carving and turning tips. Photo, chart, illustration. Sidebar on shop-tested techniques. • *Better Homes and Gardens Wood.* No. 44 (August, 1991) pp. 21-22.

Remodeling

"Attic art studio" by Kevin Ireton. Offers an inventive plan for dropping the garage ceiling to create a studio or office. Photo, diagrams. • *Fine Homebuilding.* No. 64 (Jan, 1991) pp. 84-87.

"Bed alcove" by Tony Simmonds. Offers a plan to convert attic space into a bedroom with a bed that has drawers, bookshelves and a vanity. Photos, drawing. • *Fine Homebuilding.* No. 76 (Sep, 1992) pp. 42-45.

Book Review: *Basic Home Building* . Book review on this basic guide to building or remodeling a home. Photo. Ortho Books, 352 pp. • *Home Mechanix.* No. 766 (June, 1992) p. 16.

Book Review: *Building With Junk and Other Good Stuff: A Guide to Home Building and Remodeling Using Recycled Materials* by Jim Broadstreet. Book review on a guide to throwaways that can be used as building materials. Port Townsend, WA: Loompanics Unlimited, 162 pp. • *Fine Homebuilding.* No. 67 (May, 1991) p. 104.

Book Review: *The Visual Handbook of Building and Remodeling* by Charlie Wing. Book review on a handbook covering facts about building materials. Emmaus, PA: Rodale Press, 512 pp. • *Fine Homebuilding.* No. 74 (May, 1992) p. 98.

Book Review: *Traditional Details for Building Restoration, Renovation, and Rehabilitation: From 1932-1951 Editions of Architectural Graphic Standards* edited by John Belle, John Ray Hoke, Jr. and Stephen A. Kliment. Book review on a practical guide to restoration, renovation, and rehabilitation of structures built in the era of 1932-1951. New York: John Wiley and Sons, Inc., 285 pp. • *Fine Homebuilding.* No. 65 (March, 1991) p. 108.

"Brightening a bungalow" by Rich Binsacca. Converting a 50-year-old bungalow into a modern dwelling. Photos and plans. • *Practical Homeowner.* (Sep/Oct, 1992) pp. 78-83.

"Design programs for remodeling projects" by Ivan Berger. Informative article on software programs specifically geared for remodeling projects. Photos. • *Home Mechanix.* No. 769 (Oct, 1992) pp. 24-27.

"Facelift for a loft" by Richard Ayotte. Provides a design for a cramped loft space to bring in light and space. Photos, plans. • *Fine Homebuilding.* No. 70 (Nov, 1991) pp. 80-81.

"A family at home" by Stuart Baker. Explains a remodeling project to add room for an elderly parent. Photos, plans. Sidebar on rejoining the family. • *Fine Homebuilding.* No. 65 (March, 1991) pp. 76-79.

"Floor guard" by Matt Jackson. Brief tip on protecting a terrazzo floor during remodeling. Drawing. • *Fine Homebuilding.* No. 64 (Jan, 1991) p. 30.

"A general remodel and a major addition" by Scott W. Sterl. Detailed article on the process of remodeling and adding on to a 1920s bungalow. Photos, plans. • *Fine Homebuilding.* No. 64 (Jan, 1991) pp. 38-42.

"Going up" by Michael J. Crosbie. Explains how to add a third floor to a conventional turn-of the-century house. Photos, plans, drawing. • *Fine Homebuilding.* No. 74 (May, 1992) pp. 46-49.

"Header tricks for remodelers" by Roger Gwinnup. Offers creative ideas for remodeling in unusual spaces. Drawings. Sidebar on problem solvers. • *Fine Homebuilding.* No. 62 (Sep, 1990) pp. 85-87.

"Hiring an architect" by Anne Cala. Professional advice on hiring an architect to design a remodeling project. Photos. • *Home Mechanix.* No. 741 (Jan, 1990) pp. 22-26.

"How to cut contractor costs" by Hank Spies. Detailed article on time- and money-saving ideas for remodeling projects. Drawings, charts. Sidebar on national remodeling costs. • *Home Mechanix.* No. 745 (May, 1990) pp. 28-32, 97.

"Just seven feet" by Elizabeth Lytle. How small additions can provide much extra space. Photos and drawings. • *Practical Homeowner.* Vol. V, No. 6 (Sep, 1990) pp. 42-46.

"Laguna Beach remodel" by Patrick Sheridan. Details the remodeling ideas for a 1930s stucco house in a beach community in the style of the Greene brothers. Photos, plans. Sidebar on the Gamble House. • *Fine Homebuilding.* No. 59 (Spring, 1990) pp. 83-87.

"Move up remodeling" by Ted Jones. Offers designs for additions that expand upward. Photos, plans. Sidebar on a special stair railing. • *Home Mechanix.* No. 763 (March, 1992) pp. 60-64.

"Open country" by Charlie Posoneil. Remodeling a 1940s kitchen to achieve a sense of openness. Photos. • *Practical Homeowner.* (Jul/Aug, 1992) pp. 73-75.

"Pop-top remodel" by Brian McMahon. Instructs how to recycle a roof when building a second story. Photos. • *Fine Homebuilding.* No. 72 (March, 1992) pp. 54-56.

"Raising a house addition" by Allan Shope. Describes a couple's desire to build an addition in one day with the help of friends and family. Photos, plans. • *Fine Homebuilding.* No. 59 (Spring, 1990) pp. 74-77.

"Re-siding with wood" by Hank Spies. Brief tip on re-siding and insulating a two-story house. • *Home Mechanix.* No. 744 (April, 1990) pp. 100-101.

"Rejuvenating the ranch" by Norman Kolpas. A step-by-step guide to renovating a 1920s ranch house. Photos. • *Practical Homeowner.* (Mar/Apr, 1992) pp. 50-54.

"Remodeling for the recovery" by Gary Mayk. Offers ideas to preserve and enhance the value of your home. Photos, plans, chart. • *Home Mechanix.* No. 762 (Feb, 1992) pp. 41-49.

"Remodeling protection" by Jim Barrett. Brief tip on preventing interior house damage during remodeling projects. Photos. • *Home Mechanix.* No. 748 (Sep, 1990) p. 19.

"Remodeling with paint" by Gary Mayk. Offers remodeling designs for exteriors using paint. Photos, drawings, chart. • *Home Mechanix.* No. 764 (April, 1992) pp. 48-52.

"Remodeling with windows" by Pat McMillan. Shows the transformation of a run-down hunting cabin with a wise selection of windows. Photos. • *Home Mechanix.* No. 778 (Sep, 1993) pp. 46-49.

"Row-house renovation" by Robert Van Vranken. Presents open and airy renovation plans for row-houses. Photos. • *Fine Homebuilding*. No. 82 (July, 1993) p. 69.

"Small, but sited right" by Richard Sygar. Traces the development of a small lake cottage into to a large home. Photos, drawings. • *Fine Homebuilding*. No. 75 (July, 1992) pp. 66-67.

Software Review: *Fast Track Estimating for Remodelers*, Version 2.1. Software review on a program that helps calculate estimates for residential projects. Vancouver, WA: Northwest Construction Software • *Fine Homebuilding*. No. 83 (Sep, 1993) p. 122.

"Some things bold, some things blue" by William Dutcher. Traces the transformation of a house. Photos, plans. Sidebar on shaping the design. • *Fine Homebuilding*. No. 73 (Spring, 1992) pp. 60-65.

"Sound solutions" by Bob Wessmiller. Informative article on remodeling ideas to control noise around the house. Drawings. Sidebar on Do you live near an airport? • *Home Mechanix*. No. 758 (Sep, 1991) pp. 64-71.

"Tax implications of remodeling" by Scott Brinckerhoff. An analysis of ways to limit higher tax assessments after home remodeling. • *Practical Homeowner*. Vol. V, No. 3 (April, 1990) pp. 26–28.

"Tract-house transformation" by Stan Malek. Details the transformation of a three-bedroom ranch into a spacious house. Photos, plans, drawings. • *Fine Homebuilding*. No. 62 (Sep, 1990) pp. 46-49.

"Uplifting experience" by Jim Rosenau. Description of a technique to convert a one-story home to two stories. Photos. • *Practical Homeowner*. (Nov/Dec, 1992) pp. 58-59.

"When not to do it yourself." Advice on how to avoid do-it-yourself pitfalls. Photos.

• *Practical Homeowner*. Vol. V, No. 8 (Nov/Dec, 1990) pp. 62-68.

See Also Additions; Renovation; Conservation and Restoration

Remodeling--Attics

"An attic studio apartment" by Robert Malone. Details the results of remodeling an attic. Photos, plans. • *Fine Homebuilding*. No. 60 (May, 1990) pp. 42-45.

"Attic upgrades" by Tom Hanley. An analysis of attic remodeling plans. • *Practical Homeowner*. Vol. V, No. 1 (Feb, 1990) pp. 48-53.

Remodeling--Basements

"Bold, beautiful basements" by Rhonda Chant. Reviews the various considerations in renovating a home basement into an attractive living area. Photos. Drawn sample plans. • *Canadian Workshop*. Vol. 13, No. 4 (Jan 1990) pp. 16-20.

Remodeling--Bathrooms

"27 new rules for bath remodeling" by Pat McMillan. Presents the design tips and rules for creating a safe bathroom. Photos. Drawing. • *Home Mechanix*. No. 774 (April, 1993) pp. 58-62.

"Bathing beauty" by Joseph Truini. Provides ideas for renovating a bathroom with decorative tile and new fixtures. Photos, diagrams. • *Home Mechanix*. No. 749 (Oct, 1990) pp. 48-52.

"Bathroom basics" by Ted Watson. Tips on remodeling bathrooms. Photos. • *Practical Homeowner*. (Nov/Dec, 1992) pp. 46-47.

"Stall change" by Henry Spies. Brief instructions to replace a toilet with a stall shower. Drawing. • *Home Mechanix*. No. 755 (May, 1991) p. 97.

"Sweet teen suite" by Peter James. Describes the plans for two new bedrooms and a bathroom to expand a farmhouse. Photos, plans. • *Fine Homebuilding*. No. 74 (May, 1992) pp. 60-61.

Remodeling--Bedrooms

"Simple division" by Ted Jones. Provides a design for dividing one bedroom into two rooms: one bedroom and one nursery. Photos, plans. Sidebar on installing a pocket door. Sidebar on installing padded walls. • *Home Mechanix.* No. 755 (May, 1991) pp. 57-60.

"Suite success" by Pat McMillan. Presents designs to expand bedrooms or baths without adding on to the house. Photos, plans, drawings. Sidebar on marble tiling tips from an expert. • *Home Mechanix.* No. 775 (May, 1993) pp. 70-76.

"Sweet teen suite" by Peter James. Describes the plans for two new bedrooms and a bathroom to expand a farmhouse. Photos, plans. • *Fine Homebuilding.* No. 74 (May, 1992) pp. 60-61.

Remodeling--Dangers of

"Worrisome little additions" by Lisa Iannuci. An analysis of some of the health hazards involved in remodeling, especially for pregnant women. • *Practical Homeowner.* Vol. V, No. 4 (June, 1990) pp. 16-18.

Remodeling--Entryways

"Changing entries" by Thomas F. Sweeney. Discusses remodeling a main entry. Photos, plans. Sidebar on how to build the roof arch. • *Home Mechanix.* No. 774 (April, 1993) pp. 78-82.

"Re-entry." Three designs that remodel homes by renovating entryways. Photos. • *Practical Homeowner.* (May/June, 1992) pp. 80-82.

Remodeling--Garages

"A simple coffered ceiling" by Fred Unger. Describes the renovation of a two-car garage into a library with a coffered ceiling of spruce wrapped in oak. Photos, drawings. • *Fine Homebuilding.* No. 84 (Nov, 1993) pp. 69-71.

Remodeling--Kitchens

"Custom kitchen remodel" by Paul D. Voelker. Describes a variety of remodeling ideas from the wrap-around buffets to the built-in breakfast nook. Photos, diagrams. Sidebar on quartersawn oak. • *Fine Homebuilding.* No. 58 (March, 1990) pp. 36-41.

"Labor of love" by Pat McMillan. Presents a prize-winning design for updating a kitchen. Photos, plans. • *Home Mechanix.* No. 779 (Oct, 1993) pp. 60-62,94.

"Making details count" by Joseph Truini. Offers a remodeling example for creating more space in the kitchen. Photos, plans. Sidebar on building the pantry. Sidebar on creating a solid surface counter. • *Home Mechanix.* No. 779 (Oct, 1993) pp. 46-52.

"Recipe for a kitchen remodel" by William E. Roesner. Provides a plan for remodeling a kitchen using natural materials and top-shelf hardware. Photos, plans. • *Fine Homebuilding.* No. 67 (May, 1991) pp. 72-76.

"Wide-open kitchen remodel" by Matthew Adams Longo. Highlights a kitchen remodeling plan including twenty-one windows and skylights in 200 sq. ft. Photos, plans. • *Fine Homebuilding.* No. 78 (Jan, 1993) pp. 62-65.

Remodeling--Living Rooms

"Inside-out remodeling" by Joseph Truini. Presents a design to brighten a dark living room with a sunny outdoor patio addition. Photos, diagrams. Sidebar on installing a sliding door in a block wall. • *Home Mechanix.* No. 758 (Sep, 1991) pp. 40-46.

Remote Controls

"Remote possibilities" by Matt Phair. Introduces the latest remote controls for appliances, fireplaces, and other household conveniences. Photos, chart. • *Home Mechanix.* No. 751 (Dec/Jan, 1990-91) pp. 58-61.

Renovation

Book Review: *Renovation: A Complete Guide* by Michael Litchfield. Book review on a comprehensive guide filled with professional advice on renovating houses. Prentice Hall, 640 pp. • *Home Mechanix.* No. 755 (May, 1991) p. 19.

Book Review: *Renovation: A Complete Guide, 2nd edition* by Michael W. Litchfield. Book review on this complete nuts-and-bolts approach to renovating houses. Prentice-Hall, Inc., 566 pp. • *Fine Homebuilding.* No. 65 (March, 1991) p. 106.

"Townhouse transformation" by Barbara Poutsch. Renovating a 1926 townhouse. Photos. • *Practical Homeowner.* (Mar/Apr, 1992) pp. 72-75.

See Also Conservation and Restoration; Remodeling

Renovation--Attics

"Rooms at the top" by Pat McMillan. Offers planning tips for converting an attic into a room or den. Photos, drawing. Sidebar on insulation considerations. • *Home Mechanix.* No. 773 (March, 1993) pp. 38-42.

Renovation--Barns

"New life for the Adelman barn" by Louis Mackall. Tells of the renovation of a barn into a house. Photos, diagrams. • *Fine Homebuilding.* No. 66 (Spring, 1991) pp. 60-63.

Renovation--Shaker Farmhouses

"Renovating a Shaker farmhouse" by Stephen Lasar. Presents the process of renovating an eighteenth-century farmhouse. Photos, plans, drawing. • *Fine Homebuilding.* No. 79 (March, 1993) pp. 85-89.

Repairs — *See* Maintenance and Repair

Reroofing

"Reroofing under solar panels" by Todd Smith. Offers suggestions on repairing an asphalt roof under solar panels. • *Fine Homebuilding.* No. 69 (Sep, 1991) p. 18.

Resawing

"Resawing." Useful tips for sawing thinner stock using a process called resawing. Illustrations. • *Better Homes and Gardens Wood.* No. 43 (June, 1991) p. 78.

"Resawing" by R. J. DeCristoforo. This article offers analysis of the proper techniques for resawing wood to smaller dimensions. Photos and plans. • *The Woodworker's Journal.* Vol. 15, No. 3 (May/Jun, 1991) pp. 13-16.

"Surefire resaw jig" by James R. Downing. Build your own jig to make cutting thin stock easier. Photo, diagrams. • *Better Homes and Gardens Wood.* No. 46 (Oct, 1991) pp. 80-81.

Respirators

"Respirator tips." Provides pointers on how to extend the life of respirators. Illustration. • *Better Homes and Gardens Wood.* No. 40 (Jan, 1991) p. 84.

"The woodworker's survival guide to buying respirators" by Bill Krier. Provides helpful information about the variety of respirators available and what jobs require one. Photos. • *Better Homes and Gardens Wood.* No. 40 (Jan, 1991) pp. 32-33.

Restoration — *See* Conservation and Restoration

Retaining Walls

"Great walls" by Jane Cornell. In-depth article on mortarless, retaining-wall blocks and retaining walls. Photos, drawing. • *Home Mechanix.* No. 764 (April, 1992) pp. 62-66.

Ripping

"Resawing" by R. J. DeCristoforo. This article offers analysis of the proper techniques for resawing wood to smaller dimensions. Photos and plans. • *The Woodworker's Journal.* Vol. 15, No. 3 (May/Jun, 1991) pp. 13-16.

Ripping, Radial Arm

"Featherboards assist in radial-arm ripping" by Charles Williams. Handy tip to use when ripping a thin strip from a board with a radial-arm saw. Drawings. • *Better Homes and Gardens Wood.* No. 56 (Nov, 1992) p. 18.

Rockers, Children's

"Rocking dolphins." An innovative design for a child's rocker shaped like a dolphin. Photos, plans, and materials list. • *The Woodworker's Journal.* Vol. 14, No. 6 (Nov/Dec, 1990) pp. 52-53.

"Smiley the rocking snail" by Marlen Kemmet. Instructions to build a sturdy playroom rocker for a toddler. Photos, diagrams, materials list, patterns. • *Better Homes and Gardens Wood.* No. 61 (June, 1993) pp. 58-61.

Rockers, Outdoor

"Adirondack rocker." Based on one of the publication's most popular designs, this article describes the steps in building an outdoor rocking chair. Plans and materials list. • *The Woodworker's Journal.* Vol. 15, No. 3 (May/Jun, 1991) pp. 44-47.

Rockers, Porch

"Lazy-days porch rocker" by Marlen Kemmet and James R. Downing. In-depth construction plans for a sturdy, white oak and mahogany rocker. Photos, diagrams, patterns, materials list. • *Better Homes and Gardens Wood.* No. 52 (June, 1992) pp. 58-63.

Roller Tables and Stands

"A shop-made roller table and roller stand" by Tom E. Moore. Make your own adjustable roller table and stand. Drawing. Photos. • *Woodwork.* No. 15 (May/June, 1992) pp. 66-69.

Rolling Pins

"Candy-striped rolling pins" by Marlen Kemmet. Brief article on making rolling pins with brilliant colors. Photos, materials list, drawings. • *Better Homes and Gardens Wood.* No. 55 (Oct, 1992) pp. 52-53.

Roof Eaves

"Ice-dam defense" by Henry Spies. Explains how ice dams form in roof eaves and how to prevent them. Drawing. • *Home Mechanix.* No. 769 (Oct, 1992) p. 78.

Roofs and Roofing

Book Review: *Design and Application Manual for New Roof Construction: Metric Edition.* Book review of an illustrated booklet on designing and applying shingle and shake roofs. Bellevue, WA: Cedar Shake and Shingle Bureau, 20 pp. • *Fine Homebuilding.* No. 67 (May, 1991) p. 104.

Book Review: *Roof Framing* by Marshall Gross. Book review on this title offering solid instruction on roof framing. Carlsbad, CA: Craftsman Book Company, 475 pp. • *Fine Homebuilding.* No. 60 (May, 1990) p. 106.

"Building a deck roof" by Scott McBride. Offers instructions on how to build a second-floor deck that serves as a roof for a first-floor porch. Drawing. • *Fine Homebuilding.* No. 84 (Nov, 1993) p. 12.

"Built-up cedar roofing" by Steve Dunleavy. Describes how to build a cedar roof resembling a traditional reed thatch. Photos, drawings. • *Fine Homebuilding.* No. 58 (March, 1990) pp. 67-71.

"A cascade of roofs" by John Phelps. Presents a house featuring multiple gables, long overhangs and metal roofing. Photos, plans, drawings. • *Fine Homebuilding.* No. 84 (Nov, 1993) pp. 64-68.

"Cold-roof details" by Steve Kearns. Detailed instructions on the construction of a cold roof. Drawing. • *Fine Homebuilding.* No. 65 (March, 1991) p. 14.

"Framed with concrete and glulams" by Rich Griendling. Describes an original framing technique using site-cast columns and glulam. Photos, plans. Sidebar on a woodstove becoming a fountain. • *Fine Homebuilding*. No. 77 (Nov, 1992) pp. 50-54.

"Framing a cold roof" by Steve Kearns. Instructions on how to build a cold roof, one that prevents ice damming and roof leaks. Photos, drawings. • *Fine Homebuilding*. No. 63 (Nov, 1990) pp. 42-44.

"Framing a cross-gable roof" by Scott McBride. Presents a framing plan for a cross-gable roof. Photos, drawings. Sidebar on two methods of finding backing bevels. • *Fine Homebuilding*. No. 76 (Sep, 1992) pp. 46-49.

"Framing a gable roof" by Larry Haun. Describes the process used by pieceworkers to cut and stack a roof. Photos, drawings. Sidebar on roof-framing tips. • *Fine Homebuilding*. No. 60 (May, 1990) pp. 83-87.

"Have you considered a metal roof" by Don Vandervort. An in-depth examination of the pros and cons of metal roofs. Photos. • *Practical Homeowner*. (Mar/Apr, 1992) pp. 66-71.

"Metal roofing on a flat roof" by Matt Holmstrom. Offers advice on deciding to cover a flat roof with metal. • *Fine Homebuilding*. No. 58 (March, 1990) pp. 14-16.

"Peak performance" by Joseph Truini. Describes a reroofing project replacing asphalt shingles with a fiber-reinforced cement tile. Photos. • *Home Mechanix*. No. 766 (June, 1992) pp. 64-65.

"Putting on a concrete-tile roof" by J. Azevedo. Step-by-step instructions for building a concrete-tile roof. Photos. Sidebar on cutting and breaking concrete tile. • *Fine Homebuilding*. No. 65 (March, 1991) pp. 56-61.

"Raise the roof" by Mark Alvarez. An innovative technique for using hydraulic jacks to create attic dormers or add an extra story to a building. Photos. • *Practical*

Homeowner. Vol. V, No. 3 (April, 1990) pp. 56-59.

"Razing the roof" by Jon H. Thompson. Informative article on adding a second story addition and new roof to a 40-year old house. Photos, drawings, diagram. • *Fine Homebuilding*. No. 57 (Jan, 1990) pp. 43-47.

"Roof assemblies for hot climates" by Larry Maxwell. Details a roof assembly fit for hot climates. Drawing. • *Fine Homebuilding*. No. 70 (Nov, 1991) pp. 16-18.

"Roofing with asphalt shingles" by Todd A. Smith. Instructions on laying three-tab shingles including examples of decorative roof shingles. Photos, drawings. • *Fine Homebuilding*. No. 57 (Jan, 1990) pp. 84-91.

"Single-ply roofing" by Harwood Loomis. Informative article covering the advantages of single ply membranes for the toughest roof problems. Photos, drawings. • *Fine Homebuilding*. No. 64 (Jan, 1991) pp. 43-47.

"Tile roofing" by J. Azevedo. Informative article on the various types of tile, cost, weight, and installation. Photos, drawings. Sidebar on making concrete tile. • *Fine Homebuilding*. No. 60 (May, 1990) pp. 36-41.

"Top secrets" by Joseph Truini and Judith Trotsky. In-depth article on roofing materials and their features. Photos, chart. • *Home Mechanix*. No. 764 (April, 1992) pp. 54-61.

"Venting the roof" by Kevin Ireton. Describes efficient ways to ventilate roofs. Photos, diagrams. Sidebar on the permanent ridge vent. • *Fine Homebuilding*. No. 61 (July, 1990) pp. 76-80.

Video Review: *Advanced Roof Framing* by Marshall Gross. Review of videos demonstrating advanced techniques for framing roofs. Columbia, MD: Advanced Training Services, Inc. • *Fine Homebuilding*. No. 60 (May, 1990) p. 106.

"What felt paper does" by Larry Haun. Discusses the value of using felt paper for roofing jobs to prevent leaks. • *Fine Homebuilding*. No. 84 (Nov, 1993) p. 16.

Roofs and Roofing--Maintenance and Repair

"Asbestos on the roof" by Hank Spies. Brief tip on repairing or replacing cement-asbestos shingles. • *Home Mechanix*. No. 741 (Jan, 1990) p. 84.

"Flat-roof leaks" by Henry Spies. Brief tip on preventing leaking on flat roofs. • *Home Mechanix*. No. 759 (Oct, 1991) pp. 88-89.

"Flat-roof sag" by Henry Spies. Brief article on repairing a sagging garage roof. Drawing. • *Home Mechanix*. No. 768 (Sep, 1992) p. 112.

"New life for old roofs" by Matt Phair. Presents information on latex coatings for asphalt shingle roofs. Photos. • *Home Mechanix*. No. 749 (Oct, 1990) p. 32.

"Painting metal roofs" by Matt Holmstrom. Offers tips on painting metal roofs. • *Fine Homebuilding*. No. 62 (Sep, 1990) p. 20.

"Pitched-roof sag" by Henry Spies. Brief tip on repairing a sagging garage roof. Drawings. • *Home Mechanix*. No. 762 (Feb, 1992) p. 74.

"Problems with a gravel roof" by Harwood Loomis. Offers a solution to a gravel roof that loses its gravel easily. • *Fine Homebuilding*. No. 72 (March, 1992) p. 16.

"Questionable venting" by Hank Spies. Gives advice for venting and replacing shingles on roof above a cathedral ceiling. • *Home Mechanix*. No. 745 (May, 1990) p. 93.

"Roof lichens" by Henry Spies. Brief tip on removing lichens from an asphalt-shingle roof. • *Home Mechanix*. No. 754 (April, 1991) p. 92.

"Shake-roof care" by Henry Spies. Offers instructions on how to maintain a cedar-shake roof. • *Home Mechanix*. No. 767 (July/Aug, 1992) p. 82.

"Slate roof repair" by Randy E. Medlin. Brief tip explaining a method for replacing a broken roof slate. Drawing. • *Fine Homebuilding*. No. 61 (July, 1990) p. 24.

"Strengthening plate-to-rafter connections" by Stanley H. Niu. Presents plate-to-rafter connections that will strengthen roofs during hurricanes. Photos, chart. • *Fine Homebuilding*. No. 74 (May, 1992) pp. 36-39.

Root Cellars

"Designing a root cellar" by Marc Rosenbaum. Brief instruction on how to build a root cellar in a basement. Drawing. • *Fine Homebuilding*. No. 72 (March, 1992) p. 14.

Ropes

"Rope" by Bob Stearns. In-depth article on the holding power and composition of several kinds of ropes. Photos, drawing. • *Home Mechanix*. No. 742 (Feb, 1990) pp. 79-81.

Rotary Tables

"Accessories for a rotary table" by J.W. Straight. A brief description of the various accessories useful in customizing a rotary table for a lathe or drill press. Photos and plans. • *The Home Shop Machinist*. Vol. 9, No. 4 (Jul/Aug, 1990) pp. 28-31.

"Accessories for the rotary table, part two" by J.W. Straight. See Vol. 9, No. 4 • *The Home Shop Machinist*. Vol. 9, No. 5 (Sep/Oct, 1990) pp. 26-29.

Rotary Tools

"Swing-arm support" by James R. Downing. Handy tip for supporting a motorized rotary tool. Photo, drawing. • *Better Homes and Gardens Wood*. No. 57 (Dec, 1992) p. 30.

Roughouts

"Roughouts to the rescue" by Larry Johnston. Explains the method of carving a figure or object roughly with the help of a machine. Photo. Sidebar on how roughouts have drawbacks, too. • *Better Homes and Gardens Wood.* No. 52 (June, 1992) pp. 32-35.

Router Burns

"How to dodge router burns." Brief article on how to prevent router burns on woodworking projects. Drawings. • *Better Homes and Gardens Wood.* No. 57 (Dec, 1992) p. 76.

Router Tables

"Clampless fence makes router setup fiddle-free" by Joe Bodi. Brief tip on making an adjustable fence for a router-table. Photo. • *Better Homes and Gardens Wood.* No. 59 (Feb, 1993) p. 10.

"Heavy-duty router table" by Marlen Kemmet. Detailed instructions to build a router table for your workshop. Materials list, photos, and diagrams. • *Better Homes and Gardens Wood.* No. 33 (Feb, 1990) pp. 50-56.

"Right height for a router/jigsaw table" by C. E. Rannefeld. With plywood brackets and clamps a router/jigsaw table can match the height of the work bench. Drawing. • *Woodwork.* No. 17 (Sep/Oct, 1992) p. 12.

Routers

"5 great router tricks" by Bill Krier and James R. Downing. Learn techniques for making templates for circles, louvers, frames, and other time-saving tips. Diagrams, photos, materials list. • *Better Homes and Gardens Wood.* No. 33 (Feb, 1990) pp. 34-39.

"Drill press router adapter" by Frank A. McLean. A description of a method to attach a wood router to a drill press for greater spindle control. Photos and plans. • *The Home Shop Machinist.* Vol. 12, No. 3 (May/Jun, 1993) pp. 38-42.

"For the router." A description of the different types of accessories for use with a router. Photos. • *The Woodworker's Journal.* Vol. 16, No. 1 (Jan/Feb, 1992) pp. 23-26.

"Router basics." Five helpful tips for using a router effectively. Illustrations. • *Better Homes and Gardens Wood.* No. 37 (Sep, 1990) p. 77.

"Router stands in for a surface planer" by William Kappele. Brief tip on substituting a router to cut a thin piece of stock. Drawing. • *Better Homes and Gardens Wood.* No. 53 (Aug, 1992) p. 20.

"A router-table work station" by Patrick Warner. Instruction on how to construct a router-table work station. Drawing. Photos. • *Woodwork.* No. 19 (Jan/Feb, 1993) pp. 48-53.

"Routers, routers everywhere" by Bill Krier. Extensive guide comparing the costs, effectiveness, and options of 22 different routers. Ratings chart. Photos, diagrams. • *Better Homes and Gardens Wood.* No. 33 (Feb, 1990) pp. 64-70.

"Routers—the handtools" by Graham Blackburn. A historical view of the design of routers. Drawing. Photos. • *Woodwork.* No. 19 (Jan/Feb, 1993) pp. 54-57.

"This stick-on center solves a sticky cutting problem" by Bill Lapham. Details how to cut a circular-shaped piece without leaving a hole in the middle. Drawing. • *Better Homes and Gardens Wood.* No. 65 (Nov, 1993) p. 6.

"Your first router" by Blair Hubbard. Guides the first-time buyer in choosing a router. Drawing. Photos. • *Woodwork.* No. 19 (Jan/Feb, 1993) pp. 42-47.

Routers, Plunge

"Maintaining a plunge router" by Gregg Carlsen. Offers maintenance tips for trouble-free operation. Photo. • *Fine Homebuilding.* No. 79 (March, 1993) p. 75.

"Plunge routers." Informative look at the basic components of a plunge router. Photos, illustration, chart comparing

twenty-two different plunge routers.
• *Better Homes and Gardens Wood.* No. 38 (Oct, 1990) pp. 62-65.

"Plunge routers" by Jim Barrett. This is an exhaustive review of the types of plunge routers and how to use them. Photos.
• *The Woodworker's Journal.* Vol. 16, No. 1 (Jan/Feb, 1992) pp. 72-78.

"Plunge routers" by Gregg Carlsen. Surveys the latest models of plunge routers and their features. Photo, chart.
• *Fine Homebuilding.* No. 71 (Jan, 1992) pp. 78-84.

Routing

"Accurate multiple-pass routing" by Keith P. Brown. Selected tips improve the precision of the router when doing a second pass. • *Woodwork.* No. 16 (July/August, 1992) p. 18.

Rust Prevention

"Basement rust" by Michael M. Ambrosino. A guide to inhibiting rust formation in basement workshops. • *The Home Shop Machinist.* Vol. 11, No. 6 (Nov/Dec, 1992) pp. 40-41.

"Tool-rust prevention" by Stuart E. Hof. Use blocks of synthetic camphor to keep tools rust-free. • *Woodwork.* No. 14 (March/April) p. 6.

Rust Removal

"Rust busters" by Roger Holmes. Suggestions and tips for using chemicals to remove rust from tools. • *The Woodworker's Journal.* Vol. 16, No. 2 (Mar/Apr, 1992) pp. 19-24.

"Rust removal made easy." Offers a method of rust removal using electrolysis. Illustrations. • *Better Homes and Gardens Wood.* No. 63 (Sep, 1993) p. 74.

S

Safes

"What's the right safe?" by Bill Phillips. Informative article on fire safes, burglary safes, and other types of safes. Drawing.
• *Home Mechanix.* No. 751 (Dec/Jan, 1990-91) pp. 14-15.

Safety

"Battling harmful vapors" by George Bransberg. Helpful information about harmful products and how to create a safe working environment. Drawings. • *Better Homes and Gardens Wood.* No. 39 (Dec, 1990) pp. 72-73.

Book Review: *Household Hazards: A Guide to Detoxifying Your Home* by League of Women Voters of Albany County. Book review of a recipes for household cleaners that are non-toxic. League of Women Voters of Albany County, 87 pp. • *Home Mechanix.* No. 762 (Feb, 1992) p. 37.

Book Review: *The Complete Book of Home Environment Hazards* by Roberta Altman. Book review on clearly written guide to protect the home from hazards both inside and outside. New York: Facts on File Inc., 290 pp. • *Home Mechanix.* No. 758 (Sep, 1991) p. 23.

"Hazardous waste disposal hotlines" by Timothy O. Bakke. Phone numbers and state agencies to contact for disposing of hazardous wastes in all U.S. states. Chart.
• *Home Mechanix.* No. 753 (March, 1991) p. 9.

"Home brews" by Ken Ozimek. Provides homemade nontoxic replacements for woodshop supplies. Illustration. • *Better Homes and Gardens Wood.* No. 44 (August, 1991) p. 68.

"How safe are your woodworking habits?" Test your woodworking safety savvy by taking this test. Photos. Sidebar on safety IQ. • *Better Homes and Gardens Wood.* No. 37 (Sep, 1990) pp. 70-73.

"Is benzene poisoning your home?" by Steve Lyons. An explanation of the uses and dangers of benzene. • *Practical Homeowner*. Vol VI., No. 5 (May/June, 1991) pp. 28-29.

"Lawn care safety" by John Harrington. A basic guide to the use of lawn chemicals. • *Practical Homeowner*. Vol. V, No. 5 (August, 1990) pp. 14-19.

"Little safeguards" by James Lomuscio. Tips on child proofing your home. • *Practical Homeowner*. Vol. VI, No. 7 (Sep, 1991) pp. 32-34.

"Panic button" by Carl Dorsch. Create a panic button on the off-switch to be pushed with a knee or thigh instead of hands. Drawing. • *Woodwork*. No. 19 (Jan/Feb, 1993) p. 22.

"Safety: workshop finishes pose risk" by Jim Barrett. An analysis of the dangers associated with wood finishes and the proper methods for their use. • *The Woodworker's Journal*. Vol. 14, No. 4 (Jul/Aug, 1990) pp. 18-21.

"Spotlight on tablesaw safety" by Peter J. Stephano. Specific safety advice when using a table saw. Drawings. • *Better Homes and Gardens Wood*. No. 59 (Feb, 1993) pp. 60-61.

"Tool safety tips." Brief list of guidelines for a safe woodworking environment. • *Better Homes and Gardens Wood*. No. 47 (Nov, 1991) p. 17.

"Working without pain" by Daniel Wing. Examines injuries that occur over many years incorrect posture or holding tools improperly. Photos, drawings. • *Fine Homebuilding*. No. 64 (Jan, 1991) pp. 66-69.

Safety--Bathrooms

"The safety-first bathroom" by Pat McMillan. Presents safety fixtures for bathrooms such as good traction floor coverings and adequate lighting. Photos, diagram. Sidebar—figuring on safety. • *Home Mechanix*. No. 766 (June, 1992) pp. 54-57.

Safety--Insulation

"Insulation declaration" by Joseph Truini. Brief article on safety tips for installing fiberglass insulation. • *Home Mechanix*. No. 764 (April, 1992) p. 14.

Salt & Pepper Shakers

"Salt & pepper shaker combo." This brief article offers guidance on constructing a wooden salt & pepper set. Photo and plans. • *The Woodworker's Journal*. Vol. 16, No. 2 (Mar/Apr, 1992) pp. 42-43.

Salt Water Corrosion

"Standing up to salt water" by Scott King. Solves a problem with salt water eating away at the paint and hardware on a home built on an island. • *Fine Homebuilding*. No. 68 (July, 1991) p. 16.

Saltbox Houses

"Superinsulated saltbox on the coast of Maine" by Elsa Martz. Design and plans for a saltbox house with energy-efficient features. Photos, plans. • *Fine Homebuilding*. No. 70 (Nov, 1991) pp. 54-56.

Salvaged Materials

"Salvaged in Ohio" by Clyde R. Kennedy. Details the process of building a house almost exclusively from salvaged materials. Photos, plans. • *Fine Homebuilding*. No. 66 (Spring, 1991) pp. 74-77.

Sandblasting

"Sandblasting basics" by Gene and Katie Hamilton. Brief article with information on sandblasting. Photos. • *Home Mechanix*. No. 760 (Nov, 1991) pp. 20-21.

"Sandblasting—try it once and you'll be blown away" by Bill Krier. Instructive guide for beginners on sandblasting wood, glass, plaques, ornaments, and doors. Charts, photos, pattern. • *Better Homes and Gardens Wood*. No. 34 (April, 1990) pp. 34-39.

Sanders

"Palm sander" by Jim Barrett. A tool review of six different types of palm sanders.

Photos. • *The Woodworker's Journal.* Vol. 17, No. 6 (Nov/Dec, 1993) pp. 73-77.

"Paper clips grip sandpaper on block" by Rene Stebenne. Offers a tip on making easy sandpaper changes on a hand-sanding block. Drawing. • *Better Homes and Gardens Wood.* No. 61 (June, 1993) p. 10.

"Perfomax sander" by Dennis Preston. A product review of the Perfomax sander. Photos. • *The Woodworker's Journal.* Vol. 16, No. 2 (Mar/Apr, 1992) p. 16.

"Random-orbit sanders." In-depth look at the components of a random-orbit sanders. Photos, chart with comparisons of models. Sidebar on air sanders. Sidebar on the true grit about abrasives. • *Better Homes and Gardens Wood.* No. 59 (Feb, 1993) pp. 42-47.

"Random-orbit sanders" by Terence Rucker. Evaluates the latest scratchless sanders available. Photos, charts. Sidebar on orbiting with a grinder. • *Fine Homebuilding.* No. 77 (Nov, 1992) pp. 68-73.

"Stationary belt sanders." Informative article detailing the specifications of 34 stationary belt sanders. Photo, chart. • *Better Homes and Gardens Wood.* No. 65 (Nov, 1993) pp. 58-59.

Sanders, Finishing

"Finishing sanders" by Bill Krier. In-depth analysis of the components of finishing sanders and a comparison of the latest models. Photos, chart. Sidebar on two sanding specialists for tight spots. • *Better Homes and Gardens Wood.* No. 60 (April, 1993) pp. 52-57.

Sanders, Palm

"Palm sanders" by Jim Barrett. This is a descriptive explanation of the types, uses and costs of palm sanders currently on the market. Photos. • *The Woodworker's Journal.* Vol. 15, No. 2 (Mar/Apr, 1991) pp. 18-24.

Sanders, Portable Belt

"Portable belt sanders." In-depth analysis and guide for selecting a portable belt sander. Photos, illustration, chart comparing 32 different machines. • *Better Homes and Gardens Wood.* No. 38 (Oct, 1990) pp. 74-77.

Sanders, Power

"The Fein sander" by Dennis Preston. A brief tip on using this sander. • *The Woodworker's Journal.* Vol. 16, No. 1 (Jan/Feb, 1992) p. 16.

Sanders, Spindle

"Shop-built spindle sander." This detailed article, including a materials list, provides advice on how to build a spindle sander powered with a 1/2 hp motor. Photo and plans. • *The Woodworker's Journal.* Vol. 14, No. 1 (Jan/Feb, 1990) pp. 46-49.

Sanding

"Sanding shortcuts" by Bill Krier and Jim Downing. Helpful strategies for preparing wood finishes. Photos, charts on abrasives and sanding machines, drawings. • *Better Homes and Gardens Wood.* No. 39 (Dec, 1990) pp. 62-67.

Sanding Blocks

"Shop-built sanding blocks." Describes a simple and inexpensive method of making blocks to hold sand paper. Photo and drawings. • *The Woodworker's Journal.* Vol. 14, No. 2 (Mar/Apr, 1990) pp. 40-41.

Sandpaper

"Fold tabs with a template to install sandpaper smoothly" by Elliott Bloom. Brief tip on installing sandpaper in drum sanders. Drawing. • *Better Homes and Gardens Wood.* No. 56 (Nov, 1992) p. 23.

Santa Claus — *See* Christmas Decorations

Sash Weights

"Site-cast sash weight" by Dave Marlow. Provides instructions for making a sash weight to restore an old double-hung window. Drawing. • *Fine Homebuilding.* No. 68 (July, 1991) p. 30.

Satellites Dishes, TV

"TV satellite" by David Elrich. Informative article on TV satellite installation. Photos, drawings. • *Home Mechanix.* No. 748 (Sep, 1990) pp. 78-83.

Saunas

"Exercising your options on a home sauna" by Pat McMillan. Highlights the latest sauna kits available and the process of installing a sauna. Photos. Sidebar on what's new in sauna kits. Sidebar on building a sauna from a kit. • *Home Mechanix.* No. 754 (April, 1991) pp. 78-81.

Saw Blades

"10" carbide-tipped saw blades" by Bill Krier. Analytical article on 10" carbide-tipped saw blades. Photos, comparison of saw blades. Sidebar on resharpening. • *Better Homes and Gardens Wood.* No. 63 (Sep, 1993) pp. 40-45.

"Bi-metal blades" by Merle Henkenius. Brief tip on selecting long-lasting blades for a reciprocating or sabre saw. Drawing. • *Home Mechanix.* No. 748 (Sep, 1990) p. 73.

"Brazing band saw blades" by Frank A. McLean. A guide to brazing broken saw blades. Plans. • *The Home Shop Machinist.* Vol. 12, No. 5 (Sep/Oct, 1993) pp. 44-45.

"Sawblade degumming" by Pat Percival. Simple tip to remove gum and resin from blades. • *Woodwork.* No. 17 (Sep/Oct, 1992) p. 14.

"Thin kerf blades" by Jim Barrett. This is an analytical article on the advantages of using carbide saw blades with thin kerfs (.08 to .10 inches). Photos and drawings. • *The Woodworker's Journal.* Vol. 15, No. 4 (Jul/Aug, 1991) pp. 58-62.

"Using more of a scrollsaw blade" by Dean St. Clair. Make use of an entire blade even when part of it is dull. Drawing.

• *Woodwork.* No. 15 (May/June, 1992) p. 16.

See Also specific types of saws

Saw Blades, Carbide-tipped

"Examining carbide-tipped sawblades" by Sanford Wilk. In-depth look at the design and specifications of the saw blades. Photos, chart. Sidebar on rules of thumb. • *Fine Homebuilding.* No. 72 (March, 1992) pp. 42-47.

Saw Blades--Sharpening of

"Sharpening guides and gizmos" by Jim Barrett. Advice on using bench grinder attachments, honing attachments, and drill-bit jigs. Photos. • *The Woodworker's Journal.* Vol. 16, No. 3 (May/Jun, 1992) pp. 20-25.

Saw Caddies

"Hand saw caddy" by Dennis Preston. A simple plan for a wall-mounted saw caddy. Photos and plans. • *The Woodworker's Journal.* Vol. 17, No. 3 (May/Jun, 1993) pp. 56-57.

Sawhorses

"Quickset sawhorse" by Dennis L. Collard. Offers a tip for building sawhorses that can fold up. Drawing. • *Fine Homebuilding.* No. 75 (July, 1992) p. 26.

"Sawhorse/ Outfeed table" by Dennis Preston. How to build a combination sawhorse and outfeed table. Photos, plans, and materials list. • *The Woodworker's Journal.* Vol. 16, No. 4 (Jul/Aug, 1992) pp. 58-59.

Sawing

"Extended saw table catches cut-offs, supports long work" by Dave McFarlane. Helpful tip to extend the saw table to catch small pieces or support long pieces. Drawing. • *Better Homes and Gardens Wood.* No. 53 (Aug, 1992) p. 18.

"How to rip and crosscut on a table saw" by Roger Holmes. This is a thorough explanation of good table-saw techniques for ripping wood to width and crosscutting it to proper length. Photos. • *The Woodworker's Journal*. Vol. 17, No. 6 (Nov/Dec, 1993) pp. 24-31.

Saws and Sawing

"Maintaining a worm-drive saw" by Terence Rucker. Explains a procedure to check and maintain the worm-drive saw. Photo. • *Fine Homebuilding*. No. 70 (Nov, 1991) pp. 66-67.

"The Saturday-morning panel saw" by Lee Maughan. Describes the design and materials used for an inexpensive panel saw. Photos. • *Woodwork*. No. 13 (January/February) pp. 47-49.

"Sawing straight and true" by Joseph Truini. Describes a method of making a homemade straightedge guide for sawing a long, straight cut. Photos. • *Home Mechanix*. No. 746 (June, 1990) p. 20.

See Also specific type of saw, e.g., Band Saws, Circular Saws

Saws, Compound-Miter

"A survey of compound-miter saws" by Jim Chestnut. In-depth article on the features of compound-miter saws. Photos, chart, tips on buying tools. • *Fine Homebuilding*. No. 83 (Sep, 1993) pp. 64-69.

Saws, Cut-Off

"Portable electric cut-off saws" by M. Scott Watkins. Provides information about the versatility of cut-off saws. Photos, chart. Sidebar on cutting wheels. • *Fine Homebuilding*. No. 62 (Sep, 1990) pp. 80-84.

Saws, Hole

"Hole-saw refinements" by Lloyd E. Elliott. Brief tip on making a hole saw for removing fasteners. • *Fine Homebuilding*. No. 84 (Nov, 1993) p. 28.

Saws, Japanese

"Japanese saws: eastern styles saws win converts." A detailed analysis of the types and uses of Japanese saw designs. Photo.

• *The Woodworker's Journal*. Vol. 14, No. 3 (May/Jun, 1990) pp. 12-16.

Saws, Miter

"Miter saws" by Joseph Truini. Informative article on the features of five miter saws. Photos. • *Home Mechanix*. No. 766 (June, 1992) pp. 42-45.

"Sliding compound miter saws." This tool review evaluates different types of compound miter saws. Photos. • *The Woodworker's Journal*. Vol. 17, No. 1 (Jan/Feb, 1993) pp. 68-72.

Saws, Reciprocating

"Reciprocating saw review" by Merle Henkenius. Reviews the features of a reciprocating saw. Photos, drawing. • *Home Mechanix*. No. 748 (Sep, 1990) p. 20.

Scheduling

"Hearing yourself keeps extended projects on track" by Dan Wilks. Brief tip on keeping track of your place in the process of extended projects with long interruptions. Drawing. • *Better Homes and Gardens Wood*. No. 57 (Dec, 1992) p. 23.

Schools, Finishing

"Finishing school" by Peter J. Stephano. Offers a description of a finishing school in Rosemount, MN and some finishing tips. Photos • *Better Homes and Gardens Wood*. No. 49 (Jan, 1992) pp. 46-49.

Scoops

"Carve a scoop" by Warren Asa. Instructions on how to make a hand-carved scoop. Drawing. Photos. • *Woodwork*. No. 16 (July/August, 1992) pp. 46-48.

Scrapers

"How to sharpen and use a scraper." Explains how to use a scraper for belt-sander marks and other tasks. Illustrations. • *Better Homes and Gardens Wood*. No. 56 (Nov, 1992) pp. 60-61.

"Recycle a worn plane-iron and make a new tool" by James Gauntlett. Create a scraper from an old plane-iron. Drawing. Photos. • *Woodwork.* No. 19 (Jan/Feb, 1993) pp. 74-75.

Scrapers, Wood

"Taming the hand scraper" by Roger Holmes. Instructions on using a hand scraper as an alternative to sanding. Photos. • *The Woodworker's Journal.* Vol. 17, No. 3 (May/Jun, 1993) pp. 17-20.

Screen Floors

"Removable screen floors" by Al Fink. Brief tip on making removable screens that are affixed to the undersides of the joists. Drawing. • *Fine Homebuilding.* No. 77 (Nov, 1992) pp. 30-32.

Screens

"Shoji for windows" by Rick Mastelli. Adapting Japanese rice paper shoji for window screening material. Photos. • *Practical Homeowner.* Vol. VI, No. 8 (Oct, 1991) pp. 54-55.

"Stretching screens" by David Tousain. Brief tip on how to prevent bags or sags by stretching stretch screens. Drawing. • *Fine Homebuilding.* No. 58 (March, 1990) p. 24.

Screws

"Mechanical fasteners" by Edward G. Hoffman. An explanation of the types and uses of mechanical fasteners including screws and washers. Photos and plans. • *The Home Shop Machinist.* Vol. 11, No. 2 (Mar/Apr, 1992) pp. 50-52.

"Removing broken screws and studs" by Edward G. Hoffman. Clear and simple advice on how to extract broken off screws and studs. Plans. • *The Home Shop Machinist.* Vol. 11, No. 3 (May/Jun, 1992) pp. 37-39.

"What woodworkers need to know about screws." Basic information on sizes, heads, and hole sizes for screws. Illustrations, chart. • *Better Homes and Gardens Wood.* No. 64 (Oct, 1993) pp. 68-69.

Screws, Driving

"Driving screws with a drill" by Thomas H. Jones. Brief tip on the types of drills useful for screwdriving chores. Photos. • *Home Mechanix.* No. 741 (Jan, 1990) pp. 12-14.

Scribers, Spade-bit

"Spade-bit scribers" by Rob Arthur. Brief tip on creating a scribe out of drill bits and assorted hardware. Drawing. • *Fine Homebuilding.* No. 79 (March, 1993) p. 30.

Scribing

"Basic scribing techniques" by Jim Tolpin. Explains secrets for fitting trim to uneven, unlevel, or unplumb surfaces. Photos, drawings. Sidebar on scribing the closing board. • *Fine Homebuilding.* No. 77 (Nov, 1992) pp. 58-63.

Scroll Saw Blade Holders

"Shop-made tools end inside-cutting grief" by Kenneth Fletcher. Handy tip making inside cuts easier with more effective blade holders. Drawing. • *Better Homes and Gardens Wood.* No. 57 (Dec, 1992) p. 14.

Scroll Saw Blades

"The woodworker's survival guide to buying scrollsaw blades" by Bill Krier. Guidelines for buying scrollsaw blades to match the woodworker's job. Chart, photos. • *Better Homes and Gardens Wood.* No. 34 (April, 1990) pp. 56-57.

Scroll Saw Projects

"Autumn leaves" by Susan Evarts. Instructions to create a fall foliage wall hanging. Photo, patterns. • *Better Homes and Gardens Wood.* No. 64 (Oct, 1993) pp. 70-71, 80.

"Be mine, Valentine" by John Lemieux Rose. Plans and patterns to scrollsaw a romantic silhouette for a Valentine's Day present. Photo, patterns, drawing. • *Better Homes and Gardens Wood.* No. 50 (Feb, 1992) pp. 78-79.

"Down by the old mill stream." Offers a design and pattern for a scrollsawing project in a silhouette format. Photo, pattern. • *Better Homes and Gardens Wood.* No. 45 (Sep, 1991) pp. 18-19.

"Family feud" by Mostly Victorian Design. Brief article on how to make a scrollsawed silhouette of Mom and Pop conversing. Photo, full-sized pattern. • *Better Homes and Gardens Wood.* No. 46 (Oct, 1991) pp. 18-19.

"Feathered friends mobile." An easy-to-make project for using a scroll saw to cut out bird designs for a mobile. Photo and plan. • *The Woodworker's Journal.* Vol. 17, No. 1 (Jan/Feb, 1991) pp. 58-59.

"It's a grand old flag." Scrollsaw an antique-looking decorator flag. Photo, full-sized pattern, drawing. • *Better Homes and Gardens Wood.* No. 49 (Jan, 1992) pp. 64-65.

"Kids on parade" by Elaine Hutcheson. Dynamic pattern and instructions to scrollsaw a marching band silhouette. Photo, pattern. • *Better Homes and Gardens Wood.* No. 50 (Feb, 1992) pp. 10-11.

"Letter perfect key chains." Scrollsaw a letter key chain as a gift or for yourself with these tips. Photo, drawing, illustration. • *Better Homes and Gardens Wood.* No. 46 (Oct, 1991) p. 79.

"Lure of the sea relief puzzle" by Russell Greenslade Designs. Directions and full-sized pattern for a scrollsaw project. Photo, drawing. • *Better Homes and Gardens Wood.* No. 40 (Jan, 1991) pp. 70-71.

"Nature-in-the-round" by Larry Clayton. Brief instructions and full-sized pattern for a hummingbird and flowers scrollsaw project and stand. Photo, drawing. • *Better Homes and Gardens Wood.* No. 40 (Jan, 1991) pp. 66-67.

"Ornamental metals." Describes ways to scrollsaw ornaments with soft, nonferrous metals. Photo, drawings, patterns. • *Better Homes and Gardens Wood.* No. 48 (Dec, 1991) pp. 74-75.

"Patterns, patterns, everywhere." Learn methods to turn almost any printed photograph or illustration into a scrollsaw project. Photo. • *Better Homes and Gardens Wood.* No. 61 (June, 1993) pp. 56-57.

"Sign-making made easy" by Bill Krier and Jim Downing. Design and scrollsaw your own signs with these instructions. Photos, diagrams, patterns. • *Better Homes and Gardens Wood.* No. 60 (April, 1993) pp. 40-45.

"Trains, planes, and automobiles." Provides patterns and instructions to scrollsaw three projects. Photos, patterns. • *Better Homes and Gardens Wood.* No. 42 (April, 1991) pp. 80-83.

"Wildfowl fridge magnets" by Judy Gale Roberts. Creative bird designs and instructions to scrollsaw refrigerator magnets. Photos. • *Better Homes and Gardens Wood.* No. 60 (April, 1993) pp. 68-69.

"Winter wonderland." Plans and patterns given to create a winter scene. Photo, diagrams, pattern. • *Better Homes and Gardens Wood.* No. 49 (Jan, 1992) pp. 62-63, 72.

Scroll Saws

"The cream of the crop: scrollsaws over $500" by Bill Krier. In-depth treatment of top-of-the-line scroll saws. Photos, chart with a comparison of nine scroll saws, illustrations. Sidebar on using the right stand. • *Better Homes and Gardens Wood.* No. 45 (Sep, 1991) pp. 68-73.

"Scroll saw." A product review of six different kinds of scroll saws. Photos. • *The Woodworker's Journal.* Vol. 16, No. 6 (Nov/Dec, 1992) pp. 70-77.

"Scroll saws for under $200" by Jim Barrett. A review article of nine different models of scroll saw. Photos. • *The Woodworker's Journal.* Vol. 15, No. 5 (Sep/Oct, 1991) pp. 70-75.

"Scrollsaws." Comparison of different styles of scroll saws. Photos, drawings, illustrations, chart comparing 35 different scroll saws. • *Better Homes and Gardens Wood.* No. 38 (Oct, 1990) pp. 58-61.

"Ten tips for improving your scrollwork." Brief tips increasing the precision and overall quality of your scrollwork. Drawings. • *Better Homes and Gardens Wood.* No. 41 (Feb, 1991) pp. 38-39.

Scrollsawing

"Da' Scrollers!" by Dave Kirchner. Highlights some of the basic techniques of 3-D scrollwork and two scrollers, Roy King and Scott Kochendorfer. Photos. • *Better Homes and Gardens Wood.* No. 59 (Feb, 1993) pp. 25-27.

Security Detectors

"Sophisticated security sensors" by Bill Phillips. Detailed description of home security-system detectors. Drawings, chart. • *Home Mechanix.* No. 757 (July/Aug, 1991) pp. 12-15.

Self Employment

Book Review: *Simplified Woodworking I: A Business Guide for Woodworkers* by A. William Benitez. Book review of a guide focusing on the practical side of owning a woodworking business. Austin, TX: Mary Botsford Goens (PO Box 43561) 66 pp. • *Woodwork.* No. 13 (January/February) p. 26.

Sensors, Passive-Infrared

"The ABCs of PIR sensors" by Roger Dooley. Explains the features of passive-infrared sensors for indoor and outdoor lighting systems. Drawing. • *Home Mechanix.* No. 745 (May, 1990) pp. 24-27.

Septic Additives

"Septic additives" by Henry Spies. Answers a question about additives that contain enzymes or yeast. • *Home Mechanix.* No. 765 (May, 1992) p. 81.

Septic Tank Systems

"Septic solution" by Hank Spies. Offers advice on cleaning out a cesspool system

and adding a leach field. Drawing. • *Home Mechanix.* No. 745 (May, 1990) p. 92.

Settees

"Solid-oak settee" by Marlen Kemmet. Complete instructions for building a durable and beautiful settee. Full-sized patterns included. Diagrams, photos, materials list. • *Better Homes and Gardens Wood.* No. 35 (June, 1990) pp. 60-67.

Sewing Organizers

"Needleworks" by Don Boufford. Describes how to construct a wooden sewing/needlework organizer. Table of materials. Drawn plans. Photo. • *Canadian Workshop.* Vol. 15, No. 1 (Oct 1991) pp. 34-39.

Shaker Furniture

Book Review: *The Book of Shaker Furniture* by John Kassay. Review of book on Shaker furniture. Amherst, MA: University of Massachusetts Press, 288 pp. • *Better Homes and Gardens Wood.* No. 54 (Sep, 1992) p. 94.

"Shaker chest of drawers." A detailed and complex set of plans and instructions for building a Shaker-style chest of drawers. Photos, plans, and materials list. • *The Woodworker's Journal.* Vol. 14, No. 6 (Nov/Dec, 1990) pp. 65-69.

"Shaker drop-leaf table" by Gene Cosloy. This is a brief description of the method of making a drop-leaf side table after a nineteenth-century Shaker pattern. Photo, plans, and materials list. • *The Woodworker's Journal.* Vol. 15, No. 4 (Jul/Aug, 1991) pp. 33-35.

Shaker Houses

"Three simple houses" by Dan Wheeler. Construction plans for three houses with Shaker inspired details. Photos, plans. • *Fine Homebuilding.* No. 73 (Spring, 1992) pp. 82-87.

Shapers

"The shaper" by R. J. DeCristoforo. This lengthy article describes the various woodworking uses for a power shaper. Photos and drawings. • *The Woodworker's Journal.* Vol. 14, No. 6 (Nov/Dec, 1990) pp. 20-24.

"Shapers" by Bill Krier. Examines the benefits of using shapers and comparison of ten popular models. Photos, diagrams, chart. • *Better Homes and Gardens Wood.* No. 39 (Dec, 1990) pp. 56-61.

Sheds

Book Review: *Shed, The Do-It-Yourself Guide for Backyard Builders* by David Stiles. Book review on an illustrated guide for constructing sheds. Photo. Charlotte, VT: Camden House, 142 pp. • *Home Mechanix.* No. 778 (Sep, 1993) p. 70.

"Build an outdoor closet." How to build a utility shed. Photos and plans. • *Practical Homeowner.* Vol. VI, No. 3 (March, 1991) pp. 60-62.

"Stylish sheds" by Joseph Truini. Construction plans for three storage sheds. Photos, diagrams. • *Home Mechanix.* No. 778 (Sep, 1993) pp. 64-70.

"Super sheds" by Jane Cornell. Describes several panelized sheds and how to obtain the assembly kits. Photos. • *Home Mechanix.* No. 763 (March, 1992) pp. 42-45.

"The ultimate backyard shed" by Pat McMillan. Detailed description on how to build a storage shed in the backyard. Photos, diagrams. • *Home Mechanix.* No. 758 (Sep, 1991) pp. 54-58.

Sheds, Garden

"In this corner" by Rich Binsacca. Building a garden shed that becomes part of the fence line. Photos and plans. • *Practical Homeowner.* (May/June, 1992) pp. 76-79.

Sheds, Storage

"Storage buildings" by Matt Phair. Presents five precut kits for storage buildings. Photos. • *Home Mechanix.* No. 772 (Feb, 1993) pp. 56-59.

Sheet Metal

"Drilling sheet metal safely" by Mark Francis. Brief tip on how to drill sheet metal safely and effectively. Drawing. • *Fine Homebuilding.* No. 82 (July, 1993) p. 28.

Sheet-Metal Brakes

"Site-built sheet-metal brake" by William Boyce. Describes how to build a homemade sheet metal brake. Drawing. • *Fine Homebuilding.* No. 57 (Jan, 1990) p. 28.

Shelves

"20 ways to hang a shelf." A descriptive article about the different methods that can be used in hanging shelves. Drawings. • *The Woodworker's Journal.* Vol. 14, No. 6 (Nov/Dec, 1990) pp. 31-34.

"Early American style curio shelf." This a brief tip on how to construct a three-level wall shelf in the Early American style. Photo, plans, and material list. • *The Woodworker's Journal.* Vol. 15, No. 2 (Mar/Apr, 1991) pp. 52-53.

"Glass curtain" by Joseph Truini. Introduces a novel window-wall system ideal for patios or porches. Photos, drawings. • *Home Mechanix.* No. 748 (Sep, 1990) pp. 46-48.

"Shelf sufficiency" by Joseph Truini. Presents easy-to-build storage shelves for a basement or garage. Photos, drawings, diagrams. • *Home Mechanix.* No. 748 (Sep, 1990) pp. 64-72.

"Shelf support" by David Strawderman. Offers a tip on making supports for closet shelves. Drawing. • *Fine Homebuilding.* No. 60 (May, 1990) p. 26.

"Victorian wall shelf." A quick and simple plan for the design of a small Victorian style whatnot shelf. Photo and plans. • *The Woodworker's Journal.* Vol. 14, No. 3 (May/Jun, 1990) pp. 48-50.

"Wall shelf." An easy-to-make project for building a small what-not type shelf. Photos, plans, and materials list. • *The*

Woodworker's Journal. Vol. 17, No. 6 (Nov/Dec, 1993) pp. 61-63.

"Wall-to-wall units" by Jeff Mathers. Provides detailed instructions on how to build and install wood wall shelving. Drawn plans. List of materials. Photo. • *Canadian Workshop.* Vol. 13, No. 4 (Jan 1990) pp. 46-49.

See Also Bookshelves; Storage

Shims

"Shim-shingle jig" by John Kraft. Brief tip on making shim shingles from scraps of wood. Drawing. • *Fine Homebuilding.* No. 58 (March, 1990) p. 26.

Shingles

"Algae-stained shingles" by Todd Smith. Offers a method of cleaning algae off roof shingles. • *Fine Homebuilding.* No. 63 (Nov, 1990) p. 16.

"Shim-shingle jig" by John Kraft. Brief tip on making shim shingles from scraps of wood. Drawing. • *Fine Homebuilding.* No. 58 (March, 1990) p. 26.

"Shingle TLC" by Richard E. Reed. Brief tip on cleaning old, damaged shingles. • *Fine Homebuilding.* No. 67 (May, 1991) p. 28.

"Special-effect shingles" by Ted Jones. Describes the versatility in using fancy-butt cedar shingles for newly constructed homes. Photos, drawings. Sidebar on fancy-butt shingle accents. Sidebar on Italian variations. • *Home Mechanix.* No. 756 (June, 1991) pp. 33-36.

"A wet edge" by Henry Spies. Explains why shingles curl and how to repair the cracks caused by water damage. Drawing. • *Home Mechanix.* No. 768 (Sep, 1992) p. 112.

Shingles--Maintenance and Repair

"Questionable venting" by Hank Spies. Gives advice for venting and replacing shingles on a roof above a cathedral ceiling. • *Home Mechanix.* No. 745 (May, 1990) p. 93.

Shingling

"Shingling an arch" by Dave Skilton. Handy tip on installing shingles and trimming to form a wedge shape. Drawing. • *Fine Homebuilding.* No. 57 (Jan, 1990) p. 14.

Shoe Racks

"Stackable shoe rack." A simple and easy to make plan for a two-level shoe rack. Photo, plans, and materials list. • *The Woodworker's Journal.* Vol. 14, No. 3 (May/Jun, 1990) pp. 46-47.

Shoji

"Shoji for windows" by Rick Mastelli. Adapting Japanese rice paper shoji for window screening material. Photos. • *Practical Homeowner.* Vol. VI, No. 8 (Oct, 1991) pp. 54-55.

Shop Design

"Shop layout" by Olev Edur. The author provides sample workshop floor plans, hints for more efficient work areas, and a template. Drawn plans. • *Canadian Workshop.* Vol. 13, No. 5 (Feb 1990) pp. 31-40.

Shop Mathematics

"Density, volume, dimensions = weight" by L.C. Melton. This is an analysis of the formula for fabricating metal to a specific weight. • *The Home Shop Machinist.* Vol. 9, No. 3 (May/Jun, 1990) pp. 38-39.

"Geometric construction, part five" by Edward G. Hoffman. See Vol. 10, No. 5 • *The Home Shop Machinist.* Vol. 11, No. 3 (May/June, 1992) pp. 15-18.

"Geometric construction, part four" by Edward G. Hoffman. See Vol. 10, No. 5 • *The Home Shop Machinist.* Vol. 11, No. 2 (Mar/Apr, 1992) pp. 17-19.

"Geometric construction, part one" by Edward G. Hoffman. A detailed article describing the process of marking layout lines without any measuring devices. Drawings. • *The Home Shop Machinist.* Vol. 10, No. 5 (Sep/Oct, 1991) pp. 17-19.

"Geometric construction, part three" by Edward G. Hoffman. See Vol. 10, No. 5 • *The Home Shop Machinist.* Vol. 11, No. 1 (Jan/Feb, 1992) pp. 15-17.

"Measuring with pins" by Edward G. Hoffman. This article describes the use of dowel pins as measuring devices. Drawings. • *The Home Shop Machinist.* Vol. 11, No. 4 (Jul/Aug, 1992) pp. 18-19.

"Measuring with pins, part four" by Edward G. Hoffman. See Vol. 11, No. 4 • *The Home Shop Machinist.* Vol. 12, No. 1 (Jan/Feb, 1993) pp. 16-17.

"Measuring with pins, part three" by Edward G. Hoffman. See Vol. 11, No. 4 • *The Home Shop Machinist.* Vol. 11, No. 6 (Nov/Dec, 1992) pp. 16-18.

"Measuring with Pins, part two" by Edward G. Hoffman. See Vol. 11, No. 4 • *The Home Shop Machinist.* Vol. 11, No. 5 (Sep/Oct, 1992) pp. 16-17.

"Right triangles, part three" by Edward Hoffman. An analysis of the uses of right triangle math calculations for different kinds of metal shop work. • *The Home Shop Machinist.* Vol. 9, No. 1 (Jan/Feb, 1990) pp. 20-23.

"Shop measurement, part one" by Edward Hoffman. This article offers a primer on performing all types of mathematical calculations useful in a machine shop setting. • *The Home Shop Machinist.* Vol. 9, No. 2 (Mar/Apr 1990) pp. 17-19.

Shop Measurement, part four" by Edward G. Hoffman. See Vol. 9, No. 2 • *The Home Shop Machinist.* Vol. 9, No. 5 (Sep/Oct, 1990) pp. 18-19.

"Shop measurement, part six" by Edward G. Hoffman. See Vol. 9, No. 2 • *The Home Shop Machinist.* Vol. 10, No. 1 (Jan/Feb, 1991) pp. 13-15.

"Shop measurement, part three" by Edward G. Hoffman. See Vol. 9, No. 1 • *The Home Shop Machinist.* Vol. 9, No. 4 (Jul/Aug, 1990) pp. 16-17.

"Shop measurement, part two" by Edward Hoffman. See Vol. 9, No. 2 • *The Home Shop Machinist.* Vol. 9, No. 3 (May/Jun, 1990) pp. 20-21.

"Surface finish designations, part one" by Edward G. Hoffman. This article provides an explanation of the usages and symbols for designating surface finish and smoothness. Illustrations. • *The Home Shop Machinist.* Vol. 10, No. 2 (Mar/Apr, 1991) pp. 16-17.

"Surface finish designations, part three" by Edward G. Hoffman. See Vol. 10, No. 2 • *The Home Shop Machinist.* Vol. 10, No. 4 (Jul/Aug, 1991) pp. 16-17.

"Surface finish designations, part two" by Edward G. Hoffman. See Vol. 10, No. 2 • *The Home Shop Machinist.* Vol. 10, No. 3 (May/Jun, 1991) pp. 13-15.

Shop Tables

"Shop work center" by Dennis Preston. A direct and simple set of plans for building a work table and storage area. Photos, plans, and materials list. • *The Woodworker's Journal.* Vol. 16, No. 1 (Jan/Feb, 1992) pp. 52-55.

Shop Vacs

"Piping for your shop vacuum makes cleaning up a cinch" by Dean Jenkins. Handy tip to connect a pipe system in the workshop to make vacuuming simpler. Drawing. • *Better Homes and Gardens Wood.* No. 50 (Feb, 1992) p. 18.

"What's available in low-cost dust collection systems" by Jim Barrett. This review offers a thorough analysis of the types of shop vacs on the market. Photos. • *The Woodworker's Journal.* Vol. 15, No. 3 (May/Jun, 1991) pp. 30-36.

Shopsmith Power Stations

"Combination tools-plus" by Olev Edur. Evaluates the various features of the Shopsmith Power Station. Photos. • *Canadian Workshop.* Vol. 13, No. 4 (Jan 1990) pp. 25-27.

Show Cases — *See* **Display Cases**

Shower Heads

"Low-flow shower heads" by Gene and Katie Hamilton. Offers energy-saving tips with low-flow shower heads. Worksheet. • *Home Mechanix.* No. 764 (April, 1992) pp. 16-20.

Shower Windows

"Shower window" by Henry Spies. Brief tip on protecting a wooden window in a shower. • *Home Mechanix.* No. 772 (Feb, 1993) p. 80.

Showers

"Chance of showers" by Merle Henkenius. Presents instructions for installing a new space saving shower. Photos. Sidebar on a shower of creative designs. • *Home Mechanix.* No. 749 (Oct, 1990) pp. 61-66.

"How to add a shower to a tub" by Merle Henkenius. Describes the procedure of adding a shower to a bathtub. Photos. • *Home Mechanix.* No. 769 (Oct, 1992) pp. 64-68.

"Pressure drops in the shower" by Peter Hemp. Offers an explanation for sudden pressure changes or temperature changes in a shower. • *Fine Homebuilding.* No. 65 (March, 1991) pp. 14-16.

"Retrofitting a shower-pan bed" by Peter Hemp. Describes a solution to beefing up a fiberglass shower with a thin bottom. • *Fine Homebuilding.* No. 70 (Nov, 1991) pp. 14-16.

"Small bathroom, walk-in shower" by Rich Griendling. Presents a bathroom design with a walk-in shower. Photo, drawing. • *Fine Homebuilding.* No. 79 (March, 1993) pp. 62-63.

"Super showers" by Tracy O'Shea. New ideas in shower stall design. Photos. • *Practical Homeowner.* Vol. VI, No. 7 (Sep, 1991) pp. 52-54.

"Three hour shower" by Merle Henkenius. Offers a way to add a shower to a bath or replace an old shower all within three hours. Photos, drawing. • *Home Mechanix.* No. 759 (Oct, 1991) pp. 57-60.

Shrinkage, Wood

"Detailing for wood shrinkage" by Stephen Smulski. Provides valuable information about avoiding nail pops, cracked drywall and sloping floors. Photos, drawings, diagrams. Sidebar on how moisture content changes with humidity levels. • *Fine Homebuilding.* No. 81 (May, 1993) pp. 54-59.

Sideboards

"Sideboard chest." Complete and detailed instructions for making an Early American-style sideboard. Photos, plans, and materials list. • *The Woodworker's Journal.* Vol. 16, No. 2 (Mar/Apr, 1992) pp. 38-41.

"A walnut side table" by Jeff Greef. Detailed instructions for building oval- and curved-form tables including a parts list. Photos. Drawing. • *Woodwork.* No. 17 (Sep/Oct, 1992) pp. 69-72.

"A William and Mary sideboard?" by Steven M. Lash. Presents an intriguing account of building an seventeenth century William and Mary sideboard without a model to reproduce. Drawings. Photos. Dimension specifications. • *Woodwork.* No. 14 (March/April) pp. 42-47.

Sidewalks

"Flexible walkway" by Henry Spies. Brief tip on creating a walkway to match a macadam driveway. Drawing. • *Home Mechanix.* No. 765 (May, 1992) p. 80.

"Paving without pavers" by Thomas F. Sweeney. Using poured concrete along with stamped forms to imitate paving blocks. Photos. • *Practical Homeowner.* Vol. VI. No. 7 (Sep, 1991) pp. 16-18.

"Private paths" by Joseph Truini. Presents seven paving projects for a lawn or garden. Photos, drawings. Sidebar on cutting stone and brick. • *Home Mechanix.* No. 763 (March, 1992) pp. 38-41.

Siding

Book and Video Review: *Natural Wood Siding: Selection, Installation and Finishing* by Western Wood Products Association. Review of a book and video guide to wood siding installation. Western Wood Products Association, 12 pp. • *Home Mechanix.* No. 753 (March, 1991) p. 20.

"Choosing siding" by Scott Gibson. In-depth article on the choices available for siding. Photos, chart. Sidebar on how long siding lasts. • *Fine Homebuilding.* No. 83 (Sep, 1993) pp. 40-45.

"Drying rack for siding" by Jim Gurman. Offers an idea to store siding for long periods of time. Drawing. • *Fine Homebuilding.* No. 60 (May, 1990) p. 28.

"Installing board-and-batten siding" by John Birchard. Covers the essential details to properly install board-and-batten siding. Photos, drawings. • *Fine Homebuilding.* No. 75 (July, 1992) pp. 52-56.

"Painting aluminum siding" by Henry Spies. Offers a tip on painting aluminum siding. • *Home Mechanix.* No. 771 (Dec/Jan, 1992-93) p. 81.

"Plywood siding" by Henry Spies. Brief tip on how to prevent cracking in plywood siding. • *Home Mechanix.* No. 777 (July/Aug, 1993) pp. 84-85.

"Residing an old house" by George Nash. Presents a tip on re-siding a 100-year-old Victorian house. • *Fine Homebuilding.* No. 82 (July, 1993) p. 14.

"Restaining siding" by Henry Spies. Offers three ways of restaining siding. • *Home Mechanix.* No. 770 (Nov, 1992) pp. 92-93.

"Siding holdup" by Trip Renn. Brief suggestion for siding a house with clapboards. Drawing. • *Fine Homebuilding.* No. 71 (Jan, 1992) p. 26.

"Siding over stucco" by John Decker. Provides tips on installing cedar siding over stucco. Photo, drawing. • *Home Mechanix.* No. 753 (March, 1991) pp. 16-20.

"Siding shelf" by Jim Finnegan. Brief instruction tip on building a shelf to support siding. Drawing. • *Fine Homebuilding.* No. 83 (Sep, 1993) pp. 28-30.

"Wrapping a house in vinyl" by Anne Cala. Professional advice on the advantages of vinyl siding. Drawing. • *Home Mechanix.* No. 758 (Sep, 1991) pp. 24-27.

Signs

"Colonial sign." An explanation of the patterns needed for building a Colonial-style hanging sign. Plans and materials list. • *The Woodworker's Journal.* Vol. 14, No. 4 (Jul/Aug, 1990) pp. 43-45.

"North-country signs" by James R. Downing. Instructions to create attractive, natural wooden signs for businesses or residences. Photos. • *Better Homes and Gardens Wood.* No. 62 (Aug, 1993) pp. 27-31.

"Sign-making made easy" by Bill Krier and Jim Downing. Design and scrollsaw your own signs with these instructions. Photos, diagrams, patterns. • *Better Homes and Gardens Wood.* No. 60 (April, 1993) pp. 40-45.

"A warm welcome" by Michael Mealey. Create a Southwest-style welcome sign with a router and chisel. Photo, pattern. • *Better Homes and Gardens Wood.* No. 42 (April, 1991) pp. 70-71.

Sills

"Replacing a sill on grade" by George Nash. Explains how to replace a rotting sill under a kitchen. Drawings. • *Fine Homebuilding.* No. 77 (Nov, 1992) p. 16.

Sinks

"Supporting sink cutouts" by Peter Campaner. Brief tip on preventing the sink cutouts from falling into the hole. Drawing. • *Fine Homebuilding.* No. 82 (July, 1993) p. 28.

Sinks, Double

"Double-sink upgrade" by Merle Henkenius. Detailed description on upgrading a single sink with a double sink without replacing the base cabinet. Drawing, photos. • *Home Mechanix.* No. 775 (May, 1993) pp. 17-19.

Sinks, Dry

"The oak dry sink" by Marlen Kemmet. Step-by-step instructions for this sturdy classic. Diagrams, photos, materials list. • *Better Homes and Gardens Wood.* No. 33 (Feb, 1990) pp. 40-45.

Skewers

"Sweet-tooth skewers" by David Ashe. Offers instructions on how to make skewers for caramel apples. Photos, patterns, materials list. • *Better Homes and Gardens Wood.* No. 64 (Oct, 1993) pp. 58-59.

Skylights

"Skylights in the eaves" by Anthony Simmonds. Create light-filled spaces in a house that is built in close proximity to neighboring houses. Photos, drawings. Sidebar on plants in the eaves. • *Fine Homebuilding.* No. 70 (Nov, 1991) pp. 40-44.

Slabjacking Concrete

"A lift for sunken concrete" by Matt Phair. Introduces the technique of slabjacking for sunken concrete problems. Photos, drawings. • *Home Mechanix.* No. 756 (June, 1991) p. 13.

Sledge Protectors

"Sledge bumper" by William H. Brennen. Brief tip on making a bumper on the top of the handle for a sledge hammer. Drawing. • *Fine Homebuilding.* No. 79 (March, 1993) p. 32.

Sleighs

"Snow-loving open sleigh" by Marlen Kemmet. Construct a sleek-looking classic sleigh with these instructions. Diagrams, photos, material list. • *Better Homes and Gardens Wood.* No. 39 (Dec, 1990) pp. 48-53.

Slide Boxes

"A simple slide box" by Jacob Schulzinger. Build your own inexpensive slide box for viewing slides. Drawing. Photos. • *Woodwork.* No. 19 (Jan/Feb, 1993) pp. 70-72.

Slip Cases, Magazine

"Magazine slip cases." An easy-to-make project building box-jointed magazine slip cases. Photo, plans, and materials list. • *The Woodworker's Journal.* Vol. 17, No. 5 (Sep/Oct, 1993) pp. 48-49.

Snips

"Snip tip" by Tom Law. Explains how to sharpen aviation-type metal snip tips. Drawing. • *Fine Homebuilding.* No. 79 (March, 1993) p. 30.

Snowshoes

"Making tracks" by Peter J. Stephano. Follow snowshoe maker Carl Heilman through the process of making snowshoes. Photo, drawing. • *Better Homes and Gardens Wood.* No. 48 (Dec, 1991) pp. 33-37.

Soap Dispensers

"Pump dispenser" by Ennis Mountain Woods and James R. Downing. Brief article on how to make a walnut-clad soap dispenser. Photo, diagram. • *Better Homes and Gardens Wood.* No. 46 (Oct, 1991) pp. 74-75.

Software — *See* Computer Software

Solar Energy

Book Review: *The Fuel Savers: A Kit of Solar Ideas for Your Home, Apartment, or Business* by Bruce Anderson. Book review on a handy kit of solar energy ideas for a home, apartment, or business. Morning Sun Press, 81 pp. • *Home Mechanix.* No. 762 (Feb, 1992) p. 33.

Book Review: *The Fuel Savers: A Kit of Solar Ideas for Your Home, Apartment, or Business* edited by Bruce Anderson. Book review on the basics of energy-saving ideas using solar energy. Lafayette, CA: Morning Sun Press, 81 pp. • *Fine Homebuilding*. No. 70 (Nov, 1991) p. 120.

"Seaside solar" by Peter L. Pfeiffer. Gives an example of a solar heating system for a home in New Jersey. Photos, plans. • *Fine Homebuilding*. No. 60 (May, 1990) pp. 56-59.

"Staying with solar" by Rich Binsacca. A study in adapting new solar energy systems to a house over a twenty year period. Photos. • *Practical Homeowner*. (Sep/Oct, 1992) pp. 54-59.

Solar Houses

"Practical solar design" by Debra G. Rucker. Presents a design of energy efficiency and a traditional look. Photos, plans. Sidebar on determining roof overhangs. • *Fine Homebuilding*. No. 84 (Nov, 1993) pp. 85-89.

Solar Storage

"Designing solar storage" by Marc Rosenbaum. Learn about designing an active solar-heating system. • *Fine Homebuilding*. No. 67 (May, 1991) pp. 12-14.

Soldering

"Working with lead-free solder" by Peter Hemp. Brief tip on making a clean joint with lead-free solder. • *Fine Homebuilding*. No. 57 (Jan, 1990) p. 14.

Soundproofing

"Nixing neighbor noises" by Henry Spies. Responds to a question about using blown-in insulation to soundproof walls. • *Home Mechanix*. No. 770 (Nov, 19920 p. 93.

Soundproofing Materials

"Soundproofing solution" by Henry Spies. Offers advice on soundproofing materials when installing pocket doors. • *Home Mechanix*. No. 769 (Oct, 1992) p. 79.

Space Utilization

"Space wars" by Rhonda Chant. The author describes some creative ways to organize storage space more effectively, including kitchens, study areas, laundries, and other living areas. Photos. • *Canadian Workshop*. Vol. 13, No. 5 (Feb 1990) pp. 42-48.

Spacers

"Anchor-bolt spacers" by Yon Mathiesen. Brief tip on setting anchor-bolt spacers before pouring concrete into forms for stemwall foundations. Drawing. • *Fine Homebuilding*. No. 65 (March, 1991) p. 30.

Spas

"Adding a craftsman spa room" by M. Scott Watkins. Constructions plans for spa-room additions. Photos, plans. • *Fine Homebuilding*. No. 58 (March, 1990) pp. 58-61.

"Taking the plunge" by Dean Johnson. Practical advice for installing an outdoor spa or hot tub. Photos and drawings. • *Practical Homeowner*. Vol. V, No. 4 (June, 1990) pp. 14-15.

Spice Cabinets

"Pierced-tin spice cabinet." A clear and simple explanation for building a small wall mounted spice cabinet with pierced tin doors. Photo and plans • *The Woodworker's Journal*. Vol. 15, No. 3 (May/Jun, 1991) pp. 58-59.

Spindles, Chair

"A better spindle repair" by Asaph Waterman. Describes a method of repairing broken chair spindles. Drawing. • *Woodwork*. No. 19 (Jan/Feb, 1993) p. 20.

Spokeshaves

"Spokeshaves" by Dennis Preston. This article offers a history and analysis of the use of spokeshaves for shaping and smoothing wood surfaces. Photos and drawings. • *The Woodworker's Journal*. Vol. 15, No. 2 (Mar/Apr, 1991) pp. 25-29.

Spoon Racks

"A stirring display" by David Ashe. Instructions for a display rack for teaspoons or demitasse spoons. Photo, pattern, drawings, materials list. • *Better Homes and Gardens Wood.* No. 63 (Sep, 1993) pp. 68-69.

Sprayers

"High-volume, low-pressure sprayers" by Bill Krier. Analytical article on the latest models of spraying systems. Photos, chart. Sidebar on the advantages and disadvantages of three spray-finishing options. • *Better Homes and Gardens Wood.* No. 60 (April, 1993) pp. 79-81.

Spreaders

"The spreader" by Stephen Major. Brief instructions on making a spreader to help align a studwall. Drawing. • *Fine Homebuilding.* No. 64 (Jan, 1991) p. 30.

Squares

"Pocket-sized try square" by Marlen Kemmet. Step-by-step directions to build your own precise try square. Photos, diagrams. • *Better Homes and Gardens Wood.* No. 37 (Sep, 1990) pp. 33-35.

Squares, Cylinder

"A cylinder or master square" by Frank A. McLean. A description of the uses and manufacture of a cylinder square. Photos and plans. • *The Home Shop Machinist.* Vol. 11, No. 6 (Nov/Dec, 1992) pp. 42-45.

Squares, Rafter

"Updating the rafter square" by Donald E. Zepp. Provides a new scale converting decimals to fractions and a quicker layout of hips and valleys. Photos, drawings. • *Fine Homebuilding.* No. 75 (July, 1992) pp. 50-51.

Squaring

"A tried-and-true method for squaring up stock." Helpful article on the squaring process using a jointer and table saw.

Illustrations. • *Better Homes and Gardens Wood.* No. 49 (Jan, 1992) p. 71.

Stains and Staining

"Explaining stains" by Judith Trotsky. In-depth article on conventional and new-tech wood finishes. Photos, chart. • *Home Mechanix.* No. 753 (March, 1991) pp. 53-59.

"Mixed woods in a ceiling" by Victor DeMasi. Offers instructions on how to stain mixed woods on a ceiling so the wood color matches. • *Fine Homebuilding.* No. 58 (March, 1990) p. 16.

"Products that perform." A description of new types of house stains. • *Practical Homeowner.* Vol. V, No. 3 (April, 1990) pp. 66-67.

"Texan offers more ideas on staining cherry" by Michael Barth. Brief tip on how to bring out the deep burgundy color in cherry. • *Better Homes and Gardens Wood.* No. 34 (April, 1990) p. 8.

"Working with gel stains" by Jim Barrett. This analysis outlines the pro's and con's of using a gelled wood stain product. Photos. • *The Woodworker's Journal.* Vol. 15, No. 4 (Jul/Aug, 1991) pp. 53-57.

Stair Skirtboards

"Installing stair skirtboards" by Bob Syvanen. Describes how to notch the skirtboard over the risers for a better-looking result. Drawing. • *Fine Homebuilding.* No. 68 (July, 1991) pp. 60-61.

Stairs

Book Review: *Modern Practical Stairs—Building and Handrailing* by George Ellis. Book review on a guide that offers comprehensive treatment of stairbuilding and handrailing. Hollywood, CA: Linden Publishing Co. Inc., 274 pp. • *Fine Homebuilding.* No. 64 (Jan, 1991) p. 110.

"Building an L-shaped stair" by Larry Haun. Gives construction techniques to build a stair with a three-step winder.

Photos, diagrams. • *Fine Homebuilding*. No. 67 (May, 1991) pp. 44-46.

"Clamping a staircase" by Felix Marti. Provides information on rebuilding a staircase in a renovation project. Drawing. • *Fine Homebuilding*. No. 74 (May, 1992) p. 26.

"Design guidelines for safe stairs" by Gregory Harrison. Detailed instructions and tips for building safe stairs. Diagrams. • *Fine Homebuilding*. No. 65 (March, 1991) pp. 66-68.

"Fantail deck stairs" by Jose L. Floresca. Provides instructions to build fantail-shaped deck stairs. Photos, diagram. • *Fine Homebuilding*. No. 83 (Sep, 1993) pp. 74-76.

"Fitting stair treads" by Robert Plourde. Brief tip on how to fit stair treads. Drawing. • *Fine Homebuilding*. No. 78 (Jan, 1993) p. 30.

"Flights of fancy" by David Sellers. A guide to architectural staircases. Photos. • *Practical Homeowner*. Vol. V, No. 1 (Feb, 1990) pp. 54-60.

"A freestanding spiral stair" by Steven M. White. Presents instructions to build an elegant circular staircase using ordinary shop tools and stock lumber. Photos, diagrams. Sidebar on spiral-stair layout. • *Fine Homebuilding*. No. 70 (Nov, 1991) pp. 86-91.

"Instant access" by James Appleyard. A description of the use of concrete castings to make basement steps. Photos. • *Practical Homeowner*. Vol. IV, No. 9 (Jan, 1990) pp. 62-64.

"Little plugs" by Bob Johnston. Brief tip on how to make plugs to fill in holes. Drawing. • *Fine Homebuilding*. No. 84 (Nov, 1993) p. 28.

"Making a bullnose starting step" by Stephen Winchester. Detailed instructions on how to make a double-bullnose starting step. Photos, drawings. Sidebar on installing a starting newel. • *Fine*

Homebuilding. No. 82 (July, 1993) pp. 60-63.

"Replace a stair railing" by Michael Morris. Offers information about prefabricated stairway railing kits. Photos, drawings. • *Home Mechanix*. No. 742 (Feb, 1990) pp. 42-45.

"Shrinking stringers" by Stephen Smulski. Describes how to avoid shrinking stringers when building finished stairs. Drawing. • *Fine Homebuilding*. No. 84 (Nov, 1993) pp. 14-16.

"A site-built stair" by Alexander Brennen. Design and construction plans to build a handsome staircase. Photos, diagrams, drawings. • *Fine Homebuilding*. No. 62 (Sep, 1990) pp. 42-45.

"Stair case" by Hank Spies. Brief tip on the basics of building staircase. Drawing. • *Home Mechanix*. No. 747 (July/Aug, 1990) p. 87.

"A staircase of glass and maple" by Scott McBride. Design and instructions to build a glass and maple staircase. Photos, diagrams. • *Fine Homebuilding*. No. 60 (May, 1990) pp. 74-77.

"Stairs in half the space" by Zachary Carlsen. New ideas for building compact alternating tread stairs. Photos. • *Practical Homeowner*. Vol. VI, No. 9 (Nov/Dec, 1991) pp. 28-30.

"Supporting exterior stairs" by Scott McBride. Offers a tip for hanging porch stair stringers to support stairs. Drawing. • *Fine Homebuilding*. No. 76 (Sep, 1992) p. 16.

Stairs, Stone

"A dry-laid stone stairway" by Dick Belair. Presents a crushed-rock-and-gravel method for a stone stairway. Photos, diagram. • *Fine Homebuilding*. No. 76 (Sep, 1992) pp. 60-62.

"Steps of stone" by Matt Phair. Offers instructions on how to build stone steps. Photos, diagram. • *Home Mechanix*. No. 744 (April, 1990) pp. 90-94.

Stands

"Classic column" by James R. Downing. Build a laminated pine column for indoors or outdoors with these tips. Photos, diagrams, materials list. • *Better Homes and Gardens Wood.* No. 52 (June, 1992) pp. 54-55.

Statues, Moose

"Gentle giant of the woods" by Kim Russell. Describes how to cut and sand a moose-shaped statue. Photo, patterns. • *Better Homes and Gardens Wood.* No. 64 (Oct, 1993) pp. 72-73.

Steam Baths

"All about steam baths" by Judith Trotsky. Informative article on installing a steam bath in your bathroom. Photos, drawing, chart. • *Home Mechanix.* No. 752 (Feb, 1991) pp. 78-81.

Steel Doors

"Loose screws in steel doors" by Stephen N. Denton. Brief tip showing how to tighten the screws holding the latch bolt to the edge of the door stile. Drawing. • *Fine Homebuilding.* No. 69 (Sep, 1991) p. 30.

Steel, Stainless

"Stainless steel fundamentals" by George Geneuro. A description of the varying types and properties of stainless steel. • *The Home Shop Machinist.* Vol. 10, No. 4 (Jul/Aug, 1991) pp. 28-31.

Stepstools

"Aerobic step." An easy-to-make project for an aerobic exercising step. Photo, plans, and materials list. • *The Woodworker's Journal.* Vol. 17, No. 4 (Jul/Aug, 1993) pp. 48-51.

"Stepstool/chair." How to make a chair that converts into a stepstool. Photos, plans, and materials list. • *The Woodworker's Journal.* Vol. 16, No. 5 (Sep/Oct, 1992) pp. 48-51.

Stereo Speakers

"In-the-wall stereo speakers" by Ivan Berger. In-depth guide on selecting in-wall speakers. Chart. • *Home Mechanix.* No. 760 (Nov, 1991) pp. 32-38.

Stock — *See* Building Materials; Wood; specific types of wood

Stones

"Nonrolling stones" by Bill Hart. Brief tip on anchoring smooth rocks when using them for fireplaces or walls. • *Fine Homebuilding.* No. 72 (March, 1992) p. 28.

Stones, Sharpening

"Choosing sharpening stones" by Jim Barrett. Advice on the differences between natural and synthetic oil stones. Photos. • *The Woodworker's Journal.* Vol. 17, No. 4 (Jul/Aug, 1993) pp. 22-27.

Stools

"The long and short of it." Offers a solution for wobbly four-legged chairs. Photos. • *Better Homes and Gardens Wood.* No. 53 (Aug, 1992) p. 68.

Stools, Shop

"Sit-a-spell shop stool" by Marlen Kemmet. Detailed instructions to build a padded and adjustable shop stool. Photos, diagrams, materials list. • *Better Homes and Gardens Wood.* No. 54 (Sep, 1992) pp. 70-73.

Stools, Step

"Step stool." A brief article with instructions for the construction of a utilitarian step stool. Photo, plans, and materials list. • *The Woodworker's Journal.* Vol. 15, No. 1 (Jan/Feb, 1991) pp. 54-55.

Stops, Bench

"This bench stop eliminates need for benchtop holes" by F. Eldon Heighway. Handy tip to create a bench stop instead of drilling holes in a benchtop. Drawing. • *Better Homes and Gardens Wood.* No. 57 (Dec, 1992) p. 20.

Storage

"Audio/video remote rack." A brief tip on making a small wooden tray box for holding remote control units. Photos, plans, and materials list. • *The Woodworker's Journal.* Vol. 16, No. 4 (Jul/Aug, 1992) pp. 44-45.

Book Review: *Shelving and Storage* by Tim Snyder. Book review of a helpful guide of 25 storage ideas for the home ranging from towel racks to storage benches. Emmaus, PA: Rodale Press, 360 pp. • *Woodwork.* No. 17 (Sep/Oct, 1992) p. 29.

"Cookie jar holder." Describes an easy-to-make holder for cookie jars, including materials list. Photo and plans. • *The Woodworker's Journal.* Vol. 14, No. 2 (Mar/Apr, 1990) pp. 42-43.

"Great dividers" by Matt Phair. Presents instructions to build three built-in cabinets featuring storage space. Photos, diagrams. • *Home Mechanix.* No. 753 (March, 1991) pp. 28-32.

"Kitchen spacesavers" by Kimberly Wilson. Presents a variety of space-saving accessories for the kitchen. Photos. • *Home Mechanix.* No. 754 (April, 1991) pp. 50-53.

"Lumber storage rack" by Marlen Kemmet and James R. Downing. Describes how to build a versatile lumber storage rack. Photo, diagrams, materials list. • *Better Homes and Gardens Wood.* No. 65 (Nov, 1993) pp. 42-45.

"Smart storage" by Ted Jones. Provides information about space-saving storage racks. Photos, plan, diagram. Sidebar on double-strength double doors. • *Home Mechanix.* No. 768 (Sep, 1992) pp. 44-47.

"Space wars" by Rhonda Chant. The author describes some creative ways to organize storage space more effectively, including kitchens, study areas, laundries, and other living areas. Photos. • *Canadian Workshop.* Vol. 13, No. 5 (Feb 1990) pp. 42-48.

"Storage solutions" by John Ingersoll. Provides some trade secrets from a storage expert on increasing storage space. Drawings. • *Home Mechanix.* No. 742 (Feb, 1990) pp. 27-30.

"Strategic storage" by Sharon Ross. How to create unconventional storage options. Photos. • *Practical Homeowner.* Vol. V, No. 1 (Feb, 1990) pp. 38-40.

See Also Racks

Storage Systems

"Store and order" by Dean Johnson. This article rates six different brands of room and closet storage systems. Photos. • *Practical Homeowner.* Vol. V, No. 2 (Mar, 1990) pp. 24-27.

Storage, Wall-Mounted

"Wall works" by Sally Ross. Explains how to build wall-mounted counters with drawers for storage. Photos, diagrams, drawing. • *Home Mechanix.* No. 747 (July/Aug, 1990) pp. 46-50.

Storage--Tools

"Bandsaw blade holder" by Chuck Hedlund. Brief directions to make a band saw blade holder. Photo, diagram. • *Better Homes and Gardens Wood.* No. 60 (April, 1993) p. 84.

"Clamp organizer." A brief tip for a wall mounted unit for holding clamps. Photo. • *The Woodworker's Journal.* Vol. 17, No. 5 (Sep/Oct, 1993) p. 18.

"Clamp rack." This is a brief note on how to assemble a clamp rack for a workbench. Plans. • *The Woodworker's Journal.* Vol. 15, No. 1 (Jan/Feb, 1991) p. 51.

"Clamp-storage extravaganza" by Marlen Kemmet and Richard Tollesfson. Instructions to build a storage rack for five different kinds of clamps. Photos, diagrams. • *Better Homes and Gardens Wood.* No. 63 (Sep, 1993) pp. 58-61.

"Fixture keys" by Edward G. Hoffman. An examination of the use of machined keys as aids in properly locating work pieces.

Drawings. • *The Home Shop Machinist.* Vol. 11, No. 4 (Jul/Aug, 1992) pp. 58-59.

"Hand saw caddy" by Dennis Preston. A simple plan for a wall-mounted saw caddy. Photos and plans. • *The Woodworker's Journal.* Vol. 17, No. 3 (May/Jun, 1993) pp. 56-57.

"Handy hardware hauler" by Philip Belanger. Offers instructions to make a hardware carrier from recyclable materials. Photo, diagram. • *Better Homes and Gardens Wood.* No. 61 (June, 1993) p. 16.

"Handy home for a family of pliers" by Bob Colpetzer. Brief instructions for a wall-hung pliers rack. Photo, diagram. • *Better Homes and Gardens Wood.* No. 49 (Jan, 1992) p. 20.

"Machine tool covers" by Ted Myers. Directions on how to protect machine tools with vented plastic covers. Photos. • *The Home Shop Machinist.* Vol. 11, No. 3 (May/Jun, 1992) pp. 39-41.

"Making a cutoff toolholder, part one" by Rudy Kouhoupt. A how-to guide for making a holder for a lathe cut-off tool. Photos and plans. • *The Home Shop Machinist.* Vol. 12, No. 4 (Jul/Aug, 1993) pp. 49-51.

"Palm-sander holder" by Russell Smith. Brief tip on building a palm sander holder to making sanding small projects easier. Photo, diagram • *Better Homes and Gardens Wood.* No. 46 (Oct, 1991) p. 15.

"Pantry plus" by Joseph Truini. Offers instructions for a pantry toolbox and provides creative ideas for maximizing small space storage. Photos, diagrams. • *Home Mechanix.* No. 743 (March, 1990) pp. 46-48, 61.

"Pipe clamp storage bin" by Ted Finneseth. Brief tip on constructing a storage bin for pipe clamps. Drawing. • *Woodwork.* No. 18 (Nov/Dec, 1992) p. 20.

"Plain-handy plane holder" by Kevin Hellman. Brief description on how to make a wall-hung plane holder. Diagram,

photo. • *Better Homes and Gardens Wood.* No. 50 (Feb, 1992) p. 9.

"Plastic light grid shines for screwdriver storage" by Harvey Charbonneau. Brief tip on how to organizer screwdrivers, awls, and other tools. Drawing. • *Better Homes and Gardens Wood.* No. 65 (Nov, 1993) p. 12.

"Power-cord straps" by John Schmidt. Brief tip on how to make a strap to keep extension cords coiled neatly. Drawing. • *Fine Homebuilding.* No. 82 (July, 1993) p. 28.

"A quick-change tool post system, part one" by Richard Torgerson. This descriptive article looks at the different types of quick-change tool post systems available. Photos. • *The Home Shop Machinist.* Vol. 12, No. 4 (Jul/Aug, 1993) pp. 36-42.

"A quick-change tool post system, part two" by Richard Torgerson. See Vol. 12, No. 4 • *The Home Shop Machinist.* Vol. 12, No. 5 (Sep/Oct, 1993) pp. 39-43.

"Ready wrench rack." Brief article on how to build a wrench rack that holds up to 16 wrenches. Photo, diagram. • *Better Homes and Gardens Wood.* No. 51 (April, 1992) p. 12.

"Router storage cabinet" by Dennis Preston. This project guide offers details on building a small storage cabinet for holding a power router. Photos, plans, and materials list. • *The Woodworker's Journal.* Vol. 15, No. 3 (May/Jun, 1991) pp. 37-39.

"Sanding table" by Sven Hanson. Building instructions to make a cradle to hold a sander on its side. Drawings. • *Fine Homebuilding.* No. 70 (Nov, 1991) p. 34.

"Sanding-supply organizer" by Marlen Kemmet and James R. Downing. Offers six easy-to build projects to organize sanding supplies. Photos, diagrams, patterns, materials list. • *Better Homes and Gardens Wood.* No. 56 (Nov, 1992) pp. 80-84.

"Saw hangup" by Mark White. Brief suggestion for hanging a worm-drive saw

on a sawhorse between cuts. Drawing.
• *Fine Homebuilding.* No. 71 (Jan, 1992)
p. 26.

"Saw stay straight, sharp in hanging rack"
by E.Q. Smith. Brief tip on how to
organize saws with a wall-mounted rack.
Drawings. • *Better Homes and Gardens Wood.*
No. 57 (Dec, 1992) p. 18.

"Scrollsaw-blade organizer" by John M.
Turok. Brief instructions to build an
organizer for scrollsaw blades. Photo,
diagram. • *Better Homes and Gardens Wood.*
No. 56 (Nov, 1992) p. 90.

"See-through cabinet doors" by Leon
Segal. Increase tool storage area with
acrylic doors. • *Woodwork.* No. 15 (May/
June, 1992) p. 22.

"Shelf sufficiency" by Joseph Truini.
Presents easy-to-build storage shelves for a
basement or garage. Photos, drawings,
diagrams. • *Home Mechanix.* No. 748 (Sep,
1990) pp. 64-72.

"A shop-made roller table and roller
stand" by Tom E. Moore. Make your own
adjustable roller table and stand. Drawing.
Photos. • *Woodwork.* No. 15 (May/June,
1992) pp. 66-69.

"Simple saw rack" by Merwin Snyder.
Organize the saws in your woodshop by
building a saw rack. Photos, diagrams.
• *Better Homes and Gardens Wood.* No. 48
(Dec, 1991) p. 14.

"A small-tool holder" by Bill Houghton.
Offers suggestions on storing small blades,
files, or other small tools. Drawing.
• *Woodwork.* No. 13 (January/February)
p. 14.

"Storage reel" by Ric Winters. Create a
storage reel to roll and store about 300
feet of cords and air lines. Drawing. • *Fine
Homebuilding.* No. 69 (Sep, 1991) p. 32.

"Tin-can organizers store stuff and tote it,
too" by Thomas O'Donovan. Brief tip on
how to organize screws and nails with old
aluminum cans. Drawings. • *Better Homes
and Gardens Wood.* No. 54 (Sep, 1992)
p. 12.

"Tools on wheels" by William Lego, J.
Azevedo, Paul Pieper, and Linden
Frederick. Provides instructions to make
stands with wheels for a miter-saw, radial-
arm saw, tool bench, and tool barrow.
Photos. • *Fine Homebuilding.* No. 69 (Sep,
1991) pp. 70-75.

"Universal wall-cabinet system" by James R.
Downing, Jim Boelling and Marlen
Kemmet. Construct a wall-cabinet system
for hand tools, safety equipment, and
power-tool accessories with these plans.
Photos, diagrams, materials list. Sidebar
on how to design customized tool holders.
• *Better Homes and Gardens Wood.* No. 54
(Sep, 1992) pp. 74-79.

"Workbench and portable tool chest" by
Dennis Preston. This double article gives
details on making a matching workbench
and tool chest. Photos, plans, and
materials list. • *The Woodworker's Journal.*
Vol. 14, No. 5 (Sep/Oct, 1990) pp. 62-86.

Studs

"Straightening studs" by John Riedhart.
Brief tip on fixing bowed-in or bowed-out
studs. Drawing. • *Fine Homebuilding.* No. 60
(May, 1990) p. 28.

Sump Pumps

"Water-powered sump pump" by Hank
Spies. Brief tip explaining the Home
Guard sump pump. Drawing. • *Home
Mechanix.* No. 743 (March, 1990) pp. 78-
79.

Sun Decks — *See* Decks

Sunrooms

Book Review: *Residential and Commercial
Sunrooms: 1991 Buyer's Guide* edited by Kate
Kupferer. Book review on a buyer's guide
to sunroom additions. Chantilly, VA:
Home Buyer Publications, Inc., 80 pp.
• *Fine Homebuilding.* No. 68 (July, 1991)
p. 108.

"Building with glass" by Sharon Ross. New
ideas about the use of glass in sunrooms.

Photos and plans. • *Practical Homeowner.* Vol. V, No. 2 (Mar, 1990) pp. 34-39.

"Glass act" by Joseph Truini. Describes turning a screened porch into a year-round sunroom. Photos, drawings. • *Home Mechanix.* No. 764 (April, 1992) pp. 68-71.

"A guide to sunrooms" by *Glass Magazine* Editors. Describes the steps in planning and designing a sunroom. Photos, with a table listing suppliers and services. • *The Homeowner's Guide to Glass.* No. 1 (1989) pp. 22-27.

"Sun spots" by Ted Jones and Pat McMillan. Introduces new sunroom kits and installation ideas. Photos, drawing. Sidebar on installing glass overhead. • *Home Mechanix.* No. 755 (May, 1991) pp. 48-56.

Supports, Roofing

"Staging plank supports" by Peter Evans. Brief tip on setting supports for work on the edge of a roof. Drawing. • *Fine Homebuilding.* No. 57 (Jan, 1990) p. 28.

Supports, Tool

"Swing-arm support" by James R. Downing. Handy tip for supporting a motorized rotary tool. Photo, drawing. • *Better Homes and Gardens Wood.* No. 57 (Dec, 1992) p. 30.

Supports, Work

"Work supports" by Marvin Hoppenworth. Create fold-out work supports for bulky pieces of sheet goods. Drawing. • *Better Homes and Gardens Wood.* No. 63 (Sep, 1993) p. 23.

Supports, Workbench

"Building-block supports" by George W. Early. Build supports to prevent longer pieces of wood from falling below the workbench. Drawing. • *Woodwork.* No. 15 (May/ June, 1992) p. 20.

Surveys, Home Improvement

"Home improvement survey" by Gary Mayk. An analysis of the results of a national survey about the economic value of ten different home remodeling projects. Photos. • *Practical Homeowner.* Vol. V, No. 4 (June, 1990) pp. 39-54.

Swing Sets

"Porch/yard swing." How to build a swing set with an A-frame suspension. Photos, plans, and materials list. • *The Woodworker's Journal.* Vol. 17, No. 3 (May/Jun, 1993) pp. 49-53.

Sycamore (Wood)

"Sycamore: ghost of the bottomlands" by Vern Cusban and Jack Stiles. Informative article covering the cost, availability, uses, machining and carving methods. Illustration. Chart. • *Better Homes and Gardens Wood.* No. 49 (Jan, 1992) pp. 23-24.

T

Table Saw Blades

"Thin-kerf showdown" by Bill Krier. Common characteristics of high performance thin-kerf blades including a chart with comparisons of several brands. Photos. • *Better Homes and Gardens Wood.* No. 34 (April, 1990) pp. 44-45.

"Truing a table-saw blade" by Frederic E. Bishop. Offers a helpful technique to align the blade and the fence. Drawing. • *Fine Homebuilding.* No. 61 (July, 1990) p. 26.

Table Saws

"Benchtop tablesaws" by Jim Barrett. A product review featuring nine models of table saws. Photos. • *The Woodworker's Journal.* Vol. 16, No. 5 (Sep/Oct, 1992 pp. 64-69.

"Customized tablesaw base" by Marlen Kemmet. Learn how to construct a handy and inexpensive table saw base. Photos, diagrams, pattern, materials list. • *Better*

Homes and Gardens Wood. No. 34 (April, 1990) pp. 60-63.

"Hardboard cleans up portable saw's cuts" by Jon Grasson. Brief tip to prevent a splintered edge when cutting a big sheet of plywood. Drawing. • *Better Homes and Gardens Wood.* No. 63 (Sep, 1993) p. 14.

"Shaping on a table saw" by R. J. DeCristoforo. A description of how to adapt a table saw using molding-head knives to shape pattern molds. Photos and drawings. • *The Woodworker's Journal.* Vol. 15, No. 4 (Jul/Aug, 1991) pp. 24-27.

"Tablesaws." Informative article on the inner workings of table saws and a comparison chart of 33 different types. • *Better Homes and Gardens Wood.* No. 38 (Oct, 1990) pp. 38-41.

"Tablesaws outfeed roller glides on drawer slides" by Ron Salmon. Brief tip on cutting stock that is longer than the table saw. Drawing. • *Better Homes and Gardens Wood.* No. 63 (Sep, 1993) p. 14.

Table Saws, Portable

"Portable table saws" by Bruce Greenlaw. Detailed article focusing on four lightweight direct drive bench-tops. Photos, chart. Sidebar on accessories. Sidebar on table-saw safety. • *Fine Homebuilding.* No. 64 (Jan, 1991) pp. 70-74.

Tables

"Contemporary table." Complete plans for a small, rectangular, contemporarily styled table. Photos, plans, and materials list. • *The Woodworker's Journal.* Vol. 16, No. 2 (Mar/Apr, 1992) pp. 57-59.

"Harvest table." A very detailed article on the design and construction of an Early American style dropleaf table. Photos, plans, and materials list. • *The Woodworker's Journal.* Vol. 14. No. 4 (Jul/Aug, 1990) pp. 49-51.

"A walnut side table" by Jeff Greef. Detailed instructions for building oval- and curved-form tables including a parts list. Photos. Drawing. • *Woodwork.* No. 17 (Sep/Oct, 1992) pp. 69-72.

See Also specific types of tables, e.g., Dining Room Tables, Coffee Tables

Tables, Bow-Front

"Bow-front table" by Marlen Kemmet and James R. Downing. Specific directions to construct a bow-front table with contrasting hardwoods. Photos, diagrams, materials list. • *Better Homes and Gardens Wood.* No. 65 (Nov, 1993) pp. 30-33.

Tables, Coping

"Coping table" by Grafton H. Cook. Brief tip on building a coping table. Drawings. • *Fine Homebuilding.* No. 71 (Jan, 1992) p. 24.

Tables, Farm

"Old fashioned farm table." A classic design for a long rectangular table with pull out drawer on a country pattern. Photos, plans, and materials list. • *The Woodworker's Journal.* Vol. 17, No. 5 (Sep/ Oct, 1993) pp. 50-54.

Tables, Folding

"Folding deck table." A brief article describing the method of constructing a simple folding table for outdoor use. Photo and plans. • *The Woodworker's Journal.* Vol. 14, No. 4 (Jul/Aug, 1990) pp. 37-39.

Tables, Outfeed

"Air-filtration cabinet" by Marlen Kemmet and James R. Downing. Building instructions for an air-filtration cabinet that is adjustable and can double as an outfeed table. Photos, diagrams, materials list. • *Better Homes and Gardens Wood.* No. 55 (Oct, 1992) pp. 48-51,74.

Tables, Santa Fe

"Santa Fe table." This offers a detailed exposition on the steps in cutting, shaping, assembling, and finishing a small table in the Southwestern Santa Fe-style. Photos, plans, and materials list. • *The*

Woodworker's Journal. Vol. 15, No. 1 (Jan/Feb, 1991) pp. 47-50.

Tables, Shaker

"Shaker drop-leaf table" by Gene Cosloy. This is a brief description of the method of making a drop-leaf side table after a nineteenth-century Shaker pattern. Photo, plans, and materials list. • *The Woodworker's Journal.* Vol. 15, No. 4 (Jul/Aug, 1991) pp. 33-35.

Tables, Tavern

"Tavern table." Describes how to build an Early American tavern table. Photo. Plans. • *The Woodworker's Journal.* Vol. 14, No. 1 (Jan/Feb, 1990) pp. 28-30.

Tables, Work

"Shop work center" by Dennis Preston. A direct and simple set of plans for building a work table and storage area. Photos, plans, and materials list. • *The Woodworker's Journal.* Vol. 16, No. 1 (Jan/Feb, 1992) pp. 52-55.

Tagua Nut (Wood)

"Tagua turning" by Larry Johnston and Chuck Lueggers. Learn how to create objects with the tagua nut once used to make buttons. Photos. Sidebar on teeny tagua-turning ideas. • *Better Homes and Gardens Wood.* No. 54 (Sep, 1992) pp. 54-57.

Tailstocks

"Tailstock attachments for the lathe, part one" by Frank A. McLean. A guide to the manufacture of a variety of tailstock arbors and die holders. Photos and plans. • *The Home Shop Machinist.* Vol. 12, No. 1 (Jan/Feb, 1993) pp. 46-48.

Tape Measures

"Slick tips" by Terry Mackey. Brief tip on keeping tape measures free from sand and grit. • *Fine Homebuilding.* No. 67 (May, 1991) p. 28.

Tapering

"Turning a morse taper, part three" by Rudy Kouhoupt. See Vol. 10, No. 6 • *The Home Shop Machinist.* Vol. 11, No. 2 (Mar/Apr, 1992) pp. 42-44.

Tapping Guides

"A tapping guide for a unimat" by LeRoy Nessen. A simple procedure for adapting a die holder to fit a Unimat chuck for use as a tapping guide. Plans. • *The Home Shop Machinist.* Vol. 9, No. 4 (Jul/Aug, 1990) p. 27.

Taps

"Making tap and reamer handles" by Rudy Kouhoupt. Plans for construction of handles for taps and reamers. Photos. • *The Home Shop Machinist.* Vol. 10, No. 4 (Jul/Aug, 1991) pp. 49-53.

Tax Deductions

"Strike three against home offices?" by Mark E. Battersby. An analysis of recent IRS changes affecting home machine shops. • *The Home Shop Machinist.* Vol. 12, No. 4 (Jul/Aug, 1993) pp. 34-35.

"Tax deductible home shop" by Mark Battersby. An analysis of the tax implications of the Tax Reform Act of 1986 for home shop enthusiasts. • *The Home Shop Machinist.* Vol. 9, No. 2 (Mar/Apr, 1990) pp. 38-39.

Taxes, Property

"Tax implications of remodeling" by Scott Brinckerhoff. An analysis of ways to limit higher tax assessments after home remodeling. • *Practical Homeowner.* Vol. V, No. 3 (April, 1990) pp. 26–28.

Teak (Wood)

"Teak: the topic's top seafaring stock" by Jim Boelling, Jim Downing, and Sam Radding. Informative article on the availability, cost, uses, carving and turning methods for teak. Illustration, photo. • *Better Homes and Gardens Wood.* No. 46 (Oct, 1991) pp. 33-34.

Technology

Book Review: *Appropriate Technology Sourcebook: A Guide to Practical Books for Village and Small Community Technology* by Ken Darrow and Mike Saxenian. Book review on a valuable resource for appropriate technology books. Stanford, CA: Appropriate Technology Project, Volunteers in Asia, (PO Box 4543) 800 pp. • *Fine Homebuilding*. No. 64 (Jan, 1991) p. 112.

Book Review: *The Intermediate Technology Publications/Bootstrap Press 1990 Catalog.* Book review on a guide that offers information on appropriate technology. Croton-on-Hudson, NY: ITDG (PO Box 337), 20 pp. • *Fine Homebuilding*. No. 64 (Jan, 1991) pp. 110-112.

Television Antennas

"Installing a TV Antenna" by Jim Barrett. Brief article on how to install your own TV antenna. Photos. • *Home Mechanix.* No. 743 (March, 1990) pp. 10-12.

Television Cabinets

"Get ready... get (T.V.) set... retrofit" by Larry Clayton. Explains how to install a new TV or VCR in an old console. • *Better Homes and Gardens Wood.* No. 50 (Feb, 1992) pp. 82-83.

"TV and VCR cabinet." This relatively complex project details the construction steps for making a floor-standing video cabinet with sliding doors. Photos, plans, and materials list. • *The Woodworker's Journal.* Vol. 14, No. 5 (Sep/Oct, 1990) pp. 38-41.

Tempering

"Tempering steel tools" by Joe Petrovich. This article offers a simple technique that will allow the user to temper steel cutting tools. Charts and drawings. • *The Woodworker's Journal.* Vol. 15, No. 1 (Jan/Feb, 1991) pp. 31-34.

Templates

"Handy templates" by Tom E. Moore. Suggestions for creating and using templates. • *Woodwork.* No. 14 (March/April) p. 10.

Templates, Indexing

"Indexing template for easier layout" by Edward G. Hoffman. This article describes the use of circular templates for design layouts. Drawings. • *The Home Shop Machinist.* Vol. 11, No. 1 (Jan/Feb, 1992) pp. 29-31.

Tenons

"Pull the plug on tenoning troubles" by Chuck Hedlund. Brief tip on making round tenons with a table saw, drill press or plug cutter. Drawings. • *Better Homes and Gardens Wood.* No. 65 (Nov, 1993) p. 10.

Termite Damage

"Bug busters" by Gurney Williams. How to use high temperatures to kill termites. Photos. • *Practical Homeowner.* Vol. VI, No. 5 (May/June, 1991) pp. 82-88.

"Termite termination." Brief tips on warning signs of termite damage and how to prevent infestation. Chart. • *Home Mechanix.* No. 744 (April, 1990) p. 16.

Termites

Book Review: *The Termite Report: A Guide for Homeowners & Homebuyers on Structural Pest Control* by Donald V. Pearman. Book review on a comprehensive guide to repair pest related structural problems. Pearman Publishing, 139 pp. • *Home Mechanix.* No. 764 (April, 1992) p. 29.

Book Review: *The Termite Report: A Guide for Homeowners & Homebuyers on Structural Pest Control* by Donald V. Pearman. Book review on a comprehensive guide to repair pest related structural problems. Pearman Publishing, 139 pp. • *Home Mechanix.* No. 764 (April, 1992) p. 29.

Thanksgiving Decorations

"Plate of plenty" by Pam Gresham. Directions to chip-carve a horn of plenty for the Thanksgiving holiday. Photo, pattern. • *Better Homes and Gardens Wood.* No. 65 (Nov, 1993) pp. 66-67.

"Grateful Pilgrims" by Larry Johnston and Harley Refsal. Specific instructions to carve and paint a Pilgrim couple. Photo, patterns, materials list. • *Better Homes and Gardens Wood.* No. 56 (Nov, 1992) pp. 44-47.

Thread Cutting

"Cutting left-hand threads" by Frank A. McLean. This shows how to cut left-hand threads on a lathe. Photos and plans. • *The Home Shop Machinist.* Vol. 10, No. 4 (Jul/Aug, 1991) pp. 56-58.

"Thread cutting on the lathe" by Rudy Kouhoupt. An explanation of how to use a lathe to cut threads. Photos and plans. • *The Home Shop Machinist.* Vol. 12, No. 1 (Jan/Feb, 1993) pp. 18-25.

"A thread tooling system and wiggler for the lathe" by D.E. Johnson. A thorough guide to the author's system for cutting threads on a lathe. Photo, plans, and materials list. • *The Home Shop Machinist.* Vol. 11, No. 6 (Nov/Dec, 1992) pp. 18-23.

Threading Dials

"Threading dials for cutting metric threads" by Eugene Petersen. A discussion of the use of a threading dial as a guide for cutting screw threads to metric measurements. • *The Home Shop Machinist.* Vol. 12, No. 6 (Nov/Dec, 1993) pp. 49-50.

Thumbscrews

"Making a knurled head thumbscrew" by Frank A. McLean. A quick tip on how to make a knurled thumbscrew in ten minutes. Plans. • *The Home Shop Machinist.* Vol. 11, No. 5 (Sep/Oct, 1992) p. 45.

Tileboards

"Terrific tileboard" by Jane Cornell. Provides information on using tileboard as a substitute for wood or wood-look paneling. Photos. • *Home Mechanix.* No. 760 (Nov, 1991) pp. 46-50.

Tiles

Book Review: *Tiles for a Beautiful Home* by Tessa Paul. Book review on a source of design ideas on tiles. Hauppauge, NY: Barron's Educational Series, Inc., 160 pp. • *Fine Homebuilding.* No. 62 (Sep, 1990) pp. 112-114.

"Cutting holes in tile" by Paul M. Dandini. Brief tip on cutting holes in tile for tub and shower valves. Drawing. • *Fine Homebuilding.* No. 63 (Nov, 1990) p. 28.

"Decorating tile at home" by Nancy Selvin. Brief article on decorating tile with original prints. Photos. • *Fine Homebuilding.* No. 78 (Jan, 1993) pp. 72-73.

"Removing composition tiles" by Ron Strong. Brief suggestion on removing composition tiles easily. Drawing. • *Fine Homebuilding.* No. 84 (Nov, 1993) pp. 28-30.

"Sealing tiles" by Robert Wilcoxson. Explains how to reseal tiles that have been taken up due to a refinishing project. • *Fine Homebuilding.* No. 79 (March, 1993) pp. 20-22.

"Stiffening a floor for tile" by Robert Wilcoxson. Offers a solution to a soft subfloor when considering installing tiles. Drawing. • *Fine Homebuilding.* No. 70 (Nov, 1991) p. 14.

"Tile tactics" by Joseph Truini. Describes glazed ceramic tiles and how to install them on countertops. Photos. Sidebar on creative tiling: a window-sill countertop. • *Home Mechanix.* No. 769 (Oct, 1992) pp. 48-53.

"Tools and techniques for cutting tile" by Charles Wardell. Informative article on the types of saws and cutting devices needed for shaping tile. Photos. • *Fine Homebuilding.* No. 70 (Nov, 1991) pp. 57-60.

Tiles, Bathroom

"Natural Surroundings." Using natural stone tiles for bath and shower walls. Photos. • *Practical Homeowner.* (Mar/Apr, 1992) pp. 62-65.

Tiles, Ceramic

"High-style tile" by Joseph Truini. Step-by-step instructions on laying ceramic tiles. Photos, drawing. Sidebar on a buyer's guide to ceramic floor tile. • *Home Mechanix.* No. 774 (April, 1993) pp. 84-87.

"Isolation membranes for ceramic tile" by Bob Wilcoxson. Offers advice on non-petroleum isolation membranes for ceramic tile. • *Fine Homebuilding.* No. 61 (July, 1990) p. 12.

"Planning for tile" by Herrick Kimball. Brief tip on drawing a scaled sketch before starting a tile project. • *Fine Homebuilding.* No. 72 (March, 1992) p. 26.

Tiling

"Tiling a backsplash" by Tom Meehan. Offers instructions for the preparation and layout of decorative tiles for a kitchen. Photos, plans. • *Fine Homebuilding.* No. 68 (July, 1991) pp. 67-69.

"Tiling over cracked concrete" by Bob Wilcoxson. Offers a tip on repairing cracked tile. Drawing. • *Fine Homebuilding.* No. 65 (March, 1991) p. 14.

Timber Construction

"Timber" by Roy Barnhart. A review of new trends in the construction of timber frame homes. Photos. • *Practical Homeowner.* Vol. VI, No. 8 (Oct, 1991) pp. 64-73.

Timber-Frame Houses

Book Review: *Timber Frame Homes: 1991 Buyer's Guide* edited by Kate Kuferer. Book review on a buyer's guide to timber frame anatomy, design, construction, financing the home, and selecting a framer. Chantilly, VA: Home Buyer Publications, Inc., 80 pp. • *Fine Homebuilding.* No. 68 (July, 1991) p. 108.

"Timber-frame house, shingle-style wrapper" by Lynn Hopkins. Highlights a timber-frame design with porches, dormers and roofs. Photos, plans. • *Fine Homebuilding.* No. 79 (March, 1993) pp. 50-55.

Timber Frames

"Tudor timber-frames" by Charles Landau. Addresses the problem of building a timber-framed house yet avoiding shrinkage, timber rot, and insulation problems. • *Fine Homebuilding.* No. 64 (Jan, 1991) p. 24.

Tin Punching

"Tin punching" by Bill Krier and Jim Boelling. Describes the process of tin punching. Designs included, photos, drawings. • *Better Homes and Gardens Wood.* No. 53 (Aug, 1992) pp. 42-46.

Tin Punching Projects

"Pie safe" by Marlen Kemmet and James R. Downing. Detailed article on how to construct a pie safe, complete with decorative punched-tin panels. Photos, diagram, materials list. Sidebar on how to make a pie safe look like an antique. • *Better Homes and Gardens Wood.* No. 53 (Aug, 1992) pp. 47-52.

"Teddy bear in tin." Directions to create a country-style wall hanging of a teddy bear and flag. Photo, drawing, pattern. • *Better Homes and Gardens Wood.* No. 53 (Aug, 1992) pp. 74-75.

Tires

"Tire noose" by Bruce Schwarz. Brief tip on getting a tubeless tire to inflate. Drawing. • *Fine Homebuilding.* No. 71 (Jan, 1992) p. 24.

Toboggans

"Bentwood toboggan" by Marlen Kemmet and James R. Downing. Design and building instructions for a bentwood toboggan. Photo, diagrams, materials list, drawings. • *Better Homes and Gardens Wood.* No. 46 (Oct, 1991) pp. 66-70.

Toe Screws

"Plugging a toe-screw" by Jeffrey S. Janssen. Brief tip on plugging a toe screw for handrails or other projects. Drawing. • *Fine Homebuilding*. No. 71 (Jan, 1992) p. 24.

Toilets

"Better flush systems for water-saving toilets" by Jane A. Havsy. Presents the latest water saving toilets available. Drawings. • *Home Mechanix*. No. 779 (Oct, 1993) pp. 28-30.

"Choosing an up-flush toilet" by Rex Cauldwell. Brief article on the advantages of an up-flush toilet. • *Fine Homebuilding*. No. 78 (Jan, 1993) p. 16.

"Inside flush" by Merle Henkenius. Detailed guide on water-saving toilets. Photos, drawings. • *Home Mechanix*. No. 757 (July/Aug, 1991) pp. 78-80.

"Low-flow toilets" by Amy Vickers. In-depth article on the latest water-saving toilets. Photos, charts. Sidebar on water-saving showerheads and faucets. • *Fine Homebuilding*. No. 61 (July, 1990) pp. 62-66.

"Toilet transportation" by Gary Goldsberry. Brief tip on moving a toilet in order to replace the bathroom floor covering. Drawing. • *Fine Homebuilding*. No. 84 (Nov, 1993) p. 30.

Tool Holders — *See* Storage--Tools

Tool Kits

"Buying a basic commonsense tool kit." Informative article on selecting tools for a beginning woodworker's tool kit. Illustrations, photo. • *Better Homes and Gardens Wood*. No. 63 (Sep, 1993) pp. 76-77.

Tool Stands

"Grinder stand" by Dennis Preston. How to build a wooden stand for a power grinder. Photos, plans, and materials list. • *The Woodworker's Journal*. Vol. 16, No. 4 (Jul/Aug, 1992) pp. 56-57.

"Mobilize your heavy shop tools" by Samuel W. Carson. A how-to guide for constructing a heavy-duty mobile tool stand. Photos and plans. • *The Home Shop Machinist*. Vol. 12, No. 3 (May/Jun, 1993) pp. 24-30.

Tool Tables

"One-legged helper" by Stephen E. House. Instructions for a tool table to reduce bending down when working on projects outdoors. Drawing. • *Fine Homebuilding*. No. 79 (March, 1993) p. 32.

Toolboxes

"Camper-shell toolbox" by Neal Bahrman. Brief description of how to construct a handy camper-shell toolbox. Photo, drawing. • *Fine Homebuilding*. No. 57 (Jan, 1990) p. 71.

Tools

Book Review: *The Carpenter's Toolbox* by Gary D. Meers. Book review on a manual featuring hand and power tools used for home construction and remodeling. Photos. New York: Prentice-Hall Press, 333 pp. • *Home Mechanix*. No. 747 (July/Aug, 1990) p. 28.

"Homeowners survival kit" by Roy Barnhart. A list of all the tools a homeowner might need to have on hand. Photos. • *Practical Homeowner*. Vol. VI, No. 3 (March, 1991) pp. 50-52.

"Mail-order tools" by Ron Greenman. Offers information on the rules of mail-order shopping. Drawing. • *Fine Homebuilding*. No. 62 (Sep, 1990) pp. 50-51.

"Tool-buyer's roundup" by Bill Krier. Extensive article with specification charts and helpful information for cordless drills, drill presses, jointers, portable belt sanders, routers, scroll saws, table saws, and thickness planers. Photos, charts. • *Better Homes and Gardens Wood*. No. 56 (Nov, 1992) pp. 64-78.

Tools, Antique

Book Review: *A Price Guide to Antique Tools* by Herbert P. Kean and Emil S. Pollack. Book review on a useful and complete guide for collectors of antique tools. Mendham, NJ: Astragal Press, 184 pp. • *Woodwork.* No. 17 (Sep/Oct, 1992) pp. 24-26.

Tools, Cordless

"Coming right up." Helpful tips for finding companies that recharge batteries in a short time. Illustration. • *Better Homes and Gardens Wood.* No. 42 (April, 1991) p. 84.

"Myths and facts about the care of your cordless tools." Brief article on maintaining and using cordless tools effectively. Illustration. • *Better Homes and Gardens Wood.* No. 42 (April, 1991) p. 21.

Tools, Cutting

"Teeth for rotary cutting tools" by R.S. Hodin. Short tips for making teeth for reamers and hole saws. Photos and plans. • *The Home Shop Machinist.* Vol. 10, No. 2 (Mar/Apr, 1991) p. 39.

Tools, Electrician's

Book Review: *The Electrician's Toolbox* by Rex Miller. Book review on guide to the hand tools and other equipment need for electrical projects. Photo. New York: Prentice-Hall Press, 364 pp. • *Home Mechanix.* No. 747 (July/Aug, 1990) p. 29.

Tools, Plumber's

Book Review: *The Plumber's Toolbox Manual* by Louis Mahieu. Book review on guide to the tools, pipes and fittings used by plumbers. Photo. New York: Prentice-Hall Press, 310 pp. • *Home Mechanix.* No. 747 (July/Aug, 1990) p. 29.

Tools, Power

"8 great tools" by Joseph Truini. Presents the features and advantages of eight power tools. Photos. • *Home Mechanix.* No. 766 (June, 1992) pp. 31-41, 77.

See Also specific types of tools, e.g., Saws; Clamps, etc.

Tools, Turning

"A beginner's primer on turning tools" by Larry Johnston. Helpful guide on turning tools. Photos, chart. • *Better Homes and Gardens Wood.* No. 59 (Feb, 1993) pp. 62-65.

Tools--History of

Book Review: *Selections from The Chronicle: The Fascinating World of Early Tools and Trades* edited by Emil and Martyl Pollack. Book review on the fascinating accounts collected from *The Chronicle*, a quarterly journal. Mendham, NJ: Astragal Press, 424 pp. • *Woodwork.* No. 13 (January/February) pp. 26-28.

Tools--Sharpening of

"How to sharpen turning and carving tools." Specific steps to sharpen turning and carving tools. Photos, drawings. Sidebar on how to keep your tools cool when rough-grinding. • *Better Homes and Gardens Wood.* No. 52 (June, 1992) pp. 36-41.

"Sharpen your end mills, part one" by Rudy Kouhoupt. A brief description of a technique for sharpening an end mill tool. Photos and plans. • *The Home Shop Machinist.* Vol. 9, No. 5 (Sep/Oct, 1990) pp. 42-45.

"Sharpening carving tools" by Rick and Ellen Butz. An analysis of the proper techniques for sharpening different types of cutting and carving tools. Photos. • *The Woodworker's Journal.* Vol. 17, No. 1 (Jan/Feb, 1993) pp. 24-28.

"Sharpening guides and gizmos" by Jim Barrett. Advice on using bench grinder attachments, honing attachments, and drill-bit jigs. Photos. • *The Woodworker's Journal.* Vol. 16, No. 3 (May/Jun, 1992) pp. 20-25.

Totem Poles

Book Review: *Carving Totem Poles and Masks* by Alan and Gill Bridgewater. Book review on the techniques of carving projects like totem poles and masks. New York: Sterling, 191 pp. • *Woodwork.* No. 16 (July/August, 1992) pp. 26-29.

Townhouses

"Townhouse transformation" by Barbara Poutsch. Renovating a 1926 townhouse. Photos. • *Practical Homeowner.* (Mar/Apr, 1992) pp. 72-75.

Toxins

"Test your home for toxins." Helpful guide explaining the procedure for testing homes for toxins. Information to order a test kit available. Photo. • *Home Mechanix.* No. 769 (Oct, 1992) p. 22.

Toy Boxes

"Keep-on-recycling toy box" by Marlen Kemmet, James R. Downing and Aaron Shaw. Instructions to build a recycling rolling toy-box truck. Photos, diagrams, materials list. • *Better Homes and Gardens Wood.* No. 64 (Oct, 1993) pp. 34-38.

"Toddler toy box" by Gary Walchuk. Provides detailed instructions for constructing a wooden toy box. Photo. Drawn plans, list of materials. • *Canadian Workshop.* Vol. 13, No. 5 (Feb 1990) pp. 70-75.

Toys

"Acrobatic bear folk toy." A clever design for a dancing wooden bear on string. Photos and plans. • *The Woodworker's Journal.* Vol. 16, No. 5 (Sep/Oct, 1992) pp. 54-55.

"All aboard! The wood express" by Marlen Kemmet and Richard J. Zichos. Directions to build a five car locomotive based on this prize winning design. Photos, diagrams, materials list, pattern. • *Better Homes and Gardens Wood.* No. 57 (Dec, 1992) pp. 60-65.

"The big rig." A description for constructing a toy tractor trailer truck set. Photos, plans, and materials list. • *The Woodworker's Journal.* Vol. 16, No. 4 (Jul/Aug, 1992) pp. 40-43.

"Blue ribbon tractor" by Jack Rowland. Detailed instructions on creating a tractor with a silky smooth finish. Diagrams, photo, materials list. • *Better Homes and Gardens Wood.* No. 37 (Sep, 1990) pp. 56-57.

"Classic Colonial doll house." A comprehensive and detailed set of plans for building a Colonial-style dollhouse. Photos, plans, and materials list. • *The Woodworker's Journal.* Vol. 15, No. 6 (Nov/Dec, 1991) pp. 48-52.

"Classic firetruck." A clear and concise guide to making a toy fire truck with wooden ladders. Photos, plans, and materials list. • *The Woodworker's Journal.* Vol. 16, No. 1 (Jan/Feb, 1992) pp. 62-65.

"Country wagon" by John Hetherington. Build your own wagon for decorative purposes or as a toy with these plans. Photo, diagram, patterns, materials list. • *Better Homes and Gardens Wood.* No. 44 (August, 1991) pp. 64-65.

"Custom-made building blocks" by Jeff Greef. Provides details on constructing custom-made toy building blocks for children, includes materials list. Photos. • *Woodwork.* No. 18 (Nov/Dec, 1992) pp. 70-74.

"Doll bed." Designs for the construction of an Early American style doll bed. Photos, plans, and materials list. • *The Woodworker's Journal.* Vol. 16, No. 6 (Nov/Dec, 1992) pp. 64-66.

"Dollhouse in a box" by Marlen Kemmet. Detailed instructions for a dollhouse that can be packed away in a handy case. Diagrams, photos, materials list, buying guide. • *Better Homes and Gardens Wood.* No. 34 (April, 1990) pp. 46-55.

"Dresser-top dragon." Create a whimsical wooden dragon on wheels with a personalized touch. Photo, drawing, patterns. • *Better Homes and Gardens Wood.* No. 62 (Aug, 1993) pp. 54-55.

"Farmyard favorites on a string" by Vickie Rush. Brief article on creating wooden farmyard animals. Photo, diagram, patterns. • *Better Homes and Gardens Wood.* No. 43 (June, 1991) pp. 74-75.

"Front-end loader" by Marlen Kemmet. Create an easy-to-assemble front-end loader with a pivoting-bucket assembly. Diagram, photo. • *Better Homes and Gardens Wood.* No. 41 (Feb, 1991) pp. 34-37.

"Fun-charged monster truck" by Marlen Kemmet. Step-by-step directions to create this exciting toy. Photos, diagrams, material list, drawings. • *Better Homes and Gardens Wood.* No. 35 (June, 1990) pp. 46-49.

"Horse and cart toy." This brief tip shows the method of building a simple horse and cart toy on wheels. Photo, plans, and materials list. • *The Woodworker's Journal.* Vol. 15, No. 4 (Jul/Aug, 1991) pp. 48-49.

"Kid's kitchen play center." Plans for miniature kitchen appliance, including. stove, sink, and cupboard. Photos, plans, and materials list. • *The Woodworker's Journal.* Vol. 16, No. 5 (Sep/Oct, 1992) pp. 56-61.

"Lathe-laid eggs" by Dave Hout. Describes how to turn and hollow out wooden eggs, especially with a homemade chuck. Photos, diagrams. • *Better Homes and Gardens Wood.* No. 43 (June, 1991) pp. 70-71.

"Learning my ABCs" by William Lovett. Describes how to construct a child's wooden bench and alphabet learning toy. Photo. List of materials. Drawn plans. • *Canadian Workshop.* Vol. 15, No. 1 (Oct 1991) pp. 55-56.

"The lighter side of woodworking" by Graham Blackburn. Ideas for woodworking techniques when building toys, puzzles, games, and other whimsical projects. Drawings. Photos. • *Woodwork.* No. 16 (July/August, 1992) pp. 50-53.

"Little red tote barn" by Larry Johnston. Directions to construct barn that doubles as a tote carrier for the animals and fence. Photo, drawing, materials list. • *Better Homes and Gardens Wood.* No. 61 (June, 1993) pp. 68-70.

"Livestock truck." How to build a toy livestock truck. Photos, plans, and materials list. • *The Woodworker's Journal.* Vol. 16, No. 6 (Nov/Dec, 1992) pp. 52-55.

"Marble drop" by Don Koppin. Describes how to construct a simple wooden marble drop toy for a child. Photo. List of materials. Drawn plans. • *Canadian Workshop.* Vol. 13, No. 5 (Feb 1990) pp. 49-52.

"Mighty hauler" by Kevin Atkinson. Describes how to build a toy wood truck. Materials list. Photo. • *Canadian Workshop.* Vol. 15, No. 1 (Oct 1991) pp. 53-54.

"Noah's ark." An easy-to-make project for a model of Noah's Ark complete with scroll sawn animals. Photos, plans, and materials list. • *The Woodworker's Journal.* Vol. 17, No. 6 (Nov/Dec, 1993) pp. 56-60.

"Noah's lovable ark" by Harlequin Crafts and James R. Downing. Plans to make six different kinds of wooden animals and Noah's ark. Photo, diagrams, patterns. • *Better Homes and Gardens Wood.* No. 46 (Oct, 1991) pp. 76-78.

"One lean jelly bean machine" by Tom Lewis. Innovative design and directions to construct a wooden jelly bean machine. Photos, diagrams, materials list. • *Better Homes and Gardens Wood.* No. 43 (June, 1991) pp. 80-82.

"Pegboard & mallet" by Alasdair Wallace. Furnishes detailed plans and instructions for building a wood child's toy pegboard and mallet. Photo. Drawn plans. • *Canadian Workshop.* Vol. 13, No. 4 (Jan 1990) pp. 54-55.

"Return to the round table" by Marlen Kemmet. Detailed instructions to construct a wooden castle. Photos, diagrams, materials list. • *Better Homes and Gardens Wood*. No. 39 (Dec, 1990) pp. 36-39.

"Roadster." This brief article outlines an easy-to-make roadster for a child. Photos, plans, and materials list. • *The Woodworker's Journal*. Vol. 15, No. 2 (Mar/Apr, 1991) pp. 48-51.

"Rough 'n' ready wrecker" by Marlen Kemmet and James R. Downing. Build a wooden wrecker to haul other toy vehicles that need to be repaired. Photos, diagrams, materials list, patterns. • *Better Homes and Gardens Wood*. No. 50 (Feb, 1992) pp. 68-71.

"Rugged road grader" by Marlen Kemmet and James R. Downing. Detailed instructions to construct an ideal toy for the sandbox or home. Photos, diagrams, full-sized pattern, materials list. • *Better Homes and Gardens Wood*. No. 45 (Sep, 1991) pp. 62-65.

"Sandbox excavator" by Marlen Kemmet. Complete directions to build a wooden sand excavator. Diagrams, photos, materials list. • *Better Homes and Gardens Wood*. No. 36 (Aug, 1990) pp. 52-56.

"Scroll sawn bunny rabbit puzzle." An easy-to-make project for a scroll saw. Photo. • *The Woodworker's Journal*. Vol. 17, No. 5 (Sep/Oct, 1993) p. 41.

"Sea skipper" by David Lanford. Brief article on building an easy-to-assemble floatplane. Photo, drawing, patterns. • *Better Homes and Gardens Wood*. No. 46 (Oct, 1991) pp. 58-59.

"Sports car." Complete plans for building a small, two seat, open top, roadster. Plans and materials list. • *The Woodworker's Journal*. Vol. 17, No. 4 (Jul/Aug, 1993) pp. 42-45.

"Standing-tall blocks box." Directions to construct wooden blocks tall enough to use as a booster step for toddlers. Photos, materials list, diagram. • *Better Homes and Gardens Wood*. No. 52 (June, 1992) pp. 68-69.

"Tilt action dump truck." A simple but clever design for a toy dump truck. Photo, plans, and materials list. • *The Woodworker's Journal*. Vol. 15, No. 5 (Sep/Oct, 1991) pp. 54-57.

"Toolbox 'n' tools" by Bill Kaiser. Offers directions to build a wooden toolbox and screwdriver, square and saw for children's imaginative play. Photos, diagrams, patterns, materials list. • *Better Homes and Gardens Wood*. No. 44 (August, 1991) pp. 56-59.

"Toy trio." Easy instructions for building a toy boat, truck, and helicopter. Photos, plans, and materials list. • *The Woodworker's Journal*. Vol. 17, No. 6 (Nov/Dec, 1993) pp. 49-51.

"Two toy dragsters." Detailed plans for building two types of rubber band powered wooden cars. Photos, plans and materials list. • *The Woodworker's Journal*. Vol. 14, No. 4 (Jul/Aug, 1990) pp. 40-42.

"Wagons, Ho!" by Marlen Kemmet and Scott B. Darragh. Construct a beautiful hardwood wagon with box-jointed corners and walnut trim. Photo, diagrams, materials list, patterns. • *Better Homes and Gardens Wood*. No 53 (Aug, 1992) pp. 76-80.

"What a racket!" by Phil Barley. Provides information on how to build a wood racketeer game. Materials list. Photo. • *Canadian Workshop*. Vol. 15, No. 1 (Oct 1991) pp. 50-52.

See Also specific type of Toys and Games, e.g., Trucks, Doll Houses, Puzzles, etc.

Toys, Educational

"The board of education" by Jerome Kobishop. Innovative design for a learning board teaching colors and shapes. Photo, diagrams, template. • *Better Homes and Gardens Wood*. No. 37 (Sep, 1990) pp. 58-59.

Toys, Mechanical

"Fork lift toy" by Harold Arvidson. This offers detailed plans for constructing a full operable wooden fork lift. Photos, plans, and materials list. • *The Woodworker's Journal.* Vol. 15, No. 1 (Jan/Feb, 1991) pp. 61-64.

Toys, Pull

"Grasshopper pull toy." Description of the method of building a wooden, grasshopper shaped, pull toy. Photo and plans. • *The Woodworker's Journal.* Vol. 14, No. 1 (Jan/Feb, 1990) pp. 42-43.

Toys, Push

"Cat push toy." A concise article outline the steps in creating a simple push toy shaped like a cat. Photo and plans. • *The Woodworker's Journal.* Vol. 14, No. 3 (May/Jun, 1990) pp. 54-56.

Toys, Whirligig

Book Review: *Whirligigs for Children Young & Old* by Anders S. Lunde. Review of a book on toy construction projects for youth. Radnor, PA: Chilton, 113 pp. • *Woodwork.* No. 18 (Nov/Dec, 1992) pp. 28-31.

Toys--Baggage Carts

"Toy airport baggage cart" by Clare Maginley. This is a simple how-to article for making a small child's toy baggage cart and tractor. Photo and plans. • *The Woodworker's Journal.* Vol. 15, No. 3 (May/Jun, 1991) pp. 56-57.

Train Stations

"Train-station renovation" by Mark Goldman. Explains the renovation procedure for a Carpenter Gothic exterior. Photos, drawings, diagram. • *Fine Homebuilding.* No. 81 (May, 1993) pp. 50-53.

Trains (Toy)

"All aboard! The wood express" by Marlen Kemmet and Richard J. Zichos. Directions to build a five car locomotive based on this prize winning design. Photos, diagrams, materials list, pattern. • *Better Homes and Gardens Wood.* No. 57 (Dec, 1992) pp. 60-65.

Transmissions

"Band saw transmission" by Richard Torgerson. Plans for using a transmission system to adapt a band saw for metal cutting. Photos and plans. • *The Home Shop Machinist.* Vol. 9, No. 4 (Jul/Aug, 1990) pp. 18-22.

Trays

"Barbecue tray." This article offers a simple design for a covered food tray. Plans and materials list. • *The Woodworker's Journal.* Vol. 14, No. 4 (Jul/Aug, 1990) pp. 46-47.

Trays, Cutlery

"English cutlery tray." A brief article on making a cutlery tray with mitered corners and dovetail joints. Photos, plans, and materials list. • *The Woodworker's Journal.* Vol. 14, No. 5 (Sep/Oct, 1990) pp. 54-56.

Trees

"Proper tree pruning" by Dean Johnson. A guide to the do's and don'ts of pruning trees. Photos and drawings. • *Practical Homeowner.* Vol. V, No. 3 (April, 1990) p. 12.

"Protecting your trees" by Linda P. Williams. A guide to protecting trees during construction periods. Photos. • *Practical Homeowner.* Vol. IV, No. 9 (Jan, 1990) pp. 58-59.

"Trees, a new wisdom" by Jim Rosenau. Tips on how to care for trees. Drawings. • *Practical Homeowner.* (Nov/Dec, 1992) pp. 36-41.

Trellises

"Return of the trellis" by Jonathan Fast. New ideas in designing and building garden trellises. Photos. • *Practical Homeowner.* Vol. V, No. 5 (August, 1990) pp. 74-78.

"Summer rooms" by Norman Kolpas. Ideas for building open porches, gazebos, and trellises. Photos. • *Practical Homeowner.* (Jul/Aug, 1992) pp. 78-83.

"Top-notch trellises" by Barbara McEwan, Jim Chase, and Paul Bianchina. Presents ten examples of trellises from classic arches to rustic variations. Photos, diagrams, drawings. • *Home Mechanix.* No. 744 (April, 1990) pp. 58-61.

"Trellis flashing" by Les Watts. Brief tip on making a combination flashing/anchor to repair an old trellis. Drawing. • *Fine Homebuilding.* No. 61 (July, 1990) pp. 24-25.

Trims

"Coping with rounded trim" by Anthony Patillo. Brief suggestion on how to make rounded trim to match a door. Drawing. • *Fine Homebuilding.* No. 62 (Sep, 1990) p. 30.

Trims, Door

"Trimming the front door" by Richard Taub. Provides a design for a door with custom trim. Photos, drawing. Sidebar on using hot-melt glue. • *Fine Homebuilding.* No. 79 (March, 1993) pp. 46-49.

Trowels, Power

"Operating a power trowel" by John M. Schnittker. Presents tips for operating a power trowel. Photo, drawing. • *Fine Homebuilding.* No. 83 (Sep, 1993) pp. 52-53.

Trucks (Toy)

"Mighty hauler" by Kevin Atkinson. Describes how to build a toy wood truck. Materials list. Photo. • *Canadian Workshop.* Vol. 15, No. 1 (Oct 1991) pp. 53-54.

"Over-the-road heavy haulers" by Marlen Kemmet and James R. Downing. Create a 18 wheeler tank trailer, log trailer, and semitrailer for your children." • *Better Homes and Gardens Wood.* No. 33 (Feb, 1990) pp. 72-76.

"Rough 'n' ready wrecker" by Marlen Kemmet and James R. Downing. Build a wooden wrecker to haul other toy vehicles that need to be repaired. Photos, diagrams, materials list, patterns. • *Better Homes and Gardens Wood.* No. 50 (Feb, 1992) pp. 68-71.

Trunks

"Treasure chest" by Lars Dalsgaard. Offers instructions to build an arched top treasure chest with particleboard. Photos, patterns, diagram. • *Home Mechanix.* No. 741 (Jan, 1990) pp. 71-73.

Trusses

"All trussed up" by Eliot Goldstein and Edwin Oribin. Offers instructions to build aesthetically pleasing steel-and wood box-beam trusses. Photos, diagrams, drawings. • *Fine Homebuilding.* No. 71 (Jan, 1992) pp. 74-77.

Tubing

"Aligning holes in tubing" by Neil W. Momb. Describes how to make holes in tubing all in a straight line. Drawing. • *Fine Homebuilding.* No. 81 (May, 1993) p. 26.

Tubs, Fiberglass

"Fiberglass tub fix" by Will Rainey. Instructions to build a sturdy fiberglass tub or shower to withstand strong winds or hurricanes. Drawing. • *Fine Homebuilding.* No. 68 (July, 1991) p. 30.

Tung Oil

"Tung oil: traditional favorite" by Jim Barrett. An article on the history, uses, and advantages of using tung oil for wood finishes. • *The Woodworker's Journal.* Vol. 14, No. 3 (May/Jun, 1990) pp. 21-22.

Tupelo (Wood)

"Tupelo: the wood that pioneer lumbermen left alone" by Ross Barker and John Arnes. Informative article on the availability, cost, uses, carving methods, and machining methods. Photos, illustrations, chart. Sidebar on shop-tested techniques that always work. • *Better Homes and Gardens Wood.* No. 62 (Aug, 1993) pp. 25-26.

Turning

"Green-wood turning" by Larry Johnston, Gary Zeff, and Todd Hoyer. Helpful pointers to begin green-wood turning. Photos, drawings. • *Better Homes and Gardens Wood.* No. 50 (Feb, 1992) pp. 72-75.

"Tagua turning" by Larry Johnston and Chuck Lueggers. Learn how to create objects with the tagua nut once used to make buttons. Photos. Sidebar on teeny tagua-turning ideas. • *Better Homes and Gardens Wood.* No. 54 (Sep, 1992) pp. 54-57.

"Turning Australian wood: The Banksia Nut" by Jeff Parsons. Describes how to use a wood lathe to work with the Australian Banksia nut. Photos. • *Canadian Workshop.* Vol. 13, No. 4 (Jan 1990) pp. 8-9.

"Turning between centers" by Bill Krier and Rus Hurt. Helpful tips from Rus Hurt on turning spindle projects. Photos, materials list, drawings. • *Better Homes and Gardens Wood.* No. 64 (Oct, 1993) pp. 52-57.

See Also Lathework

Turrets

"Framing a turret addition" by Patrick Rabbitt. Step-by-step instructions for constructing a turret addition to a Tudor house. Photos, drawings. • *Fine Homebuilding.* No. 68 (July, 1991) pp. 56-59.

Twisters

"The twister" by Sean Sheehan. Brief tip on making a twister to straighten out corkscrewed lumber. Drawing. • *Fine Homebuilding.* No. 77 (Nov, 1992) p. 32.

U

Underground Buildings

Book Review: *An Architect's Sketchbook of Underground Buildings* by Malcolm Wells. Review of a book filled with 400 hand-drawn sketches of underground buildings. Brewster, MA: Malcolm Wells (673 Satucket Rd.), 200 pp. • *Fine Homebuilding.* No. 65 (March, 1991) pp. 106-108.

Underground Lines

"Dousing for water lines" by Dennis T. Harbison. Brief tip for locating water, sewer, gas, or electricity lines before digging. Drawing. • *Fine Homebuilding.* No. 75 (July, 1992) pp. 26-28.

Urns

"Ageless urn" by Lee Gatzke. Instructions on how to turn a Grecian urn. Photo, diagrams, materials list, pattern. • *Better Homes and Gardens Wood.* No. 65 (Nov, 1993) pp. 60-63.

V

Vacuum Cleaners

"Piping for your shop vacuum makes cleaning up a cinch" by Dean Jenkins. Handy tip to connect a pipe system in the workshop to make vacuuming simpler. Drawing. • *Better Homes and Gardens Wood.* No. 50 (Feb, 1992) p. 18.

"Vacuum up those chips!" by Walt Dougherty. A look at the many uses of a vacuum cleaner in a machine shop. • *The Home Shop Machinist.* Vol. 12, No. 3 (May/Jun, 1993) p. 36.

"What's available in low-cost dust collection systems" by Jim Barrett. This review offers a thorough analysis of the types shop vacs on the market. Photos. • *The Woodworker's Journal.* Vol. 15, No. 3 (May/Jun, 1991) pp. 30-36.

Vacuum Systems

"Central vacuum systems" by Ed Zurawski. Provides advantages and features of central vacuum systems. Photos, drawing. • *Fine Homebuilding.* No. 60 (May, 1990) pp. 60-61.

"Install a central vacuum" by Don Vandervort. Describes how to install a central vacuum system. Photos, drawing. • *Home Mechanix.* No. 742 (Feb, 1990) pp. 48-50, 78.

Valances

"Window valance." Simple plans for the construction of wooden window valances. Photos, plans, and materials list. • *The Woodworker's Journal.* Vol. 16, No. 1 (Jan/Feb, 1992) pp. 70-71.

Valentine's Day Decorations

"Be mine, Valentine" by John Lemieux Rose. Plans and patterns to scrollsaw a romantic silhouette for a Valentine's Day present. Photo, patterns, drawing. • *Better Homes and Gardens Wood.* No. 50 (Feb, 1992) pp. 78-79.

Vanities

"Pine vanity." This descriptive article outlines the procedure for making a dresser top vanity with drawers. Photo, plans, and materials list. • *The Woodworker's Journal.* Vol. 15, No. 2 (Mar/Apr, 1991) pp. 56-58.

"Shoehorning a vanity top" by Rick Morgan. Instructions for building a vanity top when the backside of the wall is wider than the front. Drawing. • *Fine Homebuilding.* No. 68 (July, 1991) pp. 28-30.

"Vanity cases" by Pat McMillan. Presents four designs for bathroom storage. Photos, drawings, diagrams. • *Home Mechanix.* No. 774 (April, 1993) pp. 70-73.

"Vanity under glass" by Charles Metcalf. Highlights an unusual bathroom vanity combining an aluminum frame and frosted glass. Photos, drawings. • *Fine Homebuilding.* No. 84 (Nov, 1993) pp. 80-81.

Varnishes and Varnishing

"Art Carpenter's linseed-turpentine-varnish." Brief article describing Art Carpenter's favorite varnish. Photos. • *Better Homes and Gardens Wood.* No. 54 (Sep, 1992) pp. 48-49.

"Drying rack" by Daniel E. Perry. Offers a tip on building a rack to dry freshly varnished trim. Drawing. • *Fine Homebuilding.* No. 79 (March, 1993) p. 32.

"Choosing a good brush" by James Barrett. Tips on how to choose a good brush for varnishing. Photo and drawing. • *The Woodworker's Journal.* Vol. 17, No. 2 (Mar/Apr, 1993) pp. 24-27.

"High performance finishes" by Timothy O. Bakke. In-depth evaluation of new-formula deck protectors. Photo, chart. Sidebar on cleaning your deck. • *Home Mechanix.* No. 757 (July/Aug, 1991) pp. 60-63, 84.

"Lacquer that's music to your ears." Identifies some of the characteristics of fine-quality, durable lacquers. Photos. • *Better Homes and Gardens Wood.* No. 41 (Feb, 1991) pp. 52-53.

"The naturals" by Timothy O. Bakke. Provides information on clear finishes for cedar and redwood siding. Photos, chart. • *Home Mechanix.* No. 773 (March, 1993) pp. 60-62.

See Also Finishes

Vases

"Bud vases with flair" by Don Bailey. Accent your dining room or kitchen table by making an elegant wooden bud vase. Photo, drawing, patterns. • *Better Homes and Gardens Wood.* No. 48 (Dec, 1991) pp. 72-73.

"Split-turned vase" by C. Robert Taylor. Detailed instructions to turn a split-vase. Diagrams, photos • *Better Homes and Gardens Wood.* No. 40 (Jan, 1991) pp. 64-65, 88.

Veneers and Veneering

"How veneer is made: from giant log to delicate sheets" by David Loft and Abram Loft. Describes the procedures for producing different varieties of veneer. Photos. • *Woodwork*. No. 18 (Nov/Dec, 1992) pp. 44-49.

"Stone veneer on concrete block" by M. Scott Watkins. Instructions on how to lay the stone and select the right mortar for a stone veneer. • *Fine Homebuilding*. No. 84 (Nov, 1993) pp. 56-59.

"Tips and tools from France" by David Loft and Abram Loft. Brief article on the French techniques for working on veneer and tools that are used in France. Photos. • *Woodwork*. No. 14 (March/April) pp. 34-38.

"Veneering" by Roger Holmes. A comprehensive guide to all aspects of veneer work. Photos and plans. • *The Woodworker's Journal*. Vol. 16, No. 1 (Jan/Feb, 1992) pp. 27-32.

Ventilation

"The breathable home" by Lydia Cassidy. Describes factors that should be considered in improving home ventilation, including vents, fans, and insulation. Drawings. • *Canadian Workshop*. Vol. 13, No. 4 (Jan 1990) pp. 38-43.

"Venting the roof" by Kevin Ireton. Describes efficient ways to ventilate roofs. Photos, diagrams. Sidebar on the permanent ridge vent. • *Fine Homebuilding*. No. 61 (July, 1990) pp. 76-80.

Ventilation--Dryer

"Dryer vent through attic" by Mark Rosenbaum. Brief article answering a question about running a dryer vent through an attic. • *Fine Homebuilding*. No. 77 (Nov, 1992) pp. 20-22.

Ventilation--Exhaust

"Exhaust vents in a tight house" by John Hughes. Explains ventilation for a bathroom and laundry room. • *Fine Homebuilding*. No. 64 (Jan, 1991) p. 20.

Ventilation--Kitchen

"Clearing the air on kitchen ventilation" by Pat McMillan. Presents downdraft and updraft ventilators as well as hood designs. Photos. • *Home Mechanix*. No. 767 (July/Aug, 1992) pp. 64-71.

"Kitchen ventilation" by Liz Forgang. In-depth article with professional advice on selecting the proper kitchen ventilation for individual needs. Photos. • *Home Mechanix*. No. 749 (Oct, 1990) pp. 38-41, 89.

Victorian Houses

"Affordable Victorians" by Charles Miller. Provides information on building modern Victorian houses with specifications true to the Victorian-style tradition. Photos, plans. • *Fine Homebuilding*. No. 71 (Jan, 1992) pp. 70-73.

"Gingerbread houses" by Ted Jones. Describes how to restore and recreate Victorian-style homes. Photos, drawings, template. Sidebar on how to make gingerbread with a saw. • *Home Mechanix*. No. 752 (Feb, 1991) pp. 42-47.

"A newcomer on Grand Avenue" by W. Scott Neeley. Details the plans of a Victorian home built in a historic neighborhood. Photos, plans. • *Fine Homebuilding*. No. 66 (Spring, 1991) pp. 46-50.

Vise Jaws

"Productive vise jaws" by Jack Ott. A brief tip on how to make a replacement set of vise jaws. • *The Home Shop Machinist*. Vol. 10, No. 1 (Jan/Feb, 1991) pp. 43-44.

"Shop jaws" by Guy Loutard. A product review of a new type of quick-change vise jaw. Photo. • *The Home Shop Machinist*. Vol. 9, No. 3 (May/June, 1990) p. 18.

"Soft vise jaws" by James Madison. This article offers an analysis of the advantages of adding aluminum jaws to a standard vise. Plans. • *The Home Shop Machinist*. Vol. 9, No. 4 (Jul/Aug, 1990) pp. 32-35.

"Vise jaw fixtures, part one" by Edward G. Hoffman. Principles and practices associated with vise jaws. Photos and drawings. • *The Home Shop Machinist.* Vol. 11, No. 5 (Sep/Oct, 1992) pp. 56-57.

"Vise jaw fixtures, part three" by Edward G. Hoffman. See Vol. 11, No. 5 • *The Home Shop Machinist.* Vol. 12, No. 1 (Jan/Feb, 1993) pp. 52-53.

"Vise jaw fixtures, part two" by Edward G. Hoffman. See Vol. 11, No. 5 • *The Home Shop Machinist.* Vol. 11, No. 6 (Nov/Dec, 1992) pp. 54-55.

Vise Restraints

"Drill press vise restraints" by James Berger. A description of two kinds of restraints used to control vise rotation on a drill press–sliding bars and parallel linkage designs. Photos and plans. • *The Home Shop Machinist.* Vol. 11, No. 4 (Jul/Aug, 1992) pp. 45-50.

Vises

"Improving a milling machine vise" by Frank A. McLean. A guide on upgrading stock vises for milling machines. Photos. • *The Home Shop Machinist.* Vol. 10, No. 1 (Jan/Feb, 1991) pp. 56-57.

"Soft vise jaws" by James Madison. This article offers an analysis of the advantages of adding aluminum jaws to a standard vise. Plans. • *The Home Shop Machinist.* Vol. 9, No. 4 (Jul/Aug, 1990) pp. 32-35.

"Toolmakers flat vise" by Frank McLean. A brief article describing the uses for a small flat vise with horizontal jaws. Photos. • *The Home Shop Machinist.* Vol. 9, No. 1 (Jan/Feb, 1990) pp. 52-53.

"Twin lock workholding system." A product review for a new type of multi-part vise. Photo and plans. • *The Home Shop Machinist.* Vol. 10, No. 4 (Jul/Aug, 1991) pp. 10-11.

"Woodworking vises" by Bill Krier. Extensive treatment of the wide range of vises available and their features. Photos, diagrams, gripping comparison chart.

• *Better Homes and Gardens Wood.* No. 37 (Sep, 1990) pp. 42-45.

Wagons (Toy)

"Country wagon" by John Hetherington. Build your own wagon for decorative purposes or as a toy with these plans. Photo, diagram, patterns, materials list. • *Better Homes and Gardens Wood.* No. 44 (August, 1991) pp. 64-65.

"Wagons, Ho!" by Marlen Kemmet and Scott B. Darragh. Construct a beautiful hardwood wagon with box-jointed corners and walnut trim. Photo, diagrams, materials list, patterns. • *Better Homes and Gardens Wood.* No 53 (Aug, 1992) pp. 76-80.

Wainscoting

"Wainscots" by Thomas H. Jones. Presents five different types of wainscoting and how to install it. Photos, diagrams. • *Home Mechanix.* No. 771 (Dec/Jan, 1992-93) pp. 37-43.

Walking Sticks

"In praise of walking sticks" by Peter J. Stephano. Step-by-step instructions on the art of stickmaking. Photos. Stickmaking kit listed. • *Better Homes and Gardens Wood.* No. 33 (Feb, 1990) pp. 57-61.

Walkways

"Flexible walkway" by Henry Spies. Brief tip on creating a walkway to match a macadam driveway. Drawing. • *Home Mechanix.* No. 765 (May, 1992) p. 80.

Wall Anchors

"Basement-wall anchors" by Burleigh F. Wyman. Learn how to include wall anchors as basement walls are poured. Drawing. • *Fine Homebuilding.* No. 69 (Sep, 1991) p. 30.

Wall Cabinets — *See* Cabinets

Wall Shelving — *See* Shelving

Wallpaper

"Coverups for problem walls" by Judith Trotsky. Step-by-step instructions on wallcoverings that cover up cracks or damaged walls. Photos, • *Home Mechanix.* No. 750 (Nov, 1990) pp. 64-66.

"Picture-perfect wallcoverings" by Judith Trotsky. Informative article on scenic wallpaper and Lincrusta, an embossed linoleum-like wallcovering. Photos. • *Home Mechanix.* No. 771 (Dec/Jan, 1992-93) pp. 44-47.

"Recycled wallpaper" by Timothy O. Bakke. Presents a line of heavily textured wallpaper made from recycled newspaper and wood chips. Photo. • *Home Mechanix.* No. 768 (Sep, 1992) p. 33.

"Wallpaper hang-ups" by Lydia Cassidy. The author provides helpful suggestions to common problems associated with wallpapering projects. • *Canadian Workshop.* Vol. 13, No. 4 (Jan 1990) p. 70.

Wallpaper Paste

"Removing wallpaper paste" by Paul Hirsch. Offers a handy tip for removing wallpaper paste. • *Fine Homebuilding.* No. 64 (Jan, 1991) p. 30.

Walls

Book Review: *Walls & Moldings: How to Care for Old and Historic Wood and Plaster* by Natalie Shivers. Book review of handbook on fixing up plaster walls, moldings, and other areas in old homes. Washington, D.C.: The Preservation Press, 198 pp. • *Fine Homebuilding.* No. 77 (Nov, 1992) pp. 120-122.

"Building a wall on an existing slab" by Scott McBride. Brief tip on constructing a wall on a slab of concrete. Drawing. • *Fine Homebuilding.* No. 83 (Sep, 1993) pp. 14-16.

"Curing the chronic crack" by Walter Jowers. How to use fiberglass mesh tape to fix wall cracks. Photos. • *Practical Homeowner.* Vol. V, No. 3 (April, 1990) pp. 42-43.

"Forming concrete walls" by Arne Waldstein. Informative article on building forms stick by stick to save on labor and materials. Drawings. • *Fine Homebuilding.* No. 61 (July, 1990) pp. 55-57.

"Framing headers and corners" by Rob Thallon. Covers a variety of framing methods to improve the strength and energy-efficiency of walls. Photos, drawings. • *Fine Homebuilding.* No. 72 (March, 1992) pp. 57-61.

"Laying a granite-faced wall" by David Tousain. Describes techniques for using stone that is difficult to shape. Photos, drawings. • *Fine Homebuilding.* No. 58 (March, 1990) pp. 46-48.

"Raising finished walls" by Jean Dunbar. Provides tips on siding, trimming, and painting walls before erecting them. Photos, diagrams. • *Fine Homebuilding.* No. 58 (March, 1990) pp. 62-66.

"Recipe for raised-panel walls" by Rich Ziegner. Brief tip on making ornate oak paneling for walls. Drawing. • *Fine Homebuilding.* No. 82 (July, 1993) pp. 14-16.

Walls, Garage

"Recycling a wall" by Roger Gwinnup. Brief article on expanding a garage and recycling the back wall. Drawing. • *Fine Homebuilding.* No. 64 (Jan, 1991) p. 32.

Walls, Garden

"Great garden walls" by James Appleyard. A look at four different types of wood and stone retaining walls. Photos. • *Practical Homeowner.* Vol. V, No. 4 (June, 1990) pp. 66-68.

Walls, Rake

"Balloon-framing a rake wall" by Sean Sheehan. Provides a glimpse at an effective technique to increase the wind resistance for rake walls. Drawings, photos.

• *Fine Homebuilding*. No. 62 (Sep, 1990) pp. 62-63.

"Building rake walls" by Larry Haun. Offers two time-saving layout methods. Photos, diagrams. • *Fine Homebuilding*. No. 72 (March, 1992) pp. 67-69.

Walls, Rammed-Earth

"Rammed earth revisited" by Jim Rosenau. An analysis of innovations in building house walls from compacted earth. Photos. • *Practical Homeowner*. (Sep/Oct, 1992) pp. 74-77.

Walls, Retaining

"Retaining walls that last" by T.W. Brickman, Jr. Professional advice on designing and building retaining walls. Photos, drawing. • *Home Mechanix*. No. 747 (July/Aug, 1990) pp. 36-39.

Walls, Spalling

"Spalling concrete" by Alvin Sacks. Describes a solution to repair spalling concrete basement walls. • *Fine Homebuilding*. No. 71 (Jan, 1992) pp. 14-16.

Walls, Wing

"Wing-wall reinforcement" by Chris Strum. Brief tip on creating a concrete reinforcement for a wing wall. Drawing. • *Fine Homebuilding*. No. 83 (Sep, 1993) p. 30.

Walls--Curved corners

"Simple curved corners" by Scott M. Carpenter. Provides instructions to make graceful curves in white walls. Photos, drawing, diagram. • *Fine Homebuilding*. No. 83 (Sep, 1993) pp. 62-63.

Walls--Framing

"Framing walls" by Scott McBride. Detailed instructions on laying-out plans to frame walls. Photos, drawings. • *Fine Homebuilding*. No. 82 (July, 1993) pp. 42-47.

Walls--Insulating

"Basement retrofit" by Hank Spies. Brief tip on selecting insulation for a concrete basement wall. • *Home Mechanix*. No. 746 (June, 1990) p. 110.

Walls--Leaking

"Leaking brick" by Hank Spies. Brief tip on preventing water from leaking behind a veneer brick wall. Drawing. • *Home Mechanix*. No. 743 (March, 1990) p. 78.

Walnut (Wood)

"Black walnut" by Jim Boelling, Don Wipperman, Roy Kratz, Fern Weber, John Lea. Uses, availability, and overall performance profile for black walnut. Illustrations. • *Better Homes and Gardens Wood*. No. 35 (June, 1990) pp. 33-34.

Wardrobes

"Custom closet wardrobe" by Philip S. Sollman. Presents instructions to build a veneered plywood wardrobe. Photos, drawing. Sidebar on vacuum-bag veneering. • *Fine Homebuilding*. No. 83 (Sep, 1993) pp. 70-73.

"Simple closet wardrobe" by Jim Tolpin. Construction plans for a closet with shelves, drawers, and a section for hanging clothes. Photos, diagrams. • *Fine Homebuilding*. No. 78 (Jan, 1993) pp. 44-47.

Warping

"Wood movement." This is an examination of the environmental factors, such as heat and humidity, which affect wood. It also offers practical solution for protecting woodwork. Maps and charts. • *The Woodworker's Journal*. Vol. 15, No. 2 (Mar/Apr, 1991) pp. 35-37.

Water Damage

"Standing up to salt water" by Scott King. Solves a problem with salt water eating away at the paint and hardware on a home built on an island. • *Fine Homebuilding*. No. 68 (July, 1991) p. 16.

Water, Drinking

"Speaking of lead, how's your water?" Updated information on lead in drinking water. • *Home Mechanix*. No. 747 (July/Aug, 1990) p. 12.

Water Heaters

"Circulating system" by Henry Spies. Offers information about installing a gravity-fed circulating hot water system. Drawings. • *Home Mechanix*. No. 759 (Oct, 1991) p. 88.

"Electric water heaters" by Rex Cauldwell. Informative article on the features of the latest electric water heaters and maintenance tips for all models. Photos, drawing. Sidebar on water heater maintenance and troubleshooting. • *Fine Homebuilding*. No. 82 (July, 1993) pp. 54-59.

"Groaning water heater" by Peter Hemp. Brief tip on reducing the noise from a water heater. • *Fine Homebuilding*. No. 84 (Nov, 1993) pp. 12-14.

"Instant hot water" by Merle Henkenius. Informative article on installing a recirculating system to provide hot water instantly. Photos, drawing. • *Home Mechanix*. No. 762 (Feb, 1992) p. 24.

"Instant water heaters" by Henry Spies. Brief tip on arranging to have hot water quickly for showers or baths. • *Home Mechanix*. No. 759 (Oct, 1991) p. 88.

"Percolating heater" by Henry Spies. Addresses the cause of a gurgling sound coming from a water heater. • *Home Mechanix*. No. 775 (May, 1993) pp. 99-100.

"Staying in hot water" by Merle Henkenius. Describes how to install a hot-water dispenser. Photos, drawing. • *Home Mechanix*. No. 750 (Nov, 1990) pp. 68-70.

"Vacuuming a water heater" by Donna LeFurgey and Caleb Smiley. Provides a method of cleaning an electric water heater with a vacuum. Drawing. • *Fine Homebuilding*. No. 84 (Nov, 1993) p. 30.

"Water-heater anode rods" by Jay Stein. Provides information for deciding when to replace the magnesium anode of a gas hot-water tank. • *Fine Homebuilding*. No. 60 (May, 1990) p. 16.

Water Heaters, Solar

"Solar hot water for the 90s" by Marc Rosenbaum. Explains what a good quality solar domestic hot-water system is and describes the basic types of systems. Photos, diagrams. Sidebar on building custom systems. Sidebar on the new hybrids. • *Fine Homebuilding*. No. 68 (July, 1991) pp. 50-55.

"Solar water heaters" by Alex Wilson. Discusses the advantages of solar water heaters. Photos, drawings, chart. • *Home Mechanix*. No. 760 (Nov, 1991) pp. 67-72.

Water Levels

"The accuracy of water levels" by Tom Law. Explains how to accurately measure water levels. • *Fine Homebuilding*. No. 77 (Nov, 1992) p. 22.

"Low-budget water level" by Jeff Jorgensen. Create an inexpensive water level with a clear plastic jug. Drawing. • *Fine Homebuilding*. No. 70 (Nov, 1991) p. 32.

Water Pressure

"Cold shower" by Henry Spies. Brief article on how to prevent water pressure problems. Drawing. • *Home Mechanix*. No. 753 (March, 1991) p. 81.

"Under pressure" by Henry Spies. Brief tip on preventing negative pressure in water pipes. Drawing. • *Home Mechanix*. No. 763 (March, 1992) p. 82.

Water Purification Systems

"Water watch" by John P. Harrington. A guide to the various kinds of water purification and filtration systems on the market. Photos. • *Practical Homeowner*. Vol. V, No. 3 (April, 1990) pp. 22-24.

Water Quality

"Ensuring water quality" by Michael Cala. Informative article on water filters and treatment systems. Photos, drawing, chart. • *Home Mechanix*. No. 781 (Dec/Jan, 1993-94) pp. 78-83,89.

Water Supply

"Hot water quicker" by Peter Hemp. Brief article on solving the problem of getting hot water to a second-floor bathroom quicker. • *Fine Homebuilding*. No. 72 (March, 1992) p. 14.

"Power for off-grid water system" by Ezra Auerbach. Offers alternative sources of water for houses beyond the public power grid. • *Fine Homebuilding*. No. 60 (May, 1990) p. 16.

Waterproofing

"Right from the start" by Don Best. Advice for constructing dry and waterproof basements. Photos and drawings. • *Practical Homeowner*. Vol. VI, No. 5 (May/June, 1991) pp. 64-70.

Waxes and Polishes

"Protecting a new finish: a guide to waxes and polishes" by Jim Barrett. This is an introductory explanation of the different types of waxes and finishes • *The Woodworker's Journal*. Vol. 14, No. 1 (Jan/Feb, 1990) pp. 25-27.

Weather Vanes

"Fisherman whirligigs." A moderately difficult design for a weathervane whirligig. Photo, plans, and materials list. • *The Woodworker's Journal*. Vol. 15, No. 4 (Jul/Aug, 1991) pp. 44-47.

"Wily-fox weather vane" by Desiree Hajny. Brief article on how to cut a fox-shaped weather vane with a band saw or scrollsaw. Photo, diagram, pattern. • *Better Homes and Gardens Wood*. No. 44 (August, 1991) pp. 62-63.

Wedges, Dovetailed

"Making the dovetailed wedge." A description of the uses of dovetailed wedges for the prevention of cupping in wood boards. Photos and plans. • *The Woodworker's Journal*. Vol. 14, No. 4 (Jul/Aug, 1990) pp. 22-24.

Wheels (Models)

"4 fun-to-make wheels" by Jim Downing. Instructions to build wheels for model planes, cars, and monster trucks. Photos, drawings, pattern, illustrations. • *Better Homes and Gardens Wood*. No. 35 (June, 1990) pp. 40-45.

Whirligigs

Book Review: *Whirligigs for Children Young & Old* by Anders S. Lunde. Review of a book on toy construction projects for youth. Radnor, PA: Chilton, 113 pp. • *Woodwork*. No. 18 (Nov/Dec, 1992) pp. 28-31.

"Fisherman whirligigs." A moderately difficult design for a weathervane whirligig. Photo, plans, and materials list. • *The Woodworker's Journal*. Vol. 15, No. 4 (Jul/Aug, 1991) pp. 44-47.

"Two whirligigs from history" by David Schoonmaker and Bruce Woods. Brief description on how to construct whirligigs. Photos. Drawings. • *Woodwork*. No. 14 (March/April) pp. 62-67.

Whittling — *See* Wood Carving

Wicker Furniture

"Wild about wicker" by Lynda Scarrow. Presents information on how to evaluate, preserve, and restore wicker furniture. Includes list of tools and suppliers. Photos. • *Canadian Workshop*. Vol. 15, No. 1 (Oct 1991) pp. 17-27.

Willow (Wood)

"Tehal Virk's wonderful willow works" by Peter J. Stephano. Follow Tehal Virk's description of creating furniture with willow sticks. Photos. • *Better Homes and*

Gardens Wood. No. 61 (June, 1993) pp. 23-27.

Wind Storms

"The house that survived" by Gurney Williams. Description of the factors that must be considered to build a house to withstand high winds. • *Practical Homeowner.* Vol. V, No. 8 (Nov/Dec, 1990) pp. 70-78.

Window Seats

"First-class window seats" by Matt Phair. Detailed designs and construction plans for three attractive window seats and storage. Photos, diagrams. • *Home Mechanix.* No. 752 (Feb, 1991) pp. 58-63.

Window Trims

"Never-paint window trim" by Bob Wessmiller. Informative article on aluminum used for capping window trim. Photos. • *Home Mechanix.* No. 764 (April, 1992) pp. 28-29.

Windows

"Burglar-proofing windows" by Bill Phillips. Detailed instructions on securing windows from burglars. Drawings. • *Home Mechanix.* No. 774 (April, 1993) p. 14.

"Chilled glass" by Joseph Truini. Informative tip on R-value ratings for windows. Drawing. • *Home Mechanix.* No. 773 (March, 1993) pp. 22, 82.

"Deciding on window replacement" by Timothy O. Bakke. Professional advice on cutting heating and cooling costs with attention to energy-efficient windows. Photo. • *Home Mechanix.* No. 752 (Feb, 1991) pp. 12-15.

"Designing and building leak-free sloped-glazing" by Fred Unger. Presents detailed information on leak-free sloped-glazing for skylights and sunrooms. Photos, drawings. • *Fine Homebuilding.* No. 72 (March, 1992) pp. 76-80.

"Double-hungs restrung" by David Strawderman. Detailed article on repairing double-hung windows. Photos.

• *Fine Homebuilding.* No. 64 (Jan, 1991) pp. 48-49.

"Glass breakthroughs" by Timothy O. Bakke. In-depth article on the latest developments in glazing technology. Photos, diagrams, chart. Sidebar on divided-lite treatments. • *Home Mechanix.* No. 752 (Feb, 1991) pp. 55-57.

"On low-e coatings" by Paul Fisette. Provides advice on the advantage of installing low-E coating glass. • *Fine Homebuilding.* No. 64 (Jan, 1991) p. 22.

"Position of low-e coating" by Paul Fisette. Offers advice on positioning low-E coating for effective thermal performance. • *Fine Homebuilding.* No. 57 (Jan, 1990) pp. 14-16.

"Rooms with a view" by Chris Knowles. Describes how to select and install the most energy efficient windows for the home, as well as window replacement procedures. Photos. • *Canadian Workshop.* Vol. 15, No. 1 (Oct 1991) pp. 42-47.

"Selecting wood windows" by Joanne Kellar Bouknight. In-depth look at a manufactured window and how it works. Diagrams, chart. • *Fine Homebuilding.* No. 60 (May, 1990) pp. 46-51.

"Simple joinery for custom windows" by David Frane. Explains the process of using lap joinery for an eyebrow window. Photos, diagrams, drawings. • *Fine Homebuilding.* No. 76 (Sep, 1992) pp. 72-75.

"Thinking of views" by Jim Rosenau. Design ideas for installing windows in different types of rooms. Photos. • *Practical Homeowner.* (Sep/Oct, 1992) pp. 48-53.

"Window shopping" by Don Best. This article examines the newest trends in energy efficient windows. • *Practical Homeowner.* Vol. V, No. 2 (Mar, 1990) pp. 40-43.

Windows, Bay

"Building on a bay" by Joseph Truini. Describes the process of replacing a flat picture window with a bay window. Photos, drawing. • *Home Mechanix*. No. 748 (Sep, 1990) pp. 42-45.

"Framing a bay window with irregular hips" by Don Dunkley. Offers tips on calculating the tough cuts on a bay window. Photos, diagrams. Sidebar on regular and irregular hips. • *Fine Homebuilding*. No. 57 (Jan, 1990) pp. 78-83.

Windows, Double-Hung

"Keeping windows working" by Jim Barrett. Brief article with solutions to keep windows working smoothly. Photos, drawing. • *Home Mechanix*. No. 747 (July/Aug, 1990) p. 28.

Windows, Garden

"Garden windows" by Matt Phair. Describes several varieties of garden windows and how to install them. Photos. • *Home Mechanix*. No. 754 (April, 1991) pp. 62-64.

Windows, Glass Block

"Glass block for basement windows" by Matt Phair. Describes the process of installing glass block windows. Photos, drawings. • *Home Mechanix*. No. 752 (Feb, 1991) p. 30.

Windows, Palladian

"Palladian windows" by Daniel Williams. Advice on the aesthetic applications of palladian windows. Photos. • *Practical Homeowner*. Vol. VI, No. 2 (Feb, 1991) pp. 36-37.

Windows, Replacement

"Easy window upgrade" by Matt Phair. Describes a method of upgrading double-hung windows. Photos. • *Home Mechanix*. No. 767 (July/Aug, 1992) pp. 24-25.

"Matching old windows" by Walter Jowers. Tells about the process of matching windows on a circa 1740 Pennsylvania German brick home. • *Fine Homebuilding*. No. 67 (May, 1991) p. 14.

"Replacement windows" by Judith Trotsky. Surveys the features of replacement windows. Drawings. Sidebar on how to measure and order windows. • *Home Mechanix*. No. 776 (June, 1993) pp. 52-54.

"Windows: filling in the gaps" by John H. Ingersoll. Describes how to select replacement windows for the home. Photos, drawings. • *The Homeowner's Guide to Glass*. No. 1 (1989) pp. 28-33.

Windows, Tinted

"Glare repair" by Jim Barrett. Brief tip on applying tinted window film to windows to reduce solar heat and glare. Photos. • *Home Mechanix*. No. 746 (June, 1990) p. 13.

Windows, Vinyl

"Popular plastics" by Don Best. A description of vinyl framed windows. Photos. • *Practical Homeowner*. Vol. VI, No. 4 (April, 1991) pp. 68-72.

Windows--Repair and Maintenance

Book Review: *Repairing Old and Historic Windows*. Book review focusing on renovation and rehabilitation of older buildings. Photo. Washington, D.C.: The Preservation Press, 208 pp. • *Fine Homebuilding*. No. 84 (Nov, 1993) p. 124.

"Leaky window" by Hank Spies. Brief article on repairing a leaky basement window. Drawing. • *Home Mechanix*. No. 742 (Feb, 1990) p. 70.

"Panes for the ears" by Henry Spies. Provides advice on purchasing windows to block out freeway noise. • *Home Mechanix*. No. 776 (June, 1993) pp. 84-85.

"Rusting windows" by Henry Spies. Provides a brief tip on preventing steel-framed windows from rusting. Drawing. • *Home Mechanix*. No. 754 (April, 1991) p. 91.

"Trim-capping concerns" by Henry Spies. Offers information on how to cap window with aluminum so water will not collect under the aluminum. Drawing. • *Home Mechanix*. No. 759 (Oct, 1991) p. 89.

"Window condensation" by Hank Spies. Informative tip on eliminating condensation on a window frame. Drawing, chart. • *Home Mechanix*. No. 746 (June, 1990) pp. 110-111.

Wine Cellars

"Digging a basement the hard way" by Scott Publicover. Describes the procedure of excavating a wine cellar under an existing house. Photos, diagrams, drawings. • *Fine Homebuilding*. No. 81 (May, 1993) pp. 68-71.

Wiring —*See* Electrical Wiring

Wood, Australian

"Turning Australian wood: The Banksia Nut" by Jeff Parsons. Describes how to use a wood lathe to work with the Australian Banksia nut. Photos. • *Canadian Workshop*. Vol. 13, No. 4 (Jan 1990) pp. 8-9.

Wood, Found

"How to transform found wood into usable stock" by Larry Clayton. Five key steps on processing found wood. Photos, illustrations. • *Better Homes and Gardens Wood*. No. 37 (Sep, 1990) pp. 60-63.

Wood, Treated

"Post treatment" by Henry Spies. Brief suggestion for treating lumber with chemicals rather than pressure. • *Home Mechanix*. No. 755 (May, 1991) p. 97.

Wood, Tropical

"Tropical woods under fire." A critique of the controversy surrounding the continued use of wood from tropical forests for making furniture. • *The Woodworker's Journal*. Vol. 14, No. 3 (May/ Jun, 1990) pp. 26-29.

Wood, Selection of

"Buying wood" by Roger Holmes. This article offers advice on how to make knowledgeable purchases of wood stock.

• *The Woodworker's Journal*. Vol. 17, No. 4 (Jul/Aug, 1993) pp. 17-21.

"Tracking down good wood." Informative article on where professional lumber buyers seek quality stock. Illustration. • *Better Homes and Gardens Wood*. No. 61 (June, 1993) pp. 62-63.

Wood--Shrinkage of

"Wood shrinkage" by Henry Spies. Explains the cause of shrinking stock used for cabinets. • *Home Mechanix*. No. 766 (June, 1992) p. 78.

Wood--Toxicity of

"Toxic wood: Should we worry?" Informative article listing the areas of toxicity in 45 species of wood. Chart. • *Better Homes and Gardens Wood*. No. 56 (Nov, 1992) pp. 92-93.

Wood Bending

"Making curved instrument sides." This brief article outlines the process of bending wood strips to form the sides of musical instruments. Photo and plans. • *The Woodworker's Journal*. Vol. 14, No. 2 (Mar/Apr, 1990) pp. 30-31.

Wood Carving

"Barkrosing" by Larry Johnston. Introduces the carving technique called barkrosing, a Nordic decorative technique for wooden spoons or other objects. Photos. • *Better Homes and Gardens Wood*. No. 61 (June, 1993) pp. 54-55.

Book Review: *Carving the Little Guys* by Keith Randich. Book review of a source for whittling and carving figures. Greece, New York: Author (211 Woodsmoke Lane) 60 pp. • *Woodwork*. No. 14 (March/April) p. 22.

Book Review: *Carving Wildlife in Wood* by George Lehman. Book review of this guide to carving techniques for bird-carving, birds in flight. Lancaster, PA: Fox Chapel, 82 pp. • *Woodwork*. No. 15 (May/June, 1992) p. 31.

Book Review: *Sculptor in Wood: The Collected Woodcarvings of Fred Cogelow* by Bob and Mary Mischka. Book review on a delightful expressive collection of Cogelow's woodcarvings. Whitewater, WI: Bob and Mary Mischka (PO Box 336) 167 pp. • *Woodwork*. No. 13 (January/February) p. 28.

"Carving animals with Sandra Healy" by Deborah Upshaw. Features tips on carving animals. Photos. • *Woodwork*. No. 14 (March/April) p. 69.

"Getting started in carving" by Rick and Ellen Butz. A short primer on the tools and techniques used for carving wood. Photos. • *The Woodworker's Journal*. Vol. 17, No. 6 (Nov/Dec, 1993) pp. 36-37.

"Incised lettering" by Rick and Ellen Butz. A brief article describing techniques for hand lettering with cutting tools. Photos and plans. • *The Woodworker's Journal*. Vol. 17, No. 4 (Jul/Aug, 1993) pp. 28-30.

"Linen fold carving" by Rick and Ellen Butz. A description of the technique for carving linen fold patterns onto wood panels. This process requires advanced wood carving abilities. Photos and plans. • *The Woodworker's Journal*. Vol. 16, No. 6 (Nov/Dec, 1992) pp. 28-33.

"Making faces" by Larry Johnston and Harley Refsal. Specific details on how to carve faces. Photos, illustrations. • *Better Homes and Gardens Wood*. No. 45 (Sep, 1991) pp. 54-57.

"The Norwegian bachelor farmer" by Peter J. Stephano and Harley J. Refsal. Learn flat-plane carving through this rough-hewn caricature. Photos. • *Better Homes and Gardens Wood*. No. 41 (Feb, 1991) pp. 30-33, 83.

"The whittler's craft" by James E. Seitz. Learn the process of whittling. Photos. • *Woodwork*. No. 15 (May/June, 1992) pp. 52-55.

"Whittling" by Larry Johnston. Brief article on the basics of whittling. Photos,

patterns. • *Better Homes and Gardens Wood*. No. 54 (Sep, 1992) pp. 40-41.

"The woods that carvers crave" by Peter J. Stephano. Chart and brief article giving the hardness, uses, finishes, cost and availability of twelve carving woods. Photos, illustrations. • *Better Homes and Gardens Wood*. No. 45 (Sep, 1991) pp. 66-67.

Wood Carving Machines

"A wood carving machine" by John W. Snyder. An introduction to a power-operated pedestal mounted wood carving machine with multiple heads. Photos and plans. • *The Home Shop Machinist*. Vol. 11, No. 4 (Jul/Aug, 1992) pp. 34-44.

Wood Carving Projects

"A bird-in-the-hand ale bowl" by Phillip Odden. Carve your own bird-shaped ale bowl. Photos, materials list. • *Better Homes and Gardens Wood*. No. 60 (April, 1993) pp. 50-51, 82.

Book Review: *Nature in Wood* by George Lehman. Book review on carving techniques for bird-carving, birds at rest. Lancaster, PA: Fox Chapel, 40 pp. • *Woodwork*. No. 15 (May/ June, 1992) p. 31.

Book Review: *Painting Waterfowl with J. D. Sprankle* by Curtis Badger and James D. Sprankle. Book review of this resource on carving waterfowl. Harrisburg, PA: Stackpole, 240 pp. • *Woodwork*. No. 19 (Jan/Feb, 1993) p. 29.

"Carve a bluegill" by Rick Beyer. Tips on carving wooden fish from an expert carver. Drawings, photos. • *Better Homes and Gardens Wood*. No. 34 (April, 1990) p. 74.

"Carve a canvasback" by Marlen Kemmet. Step-by step instructions for carving a drake and hen wall plaque. Photos, diagrams, full-sized pattern. • *Better Homes and Gardens Wood*. No. 40 (Jan, 1991) pp. 34-37.

"Carve a cardinal" by Lindel Porter. Describes how to carve a cardinal with life-like replication. Photo, Diagram. • *Better Homes and Gardens Wood.* No. 36 (Aug, 1990) pp. 74-75.

"Carve a couple of houn' dawgs" by Bill Loftis and Larry Johnston. Follow five steps to whittle these amusing dogs. Photo, patterns, materials list. • *Better Homes and Gardens Wood.* No. 62 (Aug, 1993) pp. 58-59.

"Carve a howlin' coyote" by Max Alvarez. Whimsical design for a coyote carving. Photo, pattern, drawings. • *Better Homes and Gardens Wood.* No. 37 (Sep, 1990) p. 78.

"Carve a Santa" by Ron Ransom. Brief instructions and patterns to carve a Santa. Photos, patterns. • *Better Homes and Gardens Wood.* No. 39 (Dec, 1990) p. 78.

"Carve a scoop" by Warren Asa. Instructions on how to make a hand-carved scoop. Drawing. Photos. • *Woodwork.* No. 16 (July/August, 1992) pp. 46-48.

"Carve Shalako" by Bobbie K. Thurman. Learn how to carve a Southwest Native American symbol called a kachina doll. Photo, pattern. • *Better Homes and Gardens Wood.* No. 53 (Aug, 1992) p. 53.

"Carver's-pride trade sign" by Larry Johnston and Robert Thomas Jr. Carve a personalized trade sign with these instructions. Photo, pattern, materials list. • *Better Homes and Gardens Wood.* No. 51 (April, 1992) pp. 40-43.

"Christmas angel folk carving" by Rick & Ellen Butz. An outline of the process of carving wooden Christmas ornaments shaped like angels. Photos, drawings, and materials list. • *The Woodworker's Journal.* Vol. 14, No. 6 (Nov/Dec, 1990) pp. 48-51.

"Father Christmas wood carving" by Rick & Ellen Butz. A very complete visual guide for carving a wooden Santa Claus. Photos and drawings. • *The Woodworker's Journal.* Vol. 15, No. 6 (Nov/Dec, 1991) pp. 56-59.

"Gardening with a gouge" by John Hagensick. Brief article on how to carve realistic flowers. Photo, diagram, pattern, materials list. • *Better Homes and Gardens Wood.* No. 53 (Aug, 1992) pp. 60-63.

"Grateful Pilgrims" by Larry Johnston and Harley Refsal. Specific instructions to carve and paint a Pilgrim couple. Photo, patterns, materials list. • *Better Homes and Gardens Wood.* No. 56 (Nov, 1992) pp. 44-47.

"Here's Otto" by Larry Johnston and Desiree Hajny. Carving instructions for a life-like otter statue. Photo, drawings, materials list. • *Better Homes and Gardens Wood.* No. 46 (Oct, 1991) pp. 40-43.

"It's Western Santa" by Larry Johnston and Dave Rushlo. Detailed instructions to carve a cowboy-style Santa. Photos, patterns, materials list. • *Better Homes and Gardens Wood.* No. 48 (Dec, 1991) pp. 76-80.

"Kris Kringle goes cross-country" by Craig Lockwood. Detailed instructions to create a colorful, carved figure. Photo, patterns, materials list. • *Better Homes and Gardens Wood.* No. 57 (Dec, 1992) pp. 38-41.

"Little guy lotta fun" by Larry Johnston and Keith Randich. Directions to carve pocket-sized caricatures. Photos, patterns, materials list. • *Better Homes and Gardens Wood.* No. 63 (Sep, 1993) pp. 70-72.

"Perfect pachyderm." Specific tips on carving and painting a realistic-looking African elephant. Photos, patterns, materials list. • *Better Homes and Gardens Wood.* No. 64 (Oct, 1993) pp. 48-51, 76.

"Plate of plenty" by Pam Gresham. Directions to chip-carve a horn of plenty for the Thanksgiving holiday. Photo, pattern. • *Better Homes and Gardens Wood.* No. 65 (Nov, 1993) pp. 66-67.

"Santa Claus" by Rick and Ellen Butz. A detailed descriptive article on how to carve a wooden Santa Claus figurine. Photos. • *The Woodworker's Journal.* Vol. 17, No. 6 (Nov/Dec, 1993) pp. 38-42.

"Something new and exciting on the horizon Southwest landscape" by Andrea Miller. Pattern and directions for building a decorative accessory for your home. Photos. • *Better Homes and Gardens Wood*. No. 33 (Feb, 1990) pp. 62-63.

"Tabletop cigar-store Indian" by Peter J. Stephano, Mike Krone and Harley J. Refsal. Step-by-step directions to carve a cigar-store Indian. Photos, patterns. • *Better Homes and Gardens Wood*. No. 42 (April, 1991) pp. 38-41.

"Tips from the top" by Peter J. Stephano. Informative article giving tips from expert carvers. Photos, drawings. Sidebar on fun deserves some respect. • *Better Homes and Gardens Wood*. No. 63 (Sep, 1993) pp. 50-53.

Wood Carving Tools

"How to shop smart for carving tools" by Bill Krier. Helpful guide for beginning carvers. Chart listing specific capabilities of traditional and power carving tools. Sidebar on four woodcarving pros. • *Better Homes and Gardens Wood*. No. 44 (August, 1991) pp. 42-47.

Wood Carving--Swiss Style

"Decorative, carving Swiss style" by Larry Johnston and Wayne Barton. Learn the basics of Swiss-style carving, then try to carve a weather station. Photos, patterns, materials list. • *Better Homes and Gardens Wood*. No. 50 (Feb, 1992) pp. 44-47.

Wood Finishing

"Cosmetic advice" by Kurt Lavenson. Offers two helpful tips when caulking baseboards or painting hard to reach areas. • *Fine Homebuilding*. No. 61 (July, 1990) p. 26.

Wood Flattening

"How to flatten rough stock" by Roger Holmes. A detailed explanation of the process ripping and planing curved wood boards. Photos and plans. • *The Woodworker's Journal*. Vol. 17, No. 5 (Sep/Oct, 1993) pp. 20-24.

Wood Racks

"On-site lumber rack" by M. Felix Marti. Directions on building a sturdy lumber rack to store wood on-site. Drawing. • *Fine Homebuilding*. No. 67 (May, 1991) p. 26.

Wood Rot

"Decay resistance of exterior wood" by Stephen Smulski. Offers information on which woods resist decaying the most. Table. • *Fine Homebuilding*. No. 69 (Sep, 1991) p. 16.

"Wood-destroying fungi" by Terry Amburgey. Informative article on the fungi that can destroy wood and hints on how to prevent destruction. Photos. • *Fine Homebuilding*. No. 72 (March, 1992) pp. 64-66.

Wood Sculpture

Book Review: *Shaping Wood* by Douglas Hackett. Book review on creating a series of extraordinary sculptured designs. Blue Ridge Summit, PA: Tab, 164 pp. • *Woodwork*. No. 19 (Jan/Feb, 1993) pp. 29-31.

Wood Stoves

"Burning questions" by Steve Andrews. An analysis of new developments in environmentally friendly wood stoves. Photos. • *Practical Homeowner*. (Nov/Dec, 1992) pp. 52-57.

"Fuel for thought." Informative update on energy-efficient wood-burning stoves and clean burning fuel for the stoves. Photos. • *Home Mechanix*. No. 750 (Nov, 1990) pp. 10-12.

"Heat wave" by Joseph Truini. Presents information on how to install a woodstove and build a faux-stone chimney. Photos, diagram. Sidebar on wood stoves: engineered elegance. • *Home Mechanix*. No. 750 (Nov, 1990) pp. 46-54.

"New-tech wood stoves" by Gurney Williams. Offers designs for cleaner-burning wood stoves. Photos, drawings. Sidebar on efficient burning in three stages. Sidebar on pellet stoves: better for the environment? • *Home Mechanix.* No. 768 (Sep, 1992) pp. 62-66.

"Reconditioning a woodstove" by Gene and Katie Hamilton. Presents techniques to keep a woodstove burning efficiently. Photos. • *Home Mechanix.* No. 760 (Nov, 1991) p. 16.

Wood Treads

"Lag-shield layout" by Al Lemke. Brief tip on replacing some wood treads and risers on concrete steps. Drawing. • *Fine Homebuilding.* No. 78 (Jan, 1993) p. 30.

Woodgraining

"Decorative painted finishes" by Victor DeMasi. Provides an introduction to glazing, woodgraining, marbleizing and other finish techniques. Photos. Sidebar on marbleizing a mantel. • *Fine Homebuilding.* No. 60 (May, 1990) pp. 78-82.

Woodies

"The great woodie revival" by Peter J. Stephano. Learn how to restore wood-clad cars. Photos, references for woodie sources. • *Better Homes and Gardens Wood.* No. 52 (June, 1992) pp. 64-67.

Woodturning —*See* Lathework

Woodwork

Book Review: *52 Weekend Woodworking Projects* by John Nelson. Book review on a projects book filled with a wide range of ideas for beginner to advanced skill levels. New York: Sterling, 160 pp. • *Woodwork.* No. 15 (May/June, 1992) p. 31.

"Cutting irregularly shaped holes" by Lowie L. Roscoe. How to cut square holes in a round workpiece. Photos. • *The Home Shop Machinist.* Vol. 11, No. 6 (Nov/Dec, 1992) p. 39.

Woodwork--Stripping

"Stripping interior woodwork" by Matt Phair. Presents the safest and most effective methods of stripping interior

woodwork. Photos, chart. • *Home Mechanix.* No. 762 (Feb, 1992) pp. 50-57.

Woodworking

Book Review: *The Art of Woodworking.* Review of a series of books that cover the basic and advanced techniques of woodworking. Alexandria, VA: Time-Life Books, (20 volumes), 144 pp.) • *Home Mechanix.* No. 772 (Feb, 1993) p. 10.

See Also Carpentry or specific aspects of woodworking, e.g., Sanding, Sawing, etc.

Woodworking--Dictionaries

Book Review: *The Woodworker's Dictionary* by Vic Taylor. Book review on an excellent resource for woodworking-related information. Pownal, VT: Storey, 264 pp. • *Woodwork.* No. 16 (July/August, 1992) p. 75.

Woodworking--Encyclopedias

Book Review: *Encyclopedia of Wood Joints* by Wolfram Graubner. Book review on a valuable source of information on wood joints, including clear diagrams. Newtown, CT: Taunton, 152 pp. • *Woodwork.* No. 16 (July/August, 1992) p. 75.

Woodworking--History of

Book Review: *Selections from The Chronicle: The Fascinating World of Early Tools and Trades* edited by Emil and Martyl Pollack. Book review on the fascinating accounts collected from *The Chronicle,* a quarterly journal. Mendham, NJ: Astragal Press, 424 pp. • *Woodwork.* No. 13 (January/February) pp. 26-28.

Work Tables, Router

"Router table" by Ernie Conover. An examination of the process of building a wooden table stand with doors and shelves for holding a router. Photos, plans, and materials list. • *The Woodworker's Journal.* Vol. 16, No. 6 (Nov/Dec, 1992) pp. 47-51.

Workbenches

"The $30 workbench." This article describes the method of building a low cost work bench out of medium density fiberboard. Photo, plans, and materials list. • *The Woodworker's Journal.* Vol. 17, No. 1 (Jan/Feb, 1993) pp. 44-47.

"Labor-of-love workbench" by Marlen Kemmet. Describes how to construct a workbench with a 30 x 60" worktop and a bench-dog-and-vise system. Photos, diagrams, materials list. • *Better Homes and Gardens Wood.* No. 37 (Sep, 1990) pp. 46-53.

"Simple workbenches" by Tom Law. Presents construction plans for site-built workbenches. Photos, drawings. Sidebar on a panel-cutting table. • *Fine Homebuilding.* No. 81 (May, 1993) pp. 64-67.

"Workbench and portable tool chest" by Dennis Preston. This double article gives details on making a matching workbench and tool chest. Photos, plans, and materials list. • *The Woodworker's Journal.* Vol. 14, No. 5 (Sep/Oct, 1990) pp. 62-86.

"A workhorse of a workbench" by Marlen Kemmet and James R. Downing. Provides plans to build a laminated maple workbench. Photos, diagrams, materials list. • *Better Homes and Gardens Wood.* No. 54 (Sep, 1992) pp. 64-69.

Workshops

"A chop-saw workstation" by Scott King. Directions to build a movable table for the compound miter saw. Photo, diagram. • *Fine Homebuilding.* No. 65 (March, 1991) pp. 46-47.

"Flashing lights announce phone calls and visitors" by John Seidel and Edward DeMay. Brief tip on planning the workshop so telephone calls and visitors are heard. Drawing. • *Better Homes and Gardens Wood.* No. 64 (Oct, 1993) p. 14.

"Here it is!" Detailed suggestions for creating an effective and comfortable workshop. Photos, Sidebars on shop specs. • *Better Homes and Gardens Wood.* No. 54 (Sep, 1992) pp. 58-63.

"Home workshops that work." Offers a glimpse of several different kinds of workshops. Photos. • *Better Homes and Gardens Wood.* No. 60 (April, 1993) pp. 65-67.

Workshops--Design

"Shop layout" by Olev Edur. The author provides sample workshop floor plans, hints for more efficient work areas, and a template. Drawn plans. • *Canadian Workshop.* Vol. 13, No. 5 (Feb 1990) pp. 31-40.

Z

Zoning Variances

"Getting a variance" by Noah Derius. A description of the technicalities of zoning variances. • *Practical Homeowner.* Vol. V, No. 7 (Oct, 1990) pp. 18-20.

Title Index

A

A.O.B. House 43
ABCs of PIR sensors 145
Acadian cottage 78
Accent on lighting 101
Accessibility Book 18
Accessories for a rotary table 136
Accu-miter 71
Accuracy of water levels 178
Accurate multiple-pass routing 138
Acrobatic bear folk toy 167
Acrylic-impregnated wood 18
Adaptable Housing 5
Adapting the craftsman style 5
Adapting the Myford 33
Adapting the myford 97
Adapting Usonian 82
Adaptive behavior 20
Add the crowning touch to your projects large-scale moldings 110
Adding a craftsman spa room 152
Adding a garage 69
Adding kneewalls 93
Adding on to old houses 1
Add-on fireplace 62
Adirondack rocker 134
Adjustable bench hook 78
Adjustable cabinet jack 20
Adjustable desktop bookshelf 13
Advanced Roof Framing 135
Aeolian harp 75
Aerobic step 58
Affordable elegance 94
Affordable Victorians 174
After the flood 8
After-the-fact insulation 84
Ageless urn 172
Airbrush 3
Air-cleaning central 3

Air-drying lumber 18
Air-filtration cabinet 2
Air-hose repair 2
Airtight in Massachusetts 106
Algae-stained shingles 147
Aligning holes in tubing 171
All aboard! The wood express 170
All about steam baths 9
All the comforts 42
All trussed up 171
Allergy proofing your home 3
All-star media center 20
All-wood box 15
Alphabet soup 84
Alpine Santa 27
Alternate clamping devices 29
Alternative lumber sources 18
Alternative use for swollen biscuits 29
Aluminum fundamentals 3
America's Favorite Homes 4
America's most popular house styles 43
American home 80
Amps versus horsepower 111
Anchor-bolt clamps 29
Anchor-bolt spacers 152
And now for something completely different 35
Angle bevel 12
Annual American Family Home 43
Another decking persuader 41
Appliance drains 49
Appropriate Technology Sourcebook 162
Aquarium room divider 4
Arc in the woods 43
Arch layout 4
Architect's Sketchbook of Underground Buildings 172
Architect's Studio Companion 43
Architectural ironwork 86
Art Carpenter's linseed-turpentine-varnish 173
Art for Everyday 74

Title Index

Art of Woodworking 186
Asbestos on the roof 136
Asbestos update 6
Ash wall desk 46
Asphalt driveway resurfacing 51
Attaching plaster casts 24
Attic art studio 129
Attic studio apartment 6
Attic upgrades 6
Audel Carpenters and Builders Library 22
Audio/video remote rack 15
AutoSketch 3.0 44
AutoSketch for Windows 44
Autumn delight 86
Autumn leaves 143

B

Baby's first bed 11
Bachelor chest 26
Back-to-back baths 9
Backup power 71
Backyard Edwardian 54
Ball turning in the mill 107
Balloon-framing a rake wall 176
Band saw cutoff table 40
Band saw slow speed attachment 7
Band saw transmission 7
Bandsaw blade holder 77
Bandsawed: Through-dovetail joints 90
Band-sawn napkin holder 112
Bandsaws 7
Barbecue tray 170
Barbecue work center 23
Barkrosing 7
Baronial inglenook 62
Baseboard shims 8
Basement condensation 109
Basement flooding 8
Basement knockout 8
Basement retrofit 177
Basement rust 83
Basement-wall anchors 175
Basic frame work 67
Basic Home Building 129
Basic scribing techniques 143
Basics of clamping 29
Basics of locating 62
Basket case 94
Bathing beauty 131
Bathroom basics 9
Bathroom brushup 9
Battling a bulge in a foundation wall 66
Battling harmful vapors 138
Be mine, Valentine 143
Beam-stair 10
Beating indoor air pollution 3
Beating the heat 55
Beauty and the box 15
Bed alcove 10

Beefing up old joists 90
Before you hire a moonlighter 38
Beginner's primer on turning tools 166
Bell chuck for your lathe 28
Belt buckle and bolo set 86
Bench brushes from old brooms 17
Bench chisels 27
Benchtop lathes 96
Benchtop tablesaws 159
Beneath green gable roofs 82
Bentwood toboggan 164
Best ways to heat an addition 1
Better backing for doors 47
Better flush systems for water-saving toilets 165
Better spindle repair 25
Beyond the basic barbecue 7
Beyond the box 91
Big barn at Big River 7
Big ideas for small spaces 1
Big improvements for small baths 10
Big money game of home ownership 78
Big rig 167
Bi-metal blades 141
Bird-in-the-hand ale bowl 14
Biscuit joiner 88
Biscuit joinery basics 89
Black cherry: The poor man's mahogany 26
Black walnut 177
Block party 72
Bloom boxes 120
Blown-in wall insulation 84
Blue ribbon tractor 167
Board of education 169
Bold, beautiful basements 131
Boneyard marble 105
Book of Shaker Furniture 145
Bookshelf classics 13
Border incidents 14
Boring metal-skinned doors 482
Boring square holes 90
Bottoms-up barstools 8
Bowed psaltery 112
Bow-front table 160
Box joint jig 87
Box joints on the radial-arm saw 89
Box protects dust collector 53
Box with marquetry top 17
Boxed Lally 33
Brass inlay and brass-covered moulding 17
Brassy solution for a sloppy miter gauge 71
Brazing band saw blades 141
Breaking the rules 66
Breathable home 174
Brick repointing 17
Brick-mosaic patios 118
Brightening a bungalow 129
Bring on the bracelets 86
Bringing up the rear 123
Bud vases with flair 173

Budget bungalow 19
Bug busters 162
Build a garden pond 123
Build an outdoor closet 146
Build your own CNC controller 34
Builder's Foundation Handbook 65
BuilderGuide Software 43
Builders' Adhesives 2
Builders' blocks 81
Building a butternut kitchen 92
Building a deck roof 134
Building a dry basement 9
Building a Gothic playhouse 122
Building a hydraulic press twice, part one 125
Building a pole house 79
Building a shed-roof canopy 21
Building a tiled masonry heater 76
Building a wall on an existing slab 176
Building an exterior newel post 124
Building an L-shaped stair 153
Building and turning a bricklaid bowl 14
Building boxes 15
Building by numbers 81
Building coffered ceilings 24
Building Construction Illustrated 79
Building for unknown clients 45
Building from kits 1
Building interior doors 47
Building on a bay 180
Building rake walls 177
Building small 45
Building the panther pup 56
Building the universal pillartool 119
Building with glass 158
Building With Junk and Other Good Stuff 129
Building with pumice-crete 84
Building without barriers 5
Building wooden screen doors 48
Building-block supports 159
Built on barter 8
Built on promises 43
Built-up cedar roofing 134
Burglar-proofing windows 180
Burned countertop 39
Burning questions 185
Butler multiple boring machines 14
Butternut breadbox 15
Butternut… walnut's kissing cousin 19
Buyer's guide to faucets, spouts and showerheads 10
Buying a basic commonsense tool kit 165
Buying a biscuit joiner 89
Buying wood 102
Buzzards bay house 81

C

Cabinet shopper's survival guide 91
Cabinet with punched doors 20
Cabinet, cabinet on the wall 20
Cabinetry Basics 20

Cabriole legs 67
CAD for the small shop 34
Cameron series 164 micro drill press 50
Camino con corazon 81
Camper-shell toolbox 165
Candle holder 21
Candy-striped rolling pins 134
Cantilevered hillside house 81
Cantilevered kitchen addition 92
Cargo knots 93
Caring for Your Old House 77
Carpenter's Dream 105
Carpenter's number code 106
Carpenter's Toolbox 165
Carpenter's Dream 58
Carpenter's number code 22
Carpentry and Construction 22
Carve a bluegill 183
Carve a canvasback 183
Carve a cardinal 184
Carve a colorful feather pin 86
Carve a couple of houn' dawgs 184
Carve a howlin' coyote 184
Carve a Santa 27
Carve a scoop 142
Carve Shalako 91
Carved intarsia 85
Carver's-pride trade sign 184
Carving animals with Sandra Healy 183
Carving the Little Guys 182
Carving Totem Poles and Masks 167
Carving Wildlife in Wood 182
Cascade of roofs 134
Cast iron repair 24
Casual classics —mahogany outdoor
    furniture that will last and last 67
Casual classics—a distinctive and durable
    mahogany table 70
Cat push toy 170
Caulking and Sealants 24
C-Clamp coatrack 32
CD carousel 22
Ceiling joists for a hip roof 90
Ceiling-fan basics 59
Ceilings, the last frontier 24
Center finder 25
Central dust collection 53
Central vacuum systems 173
Cerro alloys aid in machining irregular parts 3
Chainsaws: Come out of the woods 25
Chance of showers 149
Changing entries 132
Character at cost 92
Charming Cheval mirror 108
Checkering in the mill 26
Checking lathe alignment 97
Cheery, cherry door harp 47
Cherry dropleaf dining table 46
Cherry end table 55

Title Index

Cherry letterbox 100
Cherry lingerie chest 26
Chess set 26
Chest/cupboard 26
Child's play 122
Child's stepped back cupboard 40
Child's Windsor 25
Chilled glass 180
Chimney cap 27
Chimney with a twist 27
Chiseling hinge mortises 111
Choosing a good brush 17
Choosing an up-flush toilet 165
Choosing kitchen countertops 39
Choosing sharpening stones 155
Choosing siding 150
Chop-saw workstation 187
Christmas angel folk carving 4
Cimarron 13
Circulating system 178
Clamp organizer 156
Clamp rack 127
Clamp-fishing 29
Clamping a staircase 154
Clamping scarf joints 90
Clampless fence makes router setup
    fiddle-free 137
Clamps 29, 30
Clamps on site 30
Clamp-storage extravaganza 156
Class room 68
Classic Armoire 5
Classic Colonial doll house 167
Classic column 155
Classic firetruck 167
Classic shapes for Christmas 28
Classical columns outdoors 33
Classy tissue box cover-up 16
Clean air, healthy air. 3
Cleaning concrete 35
Cleanser clean-up 30
Clear the deck 41, 109
Clearing the air on home hazards 6
Clearing the air on kitchen ventilation 174
Closet makeovers 32
Clothes tree for youngsters' aquatic playmates 32
Cluster of cottages 38
Coating concrete floors 36
Coffee table with drawers 32
Cold basement 9
Cold cabinets 91
Cold shower 178
Cold-floor cure 63
Cold-roof details 134
Collapsible basket 9
Collector's showcase 47
Collet chuck turning 28, 97
Colonial bench 11
Colonial candle box 15

Colonial sampler 33
Colonial sign 150
Colonial-style ratchet table lamp 94
Combination tools-plus 96, 148
Combustion gases: An indoor threat 33
Comfortable outdoor bench 11
Coming right up 166
Common-Sense Pest Control 118
Compact disc holder 34
Compact fluorescent lighting 56
Complete Book of Home Environment Hazards 138
Complete Do-It-Yourself Manual 103
Complete Home Restoration Manual 37
Composition panels 117
Compound angle dovetails 90
Computers in the shop 35
Concrete Formwork 35
Concrete masonry bricks 17
Condensation on diffusers 36, 46, 109
Connecticut river valley highboy, parts 1 & 2 27
Construct-a-chuck 28
Construction epoxies 58
Construction Materials 18
*Consumer's Guide to Home Improvement,
    Renovation & Repair* 103
Contemporary cradle—designed on the run 39
Contemporary farmhouse 59
Contemporary jewelry box 15
Contemporary table 160
Controlling air leakage 56
Controlling spa-room moisture 110
Convert a milling machine to CNC control 34
Convert pipe couplers into inexpensive blast gates 53
Convert your mill-drill to CNC 34
Convertible daybed 10, 41
Converting a garage into living space 69
Cookie jar holder 38, 156
Cookout kitchens 93
Cool details 56
Cool improvisation 2
Cool pool deck 42
Cooling effects of rammed-earth 38
Coping table 160
Coping with rounded trim 171
Coral cabana 19
Cordless drill/drivers 51
Cordless tool revolution 125
Cordless wonders 51
Corner for collectibles 20
Cosmetic advice 185
Cost-effective cabinet makeover 20
Costly traditions 43
Cottage in the Cotswolds 38
Cottonwood 38
Counter proposals 39
Counter punch 39
Country curio clock 31
Country clock 31
Country finishes 60

Country pie safe 119
Country pine mirror and shelf 108
Country pine table 55
Country pine writing desk 46
Country quilt hanger 126
Country shadow box 16
Country wagon 167, 175
Country-colors quilt stand 126
Courtyard connections 80
Coverups for problem walls 176
Cozy fireplace plaque 121
Cracker house in a hammock 39, 45
Cracking up 24, 103
Crawl-space concrete 35
Crawl-space moisture 39, 110
Crawl-space mold 39, 110
Cream of the crop: scrollsaws over $500 144
Create an arch 49
Create your own custom floor 63
Create zones for your hot-water heating system 76
Creative home offices 114
Credenza with charisma 39
Critter proof your home 118
Crowning touches 111
Culinary Cutting Boards 13, 40
Cultured counters 39
Curing the chronic crack 103, 176
Curing unwanted door swings 47
Curled plywood roof 123
Current cost of energy 56
Custom closet wardrobe 177
Custom kitchen remodel 132
Custom mitersaw cabinet 109
Custom paneling 117
Customized tablesaw base 159
Custom-made building blocks 13, 167
Custom-made fences for your router-table 59
Cut above the rest 13
Cutting against the grain 20, 22
Cutting clapboards 30
Cutting corners 55
Cutting corners to gain bath space 9
Cutting costs of cold floors 66
Cutting crown molding 111
Cutting edge appliances 4
Cutting holes in tile 163
Cutting irregularly shaped holes 186
Cutting left-hand threads 163
Cutting vee notches 107
Cylinder or master square 153

D

Da' Scrollers! 145
Dado-cutting tools 40
Damp masonry 110
Dampening a bouncy floor 63
Dampening drips 49
Damping duct noise 113
Daring dormers 49

Darkhouse decoys 42
Dating vintage houses 82
Daylight savings 101
Deadly lead dust 99
Decay resistance of exterior wood 125
Decentralized air conditioning 2
Deciding on window replacement 180
Deck flashing 41
Deck foundations that last 65
Deck railing planters 120
Deck-building basics 41
Deck-cleaning tips 41
Decking persuader 41
Decks with great details 41
Deckware 42
Decorating tile at home 163
Decorative floor inlays 63
Decorative painted finishes 60
Decorative, carving Swiss style 185
Decorator duck 74
Decorator oil lamps 94
Deep foundations 65
Deep freeze 67
Density, volume, dimensions = weight 147
Desert house 81
Design and Application Manual for New Roof Construction 134
Design at a discount 92
Design guidelines for safe stairs 154
Design programs for remodeling projects 129
Design under glass 46
Designing a root cellar 136
Designing and building leak-free sloped-glazing 180
Designing for a hot climate 43
Designing for tall concrete walls 36
Designing solar storage 152
Designing with kids 122
Desk clock 31
Detailing for wood shrinkage 104
Dial 0 to align jointer tables 89
Digging a basement the hard way 182
Digging out the basement 9
Display box 15
Doll bed 167
Dollhouse in a box 167
Domes sweet domes 24
Don't let upkeep get you down 104
Don't forget the blocks 13
Door jig 87
Door reinforcers 49
Doormaking Patterns & Ideas 49
Doorway defense 49
Dot houses 43
Double joist cause leak 100
Double-hungs restrung 180
Double-sink upgrade 151
Dousing for water lines 172
Doweling jigs 88

Title Index

Down by the old mill stream 144
down-to-business dust collector 53
Down-under desk clock 31
Dream keepers 10
Dresser-top coin bank 7
Dresser-top delight 15
Dresser-top dragon 167
Drill bushings 50
Drill press chuck handles 28
Drill press gets around on an easy-to-build base 50
Drill press quill lock 50
Drill press router adapter 50
Drill press vise restraints 51
Drill presses 51
Drill-bit basics 50
Drill-bit countersink 50
Drilling multiple holes in line 51
Drilling sheet metal safely 146
Drill-press dust collector 53
Drillpress table 50
Driving screws with a drill 143
Dryer air intake 52
Dryer vent through attic 174
Drying a wet slab 35
Drying rack 127
Drying rack for siding 150
Dry-laid stone stairway 154
Drywall booster shot 121
Drywall 52
Drywall detailing 52
Drywall edge trimmer 52
Duck under glass 121
Duct cleaning 52
Dust busting 53
Dust collectors 53
Dust collectors getting the most out of
    your system 53
Dust panels 54
Dust stops here — portable planer hood 53
Dutch turning 97

E

Early American candlestand 21
Early American corner cupboard 40
Early American mirror 108
Early American style curio shelf 146
Early-days sofa table 33
Earthbuilders' Encyclopedia 54
Earthship 54
Easily alarmed 3
Eastern white pine 119
Easy to make wood hinge 77
Easy window upgrade 181
Easy-build bookshelves 13
Echoes of antiquity 31
Ecoinstruction materials 18
Eco-kitchen 92
Economical framing 66
Edge-lap joints 90

Effective do-it-yourself home inspection 78
Efficiency zones for heating and cooling 76
Efficient heat pumps 76
8 great tools 166
Electric discharge machining 54
Electric radiant floors 64
Electric water heaters 178
Electric-radiant slabs and health 55
Electronic air cleaners 2
Elegance on a shoestring 79
Elegant site-built door 47
Elegant-oak dining chairs 25
Elegant-oak dining table 46
Elevating a vertical mill 108
Eli Terry shelf clock 32
Enamel spray paint 116
Enco 12X26" geared head engine lathe 96
Energy barriers 85
Energy detailing 56
Energy-efficient attic access 6
Energy-efficient hot tub 78
English cutlery tray 170
English garden set 68
Ensuring water quality 179
Entry decks 41
Environmental showcase 58
Epoxy: nearly as tough as nails and
    beautiful, too 60
Escape from Manhattan 79
Essential jigs for the table saw 87
Estimating and buying molding 111
Eucalyptus affair 58
Evaluating deck woods 41
Exact finger-joint jig 87
Examining carbide-tipped sawblades 141
Exercising your options on a home sauna 141
Exhaust vents in a tight house 174
Exhaust-fan drip 58
Exhibit under glass 74
Expert energy inspection 56
Explaining stains 153
Expressing a site 54
Extend your deck's life 41
Extended saw table catches cut-offs,
    supports long work 141
Extra bath 9

F

Fabulous fakes 18
Fabulous fences 59
Fabulous futon 69
Facelift for a loft 129
Falling eaves 67
family at home 129
Family feud 144
Fanciful flowers from found wood 74
Fanlights 59
Fantail deck stairs 42
Fantasy floors 64

Fantasy islands 91
Farmyard favorites on a string 168
Fast fences 59
Fast foundations 38
Fast Track Estimating for Remodelers 131
Faster plaster 121
Father Christmas wood carving 28
Faucet facelift 59
Faux antique crackled finish 61
Faux-turned vessels 14
Fay Jones 90
Fear of color 86
Featherboards assist in radial-arm ripping 134
Feathered friends mobile 109
Features for the '90s 4
Fein sander 140
Fence tips 59
Fences & Retaining Walls 59
Fiberglass tub fix 171
Fifty ways to vitalize your house 55
52 Weekend Woodworking Projects 20
Files and how to use them 60
Finding and Fixing Hidden Air Leaks 2
Fine print 115
Fine-feathered friend feeder 12
Finely crafted cutting gauge 71
Finish Carpentry Basics 22
Finish removers 61
Finishes for fir floors 61
Finishes for maple 61
Finishing outdoor projects 61
Finishing sanders 140
Finishing school 142
Finishing with the best 86
Finishing wood problems 60
Fireplace and chimney codes 62
Fireplace facelift 62
Fireplace facing 62
Fireplace odor 62
Fire-treating cedar shakes 24
First-class window seats 180
Fisherman whirligigs 179
Fishing rod rack 127
Fish-snake helper 55
Fishtape target 55
Fit for a queen cabriole-leg coffee table 33
Fitting in Seattle 43
Fitting small drill chucks 28
Fitting stair treads 154
5 easy pieces 41
5 easy steps to a finish that's glass-smooth 60
5 great router tricks 137
Fixture keys 91
Fixture plate for a lathe or mill 97
Flame cutter 63
Flashing a wall 63
Flashing lights announce phone calls and
    visitors 187
Flat-roof leaks 136

Flat-roof sag 136
Flexible walkway 149
Flights of fancy 154
Floor fashions 64
Floor framing for fireplaces 62
Floor guard 64, 130
Fluorescent fixes 64
Flush door face lift 47
Foam-core panels 117
Foiling oil odor 114
Fold tabs with a template to install
    sandpaper smoothly 140
Folding bandsaw blades. 7
Folding chopsaw bench 11
Folding deck table 160
Folk fiddle 60
Food-safe finishes 61
For openers 48
For projects that hinge upon their good looks
    wooden hardware 75
For the router 137
Fork lift toy 170
Forming concrete walls 176
Forstner bit holders 77
Foundation drain 65
Foundation forms that insulate 65
Foundation jacking 65
Foundation materials 65
Foundation-wall reinforcement 65
Four easy picture frames 66
Four easy-to-make kitchen projects 16
4 fun-to-make wheels 179
Four novel napkin rings 113
Fractured fiberglass 60
Frame and the panel 117
Frame-clamping jig 30
Framed with concrete and glulams 134
Framing a bay window with irregular hips 181
Framing a cathedral ceiling 24
Framing a cold roof 83
Framing a crawl-space foundation 65
Framing a cross-gable roof 135
Framing a gable roof 135
Framing a second-story addition 82
Framing a turret addition 172
Framing for garage doors 69
Framing headers and corners 176
Framing walls 177
Free pendulum clock 31-32
Freestanding spiral stair 154
Freezeproof outdoor faucets 59
French-door retrofit 67
Friendly persuader: A turned mallet for your shop 104
From blank bowl to finished bowl 14
Front door and more 47
Front yard of food, flowers, and friends 71
Front-end loader 168
Frugal four-square fixup 124
Fuel for thought 185

Fuel Savers 151
Fun at the Lathe 96
Fun furniture 69
Fun-charged monster truck 168
*Fundamentals of Building Construction
    Materials and Methods* 37
Fundamentals of Building Construction 79
Fun-in-the-sun furniture 68
Fun-to-fashion letter openers 100

G

*g.r.e.b.e.: Guide to Resource-Efficient
    Building Elements* 19
Garage conversions 70
Garage door painting 116
Garage-door update 69
Garden arbor 11
Garden windows 181
Gardening with a gouge 184
Gas-log retrofit 71
Gasping for air 3
Gearless hit 'n miss engine 57
General remodel and a major addition 130
Genius of Japanese Carpentry 22
Gentle giant of the woods 155
Geometric construction 147
Get ready... get (T.V.) set... retrofit 162
Getting a Good Home 80
Getting a handle on hammers 73
Getting a variance 187
Getting an angle on compound miters 109
Getting rid of CFCs 75
Getting started in carving 183
Giant-contour gauge 71
Gift of the belvedere 11
Gingerbread houses 174
Glare repair 181
Glass act 159
Glass additions 71
Glass block for basement windows 181
Glass breakthroughs 180
Glass curtain 146
Glossary: Energy terms 56
Glue-laminated timbers 10
Gluing oily woods 72
Gluing plaster 121
Going up 130
Goodbye to gutters 73
Gossip bench 11
Graceful goose 74
Graceful paving 13
Grandchild's clock 31
Grasshopper pull toy 170
Grateful Pilgrims 163
Great dividers 156
Great electric-drill shoot-out 51
Great garden walls 176
Great walls 133
Great woodie revival 23

Green woodworking with kids 27
Greene & Greene restoration 19
Greener carpets for better air quality 22
Green-wood turning 172
Grinder stand 165
Grinding rest for precise tools 73
Grizzly 8X18" lathe 96
Groaning water heater 178
Groundwater heating and cooling 73
Growing up in Minnesota 1
Guaranteed energy savings 56
Guide to sunrooms 159
Gumball machine 73
Gun, bookcase, and curio cabinet 20
Gusset blocks 73

H

Haertling's aspen leaf house 6
Hall tree 73
Hammered dulcimer 52
Hand planes for trim carpentry 120
Hand saw caddy 141
Hand-carved cookie molds 38
Hand-cut dovetails 90
Handsaw bracket 17
Handscrew clamps 30
Hands-on handles 74
Handy file cleaner 60
Handy hardware hauler 115
Handy home for a family of pliers 157
Handy templates 162
Hanging bird feeders 12
Hanging frameless mirrors 109
Happy-days highchair 77
Hardboard cleans up portable saw's cuts 160
Hardwood briefcase 17
Hardwood edgings for plastic laminate 39
Harvest table 47
Harvesting your own lumber 18
Have nailer, will travel 23
Have you considered a metal roof 135
Hawaiian ohana house 81
Hazardous waste disposal hotlines 75
Header tricks for remodelers 130
Healthier house plants 80
Hearing yourself keeps extended projects
    on track 104
Heart box 15
Heart of the house 92
Hearth and mantel masterpiece 62
Hearths of stone 62
Hearts-and-hares picture frame 66
Heat at your feet 77
Heat for less 76
Heat treating basics 76
Heat wave 185
Heating, Cooling, Lighting 2
Heat-seeking ducts 76
Heavy-duty router table 137

Heirloom blockfront chest 26
Heirloom jewelry box 16
Heirloom toy chest 27
Here it is! 187
Here's Otto 184
Here's a plug for end-grain joinery 89
Hickory: Tougher than nails, and versatile, too 77
Hideaway island 91
High and mighty tablesaw jig 87
High living in a small space 82
High performance finishes 60
high-caliber gun cabinet 73
Higher-security, lower-cost locks 101
High-flying photo frame 66
High-style low-maintenance millwork 108
High-style tile 164
High-styled raised panels and frames 117
High-velocity AC systems 2
High-volume, low-pressure sprayers 153
Hinge swings into action when holes require
    spacing 51
Hiring an architect 130
Holder for 13/16" dies 46
Hole-saw refinements 142
Holiday horn of plenty 77
Home brews 18, 138
*Home Building and Woodworking in Colonial
    America* 33
Home buying in the year 2001 43
Home court advantage 6
Home improvement survey 159
Home in the hills 45
Home library 13
Home Office Book 114
Home Plumbing Projects and Repairs 122
Home workshops that work 187
Homemade bench mill 107
Homemade brush features renewable foam
    'bristles 17
Homemade electric motor mount 111
Homemade hardware 75
Home-made home 18
Homemade peace of mind 30
*Homeowner's Guide to Building with Concrete,
    Brick and Stone* 105
Homeowner's Guide to Plumbing 122
Homeowners survival kit 165
Homes across America 5
Honduras mahogany 103
Horse and cart toy 168
Hot attic 6
Hot flashing 27
Hot tips on home heating systems 76
Hot water quicker 122
Hot-melt glue guns 72
Hot-melt gluing hard-to-clamp pieces 72
Hot-surface condensation 36
Hourglass 78
House in Burnaby 43

House in Friday Harbor 43
House of light 43
House on the river 80
House on the river 43
House that glass built… 72
House that healed the land 44
House that survived 180
House without barriers 5
Household Hazards 138
House-painting myth buster 116
How home inspectors can help 78
How safe are your woodworking habits? 138
How to add a shower to a tub 149
How to choose a finish 60
How to clamp tricky mitered moldings 111
How to create made-to-match cabinet
    panels 117
How to cut contractor costs 130
How to dodge router burns 137
How to flatten rough stock 185
How to hang wall cabinets 20
How to install jointer knives 93
How to level glued-up stock 100
How to rip and crosscut on a table saw 141
How to sharpen and use a scraper 142
How to sharpen turning and carving tools 166
How to shop smart for carving tools 185
How to strip rubber-backed carpet 22
How to transform found wood into usable
    stock 182
How veneer is made: From giant log to delicate
    sheets 174
Hurricane warnings 83
Hybrid cabinet construction 20
Hydronic coils for forced-air heating 76

I

Ice-dam defense 83
Ice-damming myths 83
Improved lathe drive 96
Improved post puller 124
Improving a milling machine vise 175
In praise of the well-raised bed 71
In praise of walking sticks 175
In search of the perfect door 48
In the Arts and Crafts tradition 5
In this corner 146
In tight 44
In-an-instant ornaments 28
Incised lettering 183
Incra jig pro 87
Indexing device 83
Indexing template for easier layout 162
Inexpensive power feed 112
Information resources 44
Inlaying mother-of-pearl 84
Inner space 44
Innovative outbuildings 71
Inside flush 165

Inside-out remodeling 132
Inside-out twists 74
Install a central vacuum 173
Installing a fire-safe door 48
Installing a hammer-cut stone floor 64
Installing a TV Antenna 162
Installing board-and-batten siding 150
Installing carpet yourself 22
Installing door closers 49
Installing drywall 52
Installing joist hangers 75
Installing kitchen cabinets 91
Installing locksets 102
Installing mortise locksets 102
Installing outdoor audio 6
Installing pre-hung doors 48
Installing stair skirtboards 153
Installing two-piece crown 111
Instant access 24
Instant hot water 178
Instant water heaters 178
Insulating a tight spot 85
Insulating beneath a slab 85
Insulating with recycled glass 85
Insulation declaration 85
Insulation upgrades 85
Insul-vines 85
Intarsia: The Judy Gale Roberts way 85
Intarsia project—American eagle 85
*Intermediate Technology Publications/Bootstrap
    Press 1990 Catalog* 162
In-the-wall stereo speakers 155
introduction to chairbuilding 25
Invisible door closer 48
Is benzene poisoning your home? 12
Isolation membranes for ceramic tile 164
It's a grand old flag 144
It's Western Santa 184
Itch-free insulation 85

J
Jack-shaft speed-reducer 102
Japanese saws: Eastern styles saws
    win converts 142
Jazz-up your kitchen 91
Jewel of a case 16
Jewel of a vial 63
Jewelbox bathroom 9
Jewelry chest 16
Jig and templates duplicate irregular
    shapes 87
Jigs and fixtures 63
Jigsaws 87
Joinery Basics 89
Joining tops to tables and case pieces 89
Jointer pushstick 125
Jointers 89
Junkyard motor junkie 55
Just add planning 45

Just add water 123
Just seven feet 130

K
Kalimba 91
Keeping burglars out of the garage 70
Keeping glued panels flat 30
Keeping pipe-clamps upright 119
Keeping windows working 181
Keep-on-recycling toy box 167
Keepsake jewelry box 16
Kid's kitchen play center 168
Kid's castle 122
Kids on parade 144
Kids' Adirondack chair & settee 68
Kids' modular furniture set 68
King of the caterpillars 126
Kitchen basics 92
Kitchen cabinetry 91
Kitchen cupboard facelift 91
Kitchen in the garden 93
Kitchen message center 106
Kitchen planning made perfect 92
Kitchen spacesavers 156
Kitchen ventilation 174
Kitchens that work 92
Knitter's companion featuring fine
    dovetail joinery 23
Knockdown hardware 59
Knockout bar 97
Knothole gang 85
Knurls and knurling 94
Koa jewelry chest 16
Kris Kringle goes cross-country 28

L
Labor of love 132
Labor-of-love workbench 187
Lacquer that's music to your ears 173
Lacquer that's music to your ears 94
Ladders 94
Ladies' cosmetic mirror 108
Lag-bolt cabinet leveler 100
Lag-shield layout 186
Laguna Beach remodel 130
Laid-back landscape 95
Lally boxing 33
Laminating structural timbers 94
Lamination sensation 14
Landmark Yellow Pages 77
Larger steady rest 96
Lateral support for wood beams 95
Lathe carriage stop 23
Lathe operations on a vertical mill 97
Lathe table 96
Lathe-laid eggs 168
Lathes 96
Lathe-turned hurricane lamp 94

Lawn care safety 99, 139
Lawn glider 68
Laying a granite-faced wall 176
Laying out a domed ellipse 44
Lazy-days porch rocker 134
Leaded glass-the easy way 72
Leaded-glass panels 72
Leafy lodging 12
Leaking brick 177
Leaky window 181
Learning my ABCs 168
Letter perfect key chains 91
Liberating the compact kitchen 4
Lift for sunken concrete 35
Light switch glitches 101
Light touch for kitchens 93
Lighter side of woodworking 126
Lightning protection for your home 101
Lights in the attic 6
Linen fold carving 183
Little folks desk and bench 11
Little guy lotta fun 184
Little plugs 154
Little red tote barn 8
Little safeguards 139
Livable sculpture 67
Live large, look small 19
Livestock truck 168
Living on different levels 82
Living together 33
Log houses 102
Long and short of it 25
Long horn beetles 84
Look up! 40
Looking Around: A Journey Through Architecture 5
Lookout house 79
Loose screws in steel doors 155
Louisiana country house 81
Low cost lathes 96
Low range ohmmeters 114
Low-budget water level 178
Lowdown on Asian plywood 123
Low-flow shower heads 149
Low-flow toilets 165
Low-pollution paints 116
Low-tech picture frames 66
Low-water landscapes 95
Lumber storage rack 156
Lure of the laser 95
Lure of the sea relief puzzle 144

M

Machine tool covers 157
Macintosh Construction Forum 38
Made for the shade 4
Magazine slip cases 15
Magnetic locks are hard to beat 102
Mail-order tools 165

Maintaining a plunge router 137
Maintaining a worm-drive saw 142
Maintaining Your Old House in Cambridge 37
Major's marquetry 105
Make it masonry 105
Make raised panels with your tablesaw 117
Make room for Trudy 2
Make Your House Radon Free 128
Making a bullnose starting step 154
Making a cabriole leg 100
Making a catch plate 95
Making a cutoff toolholder 98
Making a knurled head thumbscrew 163
Making a Northcoast Indian bow 14
Making a solid-surface countertop 39
Making a tombstone frame-and-panel door 48
Making a torsion box 17
Making and installing dovetailed drawers 50
Making classical columns 33
Making curved casing 23
Making curved crown 101
Making curved crown molding 111
Making curved instrument sides 182
Making dadoes 41
Making details count 132
Making drawers 50
Making faces 183
Making half-lap joints 90
Making Mechanical Marvels in Wood 106
Making of a Japanese-style plane 120
Making pin punches 125
Making plastic-laminate countertops 39
Making Rustic Furniture 68
Making space 86
Making tap and reamer handles 129
Making the cut 29
Making the dovetailed wedge 179
Making the slip joint 90
Making threads in wood 46
Making tracks 151
Manhattan comes to Sun Valley 79
Man-in-the-moon shelf clock 31
Mantels in minutes 105
Manufactured kitchen cabinets 91
Marble drop 105, 168
Marbleized masterpiece 31
Marquetry: The direct method 105
Masking before painting 116
Masonry 105
Masonry bake ovens 115
Masterpiece music box 16
Matching existing brickwork 17
Matching old windows 181
Material difference 52
Measuring with pins 148
Mechanical advantages 125
Mechanical fasteners 59, 143
Medicine kit for the yard 84

Meet the dust guzzlers 53
Mercury banned 106
Metal corrosion 38
Metal roofing on a flat roof 135
Mighty elm 55
Mighty hauler 168
Mill-drill stand 107
Milling on the lathe 98
Minnesota lake cabin 21
Miter fence 59
Miter saws 142
Mitered-moulding jig 88
Mitering curved moldings 111
Mitersaws 109
Mixed woods in a ceiling 153
Mobilize your heavy shop tools 165
Modeling home energy use 56
Modern Practical Stairs 153
Modest house in Bucks County 80
Moisture Control Handbook 109
Moisture problems in the crawl space 39
Moldy odor 39
More dishwasher disasters 47
More light, more room 44
More post pulling 124
More Power to You! A Proven Path to Electric Energy Independence 54
More solo drywall hanging 52
More than a kitchen 93
Mortise and tenon mirror 108
Mortise-and-tenon joinery 89
Mountain dulcimer 52
Mounting strips for walls 112
Move up remodeling 130
Moving sheet goods 23
Mr. Music box 112
Multipurpose doorpull jig 88
Museum-quality containers 15
Mysterious moisture 110
Myths and facts about the care of your cordless tools 166

N

Nail pickup 112
Nail stains 112
Name that fume 3
Napkin holder 113
Native American Architecture 5
Nativity scene 28, 77
Natural House Book 80
Natural Surroundings 9
Natural Wood Siding 150
Naturals 173
Nature in Wood 183
Nature's goodness wall plaque 121
Nature-in-the-round 144
Needleworks 113
Never-paint window trim 180
New 19th-century house 44

New again 18
New centering gage 69
New kitchen for an old house 93
New life for old hose 78
New Life for Old Houses 37
New life for old roofs 136
New life for the Adelman barn 133
New safe strippers 116
New skin for a plaster ceiling 24
Newcomer on Grand Avenue 174
Newest wave in compact fluorescent lighting 101
New-tech wood stoves 185
New-wave cooking 115
1991 Consumer Guide to Home Energy Savings 55
1991 National Construction Estimator 58
1993 Old-House Journal Catalog BR 36
Nixing neighbor noises 152
Nixing noises 113
No waste yard 70
Noah's lovable ark 168
No-freeze piping 119
Noise in the shop 113
Noisy floor 64
Noisy pipes 119
Nonrolling stones 155
Noodle cutter 92
No-problem pizza paddle 119
North-country signs 150
Northern red oak 114
Norwegian bachelor farmer 183
Nutcrackers suite as can be 113

O

Oak desk 46
Oak dish rack 127
Oak dry sink 151
Oak music stand 112
Oasis backyard 41
Octagonal jewelry box 16
Off the beaten track 101
Office assembly 114
Off-line electrical systems 54
Old fashioned farm table 160
Old-time icebox 83
Old-world windmill 121
Olympian display 66
On low-e coatings 180
One glue to have 58
One lean jelly bean machine 168
One whale of a cutting board 40
One-legged helper 165
One-sided clamping with pipe-c lamping 30
One-stop chopping 40
On-site lumber rack 127
Open country 93
Open the door to convenient clamping 29
Operating a power trowel 171

Ordering and installing prehung doors 48
Ornamental lettering 100
Ornamental metals 144
Ornamental plaster restoration 37
Our readers and radon 128
Out of the woods 102
Overhead drilling 51
Over-the-road heavy haulers 171

P

Paint strainer 116
Painted stone finishes 61
Painter's Handbook 116
Painting aluminum siding 150
Painting exteriors 117
Painting metal roofs 136
Painting paneling 117
Painting trim like a pro 117
Painting Waterfowl with J. D. Sprankle 183
Painting, without the pain 117
Palladian windows 181
Palm sander 139
Palm sanders 140
Palm-sander holder 157
Panelized frame, customized finish 79
Panes for the ears 181
Panic button 139
Pantry plus 118
Paper clips grip sandpaper on block 140
Passive Solar Design Strategies 43
Patching a hardwood strip floor 64
Patented Traditional & Metallic Planes in America 120
Patience and recycling 112
Patterns, patterns, everywhere 144
Paving without pavers 149
Peak performance 135
Pedestal-sized curio showcase 47
Peeling paint 36
Pegboard & mallet 118
Pennsylvania small chest 26
Percolating heater 178
Perfect pachyderm 184
Perfect-edge painting pads 116
Perfomax sander 140
Performance testing of floor finishes 61
Permanent wood foundations 65
Perpetual calendar 21
Perpetual paintbrushes 18
Petal-powered wall hanging 74
Pet-chairs for children 25
Pewter-topped potpourri bowl 14
Photovoltaic test house 56
Picking a good lock 102
Picnic table 118
Picture-book project 66
Picture-hanging jig eliminates guesswork 88
Picture-perfect wallcoverings 176

Pie safe 164
Pierced-tin spice cabinet 152
Pilgrim's-pride wall box 17
Pillar & scroll clockcase 31
Pine box 16
Pine hutch 83
Pine vanity 108
Pine wall cabinet 21
Pipe clamp storage bin 157
Pipe-clamp drywall lift 52
Pipe-cutting jig 88
Piping for your shop vacuum makes cleaning up a cinch 148
Pitched-roof sag 104
Pivot plates on carpet 122
Places in the sun 4
Plain-handy plane holder 157
Planers/molders 120
Planning for tile 164
Plant hanger from paradise 120
Plant stand 120
Plaster problems 121
Plastering Skills 121
Plastic grocery bag handles 75
Plastic injection molding machine 110
Plastic light grid shines for screwdriver storage 115
Plate joinery on the job site 89
Plate of plenty 163, 184
Plate-turning stock 122
Playful playhouse 122
Plugging a toe-screw 165
Plumber's Toolbox Manual 166
Plumbing fixtures get the lead out 123
Plumbing odors 114
Plumbing secrets 122
Plumbing with flexible pipe 123
Plunge routers 137
Plywood siding 123, 150
Pocket-door fix 48
Pocket-sized try square 153
Points of light 101
Poles for building 123
Pondside gazebo 71
Pools that do more 123
Pop-top remodel 130
Popular plastics 181
Porch reconstruction 124
Porch/yard swing 123
Porches that won't rot 124
Portable belt sanders 140
Portable circular saws 29
Portable electric cut-off saws 142
Portable table saws 160
Poshing up a Taiwanese lathe 96
Position of low-e coating 180
Post treatment 125
Post-and-beam houses 81
Pouring concrete slabs 36

Title Index

Power for off-grid water system 179
Power mitersaws 109
Power painting 116
Power washing a house 104
Power-cord straps 115
Power-tool belt clip 11
Practical Home Energy Savings 56
Practical Homeowner builds a house 44
Practical Radon Control for Homes 128
Practical solar design 45
Preservation Briefs 37
Preservative-treated wood 18
Preserving Porches 124
Pressure drops in the shower 149
Price Guide to Antique Tools 166
Private paths 65
Prize doors 48
Prize patios 118
Prize-winning plate rack 121
Problems with a gravel roof 136
Problem-solving paints and coatings 115
Productive vise jaws 174
Products that perform 153
Professional Dome Plans 47
Projects with a porpoise 45
Proper tree pruning 170
Protecting a new finish: A guide to waxes and
    polishes 179
Protecting your trees 95
Provincial bench 11
Provincial four-poster bed 11
Pueblo modern 49
Pull the plug on tenoning troubles 162
Pump dispenser 151
Purpose-made joinery. 89
Pussycat napkin holder 113
Putting on a concrete-tile roof 135

Q

Quality deck 41
Queen Anne Furniture 126
Questionable venting 147
Quick clamping jig makes fuss-free frame
    corners 66
Quick drawer fixes 50
Quick Fix Home Repair Handbook 103
Quick switch for receptacles 55
Quick-change tool post system 98
Quick-change tool post system, part one 157
Quickset sawhorse 141
Quiet Indoor Revolution 76
Quiet please 82
Quieter kitchens 93

R

R-2000: The Better-Built House 79
Radial Arm Saw Basics 127
Radial-arm saw stand 128

Radial-arm saws 128
Radiant foil 8
Radius turning attachment 98
Radon alert 128
Radon mitigation in existing homes 128
Rail thing 41
Railing against the elements 128
Rainbow hill 45
Raise the roof 49
Raising a house addition 130
Raising an eyebrow 49
Raising finished walls 176
Rammed earth revisited 54
Random-orbit sanders 140
Rasps 60
Rating your radon risk 128
Razing the roof 135
Ready wrench rack 127
Ready-reference calendar/clock 31
Recipe for a kitchen remodel 132
Recipe for raised-panel walls 117
Reciprocating saw review 142
Reclaiming your front yard 95
Reconditioning a woodstove 186
Rectifying a rotted girder 71
Recycle a worn plane-iron and
    make a new tool 142
Recycled building blocks 18
Recycled plastics find new homes 121
Recycled wallpaper 176
Recycling a wall 176
Reducing dust 53
Reducing springback 75
Redwood: The forest's elder statesman 129
Redwood potting bench 12
Re-entry 57
Refacing kitchen cabinets 91
Refining rustics 70
Refinishing Furniture 69
Refitting a door 48
Reflections 72
Reincarnating hockey sticks 74
Rejuvenating the ranch 130
Rejuvenating your deck 42
Relining a chimney 27
Relocating the laundry 99
Remodel with mirrors 108
Remodeling for the recovery 130
Remodeling protection 130
Remodeling with paint 86
Remodeling with windows 130
Remote possibilities 132
Remounting a four-jaw chuck 28
Removable high performance disks for
    your computer system 34
Removable screen floors 143
Removing broken screws and studs 143
Removing composition tiles 163
Removing exterior paint 116

Removing reluctant fasteners 59
Removing wallpaper paste 176
Renewing porcelain fixtures 123
Renovate your lawn 99
Renovating a Shaker farmhouse 133
Renovating old porches 124
Renovation: A Complete Guide 133
Repairing Furniture 69
Repairing Old and Historic Windows 181
Repairing plastic laminate 94
Repairs for sheet-vinyl flooring 64
Replace a stair railing 128
Replacement windows 181
Replacing a door jamb 86
Replacing a sill on grade 150
Replacing an inlaid gutter 73
Replacing rain gutters 73
Replicating moldings 111
Reroofing under solar panels 133
Resawing 133
*Residential and Commercial Sunrooms
    1991 Buyer's Guide* 158
Residential Indoor Air Quality & Energy 82
Residing an old house 150
Re-siding with wood 84
Resilient flooring 64
Resisting the weather on the Outer Banks 44
Respirator tips 133
Resplendent pendant 86
Restaining siding 150
Restoring the east portico of
    Montgomery Place 37
Restoring the Jacobs House 37
Retaining walls that last 177
Rethinking the cornice return 73
Retrofit damper 62
Retrofit radon reduction 128
Retrofitting a shower-pan bed 149
Retrofitting Atlas/Craftsman and other
    lathes to CNC control 35
Retro-flashing a concrete stoop 36
Return backing 52
Return of the trellis 70
Return to the round table 168
Ride the wind 74
Riding out the big one 54
Right foundation 66
Right from the start 9
Right height for a router/jigsaw table 87
Right light 101
Right triangles 148
*Right-to-Know Pocket Guide for Construction
    Workers* 19
Roadster 23
Rocking dolphins 25
Rolling interior latex wall paint 117
Roof assemblies for hot climates 135
Roof Framing 134
Roof lichens 100

Roofing with asphalt shingles 135
Room to mingle 67
Rooms at the top 133
Rooms with a view 56
Rope 136
Rotary, dual cross-slide drill press and milling
    machine table 103
Rough 'n' ready wrecker 169
Roughouts to the rescue 137
Rounding the ends 107
Router basics 137
Router stands in for a surface planer 137
Router storage cabinet 157
Router table 186
Router tenoning jig 89
Routers, routers everywhere 137
Routers—the handtools 137
Router-table work station 137
Rovi expanding mini collets 33
Row-house renovation 37
Rugged road grader 72
Rule guide for easier layout 73
Running baseboard efficiently 8
Rust busters 138
Rust removal made easy 138
Rusting windows 181

S

Safe and simple thin-strip ripper 88
Safe-and-sound customized chisel rack 127
Safety: Workshop finishes pose risk 62
safety-first bathroom 10
Sal Marino's friction-film finish for
    turned objects 123
Salt & pepper shaker combo 139
Salvaged in Ohio 79
Salvaging a small cape 21
Sam Maloof's House 81
Sample chest 26
Sandblasted wall clock 32
Sandblasting basics 139
Sandblasting—try it once and you'll be
    blown away 139
Sandbox excavator 169
Sanding shortcuts 140
Sanding table 157
Sanding-supply organizer 115
Santa Claus 28
Santa Fe bench 12
Santa Fe chair 25
Santa Fe table 33
Saturday-morning panel saw 142
Save a whale 74
Saw blade cutoff tool 40
Saw hangup 157
Saw stay straight, sharp in hanging rack 127
Sawblade degumming 141
Sawdust stripping 116
Sawing straight and true 142

Title Index

Scenic drives 51

Scrapwood eases pressure caused
    by clamp shortage 30

Scratch awl 6

Screened-porch addition 124

Screw clamps 30

Screw drills 51

Screw plugs 122

Scribe-fit plaster patch 121

Scribing extension jambs 86

Scroll saw 144

Scroll sawn bunny rabbit puzzle 169

Scroll saws for under $200 144

Scrollsaw picks up dust instead of spreading it 53

Scrollsaw-blade organizer 115

Scrollsawn bunny rabbit puzzle 126

Sculptor in Wood 183

Sea Ranch Chapel 26

Sea skipper 120

Seafarer's clock 31

Sealing creosote beams 40, 114

Sealing tiles 163

Seaside solar 152

Secret compartments 69

Secure closet 32

Seeds and such snack shop 12

See-through cabinet doors 20, 158

Selecting wood windows 180

Selections from The Chronicle 186

Septic additives 145

Septic solution 145

Set your fence accurately with this
    shop-made gauge 71

Setback thermostats 55

Setting up shop 102

Shaker bed 10

Shaker chest of drawers 26

Shaker drop-leaf table 52

Shaker oval carrier 23

Shaker tall clock 32

Shaker woodbox 16

Shake-roof care 136

Shaker-style buffet 21

Shaker-style tall chest 26

Shakey, swayey deck 42

shaper 125

Shapers 146

Shaping on a table saw 111

Shaping Wood 185

Sharp steak knives 75

Sharpen your end mills 107

Sharpening carving tools 166

Sharpening guides and gizmos 141

*Shed, The Do-It-Yourself Guide for Backyard
    Builders* 146

Shelf sufficiency 146

Shelf support 32

Shelter 79

Shelving and Storage 156

Shelving showcase 14

Sherlock ohms 100

Shim-shingle jig 147

Shingle TLC 147

Shingling an arch 147

Shoehorning a vanity top 173

Shoji for windows 143

Shoot-over decoys 42

Shop at home 44

Shop built mortise/tenoning table 90

Shop jaws 174

Shop layout 45

Shop measurement 148

Shop work center 148

Shop-built sanding blocks 140

Shop-built spindle sander 140

Shop-built window frames 66

Shopmade handscrews 30

Shop-made roller table and roller stand 134

Shop-made tools end inside-cutting grief 143

Shopsmith vs. Total Shop 102

Shoring settled foundations 65

Short branch saloon 12

Short course in flat-out fun
    plate turning 101 122

Shower window 149

Showing off 20

Shrinking stringers 154

Sideboard chest 26

Siding holdup 150

Siding hooks 78

Siding over stucco 150

Siding shelf 150

Sign-making made easy 144

Simple closet wardrobe 177

Simple coffered ceiling 132

Simple curved corners 177

Simple division 132

Simple indexing rotary table 83

Simple joinery for custom windows 180

Simple phase convertor 118

Simple saw rack 127

Simple slide box 151

Simple workbenches 187

Simplicity with style 81

Simplified valley framing 67

Simplified Woodworking I 22

Simply stated Shaker wall clock 32

Single-ply roofing 135

Single-setup drawer boxes 49

Sink-top cutting board 13

Sit-a-spell shop stool 155

Site-built kitchen 93

Site-built sheet-metal brake 146

Site-built stair 154

Site-built wire spinner 55

Site-cast sash weight 140

Site-casting concrete lintels 101

Six dovetail jigs 88

Six-cycle 'oddball' engine 57
Sizing a flue 27
Skeleton wall clock 32
Skin-tight homes 67
Skipping 18, 106, 129
Skylight bath 10
Skylights in the eaves 151
Slab leak 100
Slab-on-grade foundation for cold
    climates 65
Slant front desk 46
Slant-back cupboard 40
Slate roof repair 136
Sledge bumper 151
Sleeping beauties 11
Slick tips 161
Sliding compound miter saws 142
Slow-set epoxy 58
Small bath solutions 9
Small bathroom, walk-in shower 149
Small house on a rocky hillside 80
Small house to serve a richer life 80
Small house, big heater 77
Small t-slot nuts 113
Small, but sited right 131
Small, Maine house 82
Smallest hit & miss gas engine 57
Small-tool holder 158
Smart Kitchen 92
Smart storage 156
Smart technologies for the outdoors 95
Smiley the rocking snail 25
Smooth caulk joints 24
Sneak-a-peek periscope 118
Snip tip 151
Snow-loving open sleigh 151
Soaked ceiling 24
Soft vise jaws 174
*Software Directory for Builders
    1992* 35
Solar adobe 2
Solar hot water for the 90s 178
Solar water heaters 178
Solid-oak settee 145
Solo drywall hanging 52
Solo level shots 48
Some things bold, some things blue 131
Something new and exciting on the horizon
    Southwest landscape 185
Sophisticated security sensors 145
Sound solutions 113
Soundproofing solution 152
Southwest addition 1
Southwest tables 68
Space wars 152
Space-saving appliances 4
Space-saving clamp rack 127
Space-smart kitchens 93
Spacing deck boards 42

Spade-bit scribers 143
Spalling concrete 177
Spanning 19 ft. 1
Speak easy 85
Speaking of lead, how's your water? 178
Special delivery: letter/napkin holder 113
Special-effect shingles 147
Special-effects carpeting 22
Spiced-up spice cabinet 21
Spigot chuck 29
Spiked deck joints 42
Spindle lock for your mill/drill 102
Spirit levels 100
Splayed joinery 89
Spliced debris chute 29
Split ash baskets Maine style 9
Split-turned vase 173
Spokeshaves 152
Sports car 169
Spotlight on tablesaw safety 139
Spotlight your work with a reading lamp 94
Spreader 153
Spreading on the charm 62
Squeaking parquet floors 64
Stabilizing a cracked slab 65
Stackable shoe rack 147
Staging plank supports 159
Stainless steel fundamentals 155
Stair case 154
Staircase of glass and maple 154
Stairs in half the space 154
Standing up to salt water 104
Standing-tall blocks box 13
Standout stakes 36
Stars-and-stripes wren house 12
Starting turning 98
State-by-state radon update 128
Stationary belt sanders 140
Staying in hot water 47
Staying with solar 152
Steel band hold-ins 7
Steep-slope eyebrow dormers 49
Step stool 155
Steps of stone 154
Stepstool/chair 155
Steve Malavolta's playable artwork 126
Stick and cope doorbuilding 48
Stickley-style plant stand 120
Stiffening a floor for tile 163
Stirring display 127
Stock options 91
Stone and glass addition 2
Stone veneer on concrete block 174
Storage buildings 146
Storage by design 35
Storage reel 158
Storage solutions 156
Store and order 156
Storm and screen doors 49

Straightening concrete walls 36
Straightening studs 158
Strap-clamp for flues 64
Strategic storage 156
Strengthening plate-to-rafter connections 136
Stretching screens 143
Strike three against home offices? 114
Stripping interior woodwork 186
Strokes of genius 115
Struttin' your stuff for smoother planing 120
study in cherry 14
Stylish sheds 146
stylized rocking horse 78
Substitute caulk gun 24
Suburban refuge 44
Sucking up the small stuff 53
Sugar maple 105
Suite success 132
Summer rooms 71
Sun spots 159
Sunbaths 10
Sunburst mirrors 108
Sunny additions 1
Sunset rider deskset 46
Super ceilings 24
Super sheds 146
Super showers 149
Superinsulated in Idaho 56
Superinsulated saltbox on the coast of Maine 139
Super-simple tool transport 23
Superstamp letter holder 100
Supporting exterior stairs 154
Supporting sink cutouts 150
Supporting timber-frame posts 124
Surefire resaw jig 133
Surface finish designations 148
Surface grinding on the drill press 73
Survey of 3/8-in. variable-speed reversible drills 51
Survey of compound-miter saws 142
Survey of sidewinders 29
Sweet teen suite 131
Sweet-tooth skewers 151
Swing-arm support 136
Swiss chalets 26
Sycamore: Ghost of the bottomlands 159

T

Table lamp 94
Tablesaws 160
Tablesaws outfeed roller glides on drawer
    slides 160
Tablesaws tenoning jig 88
Tabletop armoire 5
Tabletop cigar-store Indian 185
Tabletop finishes 60
Tabletop Tom 78
Tagua turning 161
Tailstock attachment 4
Tailstock attachments for the lathe 161

Taking a load off 104
Taking care of business 19
Taking the plunge 78
Talented new trio of… portable planers 120
Tall clock 31
Taming the hand scraper 143
Taping and finishing drywall 52
Tapping guide for a unimat 46
Tassajara makeover 17
Tavern table 161
Tax deductible home shop 161
Tax implications of remodeling 161
Teak: The topic's top seafaring stock 161
Technical Carpenter 22
Technics and Architecture 5
Teddy bear in tin 164
Teddy bear music box 16
Teeth for rotary cutting tools 166
Tehal Virk's wonderful willow works 68
Tempering steel tools 162
10' carbide-tipped saw blades 141
Ten tips for improving your
    scrollwork 145
10 winning ways to work with plywood 123
Termite Report 162
Termite Termination 84
Termite termination 104
Terrific tileboard 163
Test your home for toxins 167
Testing and controlling asbestos 6
Texan offers more ideas on
    staining cherry 153
Textured drywall patch 52
Thanks for the memories 74
Thawing frozen drain lines 49
The Barn Book 8
The great bandsaw roundup 7
The Termite Report 103
Thickness planers 120
Thickness planers under $500 120
Thin kerf blades 141
Thin-kerf showdown 159
Thinking like a craftsman 20
Thinking of views 180
$30 workbench 186
31 new rules for kitchen design 92
This bench stop eliminates need for bench
    top holes 155
This old floor 64
This stick-on center solves a sticky cutting
    problem 137
Thoughts on selecting vertical mills 107
Thread cutting on the lathe 98
Thread tooling system and wiggler
    for the lathe 98
Threaded inserts go straight with simple
    installation jig 84
Threading dials for cutting metric
    threads 163

Three easy finishes for oak 61
3 fast floors 63
Three hour shower 149
Three rack-a-tiers 127
Three simple houses 145
Three smart money kitchens 93
Tile roofing 135
Tile tactics 163
Tiles for a Beautiful Home 163
Tiling a backsplash 164
Tiling over cracked concrete 164
Tilt action dump truck 53
Tilting-table dovetail jig 88
Timber 164
Timber Frame Homes 164
Timbered ceiling 24
Timber-frame house, shingle-style
    wrapper 45
Timberframe sound insulation 85
Time and materials contracts 38
Tin punching 164
Tin-can organizers store stuff and tote
    it, too 158
Tiny engines 57
Tips and tools from France 174
Tips for getting the most from your clamps 29
Tips for mess-free finishing 61
Tips from the top 185
Tips on keeping your air compressor alive
    and well 34
Tire noose 164
Tissue box cover 16
To hone or not to hone 78
Toddler cart 23
Toddler toy box 167
Toggle clamps 30
Toilet transportation 165
Tool bodies 63
Tool post grinder 72
Tool safety tips 139
Toolbox 'n' tools 169
Tool-buyer's roundup 165
Toolmakers flat vise 175
Tool-rust prevention 138
Tools and techniques for cutting tile 163
Tools on wheels 23
Top secrets 135
Top-drawer desk set 46
Topics in micromachining 96
Top-notch trellises 171
Topping it off 40
Topsy-turvy engine 57
Toucan-on-a-branch 74
Townhouse transformation 133
Toxic wood: Should we worry? 182
Toy airport baggage cart 23
Toy trio 169
Tracking down good wood 182
Tract-house transformation 131

*Traditional Details for Building Restoration,
    Renovation, and Rehabilitation* 37
Trains, planes, and automobiles 144
Train-station renovation 170
Transforming a suburban ranch 128
Treasure chest 171
Trees, a new wisdom 170
Trellis flashing 171
Trench plugs 122
Tried-and-true method for squaring up stock 153
Trim-capping concerns 181
Trimming the front door 171
Tropical woods under fire 128
Trotsky, Judith 91
Troubleshooting and Repairing Power Tools 125
Troubleshooting electric motors 112
Truing a table-saw blade 159
Truini, Joseph 41
Tudor timber-frames 164
Tumbling block quilt hanging 126
Tung oil: traditional favorite 171
Tuning an adjustable level 100
Tupelo: the wood that pioneer lumbermen
    left alone 171
Turn scraps into pincushions 119
Turning a morse taper 99
Turning Australian wood
    The Banksia Nut 7
    The Eucalyptus Slab Bowl 14
Turning between centers 172
Turning jig for better bottoms 88
Turning mesquite 106
Turning short tapers on a mill 108
Turning small boxes 15
TV and VCR cabinet 162
TV satellite 141
20 ways to hang a shelf 146
27 new rules for bath remodeling 131
Twin lock workholding system 175
Twister 172
Two new twist drills 51
Two toy dragsters 169
Two traditional inlay techniques 84
Two useful lathe dogs 95
Two useful milling accessories 107
Two whirligigs from history 179
Two-wheel deal hauls sheet goods 18

U

Ultimate backyard shed 146
Ultrasonic measuring tools 106
Unconventional traditions 44
Under pressure 178
Undercover magnet reveals tension on
    bandsaw blade 7
Underground piping tips 119
Understanding color 116
Unique home services 104
Universal band saw jig 88

Universal kitchens and baths 5
Universal table saw jig 88
Universal wall-cabinet system 21
Unusual kitchens 93
Unusual lathe dog 96
Up on the roof 42
Updating the rafter square 153
Upgrade a floor 63
Uplifting experience 131
Upper decks 42
Upward mobility 2
Use for an odd grease fitting 11
Useful follower rest 99
Using a cutoff tool 99
Using a drill guide 50
Using a handsaw 75
Using chainsaws on the job site 25
Using more of a scrollsaw blade 141
Using router bits in a drill press 12

V

V.I.P. door plaque 121
Vacuum turning 99
Vacuum up those chips! 172
Vacuuming a water heater 178
Valley framing for unequally pitched
    roofs 67
Vanity cases 10
Vanity under glass 173
Veneering 174
Venting the roof 135
Vernier protractor 125
Victorian wall shelf 146
Vinyl's revived 64
Vise jaw fixtures 175
Visual Handbook of Building and Remodeling 129

W

Wagner finecoat sprayer 116
Wagner safe-t-planer 120
Wagons, Ho! 169
Wainscots 175
Wall cabinet 21
Wall clock 31
Wall lantern 95
Wall shelf 146
Wall works 39
Wallace and Hinz 8
Wall-hung ironing board 86
Wallpaper hang-ups 176
Walls & Moldings 176
Walls Around Us 103
Wall-to-wall units 147
Walnut hand mirror 108
Walnut side table 149
Warm garage 70
Warm up to Southwest 68
Warm welcome 150

Warming trends 77
Waste not 99
Water counterbalance 101
Water watch 178
Water-based finishes 61
Water-based lacquers: the safe finish that goes
    on fast 94
Water-heater anode rods 178
Water-powered sump pump 158
Waterproofing a stone foundation 65
Waterproofing brick piers 119
Waterproofing woes 110
Water-saving showerheads and faucets 10
Wave of the future water-based finishes 61
Waxy buildup 64
Weatherization 77
Weaver's chest of drawers 27
Wedge clamps 30
Weed pots 124
Well-lit addition 1
Well-ordered cutlery case 15
Well-planted deck 42
Well-rounded door conversions 48
West coast overhang 54
Wet edge 147
What a racket! 126
What felt paper does 136
What woodworkers need to know
    about screws 143
What you really need to know about
    buying boards 18
What's available in low-cost dust collection
    systems 148
What's the right safe? 138
What's available in low-cost dust collection
    systems 53
Wheat-motif bread box 15
When 3/4 in. isn't 3/4 in 41
When architecture meets energy efficiency 45
When not to do it yourself 38
Where realism rides the waves 109
Whirligigs for Children Young & Old 179
White ash: Good wood for great sport 6
White oak: The weatherproof stock of ... 114
Whittler's craft 183
Whittling 183
Why homeowners don't hire architects 4
Wide-open kitchen remodel 132
Wild about wicker 179
Wildfowl fridge magnets 74
Wild-kingdom coatrack 32
William and Mary sideboard? 149
Wily-fox weather vane 179
Winding extension cords 58
Window condensation 182
Window dressing 111
Window shopping 180
Window valance 173
Window-mounted birdhouse 12

Windowpaned mirrors 109
Windows: Filling in the gaps 181
Windsor candlestand 21
Wing-wall reinforcement 177
Winner's circle 78
Winners 42
Winning the weed war 77
Winter wonderland 144
Wiping paint brushes 117
Wiring three-way switches 55
Wisconsin wizardry 45
Wood carving machine 183
Wood floor-vent cover 63
Wood movement 177
Wood over slab 64
Wood shrinkage 19
Wood wins in survey 19
Wood-destroying fungi 104
Wooden Boat Building Made Simple 13
Wooden clamp corners clamp corner
    better 29
Wooden kitchen utensils 92
Wooden miter boxes 16
Wood-infesting insects 84
Woods that carvers crave 183
Woodworker's Dictionary 186
Woodworker's survival guide to buying
    respirators 133
Woodworker's survival guide to buying
    scrollsaw blades 143
Woodworker's survival guide to buying
    forstner bits 12

Woodworking vises 175
Work light 101
Work supports 159
Workable window putty 126
Workbench and portable tool chest 27
Workbench helper 30
Workhorse of a workbench 187
Working spaces 114
Working with gel stains 61, 153
Working with lead-free solder 152
Working without pain 83
Workshop clock 31
Worrisome little additions 75
Wrapping a house in vinyl 150
Wrapping up your house 85
Write stuff 118

X

X and Y stops for the mill 107

Y

Yard power 99
Yardscaping 42
Yellow birch 12
You can install a home alarm system 3
Your first router 137
Your next yard tool 99
Your own special island 92
Yuletide turnings 28

Z

Zap! Dry green bowls in minutes 14

Author
Index

A

Abrams, Denny 44
Abrams, Ed 51
Abusharr, Raja 112
Acker, Steve 26, 60, 76, 118, 125
Adams, Cassandra 5, 33
Adelman, Denny 76
Albertson, Jim 100
Alexander, Rex 92
Allen, Edward 37, 43, 79
Allen, Sam 20, 89
Altman, Robert 75
Altman, Roberta 58, 138
Alvarez, Mark 47, 49, 81, 85, 114, 135
Alvarez, Max 38, 184
Ambrosino, Michael M. 83, 138
Amburgey, Terry 40, 104, 114, 185
Anderson, Bruce 151
Anderson, Donald L. 65
Andrews, Steve 117, 185
Appleyard, James 24, 36, 154, 176
Arnes, John 171
Arnott, Ann 1, 92, 114
Arthur, Rob 143
Arvidson, Harold 170
Asa, Warren 142, 184
Ashe, David 12, 66, 126-127, 151-153
Atkinson, Kevin 168, 171
Auerbach, Ezra 54, 71, 179
Avalos, Manuel 72
Ayotte, Richard 129
Ayres, Scott N. 78
Azevedo, J. 135

B

Badanes, Steve 81
Badger, Curtis 183
Bahrman, Neal 165

Bailey, Don 108, 173
Baker, Richard 127
Baker, Stuart 129
Bakke, Timothy O. 18, 42, 48, 56, 60, 75-76, 78, 85, 92, 116, 121, 128, 138, 173, 176, 180
Baldwin, John 41
Ball, Jeff 80, 84, 95, 99
Ball, John E. 22
Barden, Albie 77, 115
Barker, Ross 171
Barley, Phil 69, 126, 169
Barnett, Jim 121
Barnhart, Roy 2, 9, 41, 42, 44, 123, 125, 165
Barrett, Jim 17, 35, 46-47, 49-50, 53, 60-61, 70, 75, 88, 95, 103-104, 109-113, 116, 123, 125, 130, 138-141, 144, 148, 153, 155, 159, 162, 166, 171-172, 179, 181
Barron, Errol 81
Barth, Aileen L. 44, 80
Barth, Michael 153
Barton, Wayne 185
Battersby, Mark E. 114, 161
Beals, Joseph 33, 47, 66
Beck, Grant 17, 53
Becker, Steve 86
Beckman, Richard M. 43
Becraft, Tom 119
Beetler, Diane 92
Belair, Dick 154
Belanger, Philip 115, 157
Belke, Robert 14, 97
Bellamy, Alan 53
Belle, John 37, 129
Benaroya, David 35, 110
Benitez, A. William 22, 145
Bennett, Norman H. 107

Benzel, Mark 121
Berg, James A. 90
Berger, Ivan 6, 129, 155
Berger, James 51, 175
Best, Don 8, 76, 179-181
Beyer, Rick 26, 183
Bianco, Jeffrey Dale 79
Bigton, Else 12
Binsacca, Rich 9, 43, 129, 146, 152
Birchard, John 7, 47, 150
Birdhard, John 49
Bishop, Frederic E. 159
Black, Chris 18
Blackburn, Graham 16, 89, 126, 137, 168
Bloom, Elliott 140
Bodi, Joe 137
Boelling, Jim 6, 15, 21, 26-27, 31, 39, 50, 60, 61, 67, 75, 77, 86, 89, 103, 105, 114, 118, 161, 177
Boll, Jeff 95
Bollinger, Don 61, 63
Boness, Ken 99
Bonner, Kit 13, 125
Boucheran, Pierre H. 31-32
Boufford, Don 113, 145
Bouknight, Joanne Kellar 180
Bowan, Glenn 93
Boyce, William 146
Bradstreet, Alan 45
Brannan, Steve 47, 67
Bransberg, George 138
Brennan, Terry 128
Brennen, Alexander 82, 154
Brennen, William H. 23, 112, 151
Brewer, George 19
Brickman, T.W., Jr. 177
Bridgewater, Alan and Gill 105, 167
Bright, David 11, 42

Author Index

Brinckerhoff, Scott 43, 131, 161
Broadstreet, Jim 129
Brome, Ralph W. 8
Brook, David 2
Brooks, John 79
Brown, B. Azby 22
Brown, Craig 15
Brown, Daniel 90
Brown, Keith P. 138
Brungraber, Robert L. 124
Bryan, Susan 71, 95
Buehl, Olivia Bell 64
Burdick, William A. 63
Burgess, Chet 33
Burke, Timothy 121, 127
Bush, Brian 52
Butz, Rick & Ellen 4, 28
Butz, Rick and Ellen 28, 78, 100, 166, 183-184

C

Cala, Anne 2, 76, 130, 150
Cala, Michael 101, 179
Calvert, Robert L. 74
Cambridge Historical Commission 37
Campaner, Peter 150
Campbell, John 35
Canine, Craig 81
Capotosto, August 72, 90
Carlsen, Gregg 137
Carlsen, Larry 95
Carlsen, Zachary 154
Carlson, Glenn 122
Carlson, Peter 124
Carmody, John 65, 109
Carpenter, Scott M. 177
Carpenter, Timothy 26
Carse, David 45, 79
Carson, Samuel W. 165
Carter, Brian 27, 29
Carter, Geoffrey 37
Carver, Eric 94
Cassidy, Lydia 30, 76, 101, 174, 176
Cauldwell, Rex 123, 165, 178
Chant, Rhonda 9, 131, 152, 156
Charbonneau, Harvey 115, 157
Chestnut, Jim 22, 106, 142
Ching, Francis D.K. 5, 33, 79
Chotiner, Michael 43, 63
Christian, Jeffrey 65
Chubet, Carolyn 6, 8, 69, 70, 86, 115, 122
Clayton, Larry 37, 144, 182
Cliffe, Roger W. 127
Coffman, Pam 27
Collard, Dennis 141
Colpetzer, Bob 53, 157

Connelly, Megan 18
Connors, Sherry 74
Connors, Tim 94
Conover, Ernie 48, 186
Conway, Patricia 74
Cook, Billy S. 106
Cook, Grafton H. 160
Cook, Nick 15, 28, 96, 99
Cook, Paul R. 84
Cooper, John A. 107, 113
Cooper, Nancy 35, 44
Copeland, Gerry 19
Corbett, Arthur A. 41
Corlis, Michael 67
Cornell, Jane 62, 117, 133, 146, 163
Cosloy, Gene 52, 145, 161
Countryman, Robert 48, 102
Crane, Joseph 118
Craney, Dan 30
Crisci, Jim 84
Crosbie, Michael J. 130
Cusban, Vern 159
Cyr, Phil 41

D

Daar, Sheila 118
Dahlberg, Bob 17
Dahle, Chris 86
Dahlin, Stephen D. 63
Dalsgaard, Lars 46, 171
Dandini, Paul M. 163
Darragh, Scott B. 175
Darrah, Dennis 52, 66
Darrow, Ken 162
Davis, Michael W.R. 4
Davidson, Homer L. 125
Davidson, Leslie Barry 78, 81
Davis, Kelly 45
Davis, Michael W.R. 80
Dawson, Channing 71
Day, David 37
De Cristoforo, R.J. 12
DeBlois, Christopher 95
DeBlois, Christopher F. 1, 18
Decker, John 62, 111, 150
DeCristoforo, David 109
DeCristoforo, R.J. 7, 87-88, 90, 111, 125, 133, 145, 160
DeMasi, Victor 72, 105, 153, 186
DeMay, Edward 187
Denton, Stephen N. 155
Derius, Noah 187
DeSmidt, Gene 17, 70
DeVido, Alfredo 54
Diaz, Ana 38, 104
Dick, Robert J. 29
Dickinson, Duo 81
Diller, Donald 53

Docker, James 49
Donnelly, David 63
Dooley, Roger 63, 145
Doran, William 36
Dorn, Richard H. 49, 66
Dorsch, Carl 139
Dorsey, Lloyd 48
Dougherty, Walt 172
Downing, James R. 12, 21, 26, 31-32, 46, 53, 60, 68, 74, 87, 95, 108, 118, 121-122, 125, 127, 133, 136-137, 150, 155, 157, 159-160, 168, 179
Downing, Jim 23, 53, 61, 72, 90, 118
Downing, Larry 127
Downing, Loyal 88
Doyle, Deborah 63, 100
Dubosky, Ed 83
Duclos, Philip 57
Dufort, Robert 117
Dunbar, Jean 176
Dunkley, Don 54, 181
Dunkley, Don 24
Dunleavy, Steve 134
DuPree, Russell 82, 85
Dutcher, William 131

E

Early, George W. 159
Easley, Walt 75
Easton, Robert 5
Eck, Jeremiah 80, 115
Edur, Olev 45, 96, 147-148, 187
Effron, Edward 101
Eggleston, Howard and Mariann 74
Eich, Bill 65
Eifler, John 37, 82
Elbert, David 123
Elkins, Stephen 122
Elliott, Cecil D. 5
Elliott, Lloyd E. 142
Ellis, George 153
Elrich, David 141
Ernst, Scott 118
Evans, Peter 159
Evarts, Susan 143

F

Faner, Tim 69
Farrel, Dennis B. 58
Fast, Jonathan 70, 170
Fearn, Richard 54
Feirer, Mark 19, 65
Ferrara, Michael 70, 99
Fetchko, Joe 49, 101
Fink, Al 143
Finnegan, Jim 150
Finneseth, Ted 157
Fisette, Paul 106, 180

Fisher, E. Lee 66
Fitch, Dick 60
Flaharty, David 24, 37, 121
Fletcher, Kenneth 143
Flexner, Bob 60, 69
Floresca, Jose L. 42, 154
Flynn, Stephen 6
Foad, E.V. 89
Fontaine, Andre 5
Forgang, Liz 174
Foulkes, Robert 43
Francis, Mark 146
Francis, Robert 20
Frane, David 180
Frederick, Linden 23
Fredrickson, Marie 86
Friestad, R.W. 34-35, 106
Fulmer, Ross 49

G

Galbraith, Susan 128
Garbarino, Paula 26, 84
Gard, Richard 16
Garner, Ted 64
Gascoyne, John 50, 103
Gatzke, C.I. 14, 16, 26, 28, 98
Gatzke, Lee 172
Gauntlett, James 142
Gay, Robert 10, 100
Gaynor, John 65
Gelderloos, David 55
Geneuro, George 3, 155
Germer, Jerry 124
Gibson, Scott 150
Giles, Carl and Barbara 128
Girdler, Jeff and Leonila 74
Glades, Tommy 77
Gleason, Robert 92
Godfrey, Joe B. 66
Gold, Jeff 44
Goldbeck, David 92
Golden, Mary 63, 64
Goldey, Glenn J. 122
Goldman, Mark 170
Goldsberry, Gary 165
Goldstein, Eliot 81, 171
Gore, Robert H. 39, 45
Gozdan, Walt 115
Granseth, George 12
Grasson, Jon 160
Graubner, Wolfram 186
Gray, Alexander Stuart 59
Gray, Ralph Gareth 54, 104
Gray, W. Whitie 104
Graziani, Gary 83
Greef, Jeff 6, 13, 20, 25, 48, 94, 149, 160, 167
Green, Lee 1, 76

Greenlaw, Bruce 24, 33, 94, 160
Greenman, Ron 165
Greer, Samuel 69
Gresham, Pam 163, 184
Griendling, Rich 134, 149
Grimley, Joyce 72
Gross, Marshall 67, 134, 135
Grosser, Fred 52
Grove, Scott 41
Guazzoni, Alan 71
Guild, Bill 52
Guimond, Peter H. 6, 93
Gurman, Jim 150
Gwinnup, Roger 130, 176

H

Haberfeld, Louise 4
Hackett, Douglas 185
Haendel, Theodore 47-48
Hagensick, John 184
Hagstrom, Carl 27, 36
Hajny, Desiree 179, 184
Hall, Christopher 2, 124
Hall, David 19, 80
Hallock, Mark 88
Hamilton, Gene and Katie 56, 76, 103, 111, 115, 124, 139, 149, 186
Hamilton, Katie and Gene 24, 55, 121
Hand, A.J. 40
Hanley, Tom 6, 20, 131
Hans, George 78
Hanson, Rodney S. 110
Hanson, Sven 39, 157
Harbatkin, Lisa 91
Harbison, Dennis T. 172
Harman, Steve 101
Harmon, Frank 44, 80
Harrington, John 99, 139, 178
Harris, W. Robert 52
Harrison, Gregory 154
Hart, Bill 155
Hart, Don 74
Hartnett, Michael 93
Hartsell, Thomas L. 121
Hartzler, Neil 69
Hasek, David O. 121
Haun, Larry 13, 20, 65, 67, 73, 90, 135-136, 153, 177
Hausslein, Robert 24
Havsy, Jane A. 85, 165
Hayes, Kenneth S. 52
Hedlund, Chuck 77, 156, 162
Heighway, F. Eldon 155
Heilman, Dan 58, 105
Hellman, Kevin 157
Hemp, Peter 114, 119, 122, 149, 152, 178-179
Henderson, Gregory A. 20

Henkenius, Merle 22, 42, 47, 55, 59, 101, 122-123, 141-142, 149, 151, 165, 178
Henkinius, Merle 66
Herbertson, Ross 2, 58
Herrington, Ellen 77
Herrling, Tim 36
Hetherington, John 167, 175
Heyn, John 78
Hill, Daniel 38, 56, 111
Hill, Jeffrey O. 47
Hirsch, Paul 176
Hlavacek, Robert 85
Hodin, R.S. 166
Hof, Stuart E. 138
Hoff, Michael F., Jr. 83
Hoffman, Edward G. 29, 33, 34, 50, 59, 62, 73, 87-88, 91, 143, 147, 156, 162, 175
Hogan, Michael R. 117
Hoke, John Ray, Jr. 37
Holloway, Paul 64
Holmes, Roger 15, 20, 27, 41, 66, 89, 90, 102, 111, 117, 138, 141, 143, 174, 182, 185
Holmstrom, Matt 135, 136
Hopkins, Lynn 45, 164
Hoppenworth, Marvin 159
Hornbostel, Caleb 18
Houghton, Bill 158
House, Cathi and Steven 45
House, Stephen E. 165
Houston, Rod 39
Hout, Dave 28, 168
Howard, Thomas F. 107
Huard, Conrad 40
Hubbard, Blair 137
Hubbell, James T. 45, 79
Hudson, Walt 77
Hughes, John 174
Hunter, Linda Mason 124
Hurt, Rus 74, 92, 113, 172
Hutcheson, Elaine 144

I

Iannuci, Lisa 75, 132
Ingersoll, John 85, 156, 181
Ireton, Kevin 6, 39, 52, 58, 89, 114, 129, 135, 174
Irland, Richard 79, 82
Ivy, Robert Adams, Jr. 4, 90

J

Jackson, Albert 37
Jackson, Matt 64, 130
Jagielo, Mike 87
James, Peter 131, 132
Jantzen, Steven 1

Jedlicka, Jim 51
Jenkins, Dean 148, 172
Jensen, Don 100
Jewell, Roger 94
Johnson, Brad R. 112
Johnson, Curtis 73
Johnson, D.E. 98, 163
Johnson, Dean 67, 78, 152, 156, 170
Johnson, Thomas 55
Johnson, W. Curtis 78, 127
Johnson, Warren 123
Johnston, Bob 154
Johnston, Larry 7, 28, 31, 86, 117, 121, 137, 161, 163, 166, 168, 172, 182-184
Jones, Ted 48, 92, 114, 122, 130, 132, 147, 156, 159, 174
Jones, Thomas H. 14, 39, 50, 90, 94, 111, 121, 143, 175
Jorgensen, Henry A. 52
Jorgensen, Jeff 178
Jowers, Walter 103, 176, 181
Joyce, Tom 86
Juul, Karl 128

K

Kaercher, Bruce C. 64
Kahn, Lloyd 79
Kahn, Renee 37, 124
Kaiser, Bill 169
Kalb, Melvin L. 112
Kane, David 49
Kappele, William 137
Karten, Ron 10, 41
Kassay, John 145
Katz, Gary M. 102
Katz, Howard 1
Kaufman, David 110
Kaye, Gerald 69
Keach, Stephan 92
Kean, Herbert P. 166
Kearns, Steve 48, 79, 83, 134, 135
Keely, Arthur W. 87
Keil, Gunther 113
Kelly, Patrick H. 54
Kemmet, Marlen 3, 11, 20-21, 25-26, 30-32, 39, 45-46, 67-68, 70, 72-73, 77, 87-88, 94-95, 97, 103, 108-109, 112, 115, 118, 120, 124-126, 134, 137, 145, 151, 153, 155-160, 164, 167, 169, 175, 183, 187
Kennedy, Clyde R. 79, 116, 139
Kennedy, Stephen 65, 110, 117
Kenny, Kathleen 80
Kiley, Martin D. 58
Kimball, Herrick 39, 51, 164
King, Michael 24
King, Roy 121

King, Scott 104, 139, 177, 187
Kirchner, Dave 145
Kiser, Robert 47, 74
Kitchen, Judith L. 36, 77
Kliment, Stephen A. 37
Knowles, Chris 56, 76, 85, 180
Knutson, Gothard 7
Kobishop, Jerome 169
Kochendorfer, Scott 121
Koel, Leonard 35
Kolpas, Norman 71, 124, 130, 171
Konzo, Seichi 30
Koppin, Don 105, 168
Koprucki, Bruce G. 48
Kouhoupt, Rudy 28, 46, 50, 57, 73, 95, 97-99, 102, 106-107, 129, 157, 161, 163, 166
Kraft, John 88, 147
Kreh, Dick 66
Krier, Bill 3, 7, 12, 21, 27, 29, 40, 50-51, 53, 60-61, 67, 72, 75, 89-90, 93, 96-97, 102, 109-110, 116-117, 120, 122-123, 133, 137-141, 143-144, 146, 150, 153, 159, 164-165, 175, 185
Kuferer, Kate 164
Kupferer, Kate 158

L

La Torre, John, Jr. 111
Labs, Kenneth 65
Lagerquist, Gordon 43
Landau, Charles 164
Lanford, David 120, 169
Langsner, Drew 26
Lano, Joseph 43
Lapham, Bill 137
Lasar, Stephen 133
Lash, Steven M. 68, 149
Latta, Jay 105
Laurence, Vincent 44
Lautard, Guy 96, 125
Lavenson, Kurt 185
Law, Tom 16, 75, 151, 178, 187
Lawrence, Greg 24
Lawson, Clifton 96
Lea, John 88
Leach, Thomas 43, 80, 95
League of Women Voters of Albany County 30
Lecher, Norbert 2, 76, 101
LeFurgey, Donna 178
Leger, Gene 83
Lego, William 23, 158
Lehman, George 182, 183
Lemieux, John 143, 173
Lemke, Al 186
Leonick, John D. 52

Levine, Paul 39, 111
Levy, Debra 72
Levy, Raymond 106
Lewis, Tom 168
Litchfield, Michael 133
Lloyd, John 62
Lockhart, Brian 38
Lockwood, Craig 28, 184
Loft, Abram 174
Loft, David 174
Loft, David and Abram 17
Loftis, Bill 184
Lomuscio, James 3, 8, 38, 49, 70, 106, 108, 115, 139
London, Mark 105
Longo, Matthew Adams 132
Loomis, Harwood 135, 136
Loutard, Guy 174
Lovett, William 3, 11, 168
Lowe, Steve 101
Lowery, Bill 102, 107
Lstiburek, Joseph 109
Lueggers, Chuck 161, 172
Lunde, Anders S. 170, 179
Lustig, Jan 2
Lyell, Lanny 88
Lyons, Steve 12, 139
Lytle, Elizabeth 130

M

MacDonald, John S. 79
Mack, Daniel 68
Mackall, Louis 133
Mackey, Terry 161
Madison, James 174, 175
Magee, Vishu 84
Maginley, Clare 23, 170
Mahieu, Louis 166
Mahoney, Kevin M. 124
Major, Stephen 153
Malavolta, Steve 126
Malek, Stan 131
Maletic, V.A. 88
Malokoff, Peter 129
Malone, Robert 6, 131
Maloney, Jim 56
Mariana, Nicholas 105
Marks, Ted 82
Marlow, Dave 140
Marti, Felix 30, 47, 127, 154, 185
Martin, Dana 88
Martin, Elaine 99
Martins, Haroldo 104
Martz, Elsa 139
Marvel, Jonathan 56
Marvin, Dan 82
Marx, Robert L. 1
Mason, Audrey 98

Mason, Harold 14, 119
Mastelli, Rick 71-72, 124, 143, 147
Masterson, Jeff 50
Mastin, Bill 92
Mathers, Jeff 55, 147
Mathiesen, Yon 152
Matlosz, Anthony P. 78
Matthies, Klaus 75
Maughan, Lee 142
Maxwell, Larry 135
Mayk, Gary 17, 86, 117, 130
Mayk, George 159
McBride, Ronald E. 3, 102
McBride, Scott 21, 24-25, 44, 62, 67, 73, 101, 111, 128, 134-135, 154, 177
McClure, Paul 105
McElroy, William 59, 116
McEwan, Barbara 171
McFarlane, Dave 141
McFarlin, Peter 121
McGuffie, Robert 38
McLean, Frank A. 4, 7, 17, 28, 50-51, 69, 72, 96-99, 107, 119, 137, 141, 153, 161, 163, 175
McMahon, Brian 130
McMillan, Pat 4, 7, 9, 32, 39, 62-63, 92-93, 114, 131-133, 139-141, 146, 159, 173, 174
McNight, James S. 107
Mead, Stephen 116
Meador, Hank 54
Meagher, Ellen 37, 124
Mealey, Michael 150
Medlin, Randy E. 136
Meehan, Christopher 128
Meehan, Tom 164
Meers, Gary D. 165
Melton, L.C. 147
Menicucci, Dave 2-3, 67, 114
Metcalf, Charles 173
Metzler, Joseph G. 44, 81
Mikutowski, Michael 21
Milcahy, Michael 32
Miller, Andrea 185
Miller, Charles 19, 43-44, 59, 81, 83, 86, 104, 174
Miller, Rex 22, 166
Miller, Ron 78
Milner, Ron 73
Mischka, Bob and Mary 183
Misner, Fred 75
Moisan, Rick 21, 37
Momb, Neil W. 171
Moore, Tom E. 30-31, 88-89, 111, 134, 158, 162
Morabito, Mel 71
Morgan, Rick 173
Morrill, John 82

Morris, Michael 6, 40, 45, 64, 77, 80, 128, 154
Morse, Jeff 9
Moselle, William M. 58
Mosher, Dale F. 111
Mulfinger, Dale 21
Mulholland, Gerald 107
Mulvin, Wesley 29
Murray, Craig W. 49
Myers, Ted 55, 157
Myers, Theodore J. 114

N

Nash, George 24, 65, 67, 71, 124, 150
National Trust for Historic Preservation 36
Neeley, W. Scott 56, 174
Neill, Ira I. 23, 97
Nelson, John 20, 186
Nessen, LeRoy 46, 161
Nisson, J.D. Ned 109
Niu, Stanley H. 136
Nuding, Stephen 111
Nuess, Mike 3, 128

O

O'Donovan, Thomas 158
O'Shea, Tracy 149
Odden, Phil 12, 14, 105, 183
Odegaard, Ron 28
Odnokon, Ab 86
Olivari, Joseph 26
Olkowski, William and Helga 118
Oribin, Edwin 171
Ott, Jack 174
Owen, David 103
Ozimek, Ken 18, 138

P

Panck, Walt 14
Papa, Byron 117
Paral, Rob 73
Parker, G. Robert 5, 45
Parsons, Jeff 7, 14, 58, 78, 96, 99, 172, 182
Patillo, Anthony 171
Patrasso, Jerry 15
Paul, Tessa 163
Pearman, Donald V. 84, 103, 162
Pearson, David 80
Pellitteri, Phil 84
Penfield, Paul 94, 115
Percival, Pat 141
Perrett, Glenn 8, 78
Perry, Daniel 173
Petersen, Eugene 163
Petrovich, Joe 162
Petrowski, Elaine 92

Petrowski, Elaine Martin 115
Pfeiffer, Peter L. 55, 152
Phair, Matt 9, 11, 20, 35, 41-42, 48-49, 51, 56, 62, 65, 69, 72, 85, 91, 104, 108, 116, 120, 128, 132, 136, 146, 151, 154, 156, 180-181, 186
Phair, Matthew 10, 47, 59, 93
Phelps, John 134
Phillips, Bill 3, 49, 101, 138, 145, 180
Pieper, Paul 23
Pierce, Bruce 77
Pilaroscia, Jill 116
Platania, John 89
Plourde, Robert 154
Pollack, Emil and Martyl 166, 186
Pollack, Emil S. 166
Popovac, Vladimir 76
Porter, Lindel 184
Portland Cement Association 35
Posoneil, Charlie 92, 93, 130
Poutsch, Barbara 133, 167
Prailes, Lloyd 29
Preston, Dennis 27, 71, 87, 116, 120, 140-141, 148, 152, 157-158, 161, 165, 187
Price, Don 2
Prince, Steve 87
Provey, Joseph 4, 58, 93
Publicover, Scott 182
Purser, Michael W. 61
Pyle, Earl A. 7

Q

Quarve-Peterson, Julee 18

R

Rabbitt, Patrick 172
Raiche, Larry 74
Rainey, Will 100, 171
Raivo, Keith 113
Rand, Ellen 10
Randall, William A. 85
Randich, Keith 182, 184
Rannefeld, C.E. 87, 89, 137
Ransom, Ron 27, 184
Reed, Richard E. 90, 147
Reeves, Rick 26, 105
Refsal, Harley 119, 163, 184
Reichart, John 56
Reichert, Bob and Carolyn 12
Reilly, Peter 5
Renn, Trip 150
Rensbarger, Fran 71
Reynolds, Michael 54
Ribar, Jacob W. 17
Ricci, Thomas 124
Rider, Roy 78
Riedel, Karl 106

Riedhart, John 158
Riley, David 5
Riley, Stephen 79
Riley, Steve 69
Roberts, J. Stewart 82
Roberts, Judy Gale 74, 85, 103, 144
Roberts, S. Gary 119
Roccanova, John 112
Rockhill, Dan 100
Roesner, William E. 132
Rogers, Benjamin T. 2, 72
Rolke, William A. 24
Roopinder, Tara 30, 119
Rosauer, Harold 86
Roscoe, Lowie L. 186
Rose, Jim 19
Rose, John Lemieux 28
Rosenau, Jim 13, 40, 54, 79, 86, 115, 118, 131, 170, 177, 180
Rosenbaum, Marc 45, 52, 56, 136, 152, 174, 178
Rosenblum, Chip 75
Ross, John 85
Ross, Sally 10, 39, 50, 59, 156
Ross, Sharon 4, 44, 91, 156, 158
Roth, Eric 124
Roubal, Ted 96, 106, 123
Rowland, Jack 167
Roy, Denis 74
Rucker, Debra G. 45, 152
Rucker, Terence 140, 142
Rudd, Armin 48
Rush, Vickie 168
Rushlo, Dave 28, 184
Russell, Kim 155
Rybczynski, Witold 5

S

Sacks, Alvin 65, 177
Salmon, Ron 160
Sambrook, John 59
Saunders, Alan 77
Savage, Craig 38, 111
Savas, Gregory 49
Saxenian, Mike 162
Scarrow, Lynda 179
Schaible, Brian 29
Schendlinger, Mary 29
Schilaty, John K. 89
Schlarbaum, Pat 12
Schlender, Shelley 6
Schmidt, John 115, 157
Schnittker, John M. 171
Schoonmaker, David 179
Schultz, Glenn M. 96
Schulzinger, Jacob 102, 151
Schuttner, Scott 65
Schwarz, Bruce 164

Schweitzer, Robert 4, 80
Scolforo, Matthew 119
Seaton, Jeffrey 15
Segal, Leon 20, 158
Seidel, John 187
Seitz, James E. 183
Sellers, David 154
Selvin, Nancy 163
Settle, Jack 26
Sewall, Stephen 48
Sexton, Terry 18, 106, 129
Shafer, Jonathan F. 23
Sheehan, Sean 172, 176
Sheridan, Patrick 130
Sheriff, Edwin P. 71
Shilling, Mark 121
Shivers, Natalie 110, 176
Shope, Allan 130
Shull, Larry 107
Siegel, Carolyn Robbins 1
Silver, Chuck 38, 65
Silverstein, Murray 80
Simmonds, Tony 10, 93, 129, 151
Simpson, Bob 116
Skilton, Dave 147
Smiley, Caleb 178
Smith, Ashley 67
Smith, E.Q. 127, 158
Smith, Greg 8
Smith, Loran 30
Smith, R.W. 33, 97
Smith, Roger K. 120
Smith, Russell H. 11, 99, 157
Smith, Todd 133, 135, 147
Smith-Kim, Charles 38
Smulski, Stephen 2, 10, 18, 94, 104, 125, 149, 154, 185
Snyder, John W. 183
Snyder, Merwin 127, 158
Snyder, Tom 156
Sollman, Philip S. 14, 93, 177
Solomon, Karey 82
Sommers, Charles 77
Spear, Sherry 64
Speas, Ed 17
Spies, Henry 2, 3, 6, 9, 24-27, 36, 39, 46, 48, 52, 58-60, 62-66, 69, 71, 73, 76, 83-84, 91, 100, 103-104, 109-121, 123, 125, 128-130, 136, 145, 147, 149, 152, 154, 158, 175, 177-178, 181-182
Sprankle, James D. 183
Spratt, Steven 17
St. Clair, Dean 141
Stage, Cary 31
Starnes, Ray E. 73, 97, 108, 121
Stearns, Bob 136
Stebenne, Rene 140
Stein, Jay 2, 119, 178

Stephano, Peter J. 9, 13-14, 23, 42, 68, 85, 95, 105, 109, 113, 139, 142, 151, 175, 179, 183, 185-186
Stephen, George 37
Sterl, Scott W. 130
Stevenson, Don 59
Stevenson, Jim 38
Stiles, David 146
Stiles, Jack 159
Stodola, Rick 53
Stone, Mark Van 100
Straight, J.W. 136
Strawderman, David 32, 64, 67, 146, 180
Strong, Ron 163
Strong, Steven J. 73
Strum, Chris 177
Sullivan, Charles 37
Sundeen, Wade 61
Sweeney, Thomas F. 4, 18, 42, 84, 92, 95, 132, 149
Sygar, Richard 131
Syvanen, Bob 22, 58, 80, 153

T

Tamony, Katie 5
Taub, Richard 171
Taylor, C. Robert 173
Taylor, Steve 43, 80
Taylor, Vic 186
Tigelaar, Leffert 28
Terrell, John 79
Thallon, Rob 176
Thomas, Peter Adrian 81
Thomas, Stephan 97, 107-108
Thomsen, Jau 24
Thompson, Jack R. 8, 97
Thompson, Jim 42
Thompson, Jon H. 135
Thompson, Spencer 4
Thomsen, H. Skip 54
Thornton, Fred 43
Thurman, Bobbie K. 91, 184
Tibbets, Joseph M. 2, 54
Tillotson, Cliff 11
Timby, John I. 96
Tishman, Dan 71
Toccalino, Tony 36, 55
Tollesfson, Richard 156
Tolman, Gregory 41
Tolpin, Jim 14, 20, 100, 143, 177
Torgerson, Richard 7, 98, 157, 170
Tousain, David 143, 176
Treanor, Robert J. 21
Trim, John 42
Trinkaus, Ted 80
Trotsky, Judith 9, 22, 24, 49, 59, 70, 153, 155, 176, 181

Truini, Joseph 4, 10-11, 23, 29, 39, 41, 43, 48, 50, 62, 64, 65, 68-71, 77, 81-85, 95, 102, 105, 114, 117-118, 122, 124, 128, 131-132, 135, 139, 142, 157-159, 163-164, 180
Turner, William M. 128
Turok, John M. 115, 158

U

Unger, Fred 132, 180
Upshaw, Deborah 8, 183

V

Valbuena, Vivian 70
Van Den Branden, F. 121
Van Vranken, Robert 37, 131
Vandal, Norman 126
Vandervort, Don 42, 116-117, 123, 135, 173
Verity, Thomas 63
Vickers, Amy 10, 165
Vider, Elise 1, 41
Vienneau, Warren 94
Voelker, Paul D. 132

W

Wadham, G. 96, 97
Wagner, Bill 51
Walchuk, Gary 13, 30, 40, 50-51, 66, 87, 167
Waldstein, Arne 176
Walker, Jerry 91
Walker, Ralph T. 111
Walker, Richard B. 24, 86
Walker, Robert 116
Walker, Terence 50

Wallace, Alasdair 38, 55, 118, 168
Wallace, David 90
Wallach, Les 81
Walmsley, Brian 22
Warde, John 49
Wardell, Charles 13, 45, 52, 56, 117, 163
Warner, Patrick 137
Warren, Walt 96
Waterman, Asaph 25, 152
Watkins, M. Scott 55, 110, 142, 152, 174
Watson, Richard D. 55
Watson, Ted 131
Watts, Les 171
Weissman, David 53
Wells, Malcolm 19, 172
Wessmiller, Bob 51, 69, 105, 113, 121, 131, 180
Wessmiller, Bob and Phair, Matt 1
Westfall, Michael M. 24, 62
Westover, Allene and Harold 60
Wheeler, Dan 145
Whidden, James 33
White, Mark 18, 23, 117, 157
White, Steven M. 154
White-Hansen, Sue Ellen 81
Wilbern, Jack 128
Wilbur, C. Keith 33
Wilcoxson, Robert 163
Wilk, Sanford 29, 141
Wilks, Dan 104, 142
Williams, Charles 134
Williams, Chuck 5, 8
Williams, Daniel 181
Williams, Gurney 3, 78, 84, 162, 180, 185

Williams, John 113
Williams, Les 73
Williams, Linda P. 95, 104, 122, 170
Williamson, Andy 71
Williamson, Hugh F. 32
Willmann, Roger 11
Wilson, Alex 33, 55, 101, 178
Wilson, Glenn L. 96, 98
Wilson, Kimberly 156
Wilson, Larry 55
Winchester, Stephen 154
Winder, Kate Corbett 8
Wing, Charlie 129
Wing, Daniel 83, 126, 139
Winters, Ric 29, 158
Wipperman, Don 105
Wirth, Harry J. 82
Wodham, G. 28, 98
Wolf, Max 101
Wolfert, C.K. 36
Woodford, Eileen 37
Wyman, Burleigh F. 175
Wynn, Scott 62, 120

Y

Yoder, Robert A. 20
Yoder, Sam 17
Young, Larry S. 25
Young, Marshall R. 50, 102

Z

Zaun, Bill 120
Zepp, Donald E. 153
Zichos, Richard J. 167, 170
Ziegner, Rich 117, 176
Zurawski, Ed 173